GE180 .P53 2013
The snail darter and the dam :
33663005603077
HLC

D0651687

# DATE DUE

BRODART, CO.                    Cat. No. 23-221

*The Snail Darter and the Dam*

# *The*
# Snail Darter
## *and the*
# Dam

*How Pork-Barrel Politics*
*Endangered a Little Fish and*
*Killed a River*

Zygmunt J. B. Plater

Yale UNIVERSITY PRESS

NEW HAVEN & LONDON

Yale University Press books may be purchased in quantity for educational, business, or promotional use. For information, please e-mail sales.press@yale.edu (U.S. office) or sales@yaleup.co.uk (U.K. office).

page iii: Partially submerged silos in the reservoir created by the damming of the Little Tennessee River. (Photo © Marika Plater)

Set in Bulmer and ITC Franklin Gothic types by Westchester Book Group.
Printed in the United States of America.

Library of Congress Cataloging-in-Publication Data

Plater, Zygmunt J. B., 1943–
The snail darter and the dam : how pork-barrel politics endangered a little fish and killed a river / Zygmunt J. B. Plater.
        p.   cm.
Includes bibliographical references and index.
ISBN 978-0-300-17324-6 (hardcover : alk. paper)

    1. Environmental policy—United States.   2. Environmental legislation—United States.   3. Endangered species—Government policy—United States.   4. Rare fishes—Government policy—United States.   5. Tennessee Valley Authority.   6. Tellico Dam (Tenn.)   7. United States. Endangered Species Act of 1973.   8. United States. National Environmental Policy Act of 1969.   I. Title.
GE180.P53 2013
333.95'22—dc23                                                    2012047816

A catalogue record for this book is available from the British Library.

This paper meets the requirements of ANSI/NISO Z39.48–1992
(Permanence of Paper).

For my beloved family—Ann, Marika, Sofia

—for Anne Marie Wickham, 1946-2009

—and for all who act to protect our Earth for future generations of

plants, animals, and us

The River . . . is the living symbol of all the life it sustains or nourishes—fish, aquatic insects, water ouzels, otter, fisher, deer, elk, bear, and all other animals, including man, who are dependent upon it or who enjoy it for its sight, its sound, or its life.

—Justice William O. Douglas

Never doubt that a small group of committed citizens can change the world. Indeed, it's the only thing that ever does.

—Margaret Mead

But when the last individual of a race of living things breathes no more, another heaven and another earth must pass before such a one can be again.

—C. William Beebe

I was always taught as I was growing up that democracy is not something you believe in, not something you hang your hat on. Democracy is something you do.

—Abbie Hoffman

By the river
I try to keep alive. . . .
Sitting on the bank
the water stares back so deeply
you can hear it afterwards
when you wish. . . .

—Jim Harrison, *The Theory & Practice of Rivers*

The best way to enrage people is to force them to change their minds.

—Friedrich Nietzsche

# Contents

# *Preface*

This book grew out of a tumultuous half-dozen years when a group of my students and I at the University of Tennessee took up the cause of embattled local farmers and a river threatened by a very dubious federal dam project. Fighting to save the river and its remarkable valley, we used the federal Endangered Species Act and the snail darter, a little fish threatened with extinction, as our only available legal leverage. *The Snail Darter and the Dam* is a true-life parable, revealing major twists, turns, opportunities, and hazards, as a citizen-based public interest campaign wrestles its way through scientific, economic, political, and legal obstacles in a stubborn attempt to straighten out an enduring official mistake.

Was the battle between the Tellico Dam, being built by the federal Tennessee Valley Authority (TVA), and the little snail darter the "most extreme environmental case ever," as pundits and politicians have said? Critics have long denigrated the tiny endangered fish and the "fringe lunatics" (to quote Fox News personality Sean Hannity) who persuaded the U.S. Supreme Court to halt a "huge Tennessee Valley hydroelectric dam" that would destroy the little fish's last known natural population.

The clash happened more than thirty years ago, but Hannity and other conservatives, like Rush Limbaugh, Ann Coulter, George Will, Roger Ailes, Justice Antonin Scalia, and their cohort in Congress, still invoke the snail darter as a sarcastic put-down, using it to characterize progressive initiatives as liberal extremism. The little fish has also entered public rhetoric more broadly. A national controversy over the snail darter filled newspapers, talk shows, and television news coverage. It was one of the three biggest environmental press stories of its decade, understood then and now, even by liberals, as an example of governmental protectionism that went too far.

But what if there were a good deal more to the story than fish versus dam? Consider, for example, that TVA's Tellico Dam was relatively small, and its reservoir was designed for recreation rather than for hydroelectricity. The citizens at the heart of the fight to save the fish's river and its valley were not wild-eyed environmentalists, but rather family farmers, most of whose lands were being condemned by the federal agency so they could be transferred to a Fortune 500 corporation for resale. Ultimately a stringent high-level review concluded that the dam project had been a ruinous mistake from the very start, destroying far more economic assets and public values than the project could ever have provided.

That's not the story America heard, however. The conflict was almost always presented as "tiny fish versus huge dam"—a quick, dismissive framing of a quixotic David versus Goliath conflict. Most peoples' first reaction to the darter-dam lawsuit was a skeptical sense that the wildlife law was being hypocritically misapplied. It seemed unethical for citizens to block a federal public works project using a statute in a way that most members of Congress had clearly never intended. That idea persists to this day; eminent legal scholar and philosopher Ronald Dworkin uses the snail darter decision as a prime example of the U.S. legal system run amok.

Despite legal and economic verdicts in favor of the fish and its river valley, relentless antienvironmental industry lobbying and disappointing media coverage together helped a polarized Congress overturn the citizens' years of efforts to bring rational deliberation to the case. The river ultimately became a reservoir. The darter has survived in several transplanted locations, though it is still threatened.

Depending how one looks at it, the darter-dam conflict can be either an unbalanced campaign of self-appointed crusaders misusing a fish to serve their own obstructionist ends, or an illuminating saga showing how a tiny fish and its human advocates built a complex factual case and carried it through numerous layers of modern science, government, and politics, against large odds.

The book's narrative follows multiple concurrent threads: scientific and economic linkages between a fish and a farming community, the human drama of citizens resisting peremptory federal orders, the random power of the media, an excursion through the courts, the complexity of pork-barrel government-funded projects, and the forces within congressional establishments that shape Washington politics.

Behind the narrative, moreover, runs a basic issue of modern democratic governance: If the public knows critical facts, its representatives in government are far more likely to process issues thoughtfully and in the public interest. When the public is unaware, insider politics are free to run perversely rampant. As Madison famously wrote, "A popular Government without popular information or the means of acquiring it is but a Prologue to a Farce or a Tragedy, or perhaps both. Knowledge will forever govern ignorance: And a people who mean to be their own Governors, must arm themselves with the power which knowledge gives." The darter story reveals how contemporary Americans can play remarkable roles in improving societal governance through active engagement and heightened expectations of how we should be led and governed—and what can happen when the public doesn't have the information it needs.

Only in America could this kind of fish story happen. It's a case study of polarized politics, a powerful but imprudent press, and stalemated congressional procedures—a parable that highlights many of the strengths, idiosyncrasies, perils, and needs of our vexed modern systems of democratic governance—and it has enough twists and turns to intrigue and annoy just about everyone. A motley group of unpowerful, unwealthy people from a backwater region ultimately carried their arguments far beyond their valley farmlands, up through every branch of national government, including a battle in the Supreme Court and a novel inquisition in a special council of presidential Cabinet appointees. In fact, the citizens' Supreme Court victory is, to this day, considered one of the Court's two most significant environmental law decisions.[1]

Some technical points deserve special note:

- The book isn't designed as an academic treatise; endnotes are organized by chapter in the back pages. The book's website—www.bc.edu/snaildarter—contains a document archive, extended endnotes, notes on the various participants then and now, and a large collection of photographs and other graphics.

- Despite strenuous initial efforts to make this book an arm's-length third-person recounting of an intricate and turbulent story, the narrative worked consistently better as an account in first-person format, singular and plural. The book is a narrative history, however, not a memoir. The stars of the story are the farmers, local citizens, university students, and volunteer supporters who carried the Little Tennessee River campaign through the years.

- Reconstructed conversations occur throughout the book. The spoken lines in quotation marks have been derived, thirty years after the fact, from a variety of sources—from official transcripts and records, from notebooks I kept during the critical years of the case, and from conversations and incidents from those days as recorded or recollected by a number of participants. To get substance and tone as accurate as possible, the reconstructed conversations have been checked with the participants in as many instances as feasible. More than two dozen people who lived the story in those years have scrutinized the book to confirm the conversations' tone and accuracy. Errors that remain are of course mine, not theirs.

- The facts set out here describing agency behavior, public works economics, political maneuvers, and media responses, often seem quite lopsided. On the objective record, however, most of the facts of this particular case are indeed one-sided. The high-level God Committee (see Chapter 10) ultimately concluded that the actual merits of the dam project were slim to none. The citizens' alternative plans would have been overwhelmingly more beneficial to the public and the environment. TVA's position was primarily supported by the agency's remarkable political and media power, backed in Washington by its political allies. Virtually all TVA's justifications for building the dam were ultimately refuted by facts on the official record.

- A number of archives of materials on the Tellico Dam controversy exist, primarily at Boston College, Maryville College, and the University of Tennessee, as well as within TVA. The basic array of useful and interesting documents

and background materials is available online at www.bc.edu
/snaildarter. Two excellent compilations of information and
analysis are William Bruce Wheeler and Michael J. McDonald,
*TVA and the Tellico Dam, 1936–1979: A Bureaucratic Crisis
in Post-Industrial America* (University of Tennessee Press,
1986), and Michael R. Fitzgerald and Stephen J. Rechichar,
*The Consequences of Administrative Decision: TVA's Eco-
nomic Development Mission and Intragovernment Regulation* (University of Tennessee Press, 1983). William U.
Chandler, *The Myth of TVA* (Ballinger, 1984), examines dif-
ferential economic development in the region. A book presenting the TVA arguments in a very complimentary light
is J. Thompson and C. Brooks, *Tellico Dam and the Snail
Darter* (Spectrum, 1991). Frances Brown Dorward, *Dam
Greed* (Xlibris, 2009), is a local history of the Little Tennessee River valley and Tellico Dam based upon many oral
history interviews collected by its author. Kenneth M.
Murchison's *The Snail Darter Case: TVA Versus the Endangered Species Act* (University of Kansas Press, 2007) includes excellent and exhaustive accounting of twenty-five
years of legal proceedings in the agencies, Congress, and
courts, based on extensive reviews of published official legal
records.

   This book has profited from a host of helpers over a span of many
years, including yeoman service by Joan Shear and her colleagues at
the Boston College Law Library. More than seventy students and other
friends, unfortunately far too numerous to name, have offered ideas,
research, fact-checking, and feedback over the years. I thank you all.
A number of friends, however, deserve to be specially noted for their
truly extraordinary efforts reading and commenting on the entire manuscript. Some of these read the text when it was almost twice as long(!),
and so special thanks go to Glenn Adelson, Peter Alliman, Nathan
Bress, John Dernbach, Ailee Feber, Hank Hill, Oliver Houck, Micah
Leinbach, Ginna Mathews Mashburn, John Evon Nelson II, Patrick
Parenteau, Marika Plater, and Jesse Staniforth, and to Jean E. Thompson Black, Sara Hoover, and Jeff Schier at Yale University Press, but

most of all to my long-suffering wife and midwife, Ann, who showed me why and how this book ultimately had to be written.

Given the way the snail darter still arouses wry emotions in politicians and commentators, and the story's marked relevance to contemporary politics, readers are invited to dig further into the history chronicled here to deepen and extend the reflections that linger in the wake of the snail darter.

*The Snail Darter and the Dam*

# God Is Speaking, by Committee

JANUARY 23, 1979

A packed crowd sits hunched forward on folding chairs in a big, stark meeting room at the Department of Interior headquarters in Washington. The ceiling lights glare above eight obviously important men who sit ill at ease at a long table at the front of the room, as several staffers with flip charts and an overhead projector present maps, chronologies, analytical data, and multiple columns of big numbers.

This morning is a moment unprecedented in human history. Really. For the first time, a conscious decision is being made whether an entire species of living creatures will be condemned to extinction, or allowed to survive.

These eight men are the members of the so-called God Committee, created by Congress ten weeks earlier to resolve the problem of a notorious lawsuit from Tennessee. A small group of citizens had persuaded the Supreme Court to halt construction of the Tennessee Valley Authority's Tellico Dam because it would exterminate the entire known population of a tiny endangered perch, the snail darter.

The men sitting at the table are some of the highest-ranking officials in the nation, including members of the president's Cabinet—the secretaries of agriculture, interior, army, and transportation—the administrators of the Environmental Protection Agency and the National Oceanic and Atmospheric Administration, and the chair of the President's Council of Economic Advisers. Here they sit, told to dig into the

1

economics of the case and then declare which will prevail, the dam and its reservoir or the fish and its river.[1]

"Doesn't this just about beat anything?" Margaret Sexton whispers. Her soft Tennessee vowels add a quiet little melody to the gravelly torrent of technical talk that's been pouring for the past two hours from the bureaucrats up front. "And to think this-all started with my Daddy's hat!" Margaret, one of the volunteers defending the endangered darter and its Little Tennessee River (the "Little T"), was raised in a small farmhouse surrounded by ninety-plus acres of rich soil in the bottomlands along the river. She had moved to Washington when her fiancé, Joe, got a job there at the end of the Korean War. Down in Tennessee her parents, Asa and Nellie McCall, like several hundred other farm families in the Little T valley, continued to work the dark soil of the cool river's undulating valley—raising corn, wheat, tobacco, soybeans, alfalfa hay, black-eyed peas. Looking out over the riverside fields, here and there a visitor's eye would pick out large Native American burial mounds along the river. This had been the ancient heartland of the Cherokee, the site of nine major Cherokee villages, including Chota, their sacred place of refuge, and Tennassee Town, which gave its name to the river and the state.

Then one day fifteen years ago white cars with federal license plates began to appear along the back roads, stopping at each of the farmhouses. TVA—the federal Tennessee Valley Authority, which had been one of the most lauded creations of the New Deal—was now politically the dominant regional power in a seven-state area of the southeastern United States.

"We're buying your land for a new reservoir project," the TVA appraisers said when they came to the McCalls' farm.

"Ain't for sale," said Asa.

"Makes no sense," said Nell. "River's too shallow to get you enough power to pay for a dam."

"Yes, ma'am, but this Tellico project is for a recreational reservoir, plus we're going to have the Boeing Corporation come in and build a model city on this land. That's why we have to take all of your farm, not just the three acres we'll be flooding. The rest'll be sold for development." As TVA described it officially, the Tellico project "is expected to result in significant beneficial shifts in land use . . . to industrial, commercial, residential, and recreational development use."[2]

"You just git off our land this minute and don't come back," Asa told the TVA agents. Nell added something choicer.

Thus began the earliest chapter of a long, bitter battle between the giant federal utility and a motley collection of farmers, trout fishermen, the Eastern Band of Cherokee, history buffs, and conservationists— local people convinced from the start that TVA's small dam was an irrational mistake.

As they dug into the details of TVA's project, the farmers and their supporters unearthed more and more serious problems with the agency's plans. The project clearly made no economic sense. Alternative development designs—tourism, recreational resources, and an industrial park—could foster far more economic benefits than a dam, while keeping landowners on their farms and the river flowing.

"If people looked at this project," a frustrated Nell McCall said, "they'd see it's nuthin' but a crooked land grab."

The farmers and their allies, however, found it virtually impossible to get anyone in power to listen. They tried, fighting against the land condemnations, carpooling to Washington to testify against the project, writing letters to local newspapers. For a short time they were able to halt the project because TVA initially refused to do a required environmental impact statement. But the federal agency, supported in Washington by the pork barrel—the intricate politics of dubious federally funded projects—ultimately overrode every citizen effort to block the dam. Demoralized by a string of battles lost, the local dam fighters saw their ranks grow thinner and thinner year by year.

Then a small fish swam into the controversy, discovered under the swift currents of the lower Little T River. The fish was clearly endangered, and federal law said any federal agency action jeopardizing an endangered species violated the Endangered Species Act. After some hesitant discussions about the wisdom and consequences of using this kind of legal argument (in which, as we will see, Asa McCall's hat played a pivotal role), the farmers and their allies decided to launch one final attempt to block the dam and its real estate development project.

On the way to the Supreme Court, the citizens' case for the snail darter and its river struggled through tortuous layers of agency bureaucracy and congressional politics and trekked through three federal courts, culminating in a dramatic Supreme Court victory. But the darter's legal achievements were always obscured by an avalanche of criticism and ridicule in the media and in popular opinion. The case was inaccurately depicted as an irrational obstruction of a valuable project, a quixotic conflict between a trivial fish of no known value and a huge hydroelectric dam. The press, and even more significantly the business community and the pork-barrel lobby, reveled in the darter story, depicting the little fish as an example of environmental extremism and government regulation gone haywire. The Tellico project's economic flaws and its very dubious condemnation of farmland for resale went unnoticed in the public debate.

Reacting to the Supreme Court decision and the ensuing media hullabaloo, Congress amended the Endangered Species Act, inserting provisions creating the God Committee, empowered to review affected projects and "bring common sense to the law" by overriding endangered species protections wherever a formal economic analysis showed that human necessities outweighed the value of preserving a species.

As the day of the God Committee's economic analysis approached, the odds of an extinction verdict were unpredictable. Political insiders assumed the committee's economic review would make short work of the darter. By the time the committee got the case, TVA had already spent 95 percent of the project budget. Its heavy machinery had devastated the valley and brought the reservoir levees close to completion. With all those sunk costs, the dam should surely prevail. The darter's defenders, however, still hoped for an economic verdict that would finally show the world the realities of the federal mistake they'd been fighting for so long. The river valley could be far more valuable without the dam, while the snail darter, wiped out in all its previous habitats by sixty-eight dams, could be a canary in a coal mine—by its very existence in this last stretch of big flowing river, a sensitive natural indicator of an avoidable impending threat to human welfare.

On this January morning the staff analysts in the front of the hall finish presenting their economic charts and statistical analyses to the God Committee members. The economic merits of the darter's case have been carefully laid out in public as never before. But at this late date, so far into the game, the dam is indeed almost completed. We sit there holding our collective breath.

For an awkward moment following the presentations, the eight judges shift in their chairs in hesitant silence, glancing at one another.

"Well, somebody has to start," says Charles Schultze, chairman of the President's Council of Economic Advisers. He pauses, then continues, "The interesting phenomenon is that here is a project that is 95 percent complete, and if one takes *just the cost of finishing it* against the benefits, and does it properly, it *still* doesn't pay!—which says something about the original design!" [Laughter].[3]

The room is full of Washington insiders, all of whom know that most public works projects are built upon economic exaggerations. There's humor here in having the fictions laid out so starkly that they might now be evident to the public beyond the Beltway.

In another four minutes, based on the staff's extensive economic analysis, the committee votes unanimously against the Tellico project and in favor of the snail darter and its river.

"I hate to see the snail darter get the credit," Chairman Cecil Andrus (the Carter administration's secretary of the interior) says, "for stopping a project that was so ill-conceived and uneconomic in the first place."

Margaret is ecstatic. Back in Tennessee the farmers and their volunteer crusaders joyfully greet the news. Will this be the end of twenty-five years of battle? Will TVA and its allies finally yield and turn to alternative river development designs, with the farmers still living and working on their rich bottomlands? Will the public now see the realities of the snail darter case—that the dam's promoters are the extremists, and the fish and its defenders stand for common sense?

The verdict of the God Committee reaches Capitol Hill and the Washington media bureaus shortly before noon, but most of the evening papers and news shows do not mention the event, much less the dramatic reversal of the story as it had previously been reported. By the end of the day, however, ominous rumblings have begun deep within the marble corridors of Congress.

# CHAPTER 1

# Of Time, a River, and the Tennessee Valley Authority

200,000,000 BCE-1973

Two hundred million years ago sharp volcanic thrusts drove a long line of jagged mountains upward from the flatlands that would later become the eastern United States. Slowly over the following millennia the rains and winds softened and smoothed the heights until the Appalachians had become a great deal smaller and gentler than the Rockies, their younger relatives to the west. Though it didn't yet have a name, a good fraction of the water that shaped and drained the southern part of the mountains over that span of two hundred million years flowed westward in crevices and streams that joined together to form the Little Tennessee River.

The Little Tennessee arises in a small spring in the saddle of a north-facing ridge in the Appalachian mountains of northern Georgia, then trickles north and westward, gathering other streams as it flows through the twisting leafy green canyons of the Smoky Mountains of North Carolina and Tennessee. The Cherokee called these Enemy Mountains because beyond them from the east came other tribes' raiding parties and white invaders. Through a notch at the southern end of the Smokies, the river poured out of the mountains into the rolling lands west of the Appalachians. In 1540 the Spanish explorer Hernando de Soto, coming west from the Carolinas on his trail of discovery, had traveled along the Little T and talked with elders in a half-dozen Cherokee villages, but, finding no gold after a few days, he went south.

The Little T, coming out of the hills that by 1935 had become the Great Smoky Mountains National Park, flowed another five hours through the broad rolling landscape of America's colonial frontier to a big junction pool, where it joined the sluggish water of the Big Tennessee River on its muddy way westward to the Mississippi.

But the Little T ran clear and cool, and was filled with life. As it picked up the flow of Chief Abraham's creek in the mountains, its currents, already filled with oxygen, had taken in rich limestone water that over thousands of years had made the river a bountiful place for fish and fishermen. When twentieth century fishermen walked across the meadowlands to the river, they passed Native American mounds and ancient town sites still studded with broken potsherds, flint arrowheads, and spear points that would glisten in freshly plowed fields after a rain. In the old days, the Cherokee would hunt up in the mountains, but it was down along the banks of the Little T that they built their towns, where the river flowed through gently rolling countryside with fertile topsoil many feet deep, and the water teemed with trout.

The river flowed past the town site of Settaco, where more than a hundred warriors had built their homes and planted cornfields in 1762 when Lieutenant Henry Timberlake, a colonial British officer, first mapped the region. Across the river was Tlanumai, the cave from which, according to local folklore, two giant vultures had ruled the valley until a wise old medicine man drove them away. Farther along was Chota, described by an early white trader, James Adair, as the Cherokee's "Jerusalem and most sacred city of refuge," where God first made the Cherokee Cherokee, and where their strongest medicine was gathered. Cherokee medicine has different sources. It grows, or is dug from within the earth, or is dipped from flowing water, or is called from the air. Downstream from Chota, ten miles out from the mountains came Tennassee, the town that gave its name to the river and the state, and Toqua, with the valley's largest ceremonial mound.

In 1775 William Bartram, a young Quaker naturalist from Philadelphia, wrote upon crossing this Cherokee homeland on his 2,500-mile odyssey through the southeastern territories:

> "Perceiving the bottom or bed of the river to be level and evenly covered with pebbles, I ventured to cross over, however I was obliged to swim two or three yards at the deepest channel of it, and landed safely on the

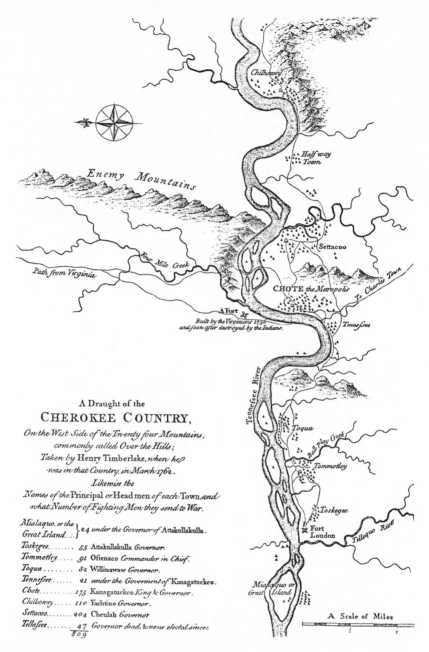

Chilhowey

Half way Town

Enemy Mountains

Four Mile Creek

Path from Virginia

Settacoo

To Charles Town

CHOTE the Metropolis

A Fort
Built by the Virginians 1756
and soon after destroyed by the Indians.

Tennefsee

Tennefsee River

A Draught of the
**CHEROKEE COUNTRY,**
On the West Side of the Twenty four Mountains,
commonly called Over the Hills;
Taken by Henry Timberlake, when he
was in that Country, in March 1762.
Likewise the
Names of the Principal or Head men of each Town, and
what Number of Fighting Men they send to War.

Toqua

Ball Play Creek

Tommotley

Toskegee

Fort
Loudon

Tellaquo River

| Town | Fighting Men | Head man |
|---|---|---|
| Mialaquo, or the Great Island | 24 | under the Governor of Attakullakulla. |
| Toskegee | 55 | Attakullakulla Governor. |
| Tommotley | 91 | Ostenaco Commander in Chief. |
| Toqua | 82 | Willinawaw Governor. |
| Tennefsee | 21 | under the Goverment of Kanagatuckco. |
| Chote | 175 | Kanagatuckco King & Governor. |
| Chilhowey | 110 | Yachtino Governor. |
| Settacoo | 204 | Cheulah Governor |
| Tellafsee | 47 | Governor dead, & none elected since. |
| | 809 | |

Mialaquo or
Great Island

A Scale of Miles

Map of the Little Tennessee River in 1762, showing Cherokee towns and warrior households along the river. Colonial British officer Lieutenant Henry Timberlake drew the map during a mission to cement an alliance with the Overhill Cherokee. The junction of the river with the Big Tennessee, where TVA built the Tellico Dam more than two hundred years later, lies fifteen miles downstream. The "Enemy Mountains" are the Smokies; Chota was the Cherokee Jerusalem; "Tennefsee" town gave its name to the river; Toskegee was the birthplace of the great Cherokee scholar Sequoyah; and Fort Loudoun, built in 1756, figures prominently in the snail darter narrative. Archaeological excavations on Mialaquo, the Great Island, revealed the Little T to be one of the two oldest sites (over ten thousand years) of continuous human habitation in the lower forty-eight states (the other: Russell Cave National Monument).

banks of a fine meadow, . . . turned out my steed to graze, and then advanced into the strawberry plains to regale on the fragrant, delicious
fruit, thereafter riding past several Cherokee towns, each centered
on a council house, "[with a] very large dome or rotunda, situated on
top of an ancient artificial mound, . . . and on every side appeared little
plantations of Corn, Beans, &c, divided from each other by narrow
strips or borders of grass. . . . I ventured to ride through their lots,
being careful to do no injury."[1]

Several hundred yards farther downstream stood colonial Fort
Loudoun, perched on a hill overlooking Toskegee town, where the great
leader Sequoyah was born, and the pool where the small Tellico River
joined the Little Tennessee. The fort was built by the British, the South
Carolina militia, and the western "Overhill" Cherokees in the 1750s and
anchored the line of western forts defending against the French and
their Ohio valley tribal allies. Lieutenant Timberlake stayed at the little
fort during his mapping missions for the crown in the 1760s. The Cherokee, protected by the fort and their British allies, farmed, fished, and
flourished in their bright meadowlands along the flowing river.

The Little T valley remained the heart of the Cherokee confederation
until the early 1800s, when migrations of colonial settlers spilled over
the Appalachians from Pennsylvania, Virginia, and the Carolinas and
out onto the westward plateaus of Kentucky and Tennessee. The assault
begun by malicious South Carolinians—who gave the Cherokee nation
blankets infected with smallpox—was finished for the Cherokee by a
surging tide of white settlers. First a series of treaties pushed many of
them southward out of the Little T valley, and then came the mass westward "removal" engineered by Andrew Jackson and his protégé Martin
Van Buren. Defying a Supreme Court decision in favor of the Native
Americans, in 1838 they sent the army to drag the Cherokee from their
green fields and down a Trail of Tears to the arid desolation of Oklahoma. Only a small number of the Overhill Cherokee were able to escape removal, hiding in the rugged mountains and later settling in a
small Cherokee community on the North Carolina side of the Smokies.

It's little wonder that trout fishermen in the late twentieth century
would fall silent as they hiked across ancient fields past burial mounds
and waded into the river's cool currents. There was no place like it.

Upriver, in the narrow canyons adjoining the national park, the federal government coordinated a chain of six hydroelectric dams on the

Little T. Outside the Smokies, the Little T meandered thirty-three miles through gently rolling flatlands, then joined the Big Tennessee River, where it met a long chain of impoundments damming all of the Big Tennessee and many of its tributaries—2,500 linear miles of river now completely backed up behind dams. But here, released from its upstream mountain valley impoundments, the last undammed stretch of the Little T flowed more than a hundred yards wide through farmlands for thirty-three miles—clear, mostly knee- or waist-deep, murmuring as its blue-green waters flowed swiftly over shoals and around gentle curves, sliding along the meadows' undercut banks. A soft fog usually lay low on the waters in early morning, the river's rippling surface resonating with the subtle splashes of fish rising unseen, as trout fed on hundreds and thousands of mayflies and caddis flies hatching in the water currents and fluttering up through the mist like a snowfall in reverse.

The Little T was an ecological treasure, preserving a barely known cross-section of hundreds of forms of life that had evolved here over two hundred million years, with traces of the humans who had lived in and around its richness for ten thousand years. Even in the 1970s Ammoneta Sequoyah and his brother Lloyd, Sequoyah's great-great-great-grandsons, both traditional medicine men in their seventies, would

A view of the uppermost section of the free-flowing Little Tennessee River, with Chota meadow at the river bend. (Courtesy of Fran Scheidt)

come here from Cherokee, North Carolina, to gather herbs surreptitiously on the riverbanks of the white farms that had taken over their tribe's homeland. In one broad stretch of river near Toqua, now called Howard's Bluff, wading fishermen in the 1970s could look down through the clear water to discover they'd been traversing an ancient Native American fish trap: a long vee of rocks and ancient waterlogged timbers still rested in the riverbed facing upstream, where Cherokee women had once stood beating the water to scare fish toward spearmen waiting at the narrow end.

Rafters floating down the river through a late summer day past old Fort Loudoun would feel the cool of the water on their knees while the heat of the sun hovered overhead. Islands provided history-laden pull-outs where canoes could be landed for picnics and cloud-gazing. In many stretches along the riverbank, glades of willow, birch, and cottonwood trees lay deep, where Cherokees once lurked in early mornings waiting for deer and elk to come to water. Down on Rose Island the archaeologists were sifting through ancient layers of human lives long gone.

At day's end, sunset backlit the rolling grain fields on the western bank of the river, punctuated by scattered barns and silos, along with the steep sides of the great burial mound at Toqua, whose shadow still stretched toward the river. Lights winked on in the windows of farmhouses in hollows across fields along the river—the homesteads of more than three hundred farm families. Some had lived here, farming the valley's rich, dark soils, since federal armies evicted the Cherokee in the 1830s. Many families were of the same Scotch-Irish stock as Davy Crockett and Daniel Boone, and Sam Houston, who grew up near the river and lived for a while there with the Cherokee. As pioneers, these families had moved south and westward, following the Appalachian mountains, as they tried to stay ahead of the town-building pressures coming from the east. When they saw the rich soils and fish-filled waters of the Little Tennessee Valley, some decided to settle here and push on no more.

Sixteen miles downstream from Great Island and old Fort Loudoun, past the broad shoals at the Coytee Spring and hundreds more acres of rich farmlands, stood an isolated slab of concrete placed there in 1968. It bridged a small side channel beside a mile-wide pasture on Bussell's Island just above the Little T's junction with the Big Tennessee. The unfinished dam wasn't very big, spanning scarcely a hundred feet. Kids

Farmland along the Little Tennessee River, with wide swaths of prime bottomland soils, USDA Grade 1 and 2 soils. (Courtesy of Fran Scheidt)

could throw pebbles over it. It had stood there awkwardly for a half-dozen years, perched on concrete legs over the channel, unconnected to anything in the broad valley—but the Tennessee Valley Authority called it Tellico Dam. If and when the agency was allowed to build earthen dikes out across the pastures beside it, walling off the main channel of the river, the waters of the Little T would slowly back up thirty-three miles, all the way to the mountains. The Little T would form a narrow, meandering impoundment, murky with algae and averaging less than twenty feet in depth. A layer of mud and water would drown the rich meadowlands along both banks of the Little T, flooding all the Native American town sites except the burial ground at Settacoo, which would be awash. The Little T would no longer be a river, but something less.

A few miles upstream from the dam's cement skeleton, in the shallow riffles of the shoals at Coytee Spring, the little secret that might make a surprising difference darted furtively among cobblestones and gravel down on the river's floor.

The Tennessee Valley Authority initially focused on big projects. Created in 1933 to pull the Appalachian region out of two centuries of economic backwardness further deepened by the Great Depression, TVA was given authority over all or part of seven Southern states by President Franklin Delano Roosevelt's New Deal, as a "federal corporation clothed with the power of government but possessed of the flexibility and initiative of private enterprise." A phalanx of young social engineers came down from the North to this national backwater, planning unprecedented governmental development initiatives and spending unprecedented amounts of federal dollars to revitalize the vast territory assigned to them. David Lilienthal, one of TVA's early leaders, liked to describe the agency's programs as "democracy on the march."[2]

TVA's two major development missions were to manufacture fertilizer to boost agriculture, and electricity to boost everything else. The young progressives were less entranced by the former goal, which got parceled off to Muscle Shoals, Alabama, so they focused instead upon electric power. Operations were based in Knoxville, Tennessee, which soon became a garden city at the edge of the Smokies.

A catalog of the region's sixty-nine potential dam sites was put together in 1934, and the first, Norris Dam, went on line in 1936, followed quickly by two dozen more hydro dams along the Big Tennessee River and its tributaries. During World War II much of the hydropower was dedicated to defense necessities, such as processing aircraft aluminum and nuclear materials. War needs quickly outstripped hydro capacity, so in the 1950s, with all the favorable hydro sites built, TVA shifted to coal-fired plants for the bulk of its power output; in the 1960s it began adding a half-dozen nuclear reactors.

By the early 1970s hydro provided less than 10 percent of TVA's electric capacity, although the big, roaring dams of the early days remained the agency's emblematic image. Along the way, the availability of cheap electricity substantially changed Appalachian society, helping to pull much of the population, especially in small towns, into the twentieth century.

During the New Deal, conservative Republicans focused their political wrath against the "socialistic experiment." They needn't have worried so much: soon enough TVA's young iconoclasts were transformed by the Appalachian Eden into utility company executives, and they became the core of the region's political establishment and social elite. They didn't move back North, and they no longer represented anything approaching socialism. To a man, federal appointees sent down to Tennessee in the early Eisenhower years with marching orders to shrink and privatize the agency did the opposite, broadly extending the agency's regional footprint. The leadership grew more stolid, backing away from earlier innovative planning and human development agendas and focusing on selling electricity.

In 1959 a congressional act converted TVA into an autonomous government entity that, unlike other federal agencies, could authorize most of its energy initiatives itself, funding them with power revenues without federal oversight. TVA was exempted from more than a dozen federal statutes, notably an exemption from federal land condemnation restrictions. Alone among government agencies TVA didn't have to go before juries to establish payment for taking private lands for its self-authorized projects. Condemnation compensation was set by TVA's own employees. When extra funds were necessary, TVA did not need to go to Congress's standing committees. It could get them in a shortcut process from the congressional appropriations committees, the home of what was traditionally known as the pork barrel for its generous funding of legislators' pet projects.

TVA preferred to be seen as having grassroots populist support. It organized and funded, among others, Citizens for TVA (CTVA), a regional civic association dedicated to backing the agency's programs. CTVA enrolled more than thirty thousand judges, mayors, state and local political leaders, newspaper editors, labor and business leaders, and power distributors. The federal agency became America's largest utility company, woven deeply into the economies and politics of its region. During Barry Goldwater's 1964 presidential campaign, when he repeated the old conservative mantra that TVA should be dismantled, business-oriented Republicans around the region howled in protest, and he quickly changed his tune.

Chairman Aubrey Joseph Wagner, called "Red" for his auburn hair, came down to TVA from Wisconsin in 1934 to take a job as a junior assistant engineer. Only twenty-two, he started working his way up through the power structure, focusing on every detail of the agency's operations and cultivating powerful friendships that helped him rise through the agency's internal politics. By 1954 Wagner was general manager and had made himself and his trusted associates the agency's controlling force. By 1962 he was already being referred to as "Mr. TVA," and his dominance became official: he was appointed chairman of the

TVA board, from which pinnacle he exercised unchallengeable authority about everything TVA did.

On Friday, February 13, 1959, Wagner called more than twenty regional TVA officials to a meeting held at a hydropower station seventy miles downriver from the agency's Knoxville headquarters. The conference room's large windows overlooked the huge Watts Bar Dam, more than a half-mile wide, which had been built in 1939.

In recent years Wagner and others had reluctantly been forced to acknowledge that TVA was suffering from internal malaise. The older generation of leadership had built a gigantic power corporation, but the brightest young engineers and planners from the valley and around the country were choosing to pursue their careers elsewhere. Building power plants for a big utility company wasn't a stirring professional aspiration. TVA morale was low, and prospects for recapturing a central regional role for the agency seemed poor. Worse, some academic economists were starting to wonder whether TVA had in fact been the savior of the region as it purported to be. In comparison with counties in surrounding states outside the agency's realm, data collected by Oak Ridge energy and economics analyst William Chandler indicated that TVA counties had statistically the same or even lower degrees of economic growth.[3]

But Wagner had an idea that might rekindle the agency's spirit and dynamism, resurrecting the image of mighty dams that had characterized TVA's glory days and giving the agency, he said, a "new mission." His memo announcing the meeting declared the agenda: Even though no suitable hydropower sites remained, TVA should pursue building more dams by imagining regional development justifications for their renewed mission. "It may be possible to demonstrate that added projects would contribute enough to further regional development to amply justify their construction," he wrote. "It may only depend on how ingenious and resourceful we can be in finding a basis for evaluating a project's usefulness. . . . Come . . . and bring all the optimism you have."[4]

Within days after that Friday the thirteenth meeting, TVA staffers had churned out a series of brainstorming proposals to bring the agency back into the dam-building business. The proposal Wagner favored was to build a small dam on the last remaining undammed stretch of the Little Tennessee, for which they'd need to conjure an inventive variety of economic development claims. The new project

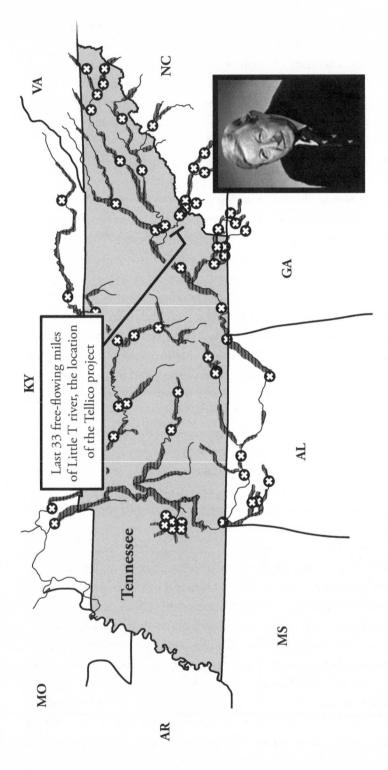

Map of federal dams in the Tennessee River system as of the late 1970s; more than sixty dams back up 2,500 linear river miles, dam to dam. Flagged section denotes the last thirty-three miles of free-flowing Little Tennessee River—TVA's Tellico project. A version of this graphic was presented to the U.S. Supreme Court in the citizens' brief. Inset: TVA Chairman Aubrey "Red" Wagner. (Map created by Nathan Bress and author; Wagner photo: Tennessee Valley Authority)

Last 33 free-flowing miles
of Little T river, the location
of the Tellico project

would be called Tellico Dam, after the little river that joined the Little T at Fort Loudoun.

Once a project has a name, it takes on a life of its own. A name gives it a concrete identity and drives bureaucratic momentum. The name "Tellico Dam" instantly provided a tangible reference for Wagner's staff. It implied highly focused capital investment and a set of stirring images—mighty concrete piers, thundering spillways, and clouds of white spume, with electrical towers in the background.

But Tellico Dam would actually be quite small, with no generators. Wagner himself, in an uncharacteristic moment of candor, admitted to a reporter that "any power or flood control benefit would be insignificant."[5] The internal TVA cost accounting showed that, after adding together total benefits for flood control, barge navigation, and power, the dam would still lose forty to fifty cents for every dollar spent.[6]

How, then, could the dam be justified? Wagner demanded that his staffers, especially the agency economists, come up with plausible-sounding economic reasons to build it, because federal law required all projects to have cost-benefit projections that theoretically could justify their expense.

Recreation quickly became the leading candidate for project justification. The waters of the Little T were cleaner than impounded stretches of river outside the mountains. Boaters and fishermen from the reservoirs surrounding the Little T might flock to a new Tellico reservoir. Wagner's staffers hypothesized net recreation benefits at more than a million dollars a year.

Several TVA economists objected that it was wrong to count recreation diverted from existing reservoirs as a net benefit, and likewise inappropriate to ignore the more promising alternative of flowing-river recreation and tourism development. Several suggestions were made for development without a dam. These included constructing a bridge (perhaps incorporating the existing pylons of an old railroad crossing so that tourists could drive up through the valley's historic sites and directly into the Smokies) and an agricultural program encouraging farmers to cultivate specialized crops for an innovative biomass energy program that a prior TVA study had shown to be feasible.

Red let loose his famous temper, denouncing the suggested alternatives and making it clear that staff could get with the new dam mission or get out. Some economists left. Those who stayed obligingly made

Wagner's projections for recreational benefits one of the Tellico Dam project's two major official justifications.

The second novel claim was a proposed model city. Athelstan Spilhaus, a noted futurist, had prepared an experimental design for a city in Minnesota that was never built. Harking back to the agency's role in the Depression, TVA planners suggested that a model industrial city of fifty thousand could be hypothesized for the banks of a Tellico reservoir, and they predicted it could generate twenty-five thousand jobs and large economic benefits. Those numbers became the repeated basis for Wagner's speeches in support of the project.

TVA gave the model city the name "Timberlake New Town," after the British officer who had mapped the Little T in 1762. Wagner enlisted the Boeing Corporation to partner with TVA in designing Timberlake and lobbying Congress to fund it. Boeing, facing stiff competition in its airplane markets, was looking for new lines of business.

TVA began to condemn sixty square miles of private lands, most of it for the potential Timberlake development. Wagner had persuaded Boeing to join him in the project on the hope (soon deflated) that Congress would provide $800 million or more to fund the model city through a national infrastructure grant program. TVA did not include the projected cost of the model city in the dam project's budget. The agency nevertheless did claim Timberlake's projected land development benefits in support of its dam, even though Boeing soon pulled out and the model city would never be built.

But why site an industrial city on a backwater in the Smokies? That's where Wagner protégé Mike Foster came in. He created the "Foster Hypothesis," which asserted that industry would inevitably come to any site where three modes of transportation were available: rail, highway, and barge channel. The Little T project was adjacent to a railroad line and two interstate highways. To justify the need for a dam, a barge channel would be dug through to the adjacent Fort Loudoun reservoir. Dissident agency economists noted that Foster's theory presented no evidence of any such success in any previous project. Even the Army Corps of Engineers, called in to confirm TVA's cost-benefit analysis, harshly criticized it as unreasonable.[7]

A variety of additional smaller project benefits were also hypothesized—water supply, flood control, power generation through a canal, wildlife benefits—though each had in fact been identified by agency staff as trivial, unnecessary, mistaken, or net losses. But these increments, like the recreation and shore land development claims, were bulked up by five dubious assumptions that Wagner's economists were ordered to apply to all their economic calculations. These stated that:

1. Without the dam project, the Little Tennessee River area would never develop economically;
2. The Tellico project would not detract from any economic benefits already enjoyed in the area;
3. If a hypothetical economic benefit *could* take place at Tellico, then it *would;*
4. All economic growth that occurred in the area after project completion would be attributable to the project; and
5. Project costs would not rise faster than the [low] annual inflation rate of the early 1960s.[8]

Using these highly questionable premises, the agency first claimed a cost-benefit ratio of 1 to 1.3—that is, over the life of the project it would produce benefits of $1.30 per $1.00 spent—and later increased this ratio to 1 to 1.7.[9] "The proposal doesn't make economic sense," argued Kerry Schell, a TVA economist who was asked to produce claimed benefit figures in a series of doubtful categories. "In economic terms it's indefensible, a big mistake." He left the agency shortly afterward and began a successful career teaching economics at the state university.

Wagner worried about local opposition to the Tellico Dam idea. While Citizens for TVA, his handpicked organization of supporters, would back the plan, the agricultural communities in and around the Little T valley might need to be persuaded because a substantial majority of the land that would be seized—almost two-thirds of the sixty square miles, more than 23,600 of the 38,000-plus acreage total—would be condemned for nonreservoir uses, primarily Boeing's Timberlake real estate development scheme. In other words, three hundred or more families would be forced to abandon some of the richest agricultural soils in the nation so that the agency could justify its development claims for the model city project. The agricultural economies of the valley and its surrounding towns would be essentially eliminated. To keep the scale of these farmland condemnations as invisible as possible, Wagner decreed that no publicly released TVA map of the project would show the actual full outline of land taken for nonreservoir uses.

Rumors about a Tellico Dam proposal occasionally leaked out of TVA in the three years after the 1959 Watts Bar meeting, but despite the agency's feverish internal planning its press office consistently assured inquiring reporters that Tellico was only one of many possible projects being studied. In late 1963, however, Wagner told his staff to create and fund a local booster group for the dam. He named it the Little Tennessee River Valley Development Association. TVA appointed three directors from each of the three adjoining counties to the association, and Wagner began briefing them informally on his exciting plans for the valley.

Chairman Wagner's statements to the press, however, were seemingly tentative: "The new project should not be built unless the people in the region want it and intend to fully develop it. . . . [Before asking Congress for funding] we want to get the reaction of the people in the area. We've had a lot of reaction and nearly all of it favorable."

Wagner prepared a promotional handout for his Little T development association emphasizing how TVA's Tellico plan would modernize the community:

> The area is now completely rural. . . . Income levels are low and typical of the Appalachian region, unemployment is high and job opportunities limited. Here then is a rare opportunity, starting from scratch, to plan and build a whole new complex of working places, living places, recreation and leisure-time facilities. . . . We will provide for our young people what I believe to be one of the greatest gifts of a free and democratic society. . . . This is the availability to young men and young women of a variety of choices as to what they may do with their lives. A society is not truly free if a young man must farm because his father farmed.[10]

Wagner traveled to Greenback, Tennessee, in September 1964 to present details of the Tellico project to the local population, convinced that with his development association's backing he could sell the idea to the local community. Instead it was a disaster. More than four hundred people had gathered for the meeting, and a parade of farmers and local townspeople went to the microphone to condemn the project proposal, declaring bitter opposition to any agency plan that would take valley lands away from their owners and out of agricultural production.

In his turn at the microphone Circuit Judge Sue Hicks, a respected local elder who had been a prosecutor in the so-called Scopes monkey trial (and who was the rumored inspiration for Johnny Cash's song "A Boy Named Sue"), lambasted Wagner for the plan's destructive effects on old Fort Loudoun, and called for a local referendum on the dam; Wagner angrily rejected the referendum idea "because this project is not just for locals." A series of fishermen spoke of this last flowing river as a regional treasure. The model city plan was treated as a joke. As a local paper reported, "No one spoke in favor of it at the meeting last night . . . and the leaders estimated that at least ninety per cent of those present were opposed to the project." Six of the nine directors of the group Wagner had created to boost his Tellico Dam declared on the spot that they'd never support it—saying that river-based development alongside the family farms would be far wiser.[11]

Wagner was enraged. The Little Tennessee River Valley Development Association and its federal funding were immediately abolished, and within a month he and his staff created a new citizen support group with more reliably supportive members, calling it the Tellico Tri-County Development Association. The directors of this new group began promoting the dam in local politics and were flown up to Washington for the first of many trips to support Tellico Dam funding at appropriations hearings.

Because Tellico wasn't a power project, TVA couldn't pay for it with power revenues, instead needing congressional funding. TVA's project justification claims were obviously problematic but good enough to win approval on Capitol Hill. Although a positive cost-benefit ratio is theoretically required by congressional rules to get a project funded by U.S. taxpayers, the integrity of agency calculations is almost never questioned. Most legislators show no desire to scrutinize the inflated economic projections that keep congressional pork barrels rolling.

In 1966 Wagner flew to Washington and was warmly received by the House appropriations subcommittee in charge of funding water projects. Ignoring the testimony of farmers and fishermen who had carpooled there to testify against the logic and economics of the dam, the subcommittee enthusiastically accepted Wagner's patchwork economic projections. It gave TVA $3.2 million, the first of many annual payments, to start the Tellico project. It was budgeted at a total project cost of $28 million, a hypothetical figure that as usual for such projects would escalate every year and ultimately reach more than $160 million.

Although the Little Tennessee River Valley Development Association had been officially disbanded, the core of the angry group gathered at Robert and Fran Dorward's house near the river in mid-October and began drafting a constitution and bylaws for a new group they called the Association for the Preservation of the Little Tennessee River. At a public meeting the following Wednesday evening at Rose Island, more than two hundred farmers, townspeople, and fishermen cheered heartfelt speeches against the dam and signed up to fight TVA under the banner of the new group.

For a coalition of rural citizens with limited experience in the national realm, the Little T preservation association showed remarkable savvy in rallying support. Over the next few years, meeting every several weeks at old Fort Loudoun, the core group formed and conducted an energetic campaign strategy. Although the group didn't have the economic expertise to challenge TVA's elaborate cost-benefit justifications—as Fran Dorward said, "All we knew is, those claims were phony"—they figured out how to pull in politically potent allies. They invited Justice William O. Douglas to visit the valley and gave him an extensive tour of farmlands, Native American mounds, river islands, and the old fort. They persuaded the Eastern Band of Cherokees across the mountains in North Carolina to join the opposition, and the Cherokees helped guide Douglas around the upper valley. Douglas vowed to carry the message back to Washington, and several weeks later prepared an article that *National Geographic* agreed to publish with photographs showing the nation what it would lose if Tellico Dam was built.[12] Making contacts through Tennessee rod-and-gun clubs, they persuaded Secretary of Interior Stewart Udall to begin a Wild and Scenic River Act study to preserve the Little T. Visiting Tennessee, Udall told local reporters that "citizens need to ask themselves whether people 50 years from now will think rivers were better left alone than impounded by second- and third-rate dams."[13]

A stream of letters poured into local newspapers from the Little T preservation group and its supporters. Small delegations of farmers and others from the group made the long road trip over the mountains to Washington to testify at each subsequent annual House appropriations subcommittee hearing, while TVA's booster groups flew overhead at taxpayer expense to do the same. As in 1966, the farmers' testimony repeatedly fell on deaf ears. When the farmers fought TVA's land condemnations in court, the local federal judge consistently decided in favor of TVA's expropriations.

The Little T activists built up a list of more than fifty organizations, national and local, that formally signed on to declare their opposition to the Tellico project. This included, remarkably, the United States Chamber of Commerce, which opposed condemnations of private lands for redevelopment, as well as multistate chapters of Trout Unlimited, and smaller groups like the Sweetwater Pig Breeders Association. They persuaded a professor at the University of Tennessee to study the economics of the dam project, which resulted in an extremely critical hundred-page economic analysis that TVA immediately and expectedly dismissed.[14] On the highways of eastern Tennessee, Charlie Tombras, an avid fly fisherman and member of the local Trout Unlimited chapter, rented twenty billboards with the block letter message "Anybody can build a dam. Only God can make a river."

The antidam activists argued forcefully that economic development without a dam would be practical and far more beneficial—continuing the family farm agriculture and trout fishing and float-boating recreational activities, and creating a tourism route up through the valley's historic sites to the Great Smokies national park, while providing locations for industrial development near the highway bridge and for residential development downstream on the western shore.

The farmers and their allies testified in numerous federal, state, and local forums against the dam, beginning in 1966. Here farmer Alfred Davis testifies in a House-sponsored hearing. (©Roger Simpson, used with permission)

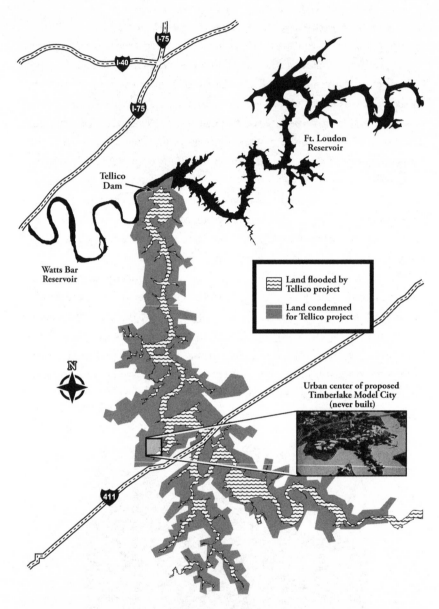

Land flooded by
Tellico project

Land condemned
for Tellico project

Ft. Loudon
Reservoir

Tellico
Dam

Watts Bar
Reservoir

Urban center of proposed
Timberlake Model City
(never built)

N

I-75
I-40
I-75
411

TVA's Tellico project total area, showing the sixty square miles of private lands taken for a reservoir-based development plan. Inset: TVA model of part of the proposed Timberlake model city, an industrial city for which TVA claimed "50,000 residents" and "25,000 industrial jobs" in its justification of the Tellico project. Indeed, most of the land taken from the valley's families was done so for planned urban development and recreational development. The cement dam structure is on a narrow channel at the top of the diagram, adjacent to Fort Loudon Dam and the backed-up waters of Watts Bar Dam. (Map created by Nathan Bress with images from TVA's environmental impact statement for "Timberlake New Community," 1974)

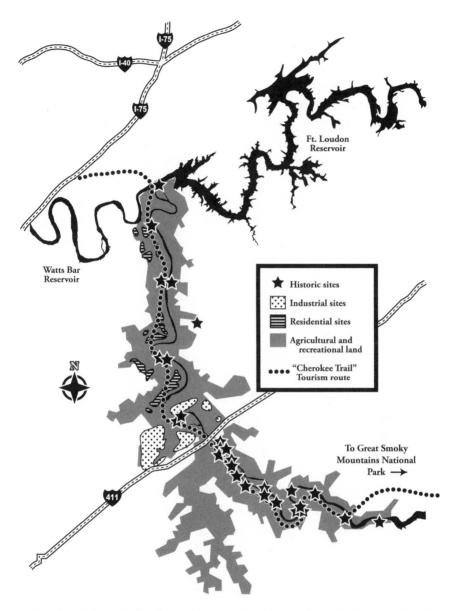

River-based alternative development proposed by citizens resisting the dam; a version of this graphic was presented to the U.S. Supreme Court in the citizens' brief. Over the years this group consistently advocated Little T valley economic development alternatives to the dam project, including river-based recreation, industrial parks, scattered residential development, and tourism—along with returning the farmers to their land. (Map created by Nathan Bress from Little Tennessee River Alliance and TVA maps)

But Wagner remained adamant. Years earlier, citizen opposition had torpedoed a dam TVA planned to build on the French Broad River, and Wagner swore this would never happen again. Land condemnations and purchases under threat of condemnation pushed inexorably through the Little T valley's farms, one by one. To divide local landowners, some families with key locations were given sweetheart cash deals and allowed to retain land adjoining the future reservoir. Other local notables were promised land or service contracts in the project area.

TVA used sticks as well as carrots. Alfred Davis, a farmer in Greenback, was audited by the IRS three times in four years. The third time he asked the auditor, "Why are you coming back here again and again? You've never found a mistake in my taxes, and last time the audit ended up giving me a refund." The auditor paused cautiously, then said, "Look, you figure it out. It's well known you're fighting that Tellico project, and TVA is a federal agency with some very powerful friends. Do you understand what I'm saying?" After the Cherokee tribal council was similarly hit with an IRS audit, the tribe lowered its profile in the coalition. Mack Prichard, an outspoken state historian desperately eager to save the historic valley, donated $200 to the Little T group. In 1972 he discovered that he'd been put on an IRS watch list because TVA reported that he'd claimed charitable deductions "illegally attempting to influence legislation."

TVA's condemnation tactics were aggressive. TVA workers painted huge demolition numbers on the sides of homes and farm buildings while families were still living and farming there, marginalized dam opponents within their communities with whisper campaigns, removed fences so cows would escape into the countryside, and burned and bulldozed emptied homes and barns to punctuate the fact that the community would never again be the same.

The agency pushed ahead with infrastructure, building a new and higher Highway 411 bridge across the river to replace the existing 411 bridge, which would be awash in a reservoir. Because the countryside was relatively low-lying in many locations, long concrete walls were erected in several places around the valley to hold in the future reservoir waters. In 1968, at the bottom of the valley where a channel curved around Bussell's Island, TVA poured the concrete structure of Tellico Dam to show the world that the reservoir was inevitable. The structure cost just $4 million to build, out of a total project cost then estimated at $59 million including land, bridges, and roads; earthen dikes and levees remained to be built to make a reservoir possible. Within TVA, Wagner's staff hoped that building the concrete structure would quiet the opposition.

It didn't. "You've still got a beautiful river here," Alfred Davis said at one of the dam resisters' meetings. "There's thousands of acres of good bottomland soils in the valley, and just an itty-bitty little cement box down there in that far-off corner." The Little T group fought on.

In 1969 Congress passed the National Environmental Policy Act (NEPA), which contained a provision that, despite showing no outward sign of having enforceable teeth, contained a hidden strength: it said major federal projects needed an environmental impact statement, and Tellico Dam didn't have one. Wagner was furious. He ordered his attorneys to insist that the environmental impact requirement did not apply to his dam: the law was passed after Tellico was planned, so they argued the law contained an implied grandfather clause exempting ongoing projects. The environmental law's prohibitions should not apply to TVA because it had been created as "an emergency agency" (they were thus claiming implied immunity from modern federal law because TVA was created to address the Great Depression). The dam, they also argued, would cause no *net* environmental harms, because the environmental *benefits* Wagner claimed for his reservoir would far outweigh whatever negatives might occur with the loss of the river. At most, TVA attorneys argued, the impact statement requirement could be satisfied by writing a simple paragraph stating the agency's conclusions.

Inspired in part by Rachel Carson's *Silent Spring*, the first Earth Day in 1970 had spawned the Environmental Defense Fund, a public-interest lawyering group funded by several large foundations. The Little T farmers and volunteers begged the year-old national group to come to Tennessee and take up the environmental impact statement case. The group's lawyers agreed, and in 1972, after six weeks of testimony on the dam's environmental problems, Robert Taylor, the trial judge, issued his ruling: Tellico was not immune from compliance with the law. He issued an injunction that stopped all work on the project until an environmental impact statement could be produced and approved by the court.

At virtually the same moment, the farmers were further buoyed by Tennessee's governor Winfield Dunn, who, responding to their pleas, sent a letter to Wagner officially requesting that TVA scrap the Tellico project:

> The best interests of the state would best be served if TVA were to discontinue plans to impound the Little Tennessee River. . . . Impoundment . . . would reduce, rather than expand, recreational opportunities in Tennessee. . . . The lands which would be inundated by the Tellico lake contain numerous sites of historical and archaeological interest, and the proposed reservoir would bury a great acreage of . . . cropland, pasturage, and woodland. . . . The Little Tennessee could best serve . . . as the focal point for a scenic river recreational gateway to the national [park] beyond. . . . Much of . . . the public monies already invested . . . can be reclaimed or turned to other uses. The Little Tennessee as it now exists is a waterway too valuable for the State of Tennessee to sacrifice.

Red Wagner responded angrily to both obstructions. He ordered his attorneys to appeal the trial court injunction and fired off a letter to the governor rejecting the state's request. "Your letter does not appear to raise any new or different factors from those which were fully considered by both TVA and the Congress before construction of the Tellico project was commenced. . . . The course of action you have proposed would sacrifice the much broader benefits which can be realized through comprehensive development as provided by the Tellico project."[15]

Wagner then lectured the governor for thirty-four paragraphs about the project's benefits in the same terms he had long been touting—a "full range" of industrial, recreational, and urban residential development benefits—and derided the river's defenders as politically insignificant. "Congress," he said (referring to the appropriations subcommittee), had heard the farmers' arguments and rejected them by approving more funds. Development of the condemned lands along the reservoir would provide nine thousand industrial jobs and sixteen thousand service jobs. The Timberlake model city (dependent, he neglected to add, on massive and unlikely taxpayer subsidies) would have fifty thousand inhabitants by 1998. His project would bring wealth to eastern Tennessee and stop the outflow of young people seeking a better life elsewhere.

Wagner's words rang with a sense of inevitability: "We expect to continue to work . . . to develop the resources of the lower Little Tennessee in a manner which will assure realization of its full potential."

As he later told an interviewer, "We had to look at the overall scope of the project and then go ahead with it. [Past] governors had supported Tellico, so it didn't make sense to say 'yes' to one governor and 'no' to another. . . . Some things should go on regardless of who is in office."

While his lawyers fought the injunction, Wagner's headquarters continued its planning, not even pausing when Boeing Corporation executives analyzed the numbers and began backing away, eventually cutting ties with TVA in 1975. Internal dissent continued to be suppressed. The agency's public relations department issued frequent briefings insisting that the reservoir project would start again as soon as the legal technicalities were overcome, and with an impact statement, if necessary. Wagner never relented on Tellico. Sixteen months after the injunction was issued his lawyers took a thick, three-volume impact statement to the court. It set out the project's claimed benefits at length, dismissed with brief commentaries all the objections raised by dam opponents, and declared all alternatives to the dam proposal inadequate because they "would result in the failure to realize the benefits that will be provided by the Tellico project, which in TVA's judgment are too valuable to be lost."[16]

The National Environmental Policy Act doesn't have the authority to veto bad projects. Once TVA provided an impact statement listing all the environmental harms its dam project might cause, and some alternatives, it had complied with the law, which contains no substantive command requiring TVA (or any agency that submits an impact statement) to avoid the environmental harms described in its impact statements. As a result, TVA was now free to continue the project as planned. Judge Taylor's quick acceptance of TVA's statement spelled the end for the farmers and their Little T dam-fighting group. They realized there were no more legal avenues to stave off the inevitable. The river and the farmlands would be lost.

Around this time I asked a staffer in the middle ranks of TVA's bureaucracy why the agency was still pushing such a mistaken dam project. "You've got to understand," he confided wryly. "It's *male menopause:* Wagner and his headquarters guys came down here thirty years ago and saw themselves as saviors lifting this region up from nothing. They desperately want to lead the pack again. Tellico's become an obsession. They get hot flashes when local people start questioning their decisions."

The Tellico Dam structure in 1975, after having been halted by
the farmers' environmental impact statement litigation; the
cost of the structure to this point: less than $4.1 million.
(Photo: Tennessee Valley Authority)

There was, however, a little-noticed line in TVA's impact statement.
It noted the possibility that one or more species of endangered fish
might live in the Little T, but concluded that "none . . . is known to exist in the project area." Eight weeks after the environmental protection
act injunction was dissolved, President Richard Nixon signed the new
Endangered Species Act into law. And one Sunday that August, standing in the middle of the Little T near Coytee Spring, University of Tennessee ichthyologist David Etnier bent down and cupped his hands
around a strange little perch he'd noticed darting among the cobbles in
the clear, flowing water.

# CHAPTER 2

# At the Old Fort
## The Start of a Small Crusade for a Little Fish

**OCTOBER 12, 1974**

Even in October, the shadows right after sunset glow warm purple in a Tennessee dusk. The headlights of our little white Fiat probe the shadows along the road as my traveling companion, law student Hank Hill, points the way down to Vonore from Knoxville across the Highway 411 bridge, then up along the west bank of the Little Tennessee River on a potholed blacktop road not wide enough for a center line. Now the headlight beams bounce up and down as we turn onto a dirt road cutting back toward the river and bump our way over rocks and ruts toward a dark knoll covered with trees. We park the car in a clearing and climb the knoll, passing through a gloomy assemblage of hemlock logs standing spiked together in sagging barricades, up to a small log blockhouse.

This scattering of fortifications is what's left of old Fort Loudoun, built here at a curve of the river in 1757, anchoring the defensive crescent of British forts that arced all the way north to Pittsburgh's Fort Duquesne, renamed Fort Pitt by the British. This hill has seen redcoats and French emissaries, white traders and Cherokee war paint. A few brutal skirmishes were fought here on the Little T, including a brief uprising of Cherokee against the British soldiers, but mostly the fort was a place of watchful wariness, a center for strategic planning, and a gathering place for the valley's inhabitants. The fort was partly restored during the early twentieth century but has since mostly settled back into spooky decrepitude, aside from the addition of a small, recently built prefab office structure.

Despite the gathering darkness, however, we still have a commanding view of the river from the old fort. The Little Tennessee is a dark silver band murmuring around the base of the hill, undulating both downstream through farmlands to the Big Tennessee, and upstream a dozen miles to the Smoky Mountains, their peaks still rosy in the sunset.

It's a Saturday in October 1974. We are here for a hastily arranged potluck supper, carrying with us an idea that may lead to a foolish decision. Before coming down to Knoxville in September 1973 as a greenhorn assistant professor of property and environmental law, I'd read about the Little T River and the TVA's Tellico Dam project. The river was described with awe in *Field & Stream* magazine—cool and clear, shallow but wide and majestic in its flow, the biggest and finest trout water east of Montana, but threatened by a dubious reservoir project. My new students in Tennessee had asked whether I'd like to fish the

Aerial view of Little Tennessee River and surrounding farmlands, circa 1970. Colonial Fort Loudoun is at left on the western bank—the frequent meeting place for dam resisters during a dozen years of conflict, and the starting point for the snail darter battle. Railway and Highway 411 bridges are in the middle distance at right. Except for the property immediately adjacent to the river, most of the farmland in this photograph was taken by TVA for resale and real estate development. (© Dean Stone, photographer, used with permission)

Little T, but I declined, knowing from experience the angst of getting to know a river only to lose it.

Although the small concrete dam structure had been erected several years earlier, nothing more had been done on the project because of the farmers' environmental impact statement lawsuit. Some dam opponents—farmers, along with fishermen, history buffs, and local conservationists—hoped the dam was dead. Encouraging reports came from Joe Congleton, an intense young Knoxville lawyer and Trout Unlimited activist devoted to the river and its trout fishing. "I keep hearing rumors from inside TVA," Congleton had told the local Trout Unlimited chapter, whose members cherished the Little T. "For certain, Boeing is pulling out of the project. Even inside TVA people are saying the dam doesn't make any economic sense. Some top TVA staffers are admitting it shouldn't be built."

For a while, Congleton's wishful thinking seemed correct. Even after TVA's attorneys persuaded the Circuit Court in Cincinnati to end the impact statement injunction in spring of 1974, the Tellico project didn't seem to be moving forward. Farm condemnation cases stayed strangely dormant, as did most of the road, bridge, and levee construction associated with the reservoir plan. The hardy survivors of the Association for the Preservation of the Little T crossed their fingers and waited.

In the fall, however, the TVA grapevine had started stirring. *Abandon Tellico Dam?!* TVA's Chairman Red Wagner had gone apoplectic when the suggestion had been cautiously raised within his staff. The design for a Timberlake model city on the shores of a Tellico reservoir would be officially presented in November. "The Tellico project will be built as planned!"

During this time Hiram "Hank" Hill, a second-year student at the University of Tennessee College of Law, was searching around for a topic for an environmental law term paper. Shaggy haired, built inside and out like one of those cherry bombs sold surreptitiously at stands on the highway south of the river, and raised at the base of Lookout Mountain near Chattanooga, Hank was bright and pugnacious. One afternoon he came to my office with a question. That past summer he had often socialized with a raucous bunch of graduate students who were studying fish biology under an eminent and equally feisty UT scientist, ichthyologist David Etnier. Hank's friends told him about a discovery that Etnier and his doctoral student Bob Stiles had made on the second Sunday of August 1973. They were wading along the shoals near Coytee Spring on the Little T when Etnier, wearing a snorkeling face mask, reached down between some cobblestones on the river bottom and grabbed a dappled, tan-colored, two-inch fish. Etnier called out to Stiles to come over and look. "Here's a darter that's never before been identified," he said. "It probably lived in other stretches of big river around here, but they'll all have been killed off now by dams. We'll have to see, but this little fish looks like she's going to be a new endangered species." Later, coming out of the river, Etnier spoke with the farmer who'd let them cross his meadows to get to the river. "Bill Kitrell was standing there with his dog, Dog," Etnier said. "I showed him the darter and told him, 'Here's a little fish that might save your farm.'" Back in the lab, Etnier confirmed that the fish he'd caught belonged to a previously unknown species of tiny perch. One student, Wayne Starnes, decided to write his Ph.D. dissertation on the fish. Because the fish's diet contained an unusually large number of very small river snails, Etnier and his students were calling their find a "snail darter."[1]

Hank described to me what his fish biologist friends had found. "The Endangered Species Act had some teeth added to it last year," he noted, "so an endangered fish might be able to block Tellico Dam. Do you think that's enough for a ten-page paper?"

I said yes, I thought it was.

Over the next few days Hank kept returning to my office with data from the fish lab and information on revisions to the Endangered Species Act, passed into law in December. The lab data was clear. Etnier, a hard-nosed scientist, had satisfied himself that the fish was a solid species, and he suspected it had been eliminated everywhere else in its natural range by dams.

TVA learned about the darter as soon as it was discovered because TVA biologists regularly worked with Etnier (in fact, he had trained most of them). They had since been sent all over Tennessee trying unsuccessfully to find other populations so the agency could say the species wasn't endangered. Etnier was relishing TVA's discomfiture. At the end of a workday, relaxing with his lab students and enjoying a beer, he waved his cigar and chortled, "Shit, this little bugger is giving TVA fits!"

Hank's research on the Endangered Species Act's legislative history unearthed evidence in the *Congressional Record* and committee reports

David Etnier (right) and several University of Tennessee ichthyology graduate students seine-netting a river shoal near Coytee Spring, where the snail darter was first discovered. Wayne Starnes (second from right) wrote his doctoral dissertation on the darter. (Courtesy of Fran Scheidt)

Netted snail darters being examined near the river shoals at Coytee Spring. (Courtesy of Fran Scheidt [right]; © Joel Sartore/joelsartore.com [left])

that most legislators assumed they were voting to protect eagles, whooping cranes, and such, but in the record a few had said more than once that the law should prohibit the harming of *any* species and be strictly enforced against federal agencies.[2] The more we mulled over the Endangered Species Act, the clearer it became that killing off the darter would be a violation of that law. Given the spirit of the times, an idea like that couldn't remain just an academic notion. Richard Nixon had just been impeached, and my mentor Joe Sax, the nation's preeminent environmental law professor, had visited UT that spring urging students to put their ideals to work. If a chance arises to put the law and your legal analysis into action on something important, he said, you go for it.

Or at least you seriously consider going for it. By late September Hank and I, along with a couple of bemused volunteers, decided that we had the law and scientific facts necessary for a legal campaign to stop the destruction of the darter and its river. Truthfully, we'd become infatuated by the possibility of using the darter in a fight to save the region's most historic river from an ill-considered, uneconomic project. But we knew a couple of amateurs couldn't handle an endangered species controversy on their own. How to proceed? The best scenario would be to give all the evidence we had to the Department of Interior in Washington, and have them enforce the law against TVA. This was their job. Given political realities, however, it was overwhelmingly unlikely that the official agency would do so. Failing that, we needed a national environmental group, with money and legal staff, to jump in and take the case to court.

Having a strong case alone doesn't get you very far in public interest litigation. A lawsuit requires money for collecting scientific evidence and for coping with avalanches of procedural assaults and informational demands from opposing lawyers. Regardless of the merits of their positions, those attorneys can crush worthy cases under unbearable burdens of "discovery" depositions and interrogatories, as well as a flood of dismissive public relations. A citizen lawsuit also requires untold hours in researching, writing, and presenting legal arguments in a gauntlet of court proceedings. What prospects for legal victory could be expected from a ragtag group led by a student with a shaky grade point average and an untenured freshman professor?

For several weeks we sent out pleas to a variety of national organizations, laying out the facts and begging for someone to take on this mission. The Environmental Defense Fund had funded and staffed the environmental impact litigation, but the group said it no longer had time or resources to offer. The National Wildlife Federation offered more hope, sending a staff attorney, Bob Golten, down to us in Tennessee. But after spending two days reviewing our legal and biological arguments, he recommended that his group turn down the case: "We believe the chances of winning such a case are slim to none."

If this battle was to be fought, it would have to be a local production.

For a grassroots legal endeavor to go anywhere, however, community participation and backup are essential. If a citizen campaign was to work, it would need a trusted core of people directly affected by the dam. For internal survivability—not to mention external credibility in the eyes of the courts, government agencies, political players, and the public at large—we needed down-to-earth people with local legitimacy. That was especially the case here, because a snail darter crusade obviously would initially strike almost everyone as outlandish. Hank, though a native Tennessean from Chattanooga, was studying at a university that many suspiciously regarded as left wing. And in my Earth Shoes and turtlenecks I was easily pigeonholed as the Northern academic carpetbagger I was. Where could we look for a core group of locals linked to the river and the valley who might support a snail darter campaign?

The answer: that's why we're at Fort Loudoun tonight, so that we can talk to the local people who had fought the dam in earlier battles. Hank had called Ken Elrod, the last president of the now dormant Association for the Preservation of the Little T. Elrod invited the remaining members to come to their accustomed gathering place to share a Saturday evening potluck supper and hear what we had to say.

We're met in front of the fort by Alice Milton, a prim ramrod of a country gentlewoman who is the self-appointed guardian of old Fort Loudoun. Tonight she has volunteered to serve again as hostess for the group's customary potluck, but clearly she has hesitations. "The dam project doesn't make any sense, and never has. I worked in Estes Kefauver's Senate office, and he held it off for years," she says. Kefauver, the coonskin-capped senator who was Adlai Stevenson's vice-presidential running mate in 1958, was from Madisonville, just down the road in Monroe County. "TVA didn't dare go forward with the Tellico project until the senator died."

But now, she says sadly, with the NEPA battle lost, she's negotiating with TVA to save as much of the fort as possible. "They're offering to lift the lower fortifications up in the air on earth fill, and rebuild every-thing with modern reconstruction. But it's all wrong," she says, steer-ing us out to the edge of the knoll to peer out over the dark valley. "The fort's always been a sentinel up here above the river. Now the barri-cades will just be sitting right on the shore of the reservoir. I hate it. But I'm working with TVA because there's nothing left to be done about it."

In the fluorescent-lit meeting room we take paper plates and fill them with macaroni and cheese, fried chicken, and three-bean salad. Elrod walks us around the room and introduces us to the approximately two dozen people who have gathered, most of them farmers. They sit quietly in disjointed clusters, making only occasional comments to one another about crops, weather, local news, and the sad facts of the on-going land condemnations.

"Did you hear? Bart Iddins gave up and sold."

"Yeah, and TVA bulldozed the Grahamses' house and barn last week. Left only the silos standing."

"They painted those big demolition numbers on the side of our house last Tuesday."

In part their general quietness is the local culture: rural Tennesse-ans don't try to stand out from their neighbors or raise their voices to entertain or impress. Relationships are built by slow accretions of ac-tions, shared experiences, and a quiet word here and there. The people here clearly feel defeated by what they've endured, and aren't eager to reawaken false hopes. They're what's left of a group of more than a hundred who would regularly squeeze into this little hall just three years ago.

Elrod asks Hank and me to explain the new idea that might do something for the Little T River valley. There is, we say, an unexpected new possibility for stopping the Tellico project. Congress has passed a new law with tough provisions in it that might give the valley another chance. It's nothing fancy; it doesn't take a lawyer to understand how it works. "Your old lawsuit was brought under NEPA," I say, "which doesn't have legal teeth; all TVA had to do was take the time to write up the paperwork. Once they did an adequate impact statement they could go ahead and build the dam. But the Endangered Species Act, if you read it carefully, has real prohibitions in it."

We pass around a paragraph, Section Seven from the Endangered Species Act of 1973, along with a picture of the little fish that is right now swimming in the darkness in riffles a dozen miles downstream. We carefully point out that at least two potential violations lie hidden within Section Seven's verbal foliage (relevant wording italicized here):

Section 7. Interagency cooperation, 16 U.S. Code 1536.

The Secretary [of Interior] shall review other programs administered by him and utilize such programs in furtherance of the purposes of this Act. *All* other *federal* departments and *agencies shall,* in consultation with and with the assistance of the Secretary, utilize their authorities in furtherance of the purposes of this Act by carrying out programs for the conservation of endangered species and threatened species listed pursuant to Section 4 [1533] of this Act and by taking such action necessary to *insure that actions authorized, funded,* or *carried out by them do not jeopardize the continued existence of* such *endangered species* and threatened species *or result in* the *destruction* or modification *of habitat* of such species which is *determined* by the Secretary, after consultation as appropriate with the affected States, to be *critical.*[3]

"Note that it says *'shall,'* not 'may,'" I emphasize. The Tellico Dam will pretty clearly "jeopardize the continued existence" of the snail darter, and it's obvious it will destroy the fish's habitat. Etnier and his students can prove both of these contentions. So the statute is being violated twice over. The dam would eliminate the entire known population of the darter in its native river habitat in the same way the others were probably eliminated one by one throughout the rest of the Tennessee River system—by dams.

There's a small chance that the Department of Interior's Fish and Wildlife Service, which has authority over the Endangered Species Act, will step in and stop TVA from finishing the dam. But if they don't, the law has a citizen enforcement provision that explicitly allows us to sue TVA ourselves. Any interested person can file an enforcement action in federal court against any federal agency breaking this law. If local federal judge Robert Taylor looks at the facts and follows the law, we figure he'll be hard-pressed not to issue an injunction against the dam.

Up to this point the idea of endangered species law enforcement is just Hank's term paper topic. If the people here decide to rally behind it, however, it could become something more. But the dam-fighting veterans sitting there in a cluster of folding chairs aren't very enthusiastic.

"That's it?" Asa McCall asks skeptically. "All these years talking about the land and the river, and now it comes down to a bitty fish?"

Old, grizzled, and clad in overalls, Asa sits beside his diminutive wife, Nell. They've been holding off the TVA condemnation marshals since the project was first announced. Whenever the TVA men stop by, the story goes, Asa meets them in his front yard with his snarling sheepdog at his side and tells them they'll have to drag him and Nell off the land; they'll never go willingly. And Nell has the phone number of a local reporter who will rush over with a camera. Although the local newspapers are hesitant to criticize the agency's dam project, a photo of two senior citizens being dragged off their land is newsworthy. TVA wants to avoid that scene, so Asa and Nell are still on their land.

Alfred Davis, sitting a couple of rows behind Asa, shares his hesitancy. "I doubt the Department of Interior will be too quick to go against TVA on this," he says. "And I'm not sure you're right about Judge Taylor either. We've been down that road before with him. It's

Nell and Asa McCall on their farm of more than ninety acres; just three of those acres would be flooded by the reservoir, while the rest of their land was condemned for resale to corporate developers. (© Roger Simpson, used with permission, smokymountainsnaturephotos.com)

kindly unlikely he'd ever decide a case against TVA. When TVA assessors came over on our place, and we said we were going to fight them in court, they said to us, 'You go right ahead. TVA has a hundred lawyers, and we also have us our own federal judge.' I do believe the only way you'll ever get another injunction is by appealing it over Judge Taylor's head, out of the valley. And we know how awful hard that can be."

Heads nod around the room. Alfred's slow, precise words carry weight with the group. He sits tall, a lanky farmer with intent blue eyes, thin sandy hair, and fair skin sunburned from working in the fields. A bachelor into his thirties, unusual in this community, he's flanked tonight by his new bride, Virginia, who nods vigorously as he talks. For more than a decade Alfred has been fighting to save his family's 180-acre farm, less than a sixth of which would be flooded by the reservoir, most being taken for the supposed Boeing real estate development. It's clear to him that just because our new idea makes sense in a law school classroom doesn't mean it's going to work in the real world. The people in this room, including his father, mother, and sister Beulah, have fought too long and have been crushed too hard to raise their hopes up once more on an idea that may not be able to bear the weight.

"Before, it was a pretty tight-knit community," says Beryl Moser, whose name as plaintiff had been on the farmers' previous lawsuit against TVA.[4] Beryl has worked his family's eighty-five acres since his father's death when Beryl was thirteen. "Everything that you needed was here. Farming, that's all I ever did want to do, you know, ever since I can remember. Pretty well everybody just wanted to go on doing what they'd done. And now we can't."

Most people in eastern Tennessee appear to accept TVA's argument that there's no alternative to the plan to dam the river. Tubby Hammontree, a farmer sitting in the corner, says ruefully, "It's gotten so most people in this area think of any of us farmers as an embarrassment, still staying on the land. They look down at their feet and shuffle, and they say, 'So much is gone already, why not just take TVA's money and let them get on with it?' "

Alfred's comments underline another reason to be skeptical. A law case is hard work. Who would do it? The fish isn't even listed as an endangered species yet, and getting it there isn't going to be easy. After that's done, the lawsuit itself is going to take a lot of preparation, organization, big money, legal expertise, and a huge amount of time.

"Environmental Defense and the Wildlife Federation say they won't do it," I'm forced to report. "Environmental Defense is burned out after three years on your impact statement fight, and the Federation thinks the endangered species argument can't win."

"But those national environmental groups are wrong," argues Hank. "The case is simple. All we have to do is show they're killing the fish! Dave Etnier and his students will do the science. We can do the legal work at UT Law School and get help on the trial work from some local attorneys." Hank is an unwaveringly positive thinker, and he is pitching his term paper hard. There's a pause. The people gathered here tonight are not inclined to argumentation, but to these veterans Hank must sound quite naïve in his optimism.

"You can't be so sure." The speaker is Jean Ritchey, a small dark-haired woman sitting in the middle of the room. "Nothing is simple when you're dealing with TVA. And I don't trust those other agencies either, any more than I trust that judge. They're all political, ever'one of them." She shakes her finger for emphasis as she talks; beside her, her husband, Ben, and their three grown daughters nod in agreement. They live on a little plateau, back from the river, in a typical eastern Tennessee single-story clapboard farmhouse with a sway-roof porch, farming 120 acres, of which only two or three will be flooded. The girls have gone to college and have found jobs in the area. Two are school-teachers. They too have been active fighters for the valley's farms.

"We've gone to talk to those committees in Congress, too," Carolyn Ritchey says. "They don't care."

"You can talk 'til you're blue in the face and they won't listen," adds Sally Ritchey.

"They just listen to TVA," says their mother.

This reminds the group of a basic reality: Red Wagner is adamant about building his dam. TVA would fight an endangered fish case in every conceivable forum. It would be a rough and intensely political battle, fought through the administrative agencies and Congress as well as in the courts and beyond, into local and state politics and the media. Even if someone attacking the dam won every court appeal, which they'd have to do, it would be clear from the start that the ultimate decision would likely be made in Washington, where people still think of TVA as the New Deal's greatest legacy.

We explain that if we start the lawsuit ourselves, we can at least count on scientific backing from inside the Department of Interior, where Dave Etnier has biologist friends who already know about the fish. Once the case is active, we'll be in a better position to persuade one of the national environmental groups to pick it up, and they'll carry on the fight in Washington. The doubt within the group, however, is palpable. They can sense we care about the farms, the valley, and the river, and have a solid technical argument based on the endangered species law. But in our enthusiasm about this new and unexpected tactic for stopping the dam, we probably aren't fully acknowledging its demands and slim chances. These veterans who have accepted a string of defeats after years of pain have a far better sense of the realities. To them, a new chance to fight on feels more like an invitation to a beating than to a victory.

And then there's the two-inch fish. "Isn't everyone going to say it's ridiculous, using a little fish like this against the dam?" says someone. The problem is obvious. The first public reaction to the news that a TVA dam is being blocked by a "minnow" will be disbelief. People will focus on a mental image of a big hydroelectric dam, essential for energy and human welfare, being stopped by a tiny creature of no apparent importance to human beings. The snail darter will thus trigger the classic fatalist cliché of unavoidable trade-off—society must choose between environment and economics, one or the other. You cannot have both. In this trade-off the snail darter reads as a metaphor for half-baked environmentalist ideals. Even its name sounds silly, an oxymoron. And Tellico Dam inevitably will be depicted as an avatar of Economic Progress.

What would people assume about the citizens who take up the darter's cause? Probably that we're hypocrites as well as fools, environmental extremists manipulating the darter to misuse the law over a technicality. But isn't that true? Isn't the fish just a fortuitous coincidence that gives us a handy weapon to fight the dam? No one tonight has talked about saving the fish for its own sake, as a fragile creature of God, or an ecological rarity deserving of protection. No one would step up for years of painful effort if the Tellico project made economic sense and the fish alone was at stake. Plus, we have to admit that Congress didn't realize what it was doing when it passed the law, and it certainly wasn't thinking about small, unfamiliar species like the darter. Section Seven would surely never have passed if Congress had realized that those key words concealed within it might be parsed to stop public works pork-barrel projects. If we want to question the dam, people will ask why we don't just confront it directly instead of through trickery. Yet there is, of course, no remaining straightforward avenue for doing so.

There's another worry: what would press coverage look like? The press plays a large role in how government treats controversies like this. "You're going to set off a real hullabaloo in the papers about this 'silly little fish,'" said local Sierra Club chair Will Skelton when we told him about the darter. "The local papers all eat from TVA's hand. They'll play up the fish angle and you aren't going to hear anything about the dam's fake economics."

"The talk radio shows are going to be bad," someone at the meeting notes. "Every lunkhead who wants to show off will phone in with wise-cracks making fun of the case." Hank says he'll be glad to phone in to debate the lunkheads, and we all can write letters to the editor and op-ed pieces to get the facts out. But even Hank can't pretend that local press and public opinion won't be a serious concern. Would the national press be any better? It needs to be; getting coverage outside the Tennessee valley would surely play an important part in how the political process handles our case.

"The national media are much better than our local media," I say hopefully. "And they're not under TVA's thumb. For the first wave of coverage no doubt they'll write 'little-fish-bites-big-dam' stories. But starting the second week they'll need more to write about. The second and third waves of the story will have to dig further into the facts—investigative stories. Everything they find will help us, not TVA. They'll discover your farms getting condemned for real estate development. That will turn the fish-dam story inside out." This is our great hope: the fish becomes a pivot that finally turns rational scrutiny onto the flimsy merits of the Tellico project.

After a half-hour of this, the conversation subtly shifts. Comments in the room turn toward the realities of what these people had been fighting for, and what would be lost along with the river. Kirk Johnson and Price Wilkins proclaim that no river in the eastern United States has the same quality of fishing. A quiet engineer from Chattanooga, Johnson belongs to the local chapter of Trout Unlimited, the fishing

organization whose members come from as far as Atlanta most weekends to wade the Little T. For the NEPA case he'd typed up an extensive history of TVA's serial misrepresentations in arguing for the dam,
and of the Little T's citizen defenders' years of fighting it. Wilkins is a
quiet, graying veteran fish biologist from the state Game and Fish Commission. The sensitive politics of the Tellico project make him hesitant
to speak, but he does. This river, he says, is the richest big-water trout
stream east of the Mississippi and a significant untapped resource for
fishing and recreation. It's seen almost no recreational development,
and it still attracts fishermen and vacationers from all over the Southeast. It's the last place left in the region for high-quality river recreation,
where troops of scouts, school kids, and families can take day-long float
trips, fish, picnic on islands, and visit the Native American sites. It's a
terrible shame to lose it.

"What it is is a crime," grunts David Scates, a gangly, taciturn
mountain man employed as a draftsman by TVA since his return from
Vietnam. He lives only for the river, but he seems embarrassed by the
sound of his exasperated voice. He has said little this evening, but
anger pushes him to add his voice now. A hundred days a year David
drives forty miles from his parents' home in Knoxville to spend time at
the Little T, often with his sidekick Larry Crisp, both ardent members
of the local Trout Unlimited chapter. David goes to fish, hunt arrowheads, or push willow-withe cuttings into riverbank areas scalped by
TVA bulldozers. Otherwise, he sits and watches the light on the Native
American mounds and mountain ridges beyond. Larry is more volu-
ble. With tears in his eyes he tells what it means to him to take his little
boy float-fishing on the river. "It just don't calculate," Larry says, "It's
like tradin' away a eagle just to get you another old crow."

The fishermen who've fought for the river over the past six years,
of whom only a few are here tonight, have different orientations. Some
are politically savvy, some aren't. Some, like Joe Congleton, have
higher education; others, like David and Larry, don't. Though virtually all are fly fishermen, some are fly-fishing purists while others occasionally use a live grasshopper, canned corn and Velveeta, or, in the
dog days of summer, a worm on the bottom. Most local Tennesseans
fish only with bait, a more passive, less-complicated technique, where
the bait does the work of luring fish. This kind of fishing can be done
lying on a bank watching clouds or sitting in a boat sipping beer. A

number of local fishermen, like David and Larry, started out as bait fishermen but over time moved into the subtlety of fly-fishing.

The Little T is extraordinary for fly-fishing, with its teeming aquatic insect life and broad shoals and riffles. Fly-fishing, especially dry fly-fishing, can be a rarefied pursuit where a lot of money can be spent attaining a graceful minimum of effort, delivering a tiny hook crafted with bits of fur and feather to mimic a delicate insect floating on the water. For some reason most fishermen involved in conservation are fly fishermen, perhaps because of the sport's special relationship with water and the personal engagement with nature it demands. Those fly fishermen joining the farmers in the fight to save the river have regularly been accused of being undemocratic elitists, separated from the interests of the majority of fishermen and, by extension, the local populace. It helps that David and Larry, visibly sons of rural Tennessee, have long been deep in this fight.

Some of the talk touches on the valley's historical resources. On this topic, too, some differences and even tensions appear among several speakers.

"You've all heard about the Cherokee," says Jeff Chapman, a young UT archaeologist. "But the real historical uniqueness of this valley is that it contains the two oldest sites of continuous human communal habitation ever discovered in the United States."

Chapman and his associate Gerald Schroedl are building national reputations as scholars of archaic American history, leading a team of excavators probing layer by layer into the valley soil at several sites along the banks of the Little T. "We've found 10,000 years of continuous human habitation at Rose Island, and at Icehouse Bottoms just upriver from here," says Chapman. "The only other site in the continent where you find human stratigraphy that old is a sheltering cave in northern Alabama, and that's the Russell Cave National Monument now."[5]

How can TVA be destroying these sites? Easily. "The National Historic Preservation Act has no teeth at all," Chapman says. "All TVA had to do to get around it was agree to fund us to do some 'salvage archaeology.' But what we're finding is of national importance. It's crazy to flood it under a reservoir." Chapman and his team aren't tenured, however, and because their department's budget relies on TVA contracts their department head, Ted Guthe, brooks no criticism of TVA. The archaeologists are willing to provide discreet help as information resources, but they won't speak against the dam to reporters, and beg not to be asked to testify in court.

Another vestige of the valley's past is present in the room: sitting alone, wearing a dark green work shirt and a string tie with a Navajo turquoise clasp, Worth Greene offers us some history. "My grandmother was full-blooded Cherokee, Qualla Band," he says. "In the early 1900s she lived in a cabin eight miles upstream from here in Chota," one of few Cherokees who had for a time been able to settle back on the river. "Lots of Cherokee today don't know much about Chota or the Little T, but I tell you, it was the most important place in all of Cherokee life. Our greatest leader Sequoyah was born in Toskegee town right at the bottom of this here hill."

Nobody knows how to speak with Greene about tonight's contemplated decision. Is he here representing the Cherokee council over in North Carolina? It doesn't seem so, but we hope they too will be interested in helping to preserve the valley. Greene is here in an ambiguous—perhaps deeply ambiguous—position. He's working as a foreman to help Chapman and Schroedl in the salvage archaeology excavation. TVA reportedly urged the archaeologists to hire him as a gesture toward pan-ethnic participation, but so far as anyone knows he's never lived in a Cherokee community.

Moreover, the kind of work Greene does with the archaeologists is an affront to many in the tribe, who see these efforts as robbing tribal graves—while helping TVA prepare to destroy the valley. The Cherokee, like most Native American peoples, consider all ancient human remains found in their homelands to be those of their tribal ancestors, and archaeological digs a desecration. Greene does not speak the old language, or practice the blended Native American–Baptist religion of the traditionalist. Nor does he hold a position in the modern Cherokee government. In fact, it's not at all clear why Worth Greene is here. No one invited him. There is a real possibility, Hank whispers, that he's a TVA spy. There's a rumor that he reports to Corydon Bell, an official in TVA's water planning division, on the ongoing internal politics of the Cherokee, and he may have been sent here to report to TVA on our potluck.[6]

Whatever the reason for his presence here with us, Greene personifies another tension as well. Although he acknowledges his ancestry, he is an assimilated modern. As with many Native American peoples, there are two opposing cultures present within the Smoky Mountain and Oklahoma branches of the Cherokee nation. The most basic distinction within many peoples, including the Cherokee, is between those who live as moderns and those who remain traditionalists. Some Native Americans live in the mainstream of American society, where their sense of being Native American may feel uncertain, an anomaly that constantly requires redefinition or that may disappear entirely. Others stay in settlements or reservations, where their status is more defined. When tourists travel through Native American areas like Cherokee, North Carolina, they buy gasoline or artisan work from cheerful red-brown salespeople, pose for photographs with locals wearing war bonnets, and speak with guides who recount the joys and sorrows of their people. These are moderns. They talk, think, and live like any other population of small-town, lower-income Americans, except that they happen to be from a town identified as Native American. Often they are fundamentalist Baptists.

But off the main roads, up in the hollows away from touring Anglos, live the traditionals. Because they've never reached much of an accommodation with the modern economy, traditionals are usually quite poor. They generally dress without ornamentation, drive beat-up pickup trucks, and are slow to speak with nontraditionals, often living with a sense of carrying on something old. The cultural stewardship of traditionals is not organized, and is not a vision fueled by hope. They live in the old culture day by day, custodians of remnants, cradling smoldering embers, with no conviction that their values and traditions will be passed on when they die. They would never come across the mountains, we knew, to join a white coalition to save the river. The Cherokee voice would have to come from moderns.

Most young Cherokee are drawn into mainstream American life. Like Greene, they spend their entire lives in the white world. A tension born of unspoken mutual reproach thus exists between moderns and traditionals. One group seems to demand to know how the other can trade away the richness of the past and a particularized identity for shiny pickup trucks and television. The opposite side silently judges their traditional brethren as pursuing an anachronistic dead-end life in which satisfaction comes vaguely, if at all, from the stubborn continuation of a doomed culture. There is never a resolution, and so long as the traditionals survive, in fewer and fewer numbers, they follow a separate path.

We deeply hope that if we begin a last fight for the river, the Chero-kee of North Carolina will help. Their official tribal council, made up of moderns, sent representatives to support the earlier litigation, and we've heard that some of the traditionals are deeply concerned. Am-moneta and Lloyd Sequoyah, who are elderly medicine men, told the tribal historian of their despair at the plan to impound the river. They still go to the water to gather medicine surreptitiously and describe the Little Tennessee as a sacred element of the tribe's spiritual world. The Cherokee word for flowing water signifies life; dammed-up water is "dead water." The brothers have told visitors that if the river at Echota stops flowing, the Cherokee religion will die, and they as medicine men will die with it.

"Thousands of great Indian artifacts are going to be lost if the river's flooded," says Roy Warren, a large, florid-cheeked retiree who seems oblivious to the fact that what he stands for is equally detested by the archaeologists, the amateur historians like Alice Milton, and the Cher-okee themselves. Warren is one of a group called pot hunters, who consider themselves amateur archaeologists, but to the Cherokee they are grave robbers, while to the professionals they are vandals. Not con-tent to scavenge just arrowheads and spear points from the surface, they chop with picks and shovels into any site that they think might yield beads, bones, or trinkets for their private collections. Stored in shoeboxes under their beds or in elaborate display cases in their living rooms, these private collections are resented by archaeologists as irre-trievable information. The original location, depths, and relationships of artifacts can never be knowable. But tonight no one criticizes War-ren's plundering. In past years he and his friends have helped fight the dam, testifying and writing letters to local newspapers. They might be helpful again if there's a new fight. If the valley is flooded, moreover, it won't make much difference who did what when the river was still flowing.

Out of all this talk tonight comes a discernible change in mood. An-ger is now venting from every corner of the room. A feeling of solidarity and renewed resistance seems to be building. It's there in a shift in wording. While earlier in the evening the people were saying "A law-suit *would* be difficult," they've now switched to "It *will* be difficult." But there are major unspoken issues lurking below this growing enthu-siasm. Isn't there a real possibility that we'll trigger a backlash? No matter how strong our endangered species case might be, if it's seen as a technicality used by hypocritical extremists, we'd ultimately lose the case—not to mention hurting the Endangered Species Act itself, and maybe more.

The nation's industrial managers, now facing effective health and pollution regulation for the first time, would clearly like to reverse the environmental tide. Their business lobbyists, however, can't talk openly about undercutting the Clean Air Act or the Clean Water Act. If they do, the public will immediately think of babies choking on smoggy air, or dirty tap water and dead fish. The image of our little endangered fish, on the other hand, might give them an opportunity. If they can characterize our snail darter as an example of environmental protection law "going too far," they can use it to weaken public support for all environmental protection policy. The ridiculous fish could become a fortuitous weapon for business lobbyists to block the national policies sparked by Earth Day and Rachel Carson's *Silent Spring.*

And how do we answer accusations of hypocrisy—the predictable claim that we don't really care about the fish, that we are just using it as a technicality? This is easy, in part: we have no choice other than the snail darter. If we're going to resist this destructive, uneconomic project, we'll use the only practical tool available—the same way they nabbed Al Capone on taxes, instead of on murder or racketeering. There's also the flip answer: "What good is a law if you can't use it?" Not to mention that the dramatic facts the media will discover in our case might actually strengthen environmental policy by demonstrating the Endangered Species Act's public interest benefits.

The political realities of American government are structured so there is no forum in which citizens can instigate meaningful official scrutiny of a pork-barrel project. Citizens certainly can't rely on Congress, where the appropriations funding committees laughed at the farmers and their supporters when they tried to tell the truth about the dam. The regular standing committees showed no interest either. The executive branch has never been eager to pry into pork barrels, and the voting booth is haplessly far removed from effectiveness. Even courts aren't a very satisfying answer, refusing as they do to review the economic merits of congressionally approved projects.

But in America, filing a lawsuit is about the only way a citizen without money or power can compel any kind of official process against a wrong. You pay the filing fee, and at least it gets you an official hearing. The judge has to listen as you lay out the legal formula "cause of action" that you think is violated, and the critical facts that fit it. Here our legal formula would be the prohibitions we've found in Section Seven of the Endangered Species Act. You get a hearing, and if the judge finds that the facts fit the law, you're supposed to win.

The group meeting this evening at Fort Loudoun represents a dramatic and essentially American phenomenon. In no other country could a band of citizens so lacking in money, social station, official position, and organizational backing matter-of-factly consider taking onto themselves the role of enforcing national law, much less against a hugely powerful defendant that itself happens to be an arm of the national government. In the 1960s, however, a legal revolution had occurred in the United States. Building on strategies that activists like Martin Luther King and Ralph Nader had employed in civil rights and consumer protection cases, citizen plaintiffs in courts around the nation persuaded judges to grant them the right to appear in court—"legal standing"—to enforce the laws against statutory violators, public and private. Caught up in the progressive populism of the decade, Congress expressly added provisions to many public interest laws—almost twenty environmental statutes, including the Endangered Species Act—granting citizens themselves the right to bring violators into federal court. Nationally, a large number of interest groups and individuals quickly began to exercise their new right as citizens to enforce statutory laws. They could step directly into the governance process without relying on the mediation of hesitant and uncertain regulatory agencies too often allied with the industries they regulated. Now any individual or any group in America could take the necessary steps to walk into court as a self-appointed private attorney-general to enforce a law, subject only to a few constitutional constraints belatedly constructed by the Nixon Supreme Court.

At this moment in eastern Tennessee, twenty-eight people sitting in a modular shed in the remnants of an eighteenth century fort planning a lawsuit against TVA represent a tremor of populist pluralism being felt across the land and starting to spread to new legal habitats around the world. We would of course be pleased to file arguments against TVA's dam project more "straightforwardly" under a "Review of Uneconomic Federal Projects Act," but Congress has never passed such a statute and never will. There are some statutes related to this area—the Farmland Preservation Act, the Historic Preservation Act, the Land and Water Conservation Act, and the Native American Religious Freedom Act—but each of these was carefully neutered in the political process so as to contain no enforceable substantive protections. For these reasons, the only effective governmental forum in our case for showing that the emperor isn't wearing clothes comes from the happenstance existence of an endangered species. But our hope is that after we establish that the Endangered Species Act conflicts with the Tellico project, the courts will ultimately look at the full case—the fish, the project's crooked economics, the attractive economic alternatives for the valley— and give us an injunction prohibiting completion of this foolish dam.

Will a victory in court end the matter? Not likely. Michigan environmental law professor Joe Sax, who champions citizen lawsuits enforcing federal laws, has written that when citizens win such injunctions in court the effect typically is to bring the issue to the attention of Congress, which is ultimately the appropriate entity to make such policy decisions. If that happens in our case, Congress will be pushed to investigate the conflicts and alternatives of the matter, and the Tellico project will finally be scrutinized on its real merits.

Does it matter that when Congress passed the law it didn't actually realize what it was doing? In short, no. Intended or not, the words the legislators used in Section Seven clearly forbid actions that threaten extinction, and the law explicitly gives citizens the right to enforce those words. We'll make the classic argument: the Endangered Species Act has a "plain meaning," and that's that. If Congress wants to change the law, it has the right to do that, but until then Section Seven, exactly as written, is the law of the land.

And it's not just a legal technicality. Our lawsuit would prevent exactly what Congress said it wanted to stop: the loss of endangered species and their critical habitats. In reminding us of the law's legislative history, Hank points out that, in hearing after hearing, witness testimony confirmed again and again that the main cause of extinction is not hunting, trapping, or poisoning—destruction of natural habitat is the primary reason, and that's precisely what TVA is doing to the snail darter.

Accusations of hypocrisy presume that environmentalists preserving endangered species should be motivated only by a limited range of "pure" impulses, valuing species solely on their individual terms. But there are many different rationales for protecting endangered species. For some, it's a religious or moral obligation for humans to steward other creatures, instead of destroying them. For others, the obligation is aesthetic, preserving the beauty and intricacy of ecological systems. The 1973 congressional hearings on the proposed law, however, tended to emphasize utilitarian justifications: because endangered species are often evolutionarily unique, they may contain chemical compounds and structures that will prove critically important in developing medicines and commercial products. The species we save today "may someday cure cancer." If we let species perish—extinction is forever—it's like burning books whose meanings we have yet to understood.

The snail darter, however, echoes an even broader utilitarian human rationale for protecting endangered species. Like the canaries carried into mineshafts in the Cumberland hills north of here in the old days to warn miners of deadly odorless methane, endangered species can act as indicators of endangered human interests. That's the point we're making—the darter and its endangered habitat identify a critical weighting of human and ecological values to show that the dam is, on balance, harmful. Because of the fortuitous existence of both the darter and the endangered species law, the public will finally have the opportunity to receive a warning about the serious mistake that is poised to destroy the economic, ecological, and cultural values of the Little T valley, and to learn of the rich alternative development options the little fish will open up for the local communities.

Of course, the law alone will not be enough to bring sense to the Tellico project and salvation to the darter and its valley. We're not foolish enough to think that. Law is only a tool. In this particular context, with such powerful political forces arrayed against us—not just TVA but all its public works pork-barrel allies in national politics—the law can only buy us leverage. The way we see it, if we can get a court injunction against the dam, the political process will have to scrutinize the project, and the truth will finally have a forum. The law can't hold up the dam forever, but it might hold it up to the light. And America might see that good ecology can be good economics, even in this seemingly most extreme of cases. On the other hand, more realistically, we could lose far more than the darter, the river, and the valley.

Well, are we going to do it? We sit there for a quiet moment looking at each other. It's Asa McCall who finally breaks the silence. Asa looks around the room and says, "Well, I never before heard of this little fish. But I say if it can save our farms, we got to give it a try." He takes off his battered hat, puts in a dollar, and passes it around the room.

Someone else agrees: "Imagine what it would be like for us to stand here in twenty-five years looking out over a reservoir, old silos sticking up from the water, muddy shorelines, erosion washing open Cherokee graves. How'd we feel saying to our grandchildren, 'We could have stopped this. We had the law. We had the facts. We had common sense and economics on our side. But we didn't have the heart for it. We didn't have enough trust in ourselves and the law to do it.' Could we bear it, to have to say that?"

Heads nod in agreement all over the room. As Asa's hat goes around the room, he turns to Ben Ritchey and says, "Nell and I probably won't live to see the end of this, but we've got our Margaret Ellen and she'll keep on fighting." When Asa's hat circles back it contains $29, enough to cover the lawsuit filing fee in federal trial court in Knoxville, with $14 left over to start the snail darter legal defense fund.

There's still one important point that remains to be settled, however. Who will be named as plaintiffs in the lawsuit? The farmers here tonight are the obvious choice, and I say so.

"No, I don't think we can do that," says Alfred Davis. "Folks around here know we were the ones that brought the other lawsuit. It'd look pretty bad in this community for us to be getting a second bite at the apple." Others nod their heads in agreement; local reaction would be far better if the case was brought by somebody new.

"But you farmers are the ones who are losing the most, and it's your story that people need to hear," we say. "If people see that Tellico's a TVA land grab, taking land away from farm families to give it to a big corporation for real estate development, they'll see that it's not about environmentalist tree huggers. The case needs to be called *Tellico Farmers versus TVA*."

"No," Alfred insists. "We just cannot do it. Don't get us wrong. We'll back you hard. We'll travel to Nashville and all the way to Washington to help you make the case. We've done that before and we'll do it again. We'll testify, we'll take reporters around our farms, into our homes. You can count on us. But people'll say it's wrong for us to be suing TVA again ourselves, or using the Little T Association name again. I'm sorry. I say, we just flat out can't do that." Heads nod again around the room in agreement with Alfred. The lawsuit should not be brought by the same people who did it before.

This is not good. Not having the farmers as the lawsuit's named plaintiffs could be a big mistake. If they're the petitioners, the press will come talk to them. If the public sees that the darter is defending private property, defending family farms from federal condemnation for a private corporate development, the whole mess that is the Tellico project would be open for scrutiny. But who are we to browbeat these veterans of fifteen years of battle against TVA? If they insist on saying no, that's how it must be. We'll try once more to find a national environmental law group to take on the case, but if that doesn't work some of us at the university will have to file the lawsuit in our own names.

In any event, the potluck supper has produced a decision: the straggling remnants of a dozen years of fighting will come together to fight once more for the river valley—and now the little fish. From this point on we'll have a small but critical mass of people from the Little T valley, Knoxville, and Chattanooga. We and the farmers will use the snail darter and the law, trying to instigate an honest accounting of a stupid, wasteful, destructive federal project. TVA's dam scheme will collapse if ever the facts about it can be publicly revealed, and that's an accounting that we can obtain in no other way.

Before going home, some of us walk quietly in the darkness to the northeast corner of the fort, peering up the valley toward the Smoky Mountains, invisible in the moonless night, the dark silver river softly curving past us down below.

"Hot damn, here we go!" crows Hank.

"Well, there's hope," I say. Before this evening I'd avoided getting to know this condemned river, but things have changed. "Next Thursday after class, how about we go fishing on the Little T?"

"Heaven help us!" might have been a more realistic response. It's not at all clear what lies ahead, nor what this night's decision might eventually mean for the fish, for the river, for the people at the fort this evening, and for the U.S.A.

# CHAPTER 3

# Pushing the Snail Darter onto the Endangered Species List

**OCTOBER 1974–OCTOBER 1975**

By the end of the Saturday night meeting at old Fort Loudoun a core group has pulled itself together to try the novel endangered species tactic. Nothing will come of it, however, unless and until we can persuade the Department of Interior to put the snail darter on the official endangered species list. If it's not on the list, it's not legally an endangered species and the law won't apply.

This "list" isn't actually a separate document. It's a collection of individual Department of Interior rules, each declaring a species officially endangered or threatened. Each listing rule has to be published in the *Federal Register,* the government's official daily record. Until now these official listings have almost always been initiated by the federal agency itself, after an internal review within the U.S. Fish and Wildlife Service, the Interior subagency with authority over the Endangered Species Act.

Dave Etnier tells us, however, that for some eligible species the Service, for various reasons, never gets around to starting the process. If and when the listing process does begin, it goes through a multistep procedure including a public "notice-and-comment" period. This can take months or years, even if the agency is enthusiastic about issuing the listing, which in our case is doubtful. TVA will surely file voluminous comments to delay or block any protection of the snail darter.

For the briefest moment we nevertheless thought that Interior would move ahead with the process and press TVA to halt construction. The

facts and law seemed clear. It soon became obvious, however, that Jean
Ritchey was right: if we waited for the appropriate people in Washington to do the job, it was never going to happen.

Etnier sent all of his laboratory data on the darter to Jim Williams,
an ichthyologist friend in the Fish and Wildlife Service's Office of
Endangered Species. Williams reviewed and passed the data over to
his section chief with a memo concluding that an urgent listing was
scientifically justified. That theoretically should have put the agency
process into motion, but Etnier soon got a call from Williams indicating we shouldn't get our hopes up. "TVA's going to fight this listing
hard," Williams told Etnier. "TVA's top scientist, Tom Ripley, flew
up to Washington to block it the morning after TVA got a copy of the
status report."

Jim Williams is one of those indispensable connections that make
citizens' forays into government possible. His primary loyalties are to
wildlife, to science, and to the law, and he's not hesitant to communicate discreetly with citizens outside the Beltway, especially when
they're recommended by someone he trusts. "I've known Ets a long
time," Williams says when I call him. "Met him years ago at a Southern
icths-and-herps meeting—ichthyologists and herpetologists. We've
co-authored some papers. Ets knows more about darters than anyone
in the country. If he says this is a good species, it's a good species."

Williams explains that TVA's scientist Ripley appeared in his office
the previous week and nonchalantly struck up a fish conversation that
was ostensibly about stoneroller minnows. "I said, 'Hey, I didn't know
you had any endangered stonerollers in Tennessee.' So he finally asked
whether I'd heard of a new darter in the Little T. I allowed as I had. He
wasn't happy. Made it clear TVA doesn't think it's a good species and
doesn't want it to be listed."

"What did you tell him?" I ask.

"I said it's science that's going to determine anything that Interior
does on this. We'll be pleased to receive as much scientific information
from TVA as they want to send us on this darter. But to my way of
thinking, TVA's going to make big trouble here."

"So will your office start the listing?" I press.

"Not any time soon," Williams says. "This issue is already identified as controversial as heck, and that means no one here will want to
stick their neck out."

Williams doesn't know who can get the ball rolling. The Endangered Species Act is a relatively new law. It incorporates a list of species
from the International Union for the Conservation of Nature in Swit-
zerland, and he doesn't expect that the office in Geneva will take much
interest in the darter. "Our agency adds species to the U.S. list from
time to time," he says, "but we're not going to be in a hurry to open a
file on a hot potato. If this thing's going to move, you'll have to be the
devils who make us do it."

I wonder aloud about a petition, and Williams agrees that it would
have as good a chance as anything. After all, everyone has a First
Amendment right to petition the government for redress of grievances.

So Hank and I sit down with Etnier and his senior graduate assistant Wayne Starnes to brainstorm about what's known of this new fish.
Etnier has pored through every university collection of bottled darters
in the country, and none has a snail darter. We worry that our fish
might be a subspecies; Ripley told Williams that TVA didn't think it
was a separate species. (The law protects endangered *sub*species as
well, but the case's emotional and political impact could be diluted if
TVA can argue the darter isn't a full species.)

"Hell, no. It's a good species," Etnier says, and launches into technical details we don't understand. He rattles off Latin names, numbers of
fin rays, differences in colors, and fin lengths. What matters, though, is
his conclusion: "There's really good species separation here!" Good.
The more separate the characteristics, the stronger the scientific consensus that they're different species.

"But when you get right down to it," he says, "it's an arbitrary distinction."

"Please don't ever use the word 'arbitrary' in court!" I protest. "If it's
a solid species, please just say it's a species."

"No," Etnier continues. "I'll say it because it's true. Every scientist
knows the lines are kind of arbitrary. We've only a rough consensus on
how much separation makes two groups into different species or just subspecies. This darter's clearly separate enough. But like I say, it's arbitrary."

"But please don't say that," I persist. "And what about the name?
Can't you call it something besides 'snail darter'? The name sounds
frivolous. Couldn't you call it the 'Tennessee darter' or the 'Sam Houston darter'?" Calling the fish a "Tennessee darter" might help with

public opinion, and would be fitting because the fish lived near the Cherokee tribe's Tennassee town. Sam Houston, hero of Texas independence, was born just a few miles north of the river.

Etnier won't budge. "No, dammit. We've been calling it a snail darter in the lab because it eats tiny snails. We're not going to change it for PR reasons." Lawyers and policy considerations are not going to affect how Etnier does his science, and it's science that matters most at this point. Etnier's lab books and Starnes's doctoral dissertation will give us all the evidence we need. After a couple hours of discussion, we formulate a working plan.

Near midnight that evening, after preparing the next day's classes, with two black cats on my lap, I'm sitting in bed, running a slight fever, and starting to draft a federal petition. How do you design a citizen petition to list a species when there's no precedent? It seems appropriate just to frame it as a request under the 1946 Administrative Procedure Act. Section 553(e) gives "any person" the right to draft or describe a proposed rule and ask a federal agency to issue it as law.[1]

What do we need to say to get a species on the endangered list? Our petition invents a five-point format for what we suppose needs to be said, in statements so disingenuously simple that the agency won't be able to duck them. The petition's addressed to Nathaniel Reed, Assistant Secretary for Fish and Wildlife, because Williams says we should go high-profile, straight to a political head.

The petition begins with the obvious:

"1. The fish currently known as the snail darter *exists*. . . ."

This seems incontestable: a good way to begin. We refer Reed to an exhibit file in the petition's appendix containing a lab photograph of the darter (*here it is*, we're saying, *you can see it*)—and followed by four dense text pages of Etnier's "meristic characteristics" physically describing the fish in excruciating scientific detail.

"2. The fish's only known location is the project area of the Little Tennessee River, a unique riverine habitat. . . ."

The attached exhibit shows a map of the river and the shoals at Coytee Spring, along with Starnes's detailed description of the site, noting that the fish has never been found anywhere else.

"3. The existing habitat appears to be critical to the continued existence of the species. . . ."

The third exhibit describes how the fish appears to need big, cleanflowing river habitat to survive, a habitat eliminated by dams virtually everywhere else in the Tennessee river system. The fish is sleekly shaped, flat-bellied, triangular in cross-section to cling to small cobbled rocks in the shallow flowing water, and feeds on tiny creatures adapted to the river bottom's cool, clean currents.

"4. Available scientific evidence indicates that the TVA Tellico project will destroy the snail darter's habitat. . . ."

TVA's bulldozing of trees along the shores, we say, is even now eroding silt onto the fish's home shoals. In the longer term, the fish's entire river habitat would be eliminated.

"5. TVA knows about the fish, its threatened status, and the Act [but continues with its timber-clearing, excavating, and construction]."

The exhibit for this assertion includes copies of TVA's timber-cutting contracts, and a letter to us from Red Wagner's chief executive officer, Lynn Seeber, saying, "We do not think that any appreciable silting of the Little Tennessee River will result from the cutting of these trees and . . . the so-called 'snail darter' has not been listed as an endangered species under the Act [nor] even been 'officially described' which is a necessary step before it can be considered for listing."

Then our petition makes the pitch: "We earnestly request [Interior] to issue an emergency notice of proposed rulemaking," asking the governor of Tennessee to agree to an expedited two-week emergency listing. We also ask Interior to notify TVA, informing the agency of the imminent listing and "asking TVA to conform its actions to the Congressional mandate" by ceasing all work destructive to the darter's habitat.

With Etnier's and Starnes's help we put the petition packet into final shape. Hank, Joe Congleton, and I sign it, send it off by express mail on January 20, and cross our fingers.

Late the very next day we get a call from Jim Williams.

"Holy cow, the shit's hit the fan," Williams proclaims. "Your petition arrived. It's being copied all over the department. It's got everything in it we need for a listing, and people don't know what to do with it. Hang on to your hats."

Then, nothing. . . . After the first week we call Williams, who re-assures us. Nothing happens in a week. He has prepared the formal listing package and sent it up. Then two weeks pass, four weeks, six weeks . . . Meanwhile, TVA crews are scalping the islands in the river.

"The file looks strong," Williams says, "but my office chief has to sign off on it, then Keith Schreiner, the Assistant Director, then the lawyers in the Interior Solicitor's Office, before it goes to the Director for approval. And then because it's controversial it will have to go up to Reed for the rulemaking signature. We'll see what happens next week."

Two weeks later, Williams calls to report that the package has been sent back with orders from Schreiner to redo it.

"So we're not going to get a two-week emergency listing?"

"No way," replies Williams. "That requires the governor of Ten-nessee's consent and this new governor will never agree to it."

What a difference one individual can make. Governor Dunn, the Republican from eastern Tennessee who fruitlessly begged TVA to stop the dam, would have approved Interior's emergency listing in a heartbeat. He's been replaced, however, by Ray Blanton, a former pav-ing contractor who often worked for TVA. Most people at the univer-sity suspect Blanton is a crook. Worse for us, he's TVA's crook.[2]

A week later, Williams reports that the package has once more been sent up, and back down. The lawyers think it needs more data. "Ac-cording to our normal procedures it's complete now," he says, "so I just don't know what to do."

Four more weeks. We filed the petition in January and it's almost May. Williams agrees things don't look so good. "We're in big trouble," he reports. "The hawks are circling above the chicken coop, and noth-ing is moving." Yesterday he was visited by someone from Tennessee Senator Howard Baker's office, and by another representing Missis-sippi Senator John Stennis. "Do you know how often senior Senate staffers come to talk to a Fish and Wildlife biologist they don't know?" Williams exclaims. "Never! And both these guys said they were very concerned about the darter listing."

What does this mean? Baker, a Republican, is Tennessee's senior senator and the Senate minority leader. Though he claims he's "objec-tive" on the dam, his staffer's appearance can be interpreted only as pressure on TVA's behalf. That's unfortunate, but understandable. But

Stennis? He's from Mississippi. Why on earth would Stennis care about the snail darter?

"Tenn-Tom," sighs Williams. "Army Corps."

Uh-oh. These cryptic-sounding words instantly change the political calculus. Stennis is a powerful old southern Democrat with seniority in the congressional committee system. He chairs the Armed Services Committee, which includes the Army Corps of Engineers. Once a Revolutionary War military unit that built fortifications and bridges, the Corps has evolved into a multibillion-dollar nationwide public works construction agency, with as much pork gravy as that role implies. The richest gravy in the two-hundred-year history of the Corps is the Tennessee-Tombigbee—Tenn-Tom—Waterway project, currently under way in Alabama.

Little known outside the region, Tenn-Tom is a $4-billion pork-barrel plan essentially to create a second Mississippi River running south from a loop of the Tennessee River, through Alabama to Mobile Bay on the Gulf of Mexico. To do this the Corps will literally have to move mountains, bringing the waters of the Big Tennessee southward while rerouting and channelizing the Tombigbee as well as a number of other pretty little Alabama rivers. The plan calls for the building of dikes and dams to create a barge route 235 miles long. Every mile of the project will flood several million federal taxpayer dollars into the coffers of local politicians, contractors, and municipalities. The political forces behind Tenn-Tom include every member of Alabama and Mississippi's congressional delegations, many of them committee or subcommittee chairs, and a vast network of allies in the Capitol's public works coalition. Seven of the locks are to be named after senior politicians in the congressional appropriations committees.

The reason the snail darter matters to these national politicians is that up to now there has been no successful legal mechanism to scrutinize the merits of massive public works projects. Citizens and outside critics can testify as much as they want at appropriations committee hearings, but the pork committees will just smile and call the next witness. Beyond the toothless environmental impact statement procedure that did little to hamper the Tellico Dam, citizens and courts have had little legal leverage regarding these projects.

The politicos know the Tenn-Tom and similar pork projects could never survive honest economic scrutiny. Until now, however, that hasn't mattered because they've always known the projects would never receive the kind of scrutiny that would threaten them. According to university economists who have reviewed its cost-benefit ratio, Tenn-Tom's multibillion-dollar cost is based on grossly exaggerated estimates of barge traffic and transit cost savings, immeasurable claims about extraordinary municipal developments predicted to flourish along the waterway, and a miserly accounting of the project's present and future costs.

As in the case of Tellico Dam's economics, the public has never heard about Tenn-Tom's financing charade. During the congressional approval process, a coalition of businesses and state and local agencies lined up alongside the Corps to paint a glittering picture of lucrative development. The local and national press aren't interested in examining the project beyond its claims. Frustrated citizen critics in Alabama have no effective forum.

But the snail darter might change that. If the Endangered Species Act is enforced as a substantive prohibition, very bad things could follow for pork-barrel politicians. The law could bring public attention to the details of these projects, leading to an unprecedented level of legitimate outside scrutiny. If the public realizes that Tellico Dam, described by TVA as a very important civic project that extremists are trying to block, is actually embarrassingly devoid of merit, then Congress might have to answer doubts about other public works projects opposed by citizens.

"I'm afraid I'm part of your political problem," says Williams. He explains that a week earlier some legislators asked for information about the possibility of endangered fish in northern Alabama rivers. Williams produced a two-page memo indicating that there were probably several, including the Alabama sturgeon, in the Tenn-Tom design corridor. Because his office chief, Ron Skoog—who would have blocked the memo—was away, assistant chief Earl Baysinger signed off on it. Baysinger wasn't a traditional, cautious bureaucrat; he himself had participated in drafting the Endangered Species Act. He told Williams to tell the truth.

"The memo caused a *huge* uproar," Williams says. "Schreiner is apoplectic. The darter listing isn't going to go anywhere for a while."

The new Ford administration is a cipher. President Jerry Ford didn't expect to be in the White House and hasn't had time to develop an agenda on much of anything. A moderate, easygoing man who wanted to calm national turmoil, he entered the Oval Office at a time of national angst. His instinct was to go slow, observing the political terrain before doing anything. But what Ford is hearing from the Nixon staffers who continue to dominate policy, Williams says, is bad for the environment and for us.

Richard Nixon, amazingly enough, behaved like an environmentalist in the early '70s, signing into law NEPA, which became the Tennessee farmers' environmental impact statement weapon. Responding to the broad popularity of the first Earth Day, Nixon's pollsters urged him to go green. Environment seemed like a safe, attractive slogan for the president, Congress, and the bureaucracy as well. Nixon signed more than thirty environmental statutes—then, now, and likely forever, more than any leader in history. "The 1970s must be the years when America pays its debts to the past by reclaiming the purity of its air, its water, and our living environment," Nixon declared. "It is literally now or never." In 1972 Nixon stood beside Representative John Dingell and Senator Mark Hatfield, known for their strong environmental stances, and declared that preserving endangered species was a top national priority. A year later he enthusiastically signed the Endangered Species Act after it passed unanimously in the Senate and with only four nays in the House.[3]

But times are changing. The national media is suggesting that the progressive mood of the '60s has started to fade in Washington, and implementation of progressive statutes is eroding. In the years following that first Earth Day, the establishment forces began to regroup. The 1972 Powell Memorandum, written for the U.S. Chamber of Commerce by Lewis Powell shortly before Nixon nominated him to the Supreme Court, became a call to arms for the old corporate order to reverse the 1960s' "socialistic" tides of progressivism in civil rights, Naderite consumerism, feminism, labor, and environmental protection.[4]

"Business," the Powell strategy declared, should "[coordinate] a sustained, major effort to inform and enlighten the American people," by financing academics, think tanks, and media, to defend "the free enterprise system . . . and the business point of view" against the progressives' "ideological warfare against the enterprise system and the values of Western society. . . . There should not be the slightest hesitation to press vigorously in all political arenas for support of the enterprise system. Nor should there be reluctance to penalize politically those who oppose it."

Echoing the Powell Memorandum, a group of oil and gas executives, along with Coors beer directors, created and financed the Heritage Foundation, a think tank with a strong media and politics agenda. A broad, increasingly sophisticated effort coordinated by the U.S. Chamber of Commerce and the National Association of Manufacturers carried the business point of view from the political capitals, where lobbying has always been effective, into the schools, colleges, and every channel of print and electronic media that shape public opinion.

In 1973 the remnants of the right-wing Goldwater coalition made a pragmatic alliance with Reverend Jerry Falwell and his evangelical movement. If evangelicals would get involved in national politics in support of business and against government regulation, the business-oriented Right—the U.S. Chamber, the American Conservative Union, and their Republican allies—would become pro-life and work to incorporate mandatory morality into federal law. Reversing his early stance, according to notes of one of his Cabinet meetings, Nixon declared in late 1973 that it was time "to get off the environment kick."[5]

Industry and its public relations firms unrolled a major effort to marginalize environmentalists and environmentalism, trying to shift the images of green activism away from the broad populism of Earth Day crowds. They depicted environmentalists as elitist birdwatchers and beaded, barefoot hippies—marginalizing caricatures the press was happy to reproduce. Television reports on environmental controversies interviewed the scruffiest ecofreaks they could find, juxtaposed with deft industry spokesmen. Meanwhile, big-budget ad campaigns denigrated environmental concerns: "Don't worry about chemicals; your body is made of chemicals." Or "Mom's apple pie is radioactive. So is Mom." Translation: only extremists worry about the environment.

It's all sadly predictable: if our case is reported as a trivial fish versus a big hydroelectric dam, as it's likely to be, the citizens defending the darter and the river will be depicted as a bunch of wild-eyed fanatics. Our group in Tennessee, however, focuses on the sensible case that can be made with the law that's on the books. The "Tennessee Endangered Species Committee," newly formed at the University of Tennessee, is recruiting volunteers for the darter crusade. The college staff and students doing the organizational work meet regularly with the farmers, spend time at the river, and hold boisterous weekly meetings and pot-luck suppers. They are supported by local flower clubs, hiking clubs, and the active local chapter of Trout Unlimited.

The darter's defenders celebrate occasional good news. Boeing has pulled out, essentially eliminating TVA's claimed land development benefits, though Red Wagner remains firm on keeping the project roll-ing. The Knoxville newspaper prints a long letter against the dam from the Oak Ridge wilderness group. Doris Gove, a graduate researcher, and Sara Grigsby, an energetic undergraduate who took on the task of organizing UT students, together design a T-shirt featuring a little snail darter being attacked by the snarling "Jaws" of a TVA shark (a takeoff on the iconic image from Steven Spielberg's recently released blockbuster movie). We sell two hundred shirts, $11 each. Supporters send letters to local newspapers, and raise comments and questions at civic associations, town halls, and TVA board meetings. Soon we have enough organization and expense money to plan a trip for me to go to Washington to push for the snail darter's listing.

Despite the political climate, we had a moment of hope for the Ford administration: Sara discovered a magazine article about Ford's Coun-cil on Environmental Quality, in which the group's senior scientist, Lee Talbot (who helped write the Endangered Species Act), was quoted as saying "endangered species have an intrinsic worth *that may be far more important than a dam project.*" Dam project? Maybe that means he's heard about our case, and his White House office will sup-port us.

After just a few days in Washington, our hope is punctured. Visiting Talbot, I discover that the "President's Council on Environmental Quality" is located in an office in a townhouse a block away from the White House, a tiny agency with a very low political profile. In theory it's the federal executive watchdog monitoring every agency's environ-mental compliance. In practice, every step forward treads on powerful toes, so the Council dares not advance much. Lee Talbot squirms when I ask how he'll help us on Tellico, where a dam directly threatens an endangered species. "We actually don't get directly involved in most of these cases," he says. "Your best bet is to go back and work with Interior."

Our Washington education is beginning. Neither the Council nor Interior wants to stick its neck out to enforce the law. When an issue

While intensive lobbying was occurring in Washington, community lobbying in eastern Tennessee was coordinated by the
University of Tennessee–based Tennessee Endangered Species Committee, which raised consciousness by writing letters
to newspapers and speaking out at TVA and other regional
meetings, and raised funds through the sale of prints of the
Exhibit #12 snail darter print and *Jaws*-inspired T-shirts,
shown here by Chuck Cook and Doris Gove (Doris Gove and
Sara Grigsby designed the T-shirt). (Jed DeKalb for the *Daily
Beacon,* University of Tennessee student newspaper; permission to use gratefully acknowledged)

smells of controversy the bureaucracy's instinct is to go slow. If the fish
isn't listed, it will have no legal duty to enforce the law. I phone Jim
Williams. "It's best you don't come over here," he says from his Fish
and Wildlife Service cubicle. "You'd get me in hot water. Citizen activists spell trouble; you're kind of persona non grata right now."

We assumed that when our petition had been submitted into the
agency process it would become the focus of some collective depart-
mental procedure, with officials bringing their shared professional experience and expertise to bear upon the science and the law of it in
an established sequence of reviews, ultimately reaching a conclusion
on the facts that the agency would then implement. That's what eighth
grade civics books say. Instead, we learn, our petition just got parked
on somebody's desk at Interior. We're lucky that desk is Jim Williams's.
He's the fish specialist, so he collects and collates the data and makes

tentative determinations on case files. But every time our case moves up the line it's kicked back down through a flinching hierarchy.

"It's political, it's just bouncing back again," Williams reports in his weekly phone call when we're back in Tennessee. "Reed knows it's solid but won't sign off on it, he just sends it down for more study. Maybe you should try to find somebody in Congress. When the Act was going through the House, John Dingell's staff were the ones pushing hardest. Maybe try them."

This is promising: Stennis and other pork-barrel legislators obstruct agency procedures, but maybe we can find others to apply counter-pressure. When we looked through the records of the original 1973 Endangered Species Act hearings, we frequently found the names of Representative Dingell, who sponsored the bill, and his Merchant Marine and Fisheries Committee's chief counsel, James Spensley. It would be hard to speak directly with the congressman himself, we figured, but why not try his lawyer? From Tennessee, we call Washington directory assistance and ask for his home phone number. It's a Saturday morning, and an unsurprised woman answers the phone and says, yes, this is Skip Spensley's home, but he can't talk about endangered species until he finishes his tennis game, in about an hour.

"This is Spensley," he answers when I call back. "Do I know you?" I explain we're from Tennessee and are frustrated by Interior's inaction on an endangered species case. "Oh, the darter," he says. He's heard rumors about us. "I figured the Act was going to start some dramatic cases but I didn't think they were going to be like this."

I explain the facts and common sense of the case—ecological treasures versus a pork-barrel dam. "Yes, yes, of course that's what's going on," he says, "but this'll be seen as just a silly minnow against a big hydroelectric dam." When I explain the stalemate in Interior, again he's unsurprised. "Public works agencies are powerful," he says. "Interior's getting the message not to raise questions about other agencies' water projects."

"Can you get Mr. Dingell to help us push this through?" I ask.

No, says Spensley. Though Dingell's our best bet out of all 535 representatives and senators in Congress, he's overloaded and can't take on a new cause that would demand months or even years of work. He sponsored the act, cares about hunting and fishing, and likes to fight, but he's already got plenty of enemies and doesn't need more, especially over an issue that's bound to lose and won't affect his factory worker constituents in Michigan. "Your dam is obviously a bad project," Spensley says, "but there's a buddy system in Congress. Stopping somebody else's project is one of the hardest things a legislator can try to do. The big reason Dingell can't help you, though," he continues, "is he's leaving the chair of the Merchant Marine committee that handles the Act. He's taking over the Special Committee on Energy. It doesn't have any wildlife jurisdiction."

This is depressing. Even the ones who wrote the law can't or won't join our cause. The endangered species statute is one of a thousand others floating out there, and it seems the only people who are paying attention to it are those who want it to go away. "So what can we do?" I ask.

"I don't know," Spensley says, "but I'll tell you this. You can't stay down there in Tennessee. You have to come up here to Washington . . ." Then he has an idea. "Do you know about the American Rivers Conservation Council? It's a citizen group that's been doing a lot on river conservation. You should come talk to them."

We immediately call them (they work weekends). A young woman's tired voice answers, "ARCC." We explain our story and she says, "You've got to talk to Brent Blackwelder. But he's not going to be off the phone for an hour. Anyway, the way he works he'll want to meet you face to face and see maps and charts and stuff like that. Look, we're putting on a dam fighters' conference here next week. Why don't you come? Eighty people are coming from all over the U.S. It's spread over three days. We do workshop sessions on strategies and tactics and on the projects they're fighting. Maybe we can do a session on your TVA dam too."

This sounds good. "How much does it cost?" I ask.

"Twenty-five bucks if you can afford it," she says. "We'll have bunks for you at the 4-H Center or sofas with activists here in town. Meals included. Most of our people can't pay what hotels charge. Come on up."

On a Friday morning a week later I fly to Washington, where the cherry trees are just beginning to blossom. As I walk east on Pennsylvania Avenue, block by block the neighborhood gets seedier. When I find 317 Pennsylvania SE, ARCC's headquarters, I'm sure it's a mistake: 317 is a Roy Rogers hamburger joint. Then I see a narrow stairway ascending through a cloud of grease smoke to an upper floor. As I round the corner at the top of the stairs I see no identifying placards, but the scene makes it clear—a packed warren of boxes, chairs, and scavenged desks, everything heaped with jumbled paper, young people hunched here and there over blinking telephones or shuttling back and forth between the room's distressed areas. This is the American Rivers Conservation Council. Letterheads on nearby desks reveal that this is also the national headquarters of EPC, the Environmental Policy Center, plus the national League of Conservation Voters.

A volunteer sitting on a folding chair beside a plywood workspace divider looks up from the document he's editing in his lap. "Can I help you?" he asks. I tell him I'm from Tennessee and he says, "Oh, we've heard about you guys. You've got to talk to Brent when he gets off the phone. I'm Dave Conrad. Let me give you the schedule for the conference."

The lectures and workshops start midday Friday, running to Sunday at noon. All the conference activities are taking place in a church basement hall three blocks away, with parties in the evenings and a dance Saturday night. All of Monday, the final day of the conference, is set aside for office visits to members of Congress. Included with the conference schedule packet—nothing fancy, it's all mimeographed paper with no slick photo handouts—are a map of places where out-of-towners can find a bed, directions to the church, and a meal card that shows the contents of boxed lunches and dinner buffets, including Jell-O for dessert. You can indicate if you prefer vegetarian meals instead.

"Brent, this is the guy from Tennessee."

"Just a minute. I'll be right with you." A hunched, thin, nerdy-looking guy with a pasty, square face, Brent is wearing a once-white shirt on its second or third day, a narrow black tie, and rumpled, drip-dry black suit trousers. He darts out of the plywood cubbyhole across to a wooden shelf of papers, retrieves a tattered report that he slides into his ratty briefcase, and sidles over to us. "Tell me about the fish," he says.

Brent Blackwelder, who works for both the Environmental Policy Center and the American Rivers Conservation Council, squints through thick glasses at a picture of the darter and a map of the Little Tennessee. With eyes flickering back and forth across the papers, he asks machine-gun questions in a flat, reedy voice that shows no trace of affect. "So they need the shoals in a big river to breed? What do they eat? Is it clear they can't live if this is impounded? Now show me the dam. It's small. A 33-mile backup? That means it's pretty flat country.

What's the cost-benefit ratio they currently claim? 1 to 1.3? That's a joke. Model city to be developed by Boeing? Pffft. That's a new one; even the Corps hasn't tried that. Has there ever been a university study of the economics? What local interests are pushing the dam? Who do you have on your side? Does Boeing have a political presence in Tennessee? Has any Tennessee representative expressed doubts about the dam publicly? Can the environmental impact statement still be challenged? Have any investigative stories come out in the press? Are you ready to bring a lawsuit? How would you pay for it? What plans have you made to follow through on this in Washington? . . ."

Brent is obviously bright, has seen boondoggles before, and knows political landscapes. In ten minutes he's digested our case in full, understands the important details, and sees the obvious shortcomings of our amateur dam-fighting group.

"You need to find a national environmental law group to carry this for you," he says flatly. I ruefully report that we've been turned down by everyone we've contacted. As the National Wildlife Federation's Golten had said, none of the big groups would take on this project if all we have going for us is the Endangered Species Act. With no more than the fish, they'd expect to lose.

"I see," he says. "That's not good."

"So can you help us?" I ask.

"Look around this room. We don't have enough money to buy desks—even if we had a place to put them. We're subleasing from EPC. We don't have a lawyer. But come to the dam-fighter sessions. We'll talk about what you can do. And after the conference is over, we'll be here, and we'll give you whatever help we can. Now excuse me, I have to go." He grabs his briefcase and dashes down the stairs for a meeting on the Hill.

Soon afterward we walk over to the church basement and are swept into a milling mass of people in jeans and hiking shoes, all wearing stick-on name tags. Young and old, farmers and canoeists, ecology students and retired dentists. Instantly there is a sense of being among friends, maybe the very first time being with so many people who share the same dilemma. Were official decisions made on the actual merits of any of the dams these people are fighting against, they'd probably win. But everyone here knows the unyielding stone walls of agency officials, politicians, and local chambers of commerce. They've seen glossy public relations campaigns boosting irrational projects, argued against faked cost-benefit project justifications, and watched local newspapers painting citizen critics as radical extremists. Everyone here understands, moreover, that unless something lucky happens, the rational arguments—and the rivers we're fighting for—will ultimately lose.

The tone of the crowd is anything but dismal, however. "Yeah, the odds are against us," a guy whose lapel sticker reads "HELLO, I'M: Brock Evans, Sierra Club" says to me. "Almost all environmental campaigns feel desperate and hopeless at the start. You can't let that get in the way. Look at everyone here, fighting for the same thing. We share stories and work on strategies."

At the dam-fighters conference Brent, the only person wearing a tie, stands on a folding chair and welcomes everyone to the second annual gathering, then asks groups to identify themselves, project-by-challenged-project. "Tellico Dam" joins a roll call of twenty projects. He notes that Tellico indicates everyone should keep an eye on the Endangered Species Act. Then he walks us through a list of workshop sessions we'll be doing over the next three days. His demeanor is wonk-square and resolutely businesslike. No talk of odds. No cursing the pork barrel. No rah-rah. There is work to be done, background Washington information to pass on, techniques to learn, and tactics and contacts to be shared.

As we move into opposite corners for individual workshops, a grinning young outdoorsman-type in a tattered plaid wool shirt comes over to say hello. His name tag identifies him as Jim Williams (the tag does not mention his Department of Interior Fish and Wildlife Service affiliation). We have spent many hours talking on the phone, but this is the first time that Williams and I meet face to face. I'd pictured him as a middle-aged professional in a conservative suit or a white lab coat, but he's scruffier than any of the farmers here.

"You can't say you saw me here," he whispers with a conspiratorial grin. "I used to work for the Alabama Conservancy, and these here are my kind of folks. But now that I'm at Fish and Wildlife there'd be heck to pay if the Tenn-Tom lobby knew I was here. Ets mentioned you were coming so I had to come by. You're going to learn a lot from these people."

Jim Williams is right. The sessions are like a graduate course in water projects: how they start and how with luck and savvy tactics citizens can challenge their political momentum. In virtually all the work-shop discussions the analysis quickly focuses on Washington. Federal laws are what provide the authority by which agencies, states, and corpo-rate allies get their power and money. As a result, the federal construction agencies—the Army Corps of Engineers, the Bureau of Reclamation, TVA—are stronger politically than most state governments. Yet it's also federal laws and courts that offer most hope for cutting through the monolithic multilevel coalitions that defend pork projects.

Out of the workshops emerges a mosaic view of government as it really works, not much resembling what we were taught in junior high. The regulatory agencies created to protect public interests are mostly reluctant to act against powerful sister agencies and their corporate backers. Some protective agencies are weak from the moment of their creation. The national Council for Historic Preservation in Interior, for example, could have intervened against Tellico Dam but it's regarded as a lightweight sop to historians. Other agencies, like OSHA, the Occupational Safety and Health Administration, start strong in a burst of public attention, and then slowly wither in power and credibil-ity, undercut by pressure from the sectors they regulate. Even huge agencies like the Environmental Protection Agency or Department of the Interior, which are made up of a dozen or more subagencies, fear the pork barrel's political power.

"Don't expect much from the Department of Interior," the ARCC volunteers tell us. "Alongside Interior's resource protection subagencies like Fish and Wildlife or the Council for Historic Preservation are much more powerful exploitation divisions like the Bureau of Reclamation—we call it 'BuWreck.' And BLM, the Bureau of Land Management—we call it the 'Bureau of Livestock and Mining.'"

Someone suggests bringing issues to the attention of the president, supposedly the top power in government. One of the Washington vol-unteers says forget it. The president hasn't been dominant in this town since Lyndon Johnson, who was sometimes loved but always feared, keeping intricate tabs on what was going on and relentlessly getting re-venge against anyone who crossed him. In the years since LBJ no one's had the same degree of control, not even Nixon, and Congress's 1974 Budget Act undercut the most basic practical power that presidents possessed. A president can still have important influence, the ARCC people tell us, but can focus on only a few headline issues at a time. He can try to direct media attention toward a policy, try to set a tone. His Cabinet appointees can have a policy effect in their agencies. But many important agencies in Washington aren't really under his control—independent agencies like the Nuclear Regulatory Commission, Interstate Commerce Commission, Federal Communications Commission, Securities and Exchange Commission, the Bonneville Power Authority, and a dozen others—and that includes the TVA. They report to Congress, not to the president. He can't remove their bosses except for gross incompetence or moral turpitude.[6]

Even in Cabinet agencies, we're told, the president gets to put his own people in only the top-level jobs—secretaries, assistant secretaries, deputy undersecretaries—the ones that change with every administration. Below them are those who do most of the real work, two million civil service employees who stay in those jobs decade after decade. "The administrative branch is like a tanker plowing along, it's inertial momentum," says ARCC volunteer Conrad, explaining that presidents rarely can change the government's course quickly. The bureaucracy wants to plow along, steering a safe, orderly course when it has to travel through stormy waters.

Conrad says, "The people you talk with in the operational offices tend to be guided more by fear of doing something wrong. They're not going to be rewarded for doing a good job enforcing the law against somebody powerful. They're afraid they'll be singled out by some senator, or editorials against their bureau, or identified as too gung-ho, loose cannons, goody-goodies. It's a survival instinct. Think of *killifish*. Have you ever looked into a creek and seen a big school of tiny minnows flashing along, totally coordinated? Each the same size, each sensing the exact moment to turn left or right, exactly together? It's a recipe for survival. If a killifish stands out because it's bigger or faster than the group it's with? Pow. Singled out, you get eaten. Stay in the mass and you're more likely to blend in and survive."

Conrad's point is that we shouldn't expect agency staffers to take up our fight just because it's the law and their agency has a duty to do something about it. There is a standard way of doing things in most agencies: keep your head down. "But don't give up on the agencies," Conrad tells the dam fighters. "You just have to be realistic. Keep pushing them. There are dozens of good people inside the agencies who can help you even if they have to keep a low profile." He's talking about people like Jim Williams, standing incognito in the crowd with a slight smile on his face. "They can let you know who's doing what, and slip you confidential documents. They can pass you pieces of useful information you'd never think of asking for. And they can take your information and put it into agency records so it might shape decisions later."

Someone in the crowd asks how you find people like that, and Conrad says you have to cultivate inside contacts, in both protective agencies and construction agencies too, if you can. "You don't just walk in the door, an unknown citizen frustrated by some water project," he says. "For them to work with you is more a danger than a duty. Look around for somebody who seems to really care about the issues. Show you know what you're talking about, that you have useful information. Show you can be trusted. Try to get to the point that a staffer feels secure calling you at home, giving you a heads-up when something good or bad is coming. We call those 'midnight phone calls.' Be very discreet." Apparently every office in Washington has a story of staffers who got burned when they gave a confidential tip to a citizen who then blabbed about it. Especially inside the public works agencies, it's a career-ending mistake. "You must never blow the cover of a staffer who's given you inside information," Conrad cautions us.

Jim Williams and I talk at the break. "Conrad is so right," he says. "You know how this listing for the darter has been derailed again and again in the sign-off process, and each failure has the name 'Keith Schreiner' tied to it? Schreiner called me in. He knows I talk to Etnier and he suspects I talk with you. He told me, 'Jim, I'm sure you want to make an end run on some of these things, but if I ever catch you on it, you're dead meat.'" Schreiner was once a very good field biologist, Williams says, but he has been promoted to associate director because his strong political instincts focus on keeping the agency out of trouble, and he's even better at that than at biology.

Williams has to be very careful. We're lucky to have him on the inside of the listing process, but he's no killifish. He already sticks out as more principled than he is careful. "We have to watch out," he says. "I can't be seen as a relay for information between you and the Department. The way they think about environmentalists they'd say I'm consorting with the enemy. I can talk openly with Etnier, because he's a scientist, but I can't with you. So I have to say I am hearing all these things through Etnier, whatever you need to pass along."

"But Jim," I say, "we've *got* to be able to talk with you. There will be things that come up fast that will come unglued if we have to wait while we find Dr. Etnier and pass messages through him."

"Listen more carefully to what I'm saying," says Jim. "People in my office have already mentioned they've seen *your* name in the phone logs when you call me. So, remember what David Conrad was saying about protecting people you work with inside the agencies? We can't have it be *you* who calls me."

"Oh, okay . . . I get it!" I say. We consider a couple of aliases and settle on the name "Chuck Cook." The real Chuck Cook is Sara Grigsby's husband, a biology student back in Knoxville. From now on, in calls to Interior's Office of Endangered Species I'll be Chuck Cook.

After the break Marion Edey, the president of the League of Conservation Voters, shifts the discussion to Congress. "Most of us who work here in Washington consider Congress the most powerful branch of government," she says. Edey spends most of her time on the Hill. In addition to running the League she's on the ARCC and EPC boards—convenient because all three groups share the same crammed space above the Roy Rogers. She speaks with the same flat tone as Brent, intense and intelligent. "They say if you distill all of the New Testament down to one word it would be 'Love.' If you distill Washington down to one word it's 'Power.' In this city you measure power not just by what people can get done, but by how other people are afraid of them. Congress isn't much afraid of the president or the courts, but the president and judges are mostly afraid of Congress."

There are 535 members of Congress (here in Washington, Edey says, you spell member with a capital "M"). They can be disturbingly unpredictable, changing a law or making a new one in just a day if they want to, and they can pass laws over the president's veto. They can block agencies' budgets for almost any reason, hit administrative officials with televised hearings with less than a day's notice, and then rake them over the coals on the evening news for things that nobody could have foreseen. They have the power to put pressure on courts by holding up funding and judicial appointments for purely political reasons. And Edey isn't just talking about Congress acting by majority votes. Many of these power plays get done by subcommittees or powerful individual members. A bill or a presidential appointment can be locked

up in a congressional committee out of courtesy to just one member.
Or a one-sentence rider that fundamentally changes a law can get added
to a money bill, invisibly, just before a vote.

"You face one of the most powerful networks in Congress: the appropriations process," she says. "You're seeing the pork barrel up close. It's
in every one of your water projects." Appropriations committees, she
explains, have the power to give or deny money to every voting district
in the United States. This makes them so powerful there's a House rule
prohibiting their members from sitting on any other committees. These
money committees, most chaired by senior Southern legislators, have
had water projects as a special favorite for the past thirty years. It's not
just water projects, though. There are pork committees for agriculture,
aerospace, highways, power transmission lines, export subsidies, and
more—all linked to powerful congressional coalitions and all largely
unnoticed by the public.

Given that voters hate paying taxes and the federal government is
sinking deeper in debt, it's surprising the appropriations committees
don't care whether their projects make economic sense. The first
twenty or so TVA dams were probably worth building, but the subsequent forty-five dams were largely a waste of taxpayer money. "Just
the opposite," Edey says. "Their power comes from *spending* federal
money. The way the pork barrel works, most people on the Hill don't
care if project benefit claims are fictions. No project has ever been given
a post-development accounting, and none ever will, because everyone
knows it'd show so many of them aren't justified."

Edey explains that most people don't realize that a network of
appropriations committees and subcommittees—paralleling the more
familiar subject matter committees—has the most constant handle on
what happens in Washington. Regular committees like the Senate Natural Resources Committee or House Interior Committee are the ones
that originate major laws and authorize programs and projects, but
they can go years without convening oversight hearings on them. The
appropriations committees, however, hold hearings every year on every
one of the ongoing projects and programs. Nothing happens if the
money committees don't give their annual approval in separate money
bills. Their subcommittee structure parallels the regular committees
almost exactly—with subcommittees for Water and Power, for Fish and
Wildlife, for Energy Development—almost a shadow Congress. And

unlike the staffs of regular committees, the appropriations staffers know exactly what's going on in each agency.

For construction agencies, lobbyists, and members who want to bring signs of their influence home to their districts, the committees that offer the most tangible help are the money guys. Appropriations committees may have been originally intended to watch the purse strings and be sure that federal tax dollars were well spent, but they quickly discovered that power comes from funding projects regardless of merits, and cutting funding for protective programs like environmental regulations that hinder these projects. There's a perverse dynamic: the construction agencies and members of Congress both have strong political incentives to justify major projects, and little incentive to worry about how much they'll really cost, or how little they'll really benefit the country.

"Actually it's more than that. It's an iron triangle," says a blond, outdoorsy-looking guy in the workshop group. He's George "Rock" Pring, an activist attorney who directs the Denver office of the Environmental Defense Fund and who also teaches part-time at the University of Colorado. He explains that political scientists use the term *iron triangle* to refer to the insider alliances that dominate Washington politics. It represents powerful three-way alliances—between a specific industry sector, the federal agency involved, and a collection of committed supporters in Congress—to extract benefits from the public for their three blocks. The industry sector gets legal support and taxpayer expenditures, the members of Congress get political support and a portion of the profits back in the form of campaign finance contributions, and the agencies get to maintain momentum as well as political clout. Heavily serviced by industry-funded lobbyists and public relations contractors, iron triangles are in place in every sector of government—in the politics of oil and gas, mining, banking, timber, chemicals and pharmaceuticals, ranch land grazing, highways, water projects, and dozens more. Pring says that an iron triangle represents an insiders' game, where the benefits extracted for the high-flying members of a triangle too often come at the expense of the rest of the nation's best interests. Public works water projects are usually initiated by government agencies like TVA, the Army Corps of Engineers, and the Bureau of Reclamation. Legislators pick up on these proposals and carry them along, supported by the economic special interests that live off them, and the projects become politically unstoppable.

"No matter how ridiculous these things are, the agency gets a trans-fusion of money and momentum when they get approved," Pring says. Ultimately it's the third block, the business sector, that drives the whole process—companies that get federal construction contracts; industries like barge transportation or irrigation whose operations are federally subsidized; real estate interests that sell land to the agencies at a profit or get free improvements to land they own; banks that get to churn land transactions; state and local politicians who run development boards or choose winners and losers in project design and construction; cham-bers of commerce whose members make money from an influx of fed-eral funds. A decisive part of the federal money that triangles absorb gets poured back into the triangles, especially in the form of lobbying and congressional campaign contributions.

"Dams are like addictive drugs to politicians," David Conrad adds. "They get praise back home when they get them approved, their bud-dies get a piece of the action, they're front and center at big ribbon cut-tings when a project is finished, and when the politicians get old or die the dams will be named after them."

A large, bearded guy unhappily agrees. He's Fred Powledge, who's researching a book on water. "It's a symbiosis," he says. "All three parts of the triangle join up in the pork process. With the connection to appro-priation committees, iron triangles are virtually unbeatable. A triangle is the strongest, most rigid geometry shape there is." The political linkage of iron triangles, he reminds us, creates nationwide networks, political megasystems where multiple iron triangles join together to discredit citi-zen efforts in any sector which affects business as usual. "Iron triangles don't like environmentalists," Powledge says. "Good luck. When you go up against them you're like mosquitoes trying to swat an elephant."[7]

"That's too pessimistic," rejoins Edey. "People can have an impact, sometimes in ways they don't foresee. If you don't bring the facts and law down on these projects, who will?" She briefs the group on specific tactics in congressional offices on Capitol Hill and the agencies. "You'll need to choose targets well," she says. "You're wasting your time if you think you can convince people inside an iron triangle to change their minds based on the public interest." The Corps isn't going to be swayed by proof that its cost-benefit calculations are dishonest. Mem-bers of Congress pushing the projects don't care either and aren't going to back off.

So where can we get leverage? "If your project involves barge facilities," she says, "look for members and lobbyists who're close to railroad and trucking industries that compete with barges. If your project destroys farmlands, try to build coalitions with farming lobbyists who'll get you into the offices of farm belt legislators. Use small-farmer lobbies, not the corporate agriculture guys who line up with the public works lobbies." Good. Tellico Dam destroys farmlands, and claims a barging benefit.

Edey hands out a list of the 535 members of Congress and their office addresses. "Plan your visits so you aren't running back and forth all over the place. If the representative has a three-digit office number, that means it's in Cannon, the old House office building. Four digits starting with '1' is the Longworth House Office Building. Starting with '2' means it's in the newest building, Rayburn. On the Senate side, three digits means the old Russell Senate Office Building, and four means the Dirksen. If you get lost, call the Hill switchboard, 224–3121."

Another good pressure point, Edey tells us, is provided by the regular committees, the ones that put the substantive laws on the books. If you can show them that the appropriations committees and public works lobbies are interfering with something they think is their turf, they can get jealous enough to fight about it. If you can convince just one member, especially someone with seniority and a committee leadership position, to take a personal interest, that may be all you need to get some leverage.

There's a visible split between Edey and Brent. She thinks the way to push the congressional process is by leveraging members' turf-protection machismo and fear. He is deeply committed to the belief that if citizens present the facts accurately, eventually the process will be guided by the merits. Both agree, however, that the press is critically important to our process.

"Try to cultivate at least one intelligent reporter who can learn your local issue and write articles that aren't just copies of press releases they get from project boosters," Brent says. "Dam promoters are afraid of bad stories in the media. They'll try to crack down on reporters who dig into project economics or political tricks. A reporter who has brains and guts *and* the support of an editor or publisher, that's worth a million-dollar lobbyist."

Edey has begun issuing an annual press release called "The Dirty Dozen," identifying the twelve worst members of Congress based on their compiled roll-call votes on environmental issues monitored by the

League of Conservation Voters. The press loves the Dirty Dozen list. It's backed by copious data and highlights congressional votes that otherwise would pass unseen in the fog of legislative process. Its rogues' gallery typically features legislators whom the press loves to pick on for other reasons too—old Southerners whose views on civil rights still reflect segregationist pasts, congressional antiregulationists, and union busters. The Dirty Dozen list always contains water project boosters. Brent says he wants ARCC to copy Edey's idea. He's preparing a survey to be published as an annual illustrated booklet of "America's Ten Worst Water Projects." If the story is picked up in national media, Congress is likely to take note of it. If we're lucky, maybe Tellico will be on his list.

That evening, the crowd in the church basement turns rowdy as beer and country music start flowing. The homogenizing spirit of the '60s is still with us. Some cross-generational dancing combinations work out, and some don't. For some volunteers the environmental movement shares some aspects with college mixers. There's an aroma of cannabis in the corner. A few newly met couples pair off.

Halfway through the evening there's a hammering at the door. In stomps a powerfully built guy in an Army Corps of Engineers uniform. Well, almost a Corps officer's uniform. On closer inspection the gold braids on his shoulders turn out to be two yellow dish sponges, and his official shirt is too short and reveals his belly hair above the plunging beltline. "I'm General Brute Thwackem, of the Yew Ess Ahmy Corps of Ingineers!" the figure booms. "I've come heah to straighten out you tree huggers on all yer Comminist criticism about our water projects. You call it Pork. We call it Progress. If you don't got you a river, we'll make you one! [Brent flicks on a slide projector that displays a photo of a canal being bulldozed through farmland.] If you got yourself a river, we'll get rid of it for you! [photo: dam construction flooding a forest] You just don' understand what yer dealing with here: God Almighty made rivers to be dammed and swamps to be drained, and He created the Corps to do the job . . ." The general turns out to be John Marlin, the original founder of ARCC, who rocks the crowd for twenty minutes with a slide show of messy pork water projects, including a photo of the Three Stooges as "agency project economists."

As the party winds down, I lean over to David Conrad. "These people—Brent, Marion, Brock, John, the others. How did they come to be here?"

"It was Earth Day, I think," Conrad says. "Brent was a grad student and saw the environment as an issue that had broad significance. He came to Washington with $400 to incorporate ARCC, hire staff, and get it going. He gets almost no salary for the work he puts in here. It isn't even his main job. He's married and has a kid. Technically his real job is teaching philosophy at a college over in Maryland. But he schedules his courses so he can teach evening classes there, and puts in all his days here at ARCC. We can't figure out when he gets to have a family life."

And Marion Edey? "She was raised as a society debutante, up in Long Island I think. I guess you could say she realized she had means but wanted some meaning, so she came here and joined Friends of the Earth. A lot of people entered the environmental movement when the civil rights marches and Vietnam War protests tapered off. I've watched Marion in meetings on the Hill. Somebody like Senator Baker will say, 'I've always supported cost accounting in energy projects,' and Marion will say 'No, that's not true. You voted against it in four key committee votes last year, and only voted for it once, last January, on the final bill after you'd tried to gut it on the Senate floor.' She says things politely but firmly and nails them dead. They know they have to treat her seriously because she really knows her stuff, even if she only has a crappy little office above the Roy Rogers."

The capital office of Friends of the Earth has been a starting point for a number of activists, but the evolution of these environmental organizations can evidently be challenging. David Brower, the charismatic old prophet of the environmental movement, formed Friends of the Earth after he was booted out of the presidency of the Sierra Club, which he'd built from a small San Francisco club into a national organization. When his mercurial style began to chafe on the bright young people he'd attracted to Friends of the Earth, Brent, Edey, and a few others jumped ship in 1971, forming the Environmental Policy Center above the hamburger shop. They created ARCC with Marlin a year later. Brower eventually was forced out of Friends too, and left for San Francisco, where he started a new group, Earth Island. Sierra Club and Friends have rebuilt their Washington offices, and everyone seems to get along now.

Since the 1960s these newer groups, together with a half-dozen older conservation organizations in the capital, have changed the national political discourse about environment. Their budgets are quite small, and their political impact depends on opportunistic interventions into legislative and administrative battles, plus media coverage, but by now they've become established junior players in congressional hearings and public policy debates.

"Most of us start out as volunteers," Conrad says. "I've never had a salary. My parents wonder why they sent me to college. But if things work out, we make ourselves a place. Brent's told me he can give me a job at ARCC and pay me maybe $125 a week. I still don't have a desk. That's how it goes in this movement. Some burn out. But we keep on growing. We've got to. If we don't do what we do, who would?"

The next Monday, we go to Capitol Hill to make contacts. No Tennessee legislator wants to talk about the dam, but we find Skip Spensley in the Merchant Marine and Fisheries Committee's wildlife subcommittee staff office. Thank you, we say: the contact with American Rivers was a very good idea. How do we push Interior to list the darter? Spensley ticks off a list of possible committees and legislators, though he guesses none of them will be responsive. But he offers some further thoughts: "You need credible threats," he says. "Maybe you could threaten to sue Interior to force the listing. And I'll try to persuade Bob Leggett, the subcommittee chair, to hold an endangered species hearing sometime this year. I doubt he'll do it. But even if he doesn't, if you tell Interior that Leggett is thinking about it, they may push the listing through to avoid looking bad."

Back home in Tennessee, we muse about what we're learning. Government isn't some inexorable process automatically responding to significant issues and forthrightly enforcing laws on the objective merits. It's much more a jumbled composite of many versions of human nature, a concatenation of people, groups, alliances, moods, and contending tribal agendas. When government actually *does* something, it seems, it's because somebody makes it happen. And who are we? I don't feel like a crusader. Rather, I feel trapped. Back at Fort Loudoun it had come down to the realization that we couldn't bear to tell our grandchildren that we had had the law, the facts, the economics, and common sense all on our side to stop the reservoir, but didn't have the courage to try. Now we're paying a price, in time, pleasure forgone (I haven't been fishing in months), and emotional energy poured down this hole. But it feels like a fight we can't abandon.

The odds? Not good. We live in a region where TVA is a dominating presence in daily life. Tennessee's daily papers never even hint that the dam's economics may be shaky or that better alternatives exist. Most people among whom we live and work assume the TVA plan makes sense, and that we are eccentric or worse. Very few people want to talk about Tellico, much less cheer us on. We've gotten used to the pained smiles and wincing looks that greet the news that we are in that group of eccentrics still questioning the Tellico Dam. Although some Tennesseans are still skeptical about the dam, they keep their heads down and seem to resent our cocky attempt to beard this lion. "Reckon you'll learn same as we did," more than one have told us. "You're just adding more hurt for yourselves, and for them you care about, when you go up against TVA." Why don't we just step away, they ask, and let the river's death sentence be executed?

In truth, some of the reasons we started this fight may not be fully admirable: revenge against agency high-handedness, and tilting at pompous institutional authority. I often see an obstreperous glitter in Hank's and Sara's eyes. But more fundamentally, the river and its valley have moved us. We've learned to know and love the snail darter as a precious survivor in a blasted ecosystem. We didn't rush thoughtlessly into the decision to litigate, and we've tried to make our preparations wisely. We're learning useful lessons in Washington. Nothing we've encountered gives us confidence to believe we'll ultimately succeed. It's just clear that nobody else will do anything to stop this destructive project.

So we push for the listing, because until the darter is on the list there will be no traction for the other stratagems we want to apply—attracting investigative press to the fish-versus-dam conflict, making overtures to railroad and farmer lobbies, finding a congressional hero who might commit time and effort to our cause. Until it's been sharpened into an actual statutory violation, the issue won't be defined as a conflict, won't have critical mass and momentum.

It turns out Spensley was serious when he said he'd help us build "credible threats." A couple days after our return to Tennessee, Spensley reports he'd mentioned to Leggett that Interior was dragging its feet on a listing because of pressure from TVA, and Leggett said something like "We'll see about *that*." Spensley suggests this means Leggett's thinking about doing something for us. We call Jim Williams and tell him he can let his bosses know (is this stretching the truth?) that Leggett is seriously thinking of calling Interior into subcommittee oversight hearings on implementation of the Endangered Species Act. That may get their attention. "You can also let them know," we add, "that unless something happens soon we're planning to file a lawsuit against Interior to force them to list the darter. That would be a messy administrative law mandamus suit [a lawsuit forcing specific government actions] that would put them all on the witness stand."

"Are you sure about this?" asks Williams. "We've been having a lot of angry talk around here this week. Schreiner and Ron Lambertson, the senior Department of Interior attorney, have really been giving us biologists the third degree. The word they're using is 'nightmare.' They say *you* guys are the enemy, that you'll end up destroying the entire Endangered Species Act over this darter. And it's real clear that Tenn-Tom is at the heart of it. The Tenn-Tom boys are going nuts about your case. Have you thought hard about what's at stake here?"

We know the risks. We might indeed end up hurting the law, and other statutes and the whole environmental movement, too, but dammit, we're *right* about Tellico. We absolutely have to do it. And if the legal system works the way it's supposed to, we will end up *strengthening* environmental law—our case will be a great example of ecology's economic benefits.

The threat of a lawsuit to force the listing isn't likely to worry Interior very much, but the threat of subcommittee hearings will. Interior knows the Endangered Species Act is the biggest statute in Leggett's Fish and Wildlife subcommittee turf, and the unpredictable chair might well call for hearings where Interior would look negligent.

Over the next few weeks "Chuck Cook" stays in daily touch with Williams, monitoring the progress of the listing procedure. The threat of hearings and a lawsuit pass up through the Service hierarchy, cursed at but slowly prompting a response.

In May, sensing that Interior might be moving toward listing, TVA tells the agency that it would be "illegal" to list the "so-called snail darter" before it has been officially published in a peer-reviewed scientific journal and given an official Latin name. (TVA's attorneys have issued an agency-wide order that the fish "must always be referred to as 'the *so-called* snail darter.' ") After some quick research by student volunteers in our undergraduate environmental law course (twenty students have been the indispensable backbone of our research efforts, half of them undergraduates), "Chuck Cook" is able to confirm to Williams three cases in which a species was officially listed before appearing with a Latin name in a scientific journal.

Meanwhile, TVA accelerates its construction work in the valley, knocking down houses and building levees. On June 3, 1975, without telling the Fish and Wildlife Service, TVA captures approximately two hundred darters from the Little T shoals and transplants them into the Hiwassee River near Chattanooga. Their biologists tell us surreptitiously that they're being told to continue efforts to relocate Little T darters elsewhere. Obviously the TVA lawyers are thinking that if they can show darters surviving in the Hiwassee and elsewhere, the species isn't endangered. They're taking the position that, at least until the fish is listed, they have no duty even to discuss the matter with Interior, and can do whatever they want with darters from the Little T. We pass that news on to Jim Williams. This bit of news proves to be too much even for the hesitant Fish and Wildlife bureaucrats in Washington. Williams reports that Interior officials, including Keith Schreiner, are furious. Given TVA's insult to Interior's territory and the reported threat of hearings and a lawsuit, Williams says, the agency leadership may be shifting position in our favor.

On June 16, 1975, Schreiner carries the official snail darter listing package into the office of Undersecretary Nathaniel Reed. Nat Reed is a silk-stocking Republican from the fringes of the millionaire enclave on Jupiter Island, Florida. Tall and thin, with a protruding Adam's apple, he's building a record as a conservationist, moderately progressive, and he hopes in the not-too-distant future to be the governor of Florida. He looks at Schreiner with dismay. He knows about the Little T because Joe Congleton and other Trout Unlimited members have been lobbying him, and he loves fly-fishing. But this case could end up aligning him in the public mind with crazies, torpedoing his standing with the GOP business establishment.

"Mr. Reed," Schreiner tells him, "this file is now complete and scientifically solid. It's time for you to sign off on it."

"This is going to cause a lot of trouble," Reed worries.

"This is what they pay you to do."

With a sigh, Reed authorizes the listing order. A "Notice of Proposed Listing for the Snail Darter" appears the next morning in the *Federal Register*. TVA draws out the rule-making review with seventy-eight pages of critical comments submitted on the very last day of the comment period, requiring another six weeks of extensive technical responses by Interior. Meanwhile, TVA continues removing 450 more darters from the Little T. But four months later, on October 9, 1975, the daily *Federal Register* publishes the notice of final rule making.

The darter is finally an official Endangered Species.

The October 9 listing is anticlimactic, however. Six days earlier I receive a desperate call from Sara reporting that at four o'clock that morning Red Wagner's bulldozers came across the fields down to the river birches at Coytee Spring, just above the darter's main spawning shoals. They drove their heavy equipment overland rather than taking the road, where they'd be seen by the Kittrell family, who were still holding out in their farm. In discussions with Interior, TVA had promised it would hold off on tree clearing in the proposed reservoir area, one of the risks to the darter noted in our petition for listing, but Wagner apparently decided to press on regardless. And where did TVA decide to start the tree cutting and bulldozing? Alongside the snail darter's primary habitat, the historic site where the Cherokee had first covenanted a treaty with the English army. By sunrise, all the trees in the grove were down, the bulldozers plowing back and forth through the spring, turning it into a cascade of mud pouring out over the darter's breeding shoals.

I immediately call TVA and am told that the agency thinks the darter doesn't deserve to be listed as an endangered species. "And even if it's listed, the law doesn't apply to Tellico," their people tell me. I demand to know why not, and I'm told, "Because when the appropriations committees gave us money, that was *Congress* telling us to go ahead and build this dam. Plus, our lawyers tell us that, technically, *Federal Register* listings aren't effective for a further 20 days, so at this point it's not illegal to keep on with our reservoir-stripping schedule."

A friend inside TVA tells us off the record that he and some of his fellow staffers are embarrassed that Coytee Spring was targeted for bulldozing. "I'm sorry. Some of the boys in the front office got carried away. They thought stripping down Coytee Spring'd break your hearts, show you who's boss. But you've got to remember: our lawyers are backing Red Wagner's position that TVA can go right ahead with construction any way it wants to. There's no legal violation."

"Yes there is," I tell them. "Your dam violates the Endangered Species Act, and Interior has told you so."

"Not the way Red's lawyers read it. Until some court orders us to stop working on Tellico reservoir, that's what Red's going to do."

# CHAPTER 4

# Trial and Tribulation in TVA's Home Court

"Do you really think," Judge Taylor winces from the bench at one point during the April trial, "that Congress would want me to stop an important project for just any endangered creature, for some *red-eyed cricket?*" The courtroom regulars chuckle in unison at the judge's witticism. Uh-oh. This doesn't sound good for us and the snail darter, telegraphing as it does that the judge thinks our case isn't serious.

Long before we got to this moment at trial, we knew who our trial judge would be, and that he would be difficult. Judge Robert Love Taylor is the only federal judge in the Eastern District of Tennessee, the home of TVA. There would be no jury, just him, because we're seeking only an injunction against TVA, not money damages. In our lawsuit, the judge's capacity for handling complexity and his ability to be even-handed are both going to pose problems. We have few illusions about our chances in the trial court.

"Taylor's absolutely going to rule against you," Will Skelton and a number of other sympathetic local lawyers had told us. "He may not be the sharpest, but he's consistent. He's ruled against TVA only once in his lifetime, and it's not likely to happen ever again." A graduate of Yale Law School, Taylor was appointed by President Harry S. Truman in 1949 after twenty-five years working in a small firm. Taylor likes to brag he has the fastest docket in America; sometimes, at the end of a trial, when the judge asks the attorneys if they are finished and they say yes, he pulls out a pretyped opinion and reads them his verdict—nothing they've said has made any difference.

No other federal judge equals his efficiency in pushing cases from initial complaint filings to final dispositions. He buries more than six hundred cases a year, which is why the federal government has never placed a second judge in this court. Efficiency doesn't necessarily mean acuity, however. As the sole federal judge sitting in a district of almost two million people—not to mention that the district also includes the headquarters of a seven-state federal agency—Taylor exercises an unusual degree of peremptory power. But in the *Knoxville Journal*'s annual professional opinion poll of local attorneys and bar associations, which evaluates Taylor along with the ninety-eight state and local judges who sit in the district's twenty-five counties, he came in last, tied with a Knoxville juvenile court judge known for falling asleep during proceedings. A slight man who wears round eyeglasses, Taylor perches in court in a long, black robe behind his broad walnut desk, peppering attorneys with questions that sometimes reveal only a fragmentary sense of what is going on in the facts and law of the cases at hand.

Taylor hasn't been without courage. On several occasions in the 1960s he handed down very unpopular rulings on school desegregation. But when it comes to TVA, Taylor has been virtually unmovable. Alfred Davis reminds us again that "when we told the TVA appraiser we'd stand and fight in court, he told us, 'Go right ahead, but we have 100 lawyers and our own federal judge.'"

The only time Judge Taylor decided against TVA was in the environmental impact statement case on Tellico Dam three years earlier. The reason for this anomaly was his late clerk, Harvey Broome. Unlike most judicial clerks, who come to the judges' chambers right out of law school, Broome was sixty-four years old and at the end of a successful forty-year legal practice when in 1965 he asked to be Taylor's clerk. Given Broome's experience, Taylor could hardly say no. In addition to being a distinguished attorney, Broome was also a nationally renowned wilderness preservation figure, cofounding and serving for a time as president of the Wilderness Society. While Broome's legal skills elevated the level of Taylor's written opinions, he'd also opened Taylor, briefly, to doubts about TVA's environmental practices. Although Harvey died suddenly in 1968, as Anne Broome, his widow, explained it to us, Taylor wrote the environmental statement decision with his late clerk's ideals in mind.

Since the end of the impact statement case, however, Taylor has been a resolute defender of TVA's legal interests, dismissing every one of the Little T farmers' condemnation challenges. Nevertheless we're approaching Taylor's court theoretically hopeful that we might win, because ours is a simple statutory lawsuit saying that the precise words of the Endangered Species Act have been violated. On the simple scientific facts and the law we clearly should win. But we need to look beyond the trial, for we cannot really expect to persuade Taylor to rule against TVA.

And it is equally obvious that even if we win, TVA will surely take this case up on appeal, as we will likewise do if we lose. It matters a great deal how we do in this first round, however. The facts proven at trial carry along with the case as it goes up on appeal, providing the factual foundation for all future legal decisions. Appellate courts almost never question the facts once they have been established by the trial court, unless they are clearly erroneous, but they do scrutinize questions of law, rethinking trial courts' legal logic.

The week after the darter's official arrival on the endangered species list, Hank Hill and I, along with a few student volunteers working out of my office or somebody's living room, spend hours analyzing and preparing for the trial stage of our legal battle. We send a "60-day notice" letter to the Department of Interior and TVA. The letter says the Endangered Species Act is being violated; if the government doesn't enforce the law within sixty days, the law gives citizens the "standing" authority to go to court to enforce the law themselves, and we'll do just that.

To get an injunction against continuation of the Tellico project we'll have to establish the basic facts of our case, showing that TVA has violated the prohibitions of Section Seven of the Endangered Species Act twice over. As we explained to the farmers at the old fort, a careful reading of Section Seven reveals four simple elements of proof needed to show a "species jeopardy" violation:

1. That a species is on the federal endangered species list—the darter now is.
2. That the defendant is a federal agency—TVA is.
3. That the agency is authorizing, funding, or carrying out some action—building a dam— . . .
4. . . . *that will jeopardize the continued existence of the species*—and we can prove that Tellico Dam will do that.

If we can prove these four elements, we've proven a "jeopardy" violation of Section Seven. The second violation is the "critical habitat" count, where all we need to prove is that the project will "destroy or modify" the species' critical habitat.

On their face, the two Section Seven violations are slam dunks. "It's a simple matter of biology," says Dave Etnier. "As far as we know, 25,000 snail darters live there and only there in the lower reaches of the Little Tennessee River." And if the river gets impounded? "They'll die out. That's why they've died out everywhere else they lived before. This darter needs clean-flowing river conditions. The best science indicates they used to live in other places in the Tennessee River system, but everywhere else is dammed up now, so they're gone."

Normal legal principles should make it easy to confirm the necessary biological facts. Congress entrusted the Endangered Species Act to the Department of Interior. Thanks to our efforts Interior has officially declared exactly those facts. A year ago, moreover, Interior officially told TVA to stop violating the Endangered Species Act and was rebuffed. What more would a court need to prove violations of Section Seven?

There are, however, problems with this seemingly simple case. First, in Taylor's court TVA's lawyers will undoubtedly try to deny every part of this logic. They will say the law doesn't apply to them or to their dam. They'll say that the law, if read properly, does not forbid jeopardizing species or harming critical habitat. They'll say those words merely require agencies like TVA to *consider* endangered species issues. As to biology, they'll hire some expensive scientists to say that the darter isn't really a valid endangered species, and that the fish would surely live happily in a reservoir, or transplanted somewhere else. Will Taylor let the TVA lawyers challenge Interior's official biological findings and the terms of Section Seven? Probably. We'll have to be prepared to prove everything from the ground up.

Moreover, it will not be enough for us just to establish the facts of the violations of Section Seven. For political as well as legal reasons, we need to establish a lot more contextual facts on the trial record to educate the public about the consequences of damming the river. The court might provide us with a forum to force a public rethinking of the entire Tellico Dam project decision. Since the farmers and other citizens have never been given a real hearing in Congress, the courtroom could provide a forum almost as strong, placing critical information in public view and raising the profile of controversy so that the political branches— legislators, agencies, and the executive—have to pay attention.

Because injunctions like the one we're seeking are "equitable" remedies, descended from the old English church equity courts, however, they typically require the court to decide not only that a defendant's act is unlawful, but also, on balance, that it's reasonable, just, and fair to issue a stop-order remedy. To get an injunction in this case, therefore, we need to present factual evidence that stopping Tellico Dam *makes sense*. Even if we prove the dam violates the law, TVA will surely argue that the dam is more important to the public than a trivial fish.

Our case can in no way end successfully if we try to balance it on what seems to many people a mere technicality. From the beginning we've known we'll have to achieve political and public recognition that preserving the darter and its river makes better practical sense than the dam. Law exists within a dynamic context of politics and public opinion, and if a legal verdict is seen as foolish and vulnerable—if our Section Seven violation is dismissed as a mere quibble—then any legal injunction we win can and will be reversed with a simple congressional roll-call vote.

For legal as well as political reasons, therefore, we'll have to counter the supposed commonsense arguments for the dam that most people are associating with this case. Neither the dam nor TVA's land speculation scheme condemning three hundred farms makes any economic sense. But to win our injunction for the legal violation, we'll have to convince a court—maybe not Taylor's, but a later court on appeal—to balance it our way. We must be able to create a record revealing the unfamiliar realities: this is an ill-considered economic development plan based on condemning hundreds of private farms for resale; river-based development alternatives preserving the darter and the valley's family farms make far more sense than TVA's trumped-up lakeside model-city plan ever did; the public's economic interests, as well as social, cultural, historical, and ecological values, will be far better served by stopping the dam; and on balance the full circumstances of protecting the darter far outweigh the exaggerated benefits of TVA's project. We need to prove much more than "dam-kills-fish."

For a long time the citizens opposing the dam have been advocating river-based development alternatives. An industrial park could easily be developed in a nonsensitive area near the main highway and rail lines. Given the valley's rich soils, enhanced agricultural production is possible. Jeff Chapman of the University of Tennessee–Knoxville archaeology department says a tourist-oriented historical trail could be a bonanza, given the valley's location beside the Great Smoky Mountains National Park. Ohio has a highly successful history-archaeology tourism program generating millions of dollars a year, and that state has no history that compares with the Little Tennessee's.

We visualize a "Cherokee Trail" route carrying tourists from the two interstate highways up through a dozen historic sites and into the national park, potentially linked to a "Circle-the-Smokies" route to Cherokee, North Carolina, before rejoining the interstates. But getting experts to testify about these alternatives is a problem. Chapman cannot testify or openly help us develop the tourism option because of TVA's pressure on his department. Other than Dave Etnier, the darter's discoverer, Dean Donald Hanson of the University of Tennessee's Department of Architecture is the lone Tennessee professor willing to testify for us as an expert. Hanson says he will state at trial that the area has valuable economic resources, and will explain what various plans for alternative development without the dam might include. Showing reasonable development options will help tip the balance in favor of an injunction.

We absolutely need the injunction. "Government today is like a nearsighted old mule," says Hank. "Unless we whack it over the head with a two-by-four the system's never going to pay attention to what's important." An injunction is what we need to deliver that whack. If we do it right, however, the trial will also help us counter the latent insinuation of hypocrisy that has dogged our case since it began—that we are suing under a law we know Congress intended only to be symbolic, and that we don't really care about the snail darter or the Endangered Species Act—we're just cynically misusing them to stop a dam we don't like. The merits of our case can answer both accusations. Congress's limited consciousness in passing the law will be vindicated by the recognition that the law works in the public interest, serving the congressionally declared policy of ecological preservation while preventing waste, saving money, and enhancing public values. We can likewise cast the darter in the public's mind as a national canary in a coal mine. But the appreciation many of us have for the darter and the Endangered

Species Act also goes further. It is inextricably spiritual and philosophical: many of us think of the darter as a piece of God's creation that
needs defending, and a manifestation of our basic interdependence
with nature that, to the ultimate detriment of human society, gets too
easily ignored.

We've found a tremendous asset in local attorney Boone Dougherty,
a descendant of Daniel Boone whom we pulled in as trial counsel at the
complaint stage. "You need someone with local trial experience to be
with you in front of Judge Taylor," Joe Congleton told us. "Boone not
only has that; he's also the judge's neighbor. He lives just down his
street from him." Boone, one of the best litigators in Tennessee, agreed
to join us after a feisty briefing by our crew at the law school. Even better, he agreed to waive his fees until such time as we may recover some
expenses, which he must know may be never. Boone quickly started
spending hours preparing evidence on the biological facts that will
establish the basic violation.

Our preparations are likewise aided by a sharp new student volunteer willing to sacrifice his time and effort for neither money nor academic credit. Peter Alliman leaned through my office door one day and
asked whether, if wasn't too much bother, he could be briefed on the
case, because he'd like to work on it. A military veteran recently returned from Vietnam and hoping to start a new life, Peter is from Iowa,
which may explain his strong empathy for the farmers of the Little T
valley. We load him down with documents and research problems, and
he doesn't grumble.

We file the complaint on a February morning. We decide to put
Hank's name first, then Plater, then Don Cohen. Don has helped in the
research and has taken over the administrative side of the case, manag-
ing logistical expenses and the revenue from T-shirt sales. So the lawsuit will be called *Hill, et al. versus TVA*. The farmers backing us won't
be listed as plaintiffs, but we'll soon add the Tennessee Audubon
Council, and Etnier and his friends have formed the Association of
Southeastern Biologists, and they'll also join our side of the case.

Taylor immediately lives up to his reputation for speed. No sooner
has he seen our complaint than he has his secretary call to set up an
immediate pretrial conference with the lawyers for both sides. From
the beginning the conference goes badly, sharply cutting back on the
case we want to present and planting potential land mines. We're

ushered into the judge's office and awkwardly take seats around his desk. The judge is wearing his Yale Law tie, and, pandering, I'm wearing mine. The judge notices. "You went to Yale?" "Yes, Your Honor," I beam. "Well, I hear they don't teach much law there these days," says the judge brusquely, and he turns toward the TVA lawyers. To them he says, "I've decided you'll be allowed to challenge all the Department of Interior's findings in this matter. This court will require plaintiffs to prove each of the biological facts of the violation they're alleging." This is bizarre. It means the judge is refusing to give a court's normal deference to the expert federal agency to which Congress assigned the Endangered Species Act (Interior) and instead is deferring to TVA, the *accused perpetrator* of the alleged violations. TVA's chief counsel, Herb Sanger, looks over at us and grins.

"No problem," whispers Boone. "With Dr. Etnier we can prove the biology of this case three times over." But the judge's decision not to extend any deference to the conclusions of the Fish and Wildlife Service will hugely complicate our task at trial. His ruling is made even worse by the fact that last week we learned TVA had persuaded Interior not to send anyone to testify in support of the department's official findings. In response we'd immediately issued a subpoena to Jim Williams, who had prepared the entire darter listing for the government. TVA, however, persuaded Taylor to quash the subpoena on grounds that it required travel of more than 150 miles for Williams. This is a defense normally raised by subpoenaed witnesses on their own behalf, not by opposing parties trying to prevent a witness's appearance! We tell the judge that Williams has agreed to travel on his own from Washington to testify for us, using several of his personal vacation days.

"That shows you, judge," says Sanger. "This government scientist is biased against TVA."

But worse, the judge tells us, that's it, period. That's the whole case. He will not allow anything more than the bare biology facts at trial. "That's what you say is violated, that this fish is endangered because of the dam. So that's the only relevant evidence, that's all we're going to talk about in court." What about the economic arguments? The breadth of the dam's harm, and the strength of the alternatives? We need to have all that put into the trial record so that it can be used in arguing for the injunction, and for the inevitable appeal. If the judge doesn't let us submit such evidence, however, the trial record's going to be reduced to bare bones. Trying to repair such factual deficits on appeal is really difficult.

"Your Honor," I say, "we need to be able to put in economic evidence. The Timberlake model city collapsed last spring, and that undercuts the project economics. If we end up proving a violation of the Act, the court will need to design a remedy, and that means there'll have to be a balance of equities between building the dam and river alternatives that protect the fish." (Although I don't say it, we're having quite a bit of trouble finding any expert in Tennessee who will testify on the dam project's economic deficiencies and alternatives, but we'll try hard to have someone by the day of trial.)

"No," says Taylor. "Courts don't have any business examining the internal economics of agency projects. I won't allow it, and the case law backs me up. That's up to Congress." Taylor doesn't realize that if the dam violates the law, he'll need to look at its economics and alternatives in order to balance whether or not to issue an injunction.

"Your Honor, part of the remedy issue here requires consideration of project alternatives. The court needs to be able to consider what alternate public benefits might be available if the dam is stopped."

"No," says Taylor. "I already went through all that alternatives material in the other case." He means the environmental impact statement case in 1972. Dean Hanson won't be allowed to testify on alternative river development designs.

"But Your Honor, in order to balance the equities—"

"You heard me," the judge cuts me off. "No more discussion of alternatives in my court. That's for TVA and Congress."

"Never mind," says Boone afterward. "I think we can still win this trial. I'll focus on proving the biology facts. You figure out legal arguments for the injunction." Over the next weeks Boone trudges through a series of depositions—pretrial interrogations of witnesses—but he's limited to the basic biological facts of the violation we're alleging.

Theoretically we could easily show that TVA "has been acting in bad faith" in actions like the agency's bulldozing of Coytee Spring, but we ultimately decide against that tactic. "Forget about trying to prove that," my mentor Joe Sax advises. "When you're up against a pillar of the establishment like TVA, courts won't go there. It would inevitably become the kind of peeing contest where you lose even if you win. Plus legally you don't need to prove bad faith when you're requiring federal agencies to comply with existing law."

The trial, starting on a Thursday morning in late April, rolls along for two days pretty much as the judge has dictated. The entire trial is focused on fish biology and whether the darter is truly endangered by the dam—which Interior has already officially established. Virtually no discussion is allowed about the project's economic deficiencies, or about the beneficial alternatives that could be developed in the river valley if, for the sake of the fish, the dam isn't built.[1]

In the courtroom Etnier and his graduate student Wayne Starnes, the two biologists who together have spent more time than anyone else on earth studying this fish, are crisply led by Boone through a presentation of the essential biological facts. By now the snail darter has an official Latin name, *Percina Imostoma tanasi* (Etnier had added "tanasi"—"Tennessee"—to compensate me for not naming it the

Courtroom artist sketch of Judge Robert Love Taylor, U.S. District Court for the Eastern District of Tennessee, Northern Division, during trial of *Hill et al. v. TVA*, April 23, 1976. (Watercolor sketch by Anna Sandhu Ray, in the collection of the U.S. District Court, Eastern District of Tennessee, Northern Division, through the kindness of Court Archivist Don Ferguson)

"Tennessee darter"), and Etnier testifies that it clearly deserves recognition as a distinct species. He talks in passionate detail about the "meristic" physical distinctions between fifteen different species of darter: all less than three inches long, some species with thirty-five vertebrae, some with thirty-six or thirty-seven, some with subocular bars (dark marks below the eye) and some without, different fin shapes and ray counts; different numbers of scale rows; and different arrangements of color and saddle-patched marking. As he testifies, Etnier indicates features of the snail darter on a beautiful watercolor print of two darters swimming amid the stones of the Little T shoals. Even though it isn't a photograph, Boone has persuaded Taylor to allow the print into evidence as Trial Exhibit #12. (We've been selling lithographs of the painting, by Dolores Roberson, for $16.)

It's clear from Etnier's testimony that he loves the details of his work and has encyclopedic knowledge of perch darters in southern waters. As to the darter's survival requirements, he and Starnes are clear and confident: darters, especially when reproducing, need cool, clear, highly oxygenated water flowing over clean gravel and sand, as well as a diet of snails, nymphs, and limpets. Damming the river into a reservoir would eliminate the fish. In summer, Etnier notes, a shallow reservoir's water gets very warm. Algae, suspended silt, and muck settle to the river bottom, blanketing spawning areas and smothering any eggs that might be laid. The water on the floor of a reservoir can become virtually devoid of oxygen.

We've urged Etnier and Starnes to use graphics in their testimony. Like most people, judges can be swayed by visual stimuli. Etnier illustrates his anatomy lessons with photos, drawings, and several specimen darters in lab vials. Starnes goes one better. Two weeks prior to the trial, snorkeling in the river with a waterproof video camera, he had the good luck to see a snail darter couple courting and spawning amid the gravels in a swift-flowing part of the Coytee Spring shoals.

Starnes throws the two-minute underwater video sequence onto a courtroom screen. The lights dim, and shaky images appear:

"This is the male, layin' here, with the female immediately in front of him . . .

"This is a bit of preliminary courtship . . .

"He is lying immediately behind her now, but she's a lot more worried about me being there than he is; he is much more intent on what he's doing." (Chuckles echo through the courtroom, as a hundred pairs of eyes peer intently into the watery boudoir.)

"Now he's doing a tail-wagging movement to get her attention off me . . .

"Now he is dropping down on her, coming over her left hindquarter here . . ." (A hush falls on the crowd.)

"Now onto her right quarter, . . . you see him place his left pectoral fin, in a cross-over maneuver, and he is stroking the tail of her body with his pectoral, . . . but, oops, she moves away . . .

"Coming up now is very heavy courtship again, and possible spawning, I think . . . They're moving in unison . . . Oh no, she moved away again . . .

"Now they go through the same maneuver again, he's stroking her with his left pectoral, then crossing over to her other side . . .

"Now there, see! . . . A violent quivering of her body. And he's waving his anal fin very violently, . . . now he's moving the sand around for egg deposit! . . .

"Okay, that's the end of it. You can turn on the lights."

The courtroom observers let out the collective breath they've been holding. Starnes explains that this is not just an aquatic sex tape, and it's not just a gambit to build empathy for the cute fish couple frolicking around in the pebbles of the river bottom. The video vividly highlights the special breeding conditions needed by this species. While filming, hunched over in the current, he'd had to struggle to hold his camera steady over the little couple in two and a half feet of fast-moving crystalline water. The video clearly shows the clean bottom pebbles and sand that would catch hold of the microscopic eggs as they squeezed out of the female and were squirted with milt from the male. If the river current stopped, he said, or if muddy water and silt settled onto this shoal, the darters' eggs sticking to substrate gravels there would lose their flow of oxygen and suffocate.

"In my opinion," concludes Starnes, "this is the only significant breeding population of this darter that we know of. If the reservoir is completed it will be completely exterminated."

TVA's lawyers' strategy on cross-examination is to score points however they can. They elicit the admission that TVA has graciously funded Starnes's studies of the darter. Under questioning, Etnier and Starnes both readily admit they personally oppose completion of the

Lithograph print of a watercolor painting by Dolores Roberson depicting a male and female snail darter *(Percina imostoma tanasi)*. It was admitted as evidence in court as Trial Exhibit #12. The print illustrates the cool, clear, shallow flowing water habitat necessary for the darter—habitat that had been eliminated elsewhere in the Tennessee river system by dams. Exhibit #12 ultimately played a cameo role later, in the Supreme Court arguments. (Collection of the author)

dam, but that hardly discredits their testimony given their obvious professional linkage to this little fish and its survival. TVA's Charlie Wagner (no relation to Red) tries to trap Etnier into misidentifying darters of several species in an assortment of jars, perhaps to undercut his expertise or to make the layman's point that these different species, and there are a lot of them, look very much alike and may not deserve special protection. But Etnier identifies each of Wagner's darters correctly.

Wagner asks Starnes about two snail darters, a male and a female, that TVA divers had collected downstream of the Tellico site. Starnes has studied those specimens. Scientifically it's not unusual to find individual fish outside their home territory. We know, moreover, that the darter's larval young drift downstream to deeper water, returning to the clear upstream shallows when it's time to spawn—sort of a miniature salmon run. Given TVA's blockage of the Little T's river channel, it's difficult for maturing darters to return to the abundant snails and spawning shoals of the Little T, and some are forced to stay in the murky downstream waters. Does finding a pair of darters below the dam structure prove the likelihood of a breeding population of darters in reservoirs?

"Not at all," says Starnes. "It's just two fish, and they were in poor condition, emaciated."

"Ah," says Wagner, "but it was spawning season. Isn't it a fact that darters appear emaciated after spawning, so these were actually reproducing?"

"I'd like to point out," says Starnes, "that the female was very gravid."

"What's gravid?" asks Wagner.

"Full of eggs. But still very skinny, and the male was gaunt."

"Gaunt? What does that mean?" asks Wagner.

"Emaciated," Starnes says.

"Oh," says Wagner. "No further questions."

The last witness for the snail darter is Interior scientist Jim Williams. His testimony starts on a sour note, for he has come to the courtroom in a plaid shirt, jacketless, planning to do some fieldwork later in the afternoon.

"I have a rule that professional men don't come into court without coats," barks Taylor.

"I think he came from Washington without a coat, Your Honor," says Boone.

"Well, that's typical of Washington," says the judge. "But I'll waive the rule for him. You may continue."

Williams first has to say he's not authorized to present any official policy positions of the Department of Interior. He's a fieldwork scientist, not a political representative. Whether or not TVA should be forced to comply with Section Seven is not something a sister federal agency wants to declare in court. Williams is here under the compromise terms of a letter from his boss, Nat Reed, using his own vacation time and testifying only about the biological facts and communications with TVA that he processed in Washington as part of the darter's official listing.

As it turns out, the most significant element of Williams's time on the witness stand is not anything he says about the agency's official process, or about TVA's efforts to transplant the darter—which he concludes have extremely uncertain prospects for success—but rather his testimony about a comment made by Tom Ripley, director of TVA's biological resources division. "In March, a year ago [the early days of the darter's listing process], Mr. Ripley indicated to me that there was little question in his mind, or in anybody's mind, that the impoundment would in fact eliminate the darter in the Tellico Dam area."

The judge (ignoring the fact that this is excludable hearsay evidence) turns to TVA attorney Tom Pedersen. "Do you concede that the reservoir will change or modify the habitat and destroy the darter itself? Do you contest that?"

The lawyer stammers that, well, "certainly it will alter or modify the presently known habitat. . . . But we think . . . the darter lives and has habitat elsewhere . . ."

To which the judge replies, "If you concede that the reservoir will change or modify the habitat and will destroy the darter, then why take up the time of the court on that issue? Why don't we go to the issues about which you are concerned, instead of taking up my time?"

Good. By the end of testimony from Etnier, Starnes, and Williams, we think the legal elements of our case have been established. It's clear that modern science knows of only one breeding population of snail darters, twenty-five thousand of them right there in the Little T where federal law has listed them, with at most only a small number of other scattered individual fish and transplants possibly surviving somewhere else in eastern Tennessee. If the dam is completed the officially listed sole known breeding population of the fish will in all likelihood be exterminated, completely gone in three years' time, the darter's maximum life span.

At the beginning of the trial's second day, to counter our biological barrage the TVA's Pedersen and Charlie Wagner present two TVA divers who describe capturing the two emaciated darters in the Watts Bar reservoir downstream of the Little T dam structure. In four weeks of diving searches, they saw a total of eight others. Compared with the living, breeding population of twenty-five thousand snail darters in the Little T, this testimony about less than a dozen darters doesn't seem very probative in biological terms, and does nothing to contradict TVA's Section Seven liability for jeopardy and destruction of the darter's officially listed Little Tennessee habitat. The TVA attorneys, however, drag it out for more than four hours.

"But wait 'til you see Ed Raney," says Etnier at the lunch break. TVA lawyers have hired eminent ichthyologist Edward Raney as their star witness in favor of the dam. For years Raney was a prominent fish biology professor at Cornell University, and then he left academia to start his own consulting company. Today he often testifies for deep-pocket clients, telling courts what his clients want judges to hear. "Among us fish biologists, we figure Raney is the only one of us who's ever become a millionaire doing fish biology," Etnier tells us. "Be prepared for him telling Judge Taylor this isn't really an endangered species, that TVA has done everything just right, and that snail darters will just love living in a reservoir."

But how, I ask, can any competent ichthyologist testify that altering the habitat of this highly adapted fish from clean-flowing river to murky sluggish reservoir conditions won't imperil its survival? "In our field," Etnier says with a wry smile, "we call these guys *biostitutes.*"

Raney is everything he was advertised to be. A big man with a shock of silver hair, sitting poised in a beautifully cut dark blue suit, he is the most imposing person in the courtroom. TVA's Pedersen deferentially leads him through his testimony, treating him like a visiting potentate stooping to bring his expertise into this scientific backwater, and Raney pontificates: Yes, he is one of the nation's most widely published ichthyologists, teaching at Cornell's zoology department for almost forty years with more than a hundred publications and an international reputation. Yes, he has examined the "so-called snail darter" and its habitat. Is the darter a separate species? Maybe not, in his opinion, Raney says. It has only minor distinctions from other darters, so maybe it's only a subspecies. Scientists disagree on how sharply to draw the lines; it's arbitrary. (This too has been a theme of TVA's lawyers, though it's beside the point, because the law protects subspecies as well as species.) Yes, he has studied TVA's program of transplanting the darter, and he is pleased to offer his professional conclusion that TVA's darter transplants into various streams around the state have been successful. (This is scientifically and legally problematic. It takes at least five years of consistent breeding to conclude probability of success, and TVA's oldest darter transplant attempt was only two and a half years ago, with only limited evidence of possible reproduction. Moreover, transplantation has little or no bearing on the legal questions at issue.) Yes, indeed, Raney says. In his opinion the darter can live perfectly well in reservoirs. (I look over at Etnier and know what he's thinking: *biostitute*.)

"So what I want to know is, would these fish survive in a Tellico reservoir?" says the judge, taking Raney's bait. The real question, of course, isn't whether particular individuals of the species could live out their lifetimes in a reservoir but whether the species itself could reproduce, maintaining its breeding cycle in subsequent generations if it didn't have a flowing river with spawning shoals and larval drift.

"Oh, yes," Raney says with a flourish as he launches into an even longer monologue.

"Wait a minute, Doctor," interjects the judge. "When you answer these questions, answer yes or no!"

When it's our turn, Boone Dougherty steps toward Raney to begin his questioning. "Is it not a fact," he asks, "that the 'stargazing darter,' the closest relative to the snail darter, does not live in reservoirs?"

"I don't know if that is true," says Raney. He launches into a long explanation of his opinion that the snail darter would live and reproduce in a reservoir, avoiding the point that its closest relative doesn't. He does not mention the critical physical differences between reservoirs and clean-flowing rivers, and keeps repeating his insistence that Etnier's conclusions about the snail darter are wrong.

"Dr. Raney, I am asking you—" says Boone, trying to get a direct answer.

"—in the case at hand where *supposedly*—" Raney sneers.

"Dr. Raney, I am asking you—"

"—this so-called snail darter only lives in the Little Tennessee—"

"Your Honor, I am asking that he be responsive," says Boone.

"—and we know—" Raney continues.

"I can't do anything with him," the judge snorts. The audience in the courtroom breaks out in laughter.

"Dr. Raney," Boone tries again. "You are answering a different ques—"

"And you are interrupting very rudely," interrupts Raney. Laughter again, at which point Raney pauses, looks around, and realizes that he is the object of the laughter.

Then Boone nails him: "Dr. Raney, have you yourself studied the critical habitat of the snail darter in the Little T River?"

"Yes, I have."

"When?"

"On two occasions."

"All right. Now, in reality your so-called predictions were determined primarily by flying over in a helicopter?"

"They were determined by being over the area in a helicopter and making very careful observations."

"And would you not agree that it is a little difficult, looking down from a helicopter, to determine, for example, the depth, the nature of the bottom, what food organisms are on the bottom, the flow and velocity of the current that would be important as to snail darter habitat?"

"Yes, that's a very wise observation on your part, sir," Raney says sarcastically.

"So that the judge can understand your observations of this area, on one occasion you took an over-flight with a helicopter, and the only other occasion that you have actually physically observed the Little Tennessee River is when one of the TVA biologists took you in an automobile on the roads up the river from where the dam is being built, and on some of those roads you can't even see the river?"

"Yes," Raney admits reluctantly.

"And the only other time that you've actually physically been on the ground was where the helicopter sits down at Coytee Spring, and you went and looked at a couple of these samples in plastic containers, stayed a little time, and then left?"

"Uh. Yes."

"Now isn't it a fact, Dr. Raney, that you have no scientific evidence that the snail darter is in any way able to reproduce in the nearby reservoirs, . . . essential in determining critical habitat?"

Raney pauses, and looks pleadingly at the TVA attorneys, who don't know what signal to give him. Raney glowers at Boone.

"I would say, yes," he finally mumbles.

Raney leaves the witness box and stomps out of the courtroom. The trial on the facts of our case against the dam is essentially over.

The courtroom laughter at Raney's expense, which always helps undercut a witness, is heartening. Given the evidence now on the record we dare to hope that Taylor, despite his personal inclinations, may be convinced that TVA has violated the law. But that means we need to present a legal argument that the violation deserves to be remedied by the issuance of a stop-order. "Your Honor," I plead, "an injunction makes solid common sense in this case. The Tellico Dam project has always been economically marginal. There are a number of very good project alternatives available for Your Honor to balance."

Peter, Hank, and I have done a memorandum of law for the judge with a dozen major cases saying that judges should balance the equities in the broad public interest when deciding on injunctions. An injunction could be an economic boon, not a disaster. This of course addresses points on which the judge has refused to hear evidence. But there's a fallback, an argument that legal principles require an injunction even if the judge doesn't balance the issues. "Your Honor, we won't repeat the precedents we cited in our trial brief. Instead at this point we base our final legal argument *only on the major case that TVA is using against us.*"

The brief filed by TVA's lawyers had focused on a 1944 Supreme Court case, *Hecht Company v. Bowles.* They argued that it authorized a judge to make the injunction decision in any way he thinks is reasonable. They used a sentence in *Hecht* saying "federal district judges . . . mold each decree to the necessities of the particular case . . . *in their sound discretion.*"[2] But we turn TVA's cited precedent against them. "If you read *Hecht* carefully, Your Honor," I say, "you'll see that in that case the defendant proved that *the statutory violations had completely stopped, and would never recur.* That's why the Supreme Court said an injunction wasn't needed in the *Hecht* case. But where statutes are involved, Your Honor, judges aren't free to decide whether or not they think Congress's law makes sense. Courts are supposed to require that statutes be complied with. If there won't be any future violations of the law, then no injunction is required. But if a defendant won't agree to comply with the statute, as TVA says it won't, that's when an injunction must be issued. That's what *Hecht* decided."

The judge looks at me blankly. "What about balancing of equities? Do you really think the members of Congress who passed this law would want us to stop an important project if it got in the way of just any endangered creature, . . . *some red-eyed cricket!?* [Laughter.] I'd like to know how much my injunction in that case five years ago cost American taxpayers!"

At this point a voice shouts from the back of the courtroom, "Fifteen million dollars, Your Honor." It's former TVA attorney Beauchamp Brogan, who now has become chief counsel for my employer, the University of Tennessee. It's evident he's still a TVA lawyer at heart, and it's clear he hasn't come to court to cheer on a junior professor from his university. No one seems bothered by his yelling from the audience seats.[3]

"This is a statutory case, Your Honor," I repeat. "Congress itself has already balanced the equities." Do I really think members of Congress weighed the prospect of particular conflicts like this? No, but we're arguing generic legal philosophy here. "Congress passed the law," I continue, "and it declared that federal projects must not destroy species." This is literally true. "If the court enforces the law with an injunction, this project will go back to Congress so they can decide what to do. That's the proper way to resolve this issue." Implicitly we're saying, "You don't need to handle this hot potato, Your Honor. As a matter of separation of powers and judicial stress avoidance, send it back to those who caused the conflict and let them handle it."

The trial ends with me making a rather self-righteous plea to higher principles of democratic justice: "In this case, Your Honor, a large federal agency has been sued by a bunch of volunteer citizens completely lacking in money and political power. We ask you to decide this case in a way that allows me to go back to my law students and say, 'Here in America, no matter what your station in life, if you prove your case on the facts and the law, even a small group of citizens can enforce a statute against violations by the most powerful agencies in the nation.' Don't make me tell my students that this is just another chapter of 'might makes right.'"

Flash cameras pop as we all troop out of the court. It's a big local story on the TV evening news, featuring a courtroom artist's watercolor rendering of Etnier looking closely at several darters in test tubes, and of Boone Dougherty embarrassing Raney. But the press coverage is, as always, disappointingly limited. The two local papers' headlines are "Darter Has Its Day in Court," and "Environmentalists Present Case in Federal Court." Nothing about the biological destruction, much less anything questioning the merits of the dam. Sara tried to get reporters to interview the farmers attending the trial, hoping the story would cover the human and economic background of the case. Nothing was mentioned about the homes and fields condemned for development by Boeing. Nothing about our development alternatives. For whatever reason—a narrow journalistic mindset, or Taylor's truncation of the trial evidence—the press coverage of the trial is all local, and all darter.

As it turns out, we have to wait a week for the judge's decision. At least he didn't pull it out of his briefcase and read it at the close of trial. While we're waiting, my dean calls me into his office. "I've received a complaint against you from the McMinn County Bar Association," he tells me. "They say you've been making speeches and soliciting money for your legal work, so they're accusing you of barratry. I've drafted a letter of apology promising you won't do so in the future. Would you please look it over and sign it?"

I stare at him. "Dean," I reply, "I suggest you write back that the professor confirms he's made many such speeches, and sold T-shirts and snail darter prints to support litigation. And tell them he has every intention of continuing to do so. He's doing what every attorney is supposed to do, making personal efforts pro bono to ensure that the laws of this nation are enforced in the public interest."

The dean blinks, taken aback. After a pause he says, "Okay, I guess that'll be alright," and drops the matter. I go back to waiting for Taylor's decision. A few mornings later, before nine o'clock, the judge's administrative clerk calls me at home. "I thought you should know. The judge has just issued his decision."

"And . . . ?"

"Dismissed. I'm sending a copy over to your office right now."

I rush to the law school and read through the opinion quickly. It's long but unenlightening. Only the conclusion is clear: "For the foregoing reasons, we conclude that plaintiffs' prayer for a permanent injunction must be denied and the action dismissed." But what are the "foregoing reasons"? Poring over the pages of the opinion, we find lots of commentary but no legal issue identified as the reason for his decision.

"We go no further," Taylor writes, "than to hold that the Act does not operate in such a manner as to halt the completion of this particular project." Does that mean he thinks the law doesn't apply to this dam, or that it does apply, but it isn't violated? Or that it applies and is violated, but he won't issue an injunction? He says, "TVA has . . . informed Congress, through its committees, about the snail darter and its position on the application of the Endangered Species Act to the project." But he doesn't say that merely telling the appropriations committee about a possible fish violation creates a statutory exemption. No judge would ever say that. And he specifically writes, "In the opinion of the Court, the Endangered Species Act *does* apply to the Tellico project."

So why isn't TVA enjoined? The judge writes that "TVA has not acted arbitrarily, capriciously . . . in continuing further implementation of the Tellico project." But as my old professor Alex Bickel used to say, "That not only misses the point, it misses the *wrong* point."

"TVA has acted responsibly, and in good faith," the judge writes. It's no surprise that the judge says this, because we chose not to present evidence of TVA's bad faith, but it's also not a legal reason to ignore the law.

Courts generally defer to regulatory agencies when reviewing their law-applying judgments, unless arbitrariness is proved. In this case, however, the judge—as we feared—is again not deferring to the official regulatory agency, Interior, but to the accused statutory violator, TVA. The opinion hints that the judge may be denying the injunction because the dam project has been under way for eight years: "At some point in time a federal project becomes so near completion and so incapable of modification that a court of equity should not apply a statute enacted long after inception of the project to produce an unreasonable result." But he doesn't say that this was so for Tellico Dam, and cannot, since he'd blocked all trial evidence about possible modifications.

The most one can say is that Taylor implies in unspecific terms that an injunction doesn't make sense to him. "Is it reasonable . . . to halt the Tellico project at its present stage of completion? We think not." The judge also presents a most unusual "finding of fact": "During the trial arguments the Court was advised . . . that the prior injunction issued by this Court cost the TVA approximately fifteen million dollars, an amount which was shocking to the Court." Where did that sum come from? It's not derived from any submitted evidence, but instead from that comment shouted out by a member of the public sitting in the courtroom! The judge also writes that "counsel for plaintiffs argues *fervently* (that'd be me) that the . . . discretion of the Court is limited to fashioning a remedy to insure compliance with the Act, not to excuse a violation thereof, *Hecht Co. v. Bowles,* . . . because Congress has expressly declared the public interest in the Endangered Species Act. . . . We cannot agree." Why not? He doesn't say.

There is, however, a silver lining to Taylor's opinion. To put our expectations in perspective and reduce them to a bare minimum, what did we really need from Taylor? Not legal holdings on the meaning of Section Seven, nor trenchant case citations on injunctions. No, all we ever needed from him were accurate conclusions on the very barest of facts. And here they are, gloriously stuck into the opinion's text along with all that stuff about not issuing an injunction: "I conclude that it is highly probable that closure of the Tellico Dam and the consequent impoundment of the river behind it *will jeopardize the continued existence of the snail darter.* Almost all of the known population of snail darters will be significantly reduced if not completely extirpated, either due to the impoundment itself or the snail darter's potential loss of reproductive ability if it is unable to adapt to a new environment."

He also writes: "Although the snail darter may continue to exist for several years after the proposed impoundment, it is highly doubtful that it would reproduce in a reservoir environment. We conclude, therefore, that the preponderance of the evidence demonstrates that closure of the Tellico Dam and the consequent creation of the Tellico Reservoir *will result in the adverse modification, if not complete destruction, of the snail darter's critical habitat.*"[4]

There it is. So what does it matter that Taylor goes on to say he won't issue an injunction? He's given us exactly the critical facts necessary to prove violation of the Endangered Species Act. If you have to lose the decision at trial, it's best to lose it on the judge's legal interpretation of law, but win the facts. The appeals court can now take the facts from the trial record and make its own legal decision. With these facts from Taylor we can tell the appeals court that it must correct the dam's violation of law with an injunction.

A local reporter calls and asks, "You told the judge you wanted to be able to tell your students that the law works for justice in the face of power. What will you tell them now that you're dismissed?"

"I'll tell them a trial verdict doesn't mean the end of the case," I say. "They'll see how a mistaken trial judge gets overturned on appeal." Am I as confident as I sound? Not really. TVA has just announced that because our lawsuit has been dismissed, they're immediately recommencing construction throughout the project area "so as to be able to complete the Tellico project as quickly as possible, as Congress has instructed us to do."

Boone Dougherty calls. He's deeply depressed. He'd obviously convinced himself over the course of the trial that if he could pin down the biological facts of the violation—which he had—the judge would listen to us and decide our way.

"Look, Boone," I tell him, "we always knew it would be like this. Think of it this way: The judge bought all *your* factual arguments. It was just *my* arguments on the law that he rejected. But we're out of Taylor's clutches now. We have all the facts we need on the record. Our case won't be in TVA's backyard anymore. Next stop is Cincinnati, as fast as we can!"

Cincinnati, Ohio, home of the U.S. Court of Appeals for the Sixth Circuit, which TVA does not own.

# CHAPTER 5

# An Appeal for Justice as
# Bulldozers Roll

JUNE 1976–JANUARY 31, 1977

"There was a meeting yesterday. Lawyers and construction engineers," reports a former student now working for TVA. "They were making plans. They said by the time you stand up to argue the appeal in Cincinnati, there won't be a single tree left standing in the reservoir area."

It's called the "sunk cost" strategy. Worried about citizen opposition, project promoters try to get as much construction done and spend as much money as possible before opponents can bring effective questions to bear. It's a basic rule of any enterprise, public or private: "a rolling stone gathers momentum." The object is to push a project until it exists as a concrete reality. Citizens get demoralized, and project promoters can say, "It's too late to turn back now." "Regrettably," the disingenuous argument goes, "by now too much has been done, too much money spent, too little of value remains, to permit consideration of any alternatives at this late date."

The sunk cost strategy recurs often in public interest law. In Memphis, 320 miles west of the Little T, the Overton Park case provided a vivid example. Fully aware of a park-protection statute, highway agencies knocked down houses and built an interstate up to the very edge of the park, then argued that it was sadly no longer feasible and prudent to go anywhere else but straight through the park. The citizens had to win a dramatic victory in the Supreme Court to stop the park's dissection. Would we need to do the same?

In the United States you have the right to appeal, but the odds are that once you've lost, you'll lose again. Like most institutions, the judicial system tends to stick with a decision once it's made. Nationwide only about 15 percent of those who lose at trial end up appealing, and of that group only about 12 percent succeed in overturning the trial court decisions. That means that less than 2 percent of all trial losers, like us, can expect to reverse their trial verdicts on appeal. The odds have never favored the darter crusade, however, so statistics are not going to scare us off now; we appeal anyway.

We immediately ask Judge Taylor for a stay, a temporary delay on reservoir construction, while we go to the federal appeals court. He immediately denies it. We file an emergency motion to the U.S. Court of Appeals for the Sixth Circuit in Cincinnati. The trial judge, we say, has established all the facts of a statutory violation, and the law will be frustrated if TVA is allowed to destroy the darter's habitat, so we request that the project be halted until the court can hear our appeal.

The appeal petition looks good, but for two long months we hear nothing from the court of appeals. In cases like this one, time is the enemy. Appeals can take months, sometimes years. TVA, however, had immediately accelerated its bulldozing, farm destruction, and road-building—actions that we argue are blatantly illegal. Under the glare of portable floodlights, TVA's construction gangs are now working by night as well as day. The agency is practicing a "when you've knocked 'em down, kill 'em" sunk cost strategy. In the same way that they'd begun bulldozing at Coytee Spring, TVA is eliminating the natural values of the flowing river to get rid of the darter, foreclose future alternative options, and break our morale. How will we talk about the river's potential for recreation and tourism once the valley is left a desolate moonscape dotted with crushed and smoldering houses, barns, brush, and trees?

Two months is a long time. One by one, groves of willows, birch, and sycamore are falling. Crews are building earthen levees and excavating the canal that will allow impounded water and boats to go into the nearby Loudoun reservoir. Appeals court judges haven't yet even told us when we can argue the appeal. After that, what will happen while we are waiting to argue the case, and then waiting some more, after the argument, for them to formulate their decision? What if, by then, there's nothing left to save?

As we wait, I get another, separate jolt. The University of Tennessee College of Law's senior faculty has voted to deny me tenure, meaning I am no longer welcome to teach at the university. It isn't my teaching or publishing, which rank high, says the dean. But tenure requires a two-thirds vote from the sixteen tenured professors, many of whom have taught here for decades. Recently the school has been hiring young progressives from up North, and there's a culture clash. Each year the senior bloc ejects one or two liberals from those up for tenure. Six professors vote against me. Peter Alliman and other students come by to commiserate, but students have no say.

"You have to understand," says one of the "old boys," a teacher of criminal law who voted against me. "You really don't fit in here. *You've never understood the moderation required of a Tennessee law professor.*"

True. Beyond my classes and writing, I am involved in more than a dozen public interest conflicts, from strip-mining and park management policies to resort development scams and recycling. Environmental issues entangle a teacher in controversy, and the school gets blamed for his activism. The dean offers that, given the late date of my dismissal, I can stay for a final year. No way. It would be purgatory to go through a year of classes stigmatized by dismissal. After several weeks of me grappling with self-doubt—among them, these old boys have two hundred years of teaching experience, so maybe they know best that I'm not cut out for teaching—a combination of luck and Joe Sax's support lands me a job in Michigan at Wayne State Law School. I'll move to Ann Arbor in late August and come back to Tennessee whenever necessary. It's only a six-hour drive.

Through June, TVA crews scrape through the valley and cut the canal closer and closer to the point where the upstream reservoir could pour in and flood the Little T. "You don't want to go down there," Peter reports. "It'll just make you cry." After the bulldozing of houses, barns, and riverbank groves, the river is full of mud.

There's more bad news. In July, Etnier and his grad student Wayne Starnes make an awful discovery: TVA's levee work closing off the north channel and diverting river flows through the dam structure's undergates have now completely choked off the darter's natural life cycle. Baby larval darters drift downstream to deep pools below the Little T, like salmon fingerlings to the sea. Later, when they have reached full size—two and a half inches—the yearling darters have migrated back upstream to their home grounds to live with their parents and eventually to spawn, beginning the cycle again. The returning young, however, now can't swim over the underwater obstacle created by the dam's subsurface foundation. Etnier quickly calls Jim Williams, and Interior orders TVA to start netting the young fish trapped below the dam and carry them back up to the flowing river. TVA demurs: "We'll put them into other rivers. This river is going to die." Ultimately some netted yearlings are trucked back to their native shoals in the Little T, some aren't. We watch, helpless.

Then, in late July, after eight excruciating weeks of watching the valley's destruction, we learn that a panel of judges has granted our request: the case will be argued in October; in the meantime all work on the Tellico project must stop until the appeal is decided. We are euphoric and start preparing the appeal brief. Two days later, however, TVA's lawyers give notice they're asking the court for an "emergency modification to the stay." There will be a hearing tomorrow before Circuit Judge Paul Weick in his hometown office in Akron, Ohio. We have to oppose this move, but how will we get there? "Don't worry," says TVA attorney Charlie Wagner. "We need you to be there. We'll give you a ride in a TVA plane."

During a long, unpleasant flight at taxpayers' expense, Wagner keeps needling us: "You have to admit your case isn't much. Look at the river valley. It's finished. Why don't you just drop this?" Herb Sanger, TVA's top lawyer, wearing a natty yellow sport coat and beige and white patent leather slip-ons, sits silently while his junior associate chides us. Later, in the judge's downtown office, Sanger does the talking. Judge Weick is almost eighty years old, and is visibly shaky. He knows nothing of the case; he just happens to be the judge on motion duty this week.

Sanger looks at Weick mournfully. "Judge," he pleads, "there are 2000 workers, blue-collar men with families, who'll be put out of work if this stay isn't modified. Congress told us to finish this dam, and we're trying to do what Congress told us to do." Sanger promises that TVA will not do anything that will *directly* harm the fish. The judge should let the bulldozing continue pending the appeals court hearing, except in the river and at the very edge of the river's banks.

We try to convey to Weick that it isn't just a question of the fish's survival. It's also about preventing destruction to the darter's critical habitat, and protecting the status quo so the public will still have options to develop the river without a reservoir if the appeals court decides the dam violates the law. Alternative development designs for the river valley, we say, are key to resolving this legal controversy. Until the appeals court rules, the destruction of the valley's trees, farms, and Native American mounds must stop to avoid dooming those alternatives.

Weick blinks uncomprehendingly and slumps in his chair as Boone Dougherty describes the fragile biology of the snail darter's life cycle. After a half-hour the judge says he thinks he sees enough about the matter to make a ruling, and he doesn't see anything in the law about encouraging alternative developments. As to the law's prohibition of critical habitat destruction, it simply doesn't register. That evening the judge's clerk calls: TVA can continue all work that doesn't risk direct physical harm to the darters.

The death watch resumes. I disconsolately pack and move to Michigan, and over a couple of weeks, with help from Peter Alliman in Knoxville, prepare a pretty good brief. However strong our arguments may be, though, bulldozers are destroying the river while we wait. Sad reports come from the farmers. Most of the working farms are now gone from within the sixty square miles of the project. The canal is almost complete, with TVA holding the last seventy-five feet of earth as a plug against the water from the adjacent reservoir.

October finally arrives. Don Cohen, who also left Tennessee and moved to Ann Arbor, drives the two of us down to Cincinnati. He shoots me a series of tough practice questions as he drives, and I try to answer them, fumbling through assorted case precedents. This is going to be difficult. A clerk in the court of appeals has passed a message: our arguments better be good, because from the tone of the conversations she's overheard, we're set to lose, three to zero.

The three judges enter the courtroom and settle themselves behind the raised mahogany bench. Wade McCree, a graduate of the Boston Latin School, is a part-time professor at the University of Michigan and the first African-American judge in the circuit. Anthony Celebrezze was Secretary of Health Education and Welfare for Lyndon Johnson before being appointed to the bench. Judge John Peck just retired but is filling in today to round out the threesome. McCree is the one who has clearly read the briefs, but he quickly stops me as I begin with an intricate argument for an injunction against the dam.

"Counsel, before you start skylarking, why don't you start from the basics and build from there? Some of us may not be as familiar with the case as you are."[1]

This is good advice. He's hinting that, especially for his brethren who haven't read the briefs, I first need to tell the essential story. So I do, pointing to the map in the back of our brief showing the valley and its Native American sites, the chart with all sixty-eight existing TVA dams, the home habitat of the darter, the possible tourist route up through the beautiful valley to the Smokies. I then take Judge Taylor's facts and pin them down: every element of a violation of the Endangered Species Act has been proved. That's it. On this record, the court has to enjoin everything that hurts the darter's critical habitat. They cannot override the statute, permitting a stark violation to continue.

Judge McCree is busily taking notes as I argue.

After I finish, Boone speaks in vivid detail for another five minutes, explaining the biological imperatives, the darter's life cycle, and destruction of the darter's critical habitat by bulldozers.

Tom Pedersen, arguing TVA's case, approaches the podium. Silver-haired and folksy, he bases his argument on plain old common sense, with a touch of condescending sarcasm. It's just crazy to stop a significant project based on a silly fish. This dam will produce enough electricity for twenty thousand homes. (This is a new tack. With the need for energy in the news, TVA is emphasizing the short canal carrying water to nearby Loudoun reservoir, and converts the relatively trivial hydro increment into a number that sounds significant to anyone who doesn't know TVA's existing capacity.)

"But isn't it true, Mr. Pedersen, that the trial judge found the fish was jeopardized and its habitat was being destroyed?" asks McCree. "Doesn't that violate the statute?"

"Yes, he did, Your Honor," Pedersen replies, "but on the facts of this case, the statute simply does not make sense. We ask you to override or amend the statute, so we can finish the dam for the public good, as Congress's appropriations committee told us to do." In Taylor's Knoxville court, this kind of argument would be enough to prevail. Will it work here in Cincinnati, out from under TVA's shadow?

There's a pregnant pause. Celebrezze glances over at McCree with a frown, then asks, "Mr. Pedersen, is that something this court is normally allowed to do—amend a statute? Isn't that a job we usually leave for the legislative branch?"

"Your Honor, TVA is just asking this court to override the statute, or repeal the statute, Your Honor, *only so far as it applies to Tellico Dam*. That's what we want."

Celebrezze frowns. McCree looks at the ceiling. Peck looks bemused.

We drive back to Ann Arbor feeling cautiously optimistic. The TVA group had looked disgusted with Pedersen after the argument. The judges had half-smiled when they passed us going to the elevator after the session was over (we waited for the next elevator). Now we must wait for their decision. It's mid-October.

But weeks drag on without a word. TVA continues energetically razing houses and barns in the project's thirty-eight thousand acres. When the families have been pulled out of their homes by U.S. marshals, TVA's front-end loaders crush the structures and, as the evictees watch, push the remains into pits and set them on fire. Only silos are left standing. At the dam the agency's engineers close all the undergates. The river had been flowing through six-foot gaps under the structure, with hinged steel plates held open by cables. Now the cables are cut and the dam's bottom-level passages are plugged shut. Impounded water begins backing up a short distance behind the dam. In compliance with Weick's order, without closure of the big gates higher on the structure, only a small pool will form. The blocked waters won't quite reach back up the river to the darter's home shoals.

David Scates calls. The stalwart volunteer who spends most of his days fishing on the Little T since returning from military duty in Vietnam is almost unable to speak. He'd been down on the lower river watching as the water pooled behind the dam. There had been a budding rosebush just at the river's edge near the dam structure, and bit by bit it disappeared under the rising water. But feeling the sunlight that still filtered down through the two feet of clear river that now covered it, the rose's flowers blossomed, for the last time, underwater. The blossoms remained there valiantly for three days. "I cried right there," he says, "seeing them blooms opening under the water as it came up."

Two more months scrape by. The valley continues to deteriorate, to the frustrated misery of our Tennessee volunteer group. But on the last day of January, we get a call from wire service reporters: the appeals judges have just decided for the darter, *3–0!* Celebrezze has written a long opinion setting out the twisting history of the conflict and declaring that this chapter must end with an injunction. McCree concurs, with a single paragraph that says it all: "The district court found that the completion of the Tellico Dam would 'jeopardize the continued existence of the snail darter,' and, therefore, we must conclude that completion of the project would violate the Endangered Species Act. The Tellico Dam project is not exempt from the provisions of the Act. . . . The case should be remanded with instructions to issue an injunction."

So why did the judges wait so long, if the case was that clear? While they dawdled, the scalped valley has been butchered. But the news—the first good thing that has happened for the river in a very long time—nonetheless brings joy to our group in Tennessee. We hold a high-spirited potluck supper celebrating the court's unprecedented decision. The dam is illegal. We are a critically necessary giant step closer to getting the farmers back on their land and restoring the fertile valley so the river can again run clear and the darter can live on. (And though TVA doesn't know it, there are already new groves of willows starting to grow back where agency bulldozers had scalped the riverbanks. David has been cutting willow withes as he drives the back roads and at least once a week he hikes the ravaged banks of the Little T, pushing hundreds of new tree seedlings into the dark soil. Many have already pushed out solid root systems, new leaves, and thin new branches, a resurrected linear forest in the making.)

Back in Michigan, I get a call from an attorney friend of Judge Mc-Cree's. "The judge wrote some things down while you were presenting your appeal," she says.

"I know," I say. "I saw him taking notes on my arguments."

"No," she laughs. "He wasn't taking notes on what you were saying. He was writing a limerick. He gave me a copy. Here it is."

> Who can surpass the snail darter,
> the fish that would not be a martyr?
> It [expletive-d] the dam,
> near the place where it swam.
> Can you think of a fish any smarter?[2]

# CHAPTER 6

# The Snail Darter Goes to Washington

**FEBRUARY 2—MARCH 15, 1977**

"Get your butts up here! You're getting killed on Capitol Hill!" It's David Conrad from American Rivers. It's February 2, three days after network evening news proclaimed an unknown minnow's surprising defeat of TVA's Tellico Dam in the federal Court of Appeals in Cincinnati.

"Brent and I just came back from the weekly meeting of environmental lobbyists on the Hill. Everyone was talking about the darter—but they're treating it as an embarrassment. There's big trouble. You need to get here, quick!"

"What's the problem? We won! Doesn't that give us some credibility?"

"No, it's the opposite. Before, only a few people knew about your case and it seemed kind of unreal. Nobody who heard about it thought you'd get an injunction. Now the press is running the story hard, but they're making your case sound crazy. The media stories are all about the size of the fish. Nobody's looking at the economics. [CBS News anchor Walter] Cronkite called your case 'frivolous' on CBS last night."

"Doesn't the court decision strengthen us politically?" I ask.

"The only credibility it gives you is with people who see you as a threat. The pork-barrel guys think the Endangered Species Act will be big trouble. They're putting out stories about how a whole bunch of silly species will kill the economy. Nothing official has happened yet, but the reaction is building on Capitol Hill, and it's bad."

"Like what?"

"It's Congress, agencies, the press—you're in trouble everywhere. The most serious threat is Senator Baker. He wants to fast-track a bill through Congress. And he's backed by Senator Stennis and the water project lobbies. They don't want the snail darter to set a precedent that blocks other projects, especially Tenn-Tom Waterway. We think we're going to see a quick-strike bill, a poison dart to kill off your Tellico injunction. After that, some of them will try to repeal the whole Act." Conrad explains that Baker is backed by antiregulation industry groups from a variety of pork politics beyond water projects. Endangered species are found in lots of places, and could bring scrutiny into sacred programs and projects all over the country.

Industry people are naturally pleased at the way the press is reporting our case, and headline writers are picking up on it sarcastically: "Minnows v. Progress," "The Snail Darter Versus $100 Million TVA Dam," "Tennessee Dam Squeezed Out by 'Sardine,'" and "Will the Protection of Animals and Plants Peril Homo Sapiens?" It's coming across as an example of extremism they can use to make all environmental regulations look bad. "Everybody, and I mean *everybody,* is making fun of your fish," Conrad says. "We can hardly turn around without being called 'snail-darter people' or hearing jokes about how this or that's 'silly as a snail darter.' The press is playing it for all it's worth. It's too good to miss. A trivial fish stopping big technology."

"What about the new administration?" I ask. Ten days earlier the candidate who had campaigned as an environmentalist was sworn in as president. "Jimmy Carter stopped a pork dam in Georgia. He talks about good science and honest economics."

"The Carter people are confused," Conrad says. "They've been in their offices barely a week and here comes this mess. They're mostly saying the right things, but Washington veterans are telling them about political strategy. It's not environmentalists they need to worry about. They could fold on this in a minute. [Interior] Secretary Andrus looks like he wants to back down on endangered species. He called you 'misguided environmentalists' on *Face the Nation* yesterday. Interior is saying maybe the Act shouldn't apply to ongoing projects, and they're thinking about putting that into their regulations. Other agencies like the Forest Service and the Bureau of Land Management realize the Act threatens them as well as TVA. They're starting to talk about cutting endangered species law too."

"What should we do?" I ask.

"Anne Wickham says the key is for you to make sure people in Washington know a lot more about you and your fish."

"Who's Anne Wickham?" I ask.

"Conservation director at Friends of the Earth," Conrad explains. "Works on wildlife and political pork. Useful person to know. She says the problem is no one on the Hill knows the facts. Brent Blackwelder and I told her and the others what we knew about Tellico's economics, and none of them had heard any of it before. Even people on your side thought it was a big hydroelectric dam. Anne says to get your sorry butts up here. That's the way she talks. She says—and we think she's right—it'll have to be you guys who educate people on the Hill and the agencies and the press about this."

"But can't the big environmental groups get on it? There must be nine or ten citizen groups in Washington that care about wildlife and stopping water projects."

"You don't understand. The real fight is just beginning. Now it's political. And most environmental groups are really p.o.'ed at you, because they're going to be forced to defend the Act against attacks all over the place. No one had budgeted the time or resources to do that this year. For the Act's first big test case you've stuck them with a story that looks weak. The fish is too small and the facts are too complicated. Half a dozen groups will try to help, but they care about the Act, not the darter. They resent you. Some will be tempted to trade off your case to buy the Act some time. Anne Wickham likes the sound of your case, but she and Friends don't have any time either. It's got to be you guys who make the case for the darter in Washington, or it won't be made."

"If we're able to come to Washington, where do we focus first?" I ask. "The agencies? Congressional offices? Media? Or should we focus on briefing enviro groups?"

"Are you kidding? You've got to focus *on all of them*," Conrad says, exasperated. "This isn't a law school seminar. You can't take things one at a time. Washington works like a bunch of aircraft carriers plowing along side by side, all coming at you fast. If your group cares about the snail darter you have to handle *them all*. Any one of them could kill your case off in a flash, even this week. You need to get credible in Washington, right now. Across the board." If he is right, we somehow have to get our message into each power structure in the civics books. It's crazy. We're backwater amateurs, with no funding or political support.

We hear the same thing from Kathi Korpon, a young new staffer we telephone at the Senate subcommittee on resource protection after we find her name in a news story. She's working for John Culver, a newly elected, very progressive senator from Iowa, and she seems very sympathetic. "Senator Baker's staffers are working hard to slide through a Tellico exemption overturning your injunction," she confirms. "They're getting help from agency people in Interior, drafting a bill, and they want to do it without hearings. On the committee, we don't know what to say. If you have good arguments, we need to hear them."

That night, Sara Grigsby, Hank Hill, Peter Alliman, and I caucus by phone. We trust Conrad, Brent, and Korpon's evaluation. Our darter has raised its head enough to become a target for some very big guns. Plus we've put the Endangered Species Act into the crosshairs, just as many people were afraid we would. It seems unfair, though. We won our case on the facts and on the precise terms of the statute passed by Congress. Isn't government supposed to pick up the issue now and examine it carefully, then forge a rational conclusion? If Congress ever looks at the economics and policy, the fish and the river will surely prevail. But the political process wants to flick us away without even a hearing. Interior, the agency that's supposed to enforce the law, wants to sidestep us, and power players like Baker want to amend the law without revealing embarrassing facts. How can we handle this? We've always hoped the national environmental groups would be forced to save our bacon, our lawsuit making them hostages, forcing them into active defense of the darter. What we hadn't realized was how limited the national groups' resources were, stretched across too many issues. Washington's environmental groups won't ever absorb enough of the details to defend the darter's case successfully on Capitol Hill.

I am, frankly, scared by the thought of trying to establish a credible Washington lobbying presence. Every other organization has some kind of institutional backing and at least a survival budget, but we have neither. Our assets are a little group in Tennessee selling T-shirts and holding potluck fund-raisers—plus what little credit remains on my Visa card. Yet we're the ones who know our bizarre, complicated case best.

Guilt, too, pushes us toward Washington. We feel responsible for putting the entire Endangered Species Act at risk. It's a peril of citizen suits. If anybody can file suit against alleged violators, the evolution and fate of a regulatory statute can be shaped by self-appointed vigilantes like us. Now that our case has exploded with fallout for the world's most progressive wildlife law, we can't scuttle away and leave people we respect to handle the destruction. Acting alone, we'd authorized ourselves to take the darter's fate to court under the Endangered Species Act—so we ourselves must try to carry the case onward in Washington.

In Detroit the next day, I approach my dean, Don Gordon, and ask if he can change my teaching schedule for the rest of the academic year so I can spend half of each week in Washington. I promise him I will fully cover my teaching and advising duties. I can sandwich the ninety students in my two courses into class sessions on Mondays and Tuesdays, days and evenings, then fly to Washington, where I'll be available by phone for the rest of the week. In Tennessee this proposition would have gotten me tongue-lashed, but even though I'd been in Michigan less than six months, the dean says, "Sounds reasonable to me."

A week and a day after the court of appeal's announcement, I take a morning flight to Washington's National Airport, bringing the snail darter crusade to the District of Columbia.


## Anne Wickham

My first stop is the office above the Roy Rogers burger joint to see Brent and Conrad. There's no available space in that tightly packed warren, so Brent has phoned Anne Wickham across the street asking if we could have a desk at Friends of the Earth, and she said maybe, on a trial basis. Over the phone yesterday her advice was blunt: "Educate, educate, educate. If you don't educate people here fast, you are going to lose everything—the darter, the river, and the Act, too."

Anne isn't there when I walk into Friends of the Earth. "She's on the Hill," says a volunteer. "You can have the desk under the stairwell." Friends is slightly bigger than the offices above the Roy Rogers. It has the usual white-plastered walls and plywood room dividers festooned with notes, photos, and cartoons. Volunteers work around stacks of files, and telephones are ringing. In a back room full of books and loose papers is a coffee maker and a photocopier; there's a single bathroom for more than two dozen people.

"Welcome," says Eric Lynstrom, who works by the copy machine. "I'm working on utility corridor herbicide issues."

"What's that?" I ask.

"Utility companies use chemicals to kill off vegetation under power lines so they don't have to do maintenance. The chemicals are toxic and get into groundwater. Genetics and cancer. But the power and chemical industries make it difficult to talk on the Hill about regulation."

"Who's pushing for regulation?"

"Uh, mostly me, I guess," he says. "Environmental groups don't have people on staff to focus on it. Friends of the Earth gave me this desk and a phone. My parents pay my rent in a boardinghouse."

"Is there somebody from Tennessee here?" shouts the volunteer at the phone console. Anne is calling from her meeting on the Hill. I pick up the phone.

"This is Anne," a voice barks. "Do you have a fact sheet ready?"

I explain that I have maps and legal documents in my leather bag, along with photos and a report on the dam's economics from the impact statement lawsuit.

"No, no, no. You need something concise, no more than two pages, laying out the whole argument for people on the Hill. Do it! I'll be back in an hour."

Lynstrom shows me the rest of the office, which also houses the headquarters of the National Clean Air Act Coalition. In one corner a guy is working on issues involving Native Americans and the environment, and upstairs are people working on national forest issues, international environmental matters, and World Bank projects. There are dozens of issues being processed in this small space. Rafe Pomerance is president of Friends and runs the office. Up close, this epicenter of the "National Environmental Movement," demonized on talk radio, looks like the household of the Old Woman Who Lived in a Shoe.

Two hours later, as I finish a fact sheet on Tellico, there's a clatter of metal tubing on brick in the doorway and a shrill "Goddammit!"

"Anne's back," the young woman at the phone console calls out cheerily. The door is wedged open by a blonde-haired woman in a wheelchair trying to retrieve an arm crutch that has gotten stuck in the doorjamb while an intern pushes the chair from behind to help get its front wheels over the threshold. The chair bumps through the door and she wheels through.

"You're Zyg? I'm Anne. Show me your fact sheet."

She's a decisive editor. "This paragraph's good; that one's crap. That one too. You're not writing this for a law review. Write so congressional staffers and committees get the full picture, fast. So they know the issues, and which facts are key. And put information contacts here in Washington—the phone number here at Friends, Brent at American Rivers, and put me on it too. Now tell me about the darter. And the farmers and the Cherokees."

Like Brent Blackwelder, Anne is a very quick study. She says, "If people know these facts, you win. But they don't, so you have to educate them. Do you have a plan? Who are you going to meet with today and the rest of the week?"

I tell her the five appointments I've arranged for the day, and that Hank, Peter, and Boone Dougherty are flying in from Tennessee the next day to talk with the senators and several representatives from Tennessee.

"Your schedule for today is a waste of time, except Skip Spensley in the House merchant marine committee," says Anne. "Lee Talbot at the Council on Environmental Quality won't help you much. CEQ's too small. Rick Herod in Baker's office is just an errand boy; the senator doesn't listen to him. Anyway, forget Baker. He's working for TVA and won't change his mind. Clifford Allen, who represents Nashville, hates TVA, but this isn't in his district and he doesn't have the political capital to go against the rest of the delegation. Your Tennesseans will waste their time talking to the state delegation.

"And Jim Williams at Fish and Wildlife is out of the loop in Interior. People know he's talking to you. There's a better contact inside Interior. Cynthia Wilson. She's the one who taught me about Washington when I got here. She was at Audubon before the election and just got a position in the secretary of interior's office. She says the leadership at Interior is worried about the Endangered Species Act. They're thinking about issuing regulations that will make political compromises. You're likely to be the first. You need to get good information into the interior secretary's office, fast. And I'll try to get you connected to someone in the White House. You need the president's Domestic Pol-

icy Council to know the issues so they can ride herd on Interior and
other agencies who're even more scared of the Act. But Spensley, he's
different. He knows everyone, and knows how to leverage them."

Anne really knows her Washington. Each of her pronouncements
proves to be right on. The tone of the meeting with Baker's Herod is
shallow and snide. No interest in project economics, and repeated gleeful warnings from him that the angry senator will probably crush us
with a legislative rider exempting Tellico Dam from the law. Herod
quotes Baker: "When Congress passed that law, we intended to protect
big warm fuzzy animals like eagles and grizzlies, not little, cold, slimy
things—and the Act's not supposed to stop ongoing projects." Representative Allen fulminates against TVA but says he can't do anything
for us. Jim Williams at Interior reports he's been taken off the darter
and given dull work on catfish. He says Interior is finalizing regulations
that will let agencies with ongoing projects like Tellico exempt themselves from the law.

But Skip Spensley in the House committee is again helpful. He
arranges a brief meeting with subcommittee chair Robert Leggett,
suggesting beforehand that I emphasize Cherokee history and
schoolchildren floating down the river on field trips—"Leggett likes
those issues"—as well as the fish. When we get in to talk with Leggett,
he listens to us for maybe six minutes, mumbles something about protecting the law, and scurries off. "I think he'll be able to do something
for you later on," says Spensley. "He's looking to leave a legacy when he
leaves Congress, and the Endangered Species Act may be it."

Spensley also introduces Jenna Christy, a graduate student working
on endangered wildlife; she's interning with the subcommittee and is
immediately excited about Tellico. She's been hoping the Endangered Species Act would heat up as an issue. She knows a lot about
zoology—she's doing her dissertation on bog turtles—and the darter
has a complex ecological niche and life cycle. We tell her that if she
visits Tennessee she can go on a collecting trip with Dave Etnier and
actually see the endangered fish. In two years of looking she has never
actually found a bog turtle—also an endangered species—in the wild.
Christy agrees to keep daily tabs for us on the law's congressional politics from her vantage point in Leggett's subcommittee. She can ask for
documents from Interior in Leggett's name, which may give us easier
access to agency material. She'll also bring our issue to the attention of

the congressional Environmental Study Conference, a bipartisan group made up of about seventy legislators concerned with environment issues, and their staffers, each office kicking in a few hundred dollars a year to support the group as an informal congressional environmental forum.

"I think Skip is right," she tells us. "Leggett doesn't know much about the Act, but he senses it can be his legacy. It's an open secret he's not coming back next Congress. The newspapers in southern California discovered that the woman he's been introducing as Mrs. Leggett here in Washington isn't the same Mrs. Leggett they know in San Diego. But I suspect he'll be willing to do things for you. And I get along well with Ed Forsythe, the senior Republican on the subcommittee. Let me know when you need things and I'll find the right moment to ask for them."

Back at Friends of the Earth I ask Anne for her advice on where to go from here. "Interior," she says. "Cynthia will get you a meeting. The White House, too. I think I can get you a meeting in the President's Domestic Council. Now you need to find a base in the Senate. And work the press. Walter Cronkite is God around here. When he calls you 'frivolous' on the six o'clock news, it means you're in trouble and you have to turn them around.

"But look. You can't just focus on a dozen people," Anne warns, warming to what amounts to a tutorial. "Get your facts out to every congressional office where you might find active support. That's probably more than a hundred offices. Staffers need to know what's going on. Personal visits, not just fact sheets. Any one of them might have an opportunity sometime to say something that'll make a difference. And you need to poke around in agencies besides Interior to see if you can find broader support for the Act. If Interior thinks it's alone on this it won't be an active ally.

"And reporters, you can't talk to enough of them. You need good press wherever you can find it. Turn the story around. Look at the way our opposition gets their message out. They spend millions on public relations firms that get their message into papers and broadcasts all over the country. They create a climate of public opinion around their issues. You don't need just one story telling the truth about Tellico. You need a bunch of stories feeding off each other to show the dam isn't worth it.

Anne Wickham's 1967 AMC Hornet, shown parked in front of the White House for a meeting in the Old Executive Office Building next door. The car's handicap driving accessories are affixed to the steering wheel by duct tape, which also (nearly) holds shut the passenger-side front door. Inset: Anne Wickham herself, the snail darter campaign's primary source of advice and assistance in Washington, DC. (Courtesy of Wickham family)

"Another thing. Wear a suit. Why do you think I wear tweed skirts and blouses with little lace trims instead of my love beads? If you want people to think the fish has serious representation here, you can't look like a tourist. You're a professional, and professionals on the Hill wear suits.

"Remember, you don't represent money or power to these people, so they have to trust you as a person and a source of information. People need to get to know you, know you're rational, not nuts. That you know your stuff. In this town people who have factual data in hand get listened to. Staffers on the Hill love to know facts. If you've given them information so they know the important questions and the answers, and no one else does, things are more likely to go your way. But protect your credibility. You have to give them good information, fact sheets, maps, and charts. Explain the details to them and the big picture. God help you if you give them inaccurate information. If you do, you'd better be the first one, not the second, to get right back and tell them so. It'll hurt, but it'll validate you to them for the next time. These staffers expect to get crappy information from industry lobbyists. Everyone knows they're bought and paid for. But if you're an environmentalist, all you have is your credibility. Don't blow it."

Hank, Peter, and Boone arrive from Tennessee for two days in Washington. They don't want to tell me how the river is looking back home. "It'd break your heart." But I push. Their description of the scalped and ravaged valley puts a claw in my stomach as I think of the realities hanging upon what we do here. They're convinced it's still worth trying to push the Tennessee congressional delegation on Tellico, so that's where they'll focus. Boone thinks his advocacy will carry some weight with the Tennessee senators, Baker and James Sasser. Hank and Peter will go to five other offices.

At each stop the Tennesseans are greeted hospitably. Some staffers are from down home and are about the same age as Hank and Peter, and Capitol Hill office staffers are told to be gracious to visiting constituents from "the district." Moreover, most of these staffers appreciate seeing real people who give them a refreshing break from the tide of Washington professionals appearing with political agendas in hand. Some of the Tennessee delegation's staffers seem genuinely interested in the facts of Tellico. Their bosses, however, won't budge. TVA is a dominating part of their state's social and economic base. It isn't to be crossed. They tell us there'll be a push to override the law in Congress, and they'll observe the debate with interest. But they won't help us raise questions about TVA's dam. With the shadow of TVA overhead, time spent talking to the Tennessee delegation is wasted.

That evening we gather at Tennessee friend Bob Lynch's apartment, where Hank and Peter are crashing for the night. We talk about how not to waste the next day. We consider Representative John Murphy, from New York City, whom Anne had recommended and who's taking over as chair of the Merchant Marine and Fisheries Committee, overseeing endangered species. Murphy, Anne had told us, personifies the unholy mixture reflected in the committee's name. He's rooted in the corrupt politics of shipbuilding contracts and knows nothing about wildlife. "Leggett on the subcommittee sounds as if he'll be useful to us," Anne said, "but if we can get the full committee chair on our side that will be better." She has begun saying "we." That is a very good sign.

While Peter and Hank are working on Murphy and visiting Tennessee congressional offices, I'll go to the secretary of interior's office, then to some potentially significant non-Tennessee House offices, and finally to senior staffers on the Senate Environment and Public Works Committee.

It's a long, tiring day. In visits to congressional offices a succession of representatives and aides concedes that we're probably correct on the facts, but their office won't take up the issue. Even Mo Udall, the gutsy progressive congressman from Arizona whose brother Stewart had been the greatest interior secretary in recent memory, is apologetic but firm. It's not his turf. Without a single Tennessee legislator supporting us it's hard to convince others to help.

When we meet that evening to compare notes, however, Hank is ebullient. "Total waste of time in the Tennessee offices," he reports. "Senator Sasser's not going to back us because of Baker, even though his legislative assistant told me the senator knows the dam's a pile of crap." Like many staffers, Sasser's bright legislative assistant Dick Lodge obviously wishes that the processes of government were shaped by facts and logic. Instead he's forced to defend his boss's timid shifts in the political winds. The senator won't take a stand with us "unless you can make it safe for him, and you can't." On the House side, a sympathetic staffer for John Duncan, the consistently passive legislator who represents two counties touching our river, tells us Duncan will never buck TVA. So why is Hank so jovial? "It's Jack Murphy!" he chuckles. "Chairman Murphy is a scurrilous bastard. He's a real crook. It's obvious. We got along *great!*" Apparently Murphy had granted them ten minutes, which had then stretched out to more than an hour as Hank told tales about Tennessee politics, vilifying TVA and its dirty tricks and recounting the guerrilla warfare that the farmers and fishermen had been waging right back at the colossus. Murphy loved it all. He'd invited them to come back again soon, and Hank and Peter promised they would.

I hadn't been so successful. Through Cynthia Wilson's efforts I'd met with Secretary Andrus's deputy, Larry Meirotto. He asked a few pro forma questions and kept looking at his watch. The department is aware of the situation, he said, ushering me out, although it's clear he doesn't know anything about the dam project. If Interior's new appointees are supposed to be our friends, we're in trouble.

So what should we make of what occurred in the Senate committee office later that day? Anne had gotten me an interview that morning with one of Senator Edmund Muskie's committee aides, John Freshman. Anne explained that because Muskie and his environmental committee had sponsored the Endangered Species Act and many other environmental statutes, his staff should be briefed on this latest controversy. We needed Senate allies besides John Culver's aides, and Freshman had helped Muskie oversee two of the nation's most complex statutes, the Clean Air and Clean Water Acts. When Freshman came out of the inner office to greet me, however, he immediately announced he was sorry but could give me only two minutes. There was a major reorganization plan to be finalized this morning, he said, giving me "the look." We'd been getting used to the look: an impatient furrowing of the brow, squinting eyes, and mouth shaped into half impatient scowl and half knowing smile. The look says: "You're one of those wackos from Tennessee who used that little fish technicality to stop a big hydroelectric dam. You're so off the wall that no environmental group will help you in court, and now no one except Anne Wickham wants to get within ten feet of your case. You'll soon be a footnote to history."

It's always painful to be condescended to, but it's excruciating when those condescending to you don't know what they're talking about.

"I'm sorry," said Freshman, "but I'm really not in a position to help you." His boss, Senator Muskie, he reminds us, is leaving his environmental chair to take over the budget committee, and anyway, even though Muskie believes in the law, he's heard that an endangered plant is blocking the hydroelectric Dickey-Lincoln Dam in Maine, and he's deeply committed to publicly owned power.[1]

Freshman was polite (barely) but dismissive. Like most Hill staffers he was a political junkie who could give insider-wisdom verdicts on virtually any topic. By now the Washington papers had painted our picture—a fishy gimmick blocking economic development—and every week there was another story about another silly-named species that might cause trouble, adding to the hullabaloo about our darter. In his boss's Maine, it was the worrisome endangered plant in the Dickey-Lincoln project area called Furbish's lousewort.

As he said "lousewort," Freshman rose to leave.

"But wait," I bleated. "Anne says you have a sense for political strategy . . . but you don't seem to see what's going on here! She says

Muskie always argues it's wrong to see everything as a trade-off between environment and economics, but that's exactly what you're doing. And you've got it totally backwards. Could you please look at this for just one more minute?" At this point I rolled out a topographical map of the Little T: there's the small dam structure in a corner, then thirty-three miles of river and valley farmland, with the TVA land condemnations outlined in magic marker showing how much private land is being taken for the project and how little of it would be for the reservoir. I pointed to the little dam. "Do you know the primary purpose of Tellico Dam?"

"Electricity, right?"

"No, *recreation,* supposedly. And second, having the Boeing Corporation develop a model city called Timberlake on all this farmland they're condemning—except the model city plan collapsed two years ago. That's two-thirds of the claimed benefits right there. Look, here's the official cost-benefit ratio. Barges are supposed to add a little. There are no generators, though a bit of power could come from running water through a canal to another dam. Tellico is a marginal, last-gasp project. There are already twenty-four dams within fifty miles of Tellico! And for the alleged real estate development project they're throwing three hundred farm families off more than twenty thousand acres of prime agricultural lands."

Our Tellico pitch is starting to become automatic. We need to lay out facts quickly that will complicate the little-fish-big-dam image that our listeners thought they knew. I'm carrying a beat-up leather satchel stuffed with enough papers to cover a small dam—a fat mailing tube of maps, a sheaf of economic reports, pictures of the darter, notebooks, copies of our current position paper, along with markers, pens, tacks, tape, and breath mints. Deploying this arsenal, we try daily to flip the conventional story. Who are really the ones being extreme and irrational here, we ask? It's the TVA people, not us. We're the ones trying to make economic as well as ecological sense.

Our standard Tellico spiel has five points leading to the conclusion that the dam project doesn't make economic or common sense—while the alternate options preserving the endangered species do. Here's the pitch:

- Endangered species are canaries in a coal mine, sensitive natural indicators of human welfare as well as ecology.

- Tellico is primarily a recreation and land development project, not a power dam.
- Three hundred-plus farm families are being forced off their prime agricultural lands for a mythical model city, a plan that was abandoned in 1975 as economically untenable.
- Extremely valuable river-based project development alternatives exist to save the darter, get farmers back on their land, producing far greater recreational, agricultural, tourism, and commercial development benefits than a dam—proving that the Endangered Species Act makes economic sense.
- TVA consistently refuses to consider any options except its original dam-based plan that will destroy the darter, the river, and the valley farmlands.

The obvious conclusion—*The snail darter injunction should be upheld, for river-based development.* It's our pork-barrel opponents who are the cynical extremists.

After five minutes of this barrage, people either get pulled into the details of our dilemma, focusing inquisitively on the maps, charts, and political landscape, or they back away in political discomfiture. In this case Freshman sat back down and leaned over the map. "Do you have more time?" he asked. "There are a couple of other people I think we ought to bring in on this." At his call came Leon Billings, Muskie's chief committee aide, and Len Stewart, Colorado Senator Gary Hart's legislative aide.

"Oh, a snail darter person," Stewart winced as soon as we'd been introduced.

"No, wait," said Freshman, turning to me. "Show them what this case is really about."

After almost an hour more, covering every challenge they could think of, the committee staffers sit back in agreement. "If what you're saying is true, this case is a lot more than it's been cracked up to be," Freshman said. "None of this is out on the table, though. Nobody knows about it. Even if they did, it's hard to process. It's just too complicated for people to understand. You need a way to present the bottom line in some credible way. And you need to be credible yourselves so members will take you seriously. Baker is going to try to ram an exemption bill through in the next few weeks."

"Can you help us?"

"Not much. We're moving with Muskie over to Budget, and Hart is tied up with other issues. We can make some phone calls for you. The new chair is Jennings Randolph from West Virginia. He won't be much help, but John Culver, the new resource subcommittee chair, might be. We'll let him and his staff know this is a significant case. But you really need to rally environmental groups to stand with you, and get some good press. If you don't change the way things are now, you're dead."

This session took more than two hours. What did it gain us? Maybe just free advice, and perhaps supportive phone calls from three staffers who made it clear they aren't going to be doing much on the endangered species issue. As I leave I wonder if these three didn't just give me that time so they'd learn things about the controversy that no one else knew. Being in the know is one of the valuable currencies that build the ego accounts of staffers on the Hill.

"No, they probably weren't wasting your time," says Brent Blackwelder later that evening, after Peter, Hank, and Boone leave for Tennessee. "They'll brief Muskie's right-hand guy, Tom Jorling, on the issue, and that can't hurt. Maybe even Muskie himself. And John and Len will probably make some phone calls to help with the new committee. They can also make a difference with some of the environmental groups. And Hank and Peter's visit with Murphy was definitely not a waste of time."

Trying to get traction in Washington isn't easy. In two days we've run all over town, spoken in person with more than forty people in Interior, the Council on Environmental Quality, and the House and Senate. We've also talked by phone with almost a dozen more with whom we weren't able to arrange face-to-face meetings, and we cold-called reporters in Washington and New York whom Anne or Brent thought might pick up on the details of the Tellico story. Victor Neufeld of ABC News in New York expressed some interest. Add it up, however, and we're still running around directionless.

"Brent," I ask, "what are we supposed to be accomplishing here? There are thousands of people in this town we could talk to about Tellico if we had the time, which we don't. We need to focus. On what?"

"There's no simple answer. Remember you're operating in four or five separate Washington networks simultaneously—courts, Congress, key agencies, the press, and the environmental movement. Think of what will get you where you need to go: first, you've got to stay alive. You have to protect that injunction. You can't let the agency undercut you or let Congress reverse your court order with a quick strike amendment. Then you have to start turning around peoples' perception of the case—the way you guys did with Murphy and Muskie's staffers—so they see that the darter, the river, and the Act make more sense than the dam. And you have to pin it down politically, consolidate it. Eventually you'll have to get the dam deauthorized and your river-based plan for Tellico made official. That way you can work on getting the valley developed positively, make it a success story for the Act and environmental policy.

"For starters," he asks, "how are you doing in federal court?"

"Nothing's moving in the courts," I say. TVA will surely try to appeal the court of appeals injunction to the Supreme Court, but that will take at least six months until the Court's fall term, and probably longer.

"Good. That means your immediate threats just come from Interior and Congress. The agency could cut the case out from under you by fudging the regulations or delisting the darter. I bet they're getting a lot of pressure to do that. And Congress can change your law with a snap of its fingers. The way Baker's talking, you've got to worry about a quick override like that blackbird bill." Brent describes how a year ago it had taken Congress only a day—start to finish, just one day, no hearings—to pass a law allowing Fort Knox in Kentucky to spray a killing solution onto millions of starlings that had decided to roost in rookeries around the federal facility. The speckled black birds were ecological imports multiplying by the millions after an eccentric Anglophile transplanted a dozen of those English starlings into New York's Central Park in the 1890s. They had few natural predators, they decimated native species in many parts of the nation, and they were dumping hundreds of pounds of guano onto the trees and sidewalks of Fort Knox. Pushed by intense daily media coverage of the gooey mess, Congress quickly passed an exemption setting aside all laws and regulations that would have required time and study before spraying the birds.

Brent was undoubtedly right. Given the media's repackaging of pork-barrel antienvironmentalists' public relations materials, a vote in Congress on Tellico Dam today would mean we'd lose in an avalanche. "Your first job is to block the immediate threats in Interior and Congress. After that, you start building a factual record to change the way

Washington thinks about the darter. Congressional hearings, agency briefings."

Echoing Freshman and Stewart, Brent adds that we need to get the environmental groups more actively on our side. Since Earth Day, the environmental NGOs—nongovernmental organizations—have become a political bloc that members of Congress know can sometimes hurt them. Environmental groups gave Carter his early momentum and helped elect him. Right now most of the environmental groups think we're nothing but a headache.

"You need to persuade the press, too, get them to look beyond the snail darter jokes and all the silly-named species people are saying will block progress," he says. The press is Washington's most important information system, wielding more power than official white papers and hearings. Congress knows a story in the media is being seen by the grassroots public. The public cares about issues based on how they are being covered. If our issue is being portrayed as frivolous, if the facts aren't getting out, politicians will just continue to play the insider games. Thus our battle plan for the second week is short-term survival. We'll work in the interlocking networks of agencies, Congress, environmental groups, and the press—and also on the home front in Tennessee.

News from Tennessee is grim. Apparently claiming they had received no official notice of the injunction order, TVA continued working on dam construction after the court of appeals decision and kept bulldozing the valley. On February 17, more than two weeks after the court's ruling, the agency dynamited historic Lookout Rock at Fort Loudoun, saying it would be a hazard to future navigation and its removal wouldn't hurt the snail darter.

I speak on the phone with an insolent TVA attorney, who says TVA acknowledges that for the time being it must protect the darter in the river, but adds that the agency has no reason to preserve the existing condition of the valley because eventually the reservoir will be built. I tell him any continued work on a reservoir is illegal, and undercuts alternative development options for the valley. On February 24, Boone and Peter get a fairly strong protective order from Judge Taylor, but the valley looks bad. Given the condition of the project area, local press coverage, and TVA's continuing implacable insistence that a dam will be built, virtually no one in eastern Tennessee realizes that attractive economic alternatives exist.

Over the next two weeks we focus on Interior and Congress. Of the two, Congress is more dangerous. Baker's top aide, Jim Range, has gotten to every office, every staffer, even over on the House side, before we do. Staffers look at us skeptically: "Jim Range says that Baker is furious about Tellico Dam and that this is a silly lawsuit and Baker has the votes to override the law right now. It's Tennessee's business and other members should back off, defer to Baker and the rest of the Tennessee delegation." There's already one exemption bill in the hopper, submitted by Representative Robin Beard from western Tennessee, striking the Tellico Dam, Tenn-Tom, and middle Tennessee's Duck River Dam from the Endangered Species Act. Although Beard is a lightweight, and that bill will go nowhere, we nevertheless feel like we've landed on a conveyor belt that's yanking our feet out from under us. The big boys are getting into the game, and it's starting to move fast.

Skip Spensley and Jenna Christy give us an hour to brainstorm how to slow down the volatile congressional battlefield. "You have two big arguments," says Spensley. "Congress shouldn't act until there have been *hearings*. And they shouldn't take this case on until they know what the *Supreme Court* is going to do." The prospect of congressional hearings argues against a quick override bill: if congressional committees approve an amendment without hearings, the environmental groups could make the bill look like a kangaroo court, an embarrassment. "If you get some members calling for hearings," Spensley says, "that'll give others a good excuse to hold off, 'to look the issue over and give it due process.'" We should also push the legislators to "wait and see what the Supreme Court does." That too makes powerful sense as a message to the politicians: a battle over a quick-strike bill could be messy—why bother, if the Supreme Court might make the case go away?

At this point Chairman Leggett walks into the subcommittee staff room and asks what we're discussing. "Baker wants an override? Sounds like that goddam blackbird bill," he grunts as he turns back toward his office. "I got rolled on that one. Passed the damn law without a hearing, and they didn't know what they were doing. Most of the birds didn't even die when they sprayed them. Just hung around sick, making an even sorrier mess. I'm going to tell anybody who wants us to do that again to go sit in some bird shit. We need oversight hearings on this—and the whole damn Act. See how it's working, not just this one case."

"There you have it!" says Spensley as Leggett disappears into his back office. "Those are the arguments: 'Wait for hearings and the Supreme Court, no need to rush.' Leggett will say that to the House leadership. You should get the Senate subcommittee chair to do the same. And go talk to Frank Potter. He's Dingell's guy. Even if his boss is moving over to Energy it might be a good idea to have him backing up Leggett on this."

In Senate subcommittee quarters, Kathi Korpon sits me down with Dick Oshlo, Senator Culver's legislative aide. Likewise young and a quick study, he shows immediate interest in the Tellico maps, facts, and history. "The senator's just gotten on this committee and doesn't know much about the Act," Oshlo explains (meaning Culver probably knows nothing at all about it). "But this could be the first big issue for his subcommittee. Culver studies hard. Takes this stuff home with him. In a week he'll know more about it than anyone else on the Hill. And I think he'll fight to defend his committee's turf even though he's new here and Baker's the senior Republican."

Culver comes into the staff room while we're talking, and Oshlo and Korpon make a quick introduction.

"What's this I'm hearing about snail darters?" the senator asks, but doesn't pause for an answer. Big and brusque, he carries his Harvard fullback frame slightly forward on his feet. He speaks easily but is in a hurry to move on. "You keep these members of my staff informed, OK?"

"We're worried about a fast-track exemption bill," we say to his departing back.

"We'll see about that," Culver barks, and disappears.

"I think he'll get into this," Oshlo says. "I think he's interested. Give me some maps and fact sheets and I'll start briefing him."

"It would also help to know how many other projects have had trouble with the Endangered Species Act," Korpon adds. "We need to be able to show the senator that the Act's workable, so he'll be justified in holding oversight hearings rather than letting an exemption bill sail through."

Over on the House side I make an appointment with Frank Potter, Dingell's chief of staff. On the phone he'd said, "Why do you want to talk with me? Mr. Dingell is giving up his chair on endangered species." Potter's tone is evasive, almost surly. I persist, saying he knows the law's background, and that may be helpful to us. Entering the office, I see a disheveled middle-aged man at a messy desk. He has clearly been around a while, watching waves of bright, high-energy young people fight their way into the ranks of Capitol Hill staffers, build up their rolodexes and momentum, and hustle onward. Potter has stayed at Dingell's side for more than a dozen years.

"When Mr. Dingell wrote Section Seven he knew what he was doing," Potter says. "He wrote it so it wouldn't emphasize stopping federal projects." (That's putting it delicately. Dingell knew that Section Seven had teeth, which means its rambling text was an act of intentional camouflage.) "He put testimony into the record showing it could be used that way." We'd cited that in court. "We hoped the first cases would be about cranes or bears or eagles," Potter says, "not something insignificant." Potter is echoing what Spensley told us the first time we talked. I launch into the standard disquisition on why the darter isn't insignificant, why the Tellico case is a superb demonstration of how using the Endangered Species Act makes economic sense even though at first glance it's extreme. He looks uninterested. But when I make a move to leave, he says, "No, sit back down. Look, you need to make a clearer link to human utility. In the House report on the 1973 bill, we said how endangered species are like canaries in a coal mine. They should be protected for what they can tell us about human welfare as well as for ethics or whatever. Emphasize that. And send a letter to Dingell right away saying you've talked to me and I advised you to talk with Leggett and Murphy. Dingell will want to think you came to him first." Potter doesn't have great respect for Leggett and Murphy. "Neither of them understands the issues, but you might get them to fight end runs around their committee. They'll need Dingell for any battle on the merits. He'll stand up with them to block a blackbird bill on your darter. And Dingell's strong. You should see members cower when he's mad."

Potter has become enthusiastic. He says getting Dingell enthused about our case will help on the Senate side as well. Potter tells an old saw about the difference between the House and Senate. Members of the House, he says, are generally brighter than the dimmer bulbs over in the Senate, so when one not especially intelligent representative recently left the House for the Senate it was said that he actually raised the average IQ of both chambers. "Leggett's an exception, not all that sharp, but I think Dingell will firm him up, and a lot of people will heed what Dingell says."

When I tell Spensley about my time with Potter, he isn't surprised. "Frank wants you to think he's a crusty old grouch," he says, "but he really believes in species conservation, much more even than his boss. They say Dingell shoots wildlife in Africa on Safari Club junkets, probably including some endangered species. He comes from a Detroit-area factory district and isn't always on your side in environmental battles. But Potter wants you and your darter to win. When he says he thinks Dingell will help, he means he'll push Dingell to help you, and Dingell will.

"Potter talked about Dingell writing Section Seven and seeding the record with examples of federal actions to be blocked," Spensley continues. "Guess who *really* wrote Seven—it was *him*. Frank did it, along with Tom Garrett's help over at Friends of the Earth, and Lee Talbot, Chip Bohlen, and Earl Baysinger. Frank and Tom drafted Section Seven on the back of a lunch bag. Potter and the other three made sure it didn't get changed in the committee process, or even noticed. You'll see. Potter will make sure Dingell fights to save their baby."

## Pursuing the Executive Branch

In Interior the situation doesn't look good. On February 28 TVA filed a petition to delist the darter and its critical habitat, arguing that its transplants to two other rivers, done without Fish and Wildlife's permission, have eliminated the threat of extinction. The Little Tennessee River, moreover, is no longer feasible habitat, TVA says, because it had, inadvertently, cut off the darter's life cycle in the process of diverting the Little T's flow through the bottom of the dam. Now that the river's been altered it's too late to save them; it's become an unsuitable habitat. Jim Williams says Interior is going to let TVA catch more yearling fish trying to return upstream to breed, and haul them away to the Holston River. Even more distressing, Korpon from Culver's office reports that Jim Range has pushed Interior's Keith Schreiner to draft a bill exempting Tellico from the law. We're perplexed. Why would Interior's Fish and Wildlife Service, the agency entrusted with enforcing the Endangered Species Act, draft amendments undercutting it?

Apparently Range has been browbeating the Service about how the whole law will perish unless the agency addresses the need for "reasonable flexibility." So Schreiner and some unknown agency attorneys have prepared an exemption bill.

There are other problems with Interior. Secretary Andrus still won't meet with us, and has been commenting to reporters about "unbalanced environmentalists." He hasn't backed off the proposed regulation that notes "the waste that can occur if an advanced project is halted"—the "affected agency" (meaning TVA, not Interior or the courts) should itself decide whether its project's "degree of completion" allows the law to be overridden. When I suggest to Ron Lambertson, the Service's attorney, that the best defense of the law is to show congressional committees evidence that it's working—evidence that dozens of potential conflicts have been resolved through Interior's interagency negotiation, while TVA is one of very few examples of impasse—he tells me that Interior doesn't have that data and isn't interested in collecting it.

The executive branch, which we confidently thought would be lurching over to our side as soon as Jimmy Carter took office, isn't doing that. Bureaucracy doesn't follow a new agenda unless the new team in town cracks a whip, which the Carter people haven't done. We'd thought we would have opportunities to get through to the Carter White House. When Hank Hill first flew to Washington after the court of appeals decision, he found himself across the aisle from a young, attaché-case-carrying good ol' boy who turned out to be Hamilton Jordan, Carter's new chief of staff. The jovial Tennessean and the wisecracking Georgian hit it off. When Hank explained what we were doing with the Tellico case and how it was going to lead to a big fight over the Endangered Species Act, Jordan sounded encouraging. He was no ecofreak, he said, but his boss had this thing about the environment. "I think this is the kind of thing we'll want to take on," Jordan told Hank. "Here's my phone number in the West Wing and Stu Eizenstat's in the Domestic Council. Give me a call." Hank called the next morning, and again over the next few days, but never got through to Jordan or any of the staffers.

The second week we're in Washington, Sara Grigsby calls from Tennessee with an exciting idea to crack through the executive impasse. Carter's press office has announced he'll do an on-air call-in program on March 5 to hear directly from citizens at the start of his term. Carter is a fresh populist breeze blowing into the swamps along the Potomac. With his straight-shooting grassroots common sense, his back-to-the-people inauguration walk down Pennsylvania Avenue, and his announcement that he wants to rethink federal government from top to bottom, the new president has momentarily set Washington on its heels. Sara and a bunch of other volunteers start dialing the White House 800-number an hour before the show, ready to tell the president the real story of Tellico Dam and the snail darter. Over the next two hours, Jimmy Carter hears from forty-two callers from twenty-six states, with twenty million people listening in. Sara's lively Tennessee drawl, however, never makes it through to 1600 Pennsylvania Avenue and the world.

Looking for more prosaic executive pressure points, I visit Agriculture's Rupert Cutler, recently appointed Carter's assistant secretary in charge of the U.S. Forest Service. The Carter people wanted to find an assistant secretary from the heartland serious about bringing modern environmental accounting into federal bureaucracy. I'd given lectures to Cutler's Resource Management class at Michigan State the previous spring. "I had forty-five students then. Now I have twenty-five thousand employees under my command!" he chortles. Among other policy initiatives, he wants to integrate endangered species protection into management of all national forests. "Let's see if the Department of Agriculture can be an ally in environmental protection for a change."

Cutler's agency isn't central to endangered species law, but the visit proves worthwhile. "You're having trouble with Interior, and CEQ isn't doing anything?" he asks. "Call Steve Jellinek at CEQ. Tell him I sent you, and see if he'll open some doors." Is this how government works, I wonder—personal networks? As soon as I contact Jellinek, we're welcome at the president's Council on Environmental Quality. "Cutler sent you? OK," Jellinek says. "Poor old Rupe. He's sitting on top of a den of loggers who think the word 'ecosystem' is a communist plot." Jellinek links us to the Council's wildlife issues attorneys. They look at our case's ecology and economics and make calls to the president's Domestic Policy Council, telling them to pay attention to the merits of our case.

## The Enviros: Gunners, Tree Huggers, and "Humaniacs"

Anne Wickham had told us to talk with every environmental group in town. By now it's clear that Friends of the Earth, in its dilapidated row house office—and American Rivers/Environmental Policy Center/ League of Conservation Voters, the oddball consortium above the Roy Rogers grease pit—are our bottom-line supporters in Washington, our indispensable base of operations and guidance. "The environmental movement is taken seriously on the Hill," Anne says, but if the groups take divided stands on Tellico and the Act, that will tell politicians they can dump us without getting much backlash from the greens. "The problem is, some groups don't like each other. You have to make clear to each of them that you're just interested in doing the best job for the Act and your fish."

Anne and Brent arrange introductions and give us a strategy for each group. "Approach each one on its own terms," Anne says, "but make them all accept that the darter case isn't going away, so it needs to be fought by everyone. Talk to people who do environmental lobbying on Capitol Hill, not the environmental lawyers. The enviro lobbyists are crucial. Mostly young, but they know best how to get through to Congress."

The most important group for us is the National Wildlife Federation. Next to the National Rifle Association, the National Wildlife Federation has more money and more political pull than any other such group. The Federation gets its money and clout from almost a million individual members, from chapters in every state, and from its *Ranger Rick* magazine, which goes to more kids than any other environmental publication. The Federation has a split personality, however. Many individual members are tree huggers, but they don't get to vote on how the Federation is run—only the state chapters do, and they're typically rod and gun clubs, not environmental activists. Here in the Washington office, though, the group's leaders are active environmental players. President Tom Kimball drives around in a chauffeured car, and regularly meets with senior senators and department secretaries; many of the enviro groups' leaders like so-called power lunches. The Federation rarely joins coalitions because it doesn't like anyone else speaking for it, but on occasion it has coordinated some of the country's biggest fights for air quality, water pollution control, and wildlife.

"If you get the Federation to go along with you, you'll get most of the conservative green groups," Anne says. She's set up a meeting in the Senate cafeteria with Martha Pope, the group's wildlife lobbyist. "Martha's a young pro. She'll give you the third degree, wanting to know whether

you're a 'humaniac'—that's what rod and gun types call the animal protection groups, the humane societies. The Federation doesn't trust the
animal groups' emotionalism. But if Martha likes you she'll tell the other
Federation lobbyists to work with you. And Ollie Houck and Pat Parenteau are Federation lawyers, but they're good people. Ollie is vice president and general counsel. Pat's starting a whooping crane lawsuit in
Nebraska. I've heard him testify on the Hill. He sounds like Dingell,
smart and powerful."

Martha Pope grills me over coffee in the Russell Senate Office Building cafeteria. She waves away the maps and charts. "No, no, I don't
want to talk about that yet. What I want to know is, what if a species is
blocking construction of a hospital, or a highway that's needed for access to some mountain community? Do you believe the Act should still
apply?"

"If you're asking," I say, "whether I think the law makes species
protection the top priority, overriding human welfare, no." She nods,
agreeing.

"If it's a conflict," I say, "and human necessity requires the extinction of a species, so be it. At that point I think we regretfully have to
say the species has to give way. If it's all or nothing, humans are clearly
more important."

"Good." Martha leans back. "I thought you were going to be one of
those people saying humans don't have that right."

"Well, humans have to have that right. But in most cases you aren't
going to face that kind of choice. There are going to be lots of cases
where the threat is being driven by mere convenience or profit-
maximizing. That's not enough reason to sacrifice a species. Even where
there's pressing human necessity, you usually can modify projects so the
conflict disappears. Change the location, the timing, the design."

Martha's eyes narrow. This means she needs to test my purported
flexibility some more. "OK. Tell me then, where do you personally
draw the line?" she asks. "Are you ready to accept there'll be cases
where species will have to be sacrificed?"

"Yes, probably. But remember, there are going to be many more
cases where saying 'humans-over-animals' is just a convenient argument to blow off the Act. If the Act's to mean anything it's inevitably
going to block some human development projects. The challenge is to
develop procedures and standards to make rational decisions. Stark

conflicts are going to be rare. Take our snail darter—it's supposedly the most extreme trade-off ever, but on the facts there's a strong case that you don't need to make a trade-off. It can be a win-win."

I roll out maps and charts. By this point Martha is ready enough to listen to the details. She asks a few technical questions. She clearly still wonders, however, how extreme our position is going to be in practice. Her skepticism is both personal and professional. We obviously want to make her and the National Wildlife Federation our allies, sharing confidences and strategies, opening her organization's national publicity and lobbying resources to us. But she doesn't want to waste time working on this issue with someone whose rationality is suspect, with whom she can't let down her guard. If she allows herself and her organization to be aligned with us, and we say something farcical to a reporter or a congressional committee, her credibility on the Hill, along with the Federation's, will be tarred by association.

"Look," I say. "Check out the legal arguments we've been making, that we'll make again if this goes to the Supreme Court. The proper way to do this, if there's an unresolvable conflict between a species and a development project, is to enforce the law and then bring it to Congress, where the merits can be fully explored in hearings. The Act isn't absolute, but it isn't supposed to be a casual decision tossed off by an agency official in some technical department, or by an unelected judge who isn't equipped to make science and policy decisions."

"You don't know much about Congress, do you?" she jabs. "This idealized review you're talking about—these guys don't work that way. Nobody listens with open minds to detailed investigations. Members who come to hearings like that already have axes to grind one way or another."

"Let's at least hold a strong position on this dam and the Endangered Species Act until the outcome in court is pinned down," I say. "If our case gets flushed before then, the Act gets weakened for everyone. We can't afford that."

Martha is hesitant. She confides that Baker's Jim Range has been lobbying her hard, trying to keep the Federation from supporting the darter. She didn't need to tell me that, so perhaps that's a sign she trusts us. "Range tells me the farmers were giving up farming anyway," she says. "He says TVA's cost-benefit estimates are good. He says you're just an isolated bunch of disgruntled leftists from the North."

"All crap," I say. "Anything you hear from Range, check with us. From what we're hearing, he peddles as much of TVA's line as he can sell. That's usually barefaced lies about the case, whatever they can slide by. Like saying the project is designed to create twenty-five thousand jobs, without saying that their industrial city plan has collapsed. If you don't know the facts, though, he comes across as authoritative and powerful, and charming."

"He *is* charming, and Baker is powerful," Martha says. "Isn't it true what he says, that local polls show the majority of people support the dam?"

"That's true now, yes."

"Well?"

"Look," I plead, "you think it's frustrating for us trying to bring the facts of this story to the Hill with the national press just yodeling about the little fish and the huge dam? You should see how it is back in Tennessee! Living under the shadow of TVA is even more frustrating, because we can't even get an investigative story from reporters who live only thirty miles from the dam and know better. TVA has given more than $100,000 to the local organization of dam boosters it set up to keep up a drumroll for the project, and they're the ones, along with the TVA press office, who get the local media coverage.

"And opinion polls?" I continue, "What do you think happens when TVA pollsters ask people in eastern Tennessee: 'Now, with $100 million and eleven years spent on constructing the Tellico Dam project, do you think it should be stopped for a little fish, or finished to provide its benefits for the public?' Give me a break. It's no surprise most local people now say, 'Finish it.' Think what a difference it'd make if a newspaper poll asked, 'If developing the Tellico project without a dam would create more economic benefits than the dam, salvaging most past expenditures and getting farmers back on their land, would you still prefer a dam?' Most people in eastern Tennessee have never heard there are better options for development without a dam. We need help getting out the facts. But getting them out at the national level may be the only way we'll ever get them through to the local public. Your federation could really help us there too, not just on the Hill." It seems that Martha understands the dam's demerits, and is somewhat reassured about working with us. We promise to keep in touch and coordinate plans. The rest of the day we work on making additional contacts with congressional offices, people in Interior, and reporters.

Over the next ten days we speak to almost twenty national environmental organizations. Some of the visits are intriguing and long.

The session with Christine Stevens of the Humane Society is at her beautiful home in Georgetown. The nation's most influential "humaniac," she's married to the chair of the Kennedy Center, who at one time owned the Empire State Building. Their home boasts carved woodwork, velvet upholstery, and exquisite wallpaper, a striking contrast with the offices and homes of environmentalists we've seen. Over the marble mantelpiece there's a painting by the French artist Maurice Utrillo. On the facing wall there's a Monet: the west façade of Rouen cathedral. They are not reproductions. Stevens bustles in and says, yes, yes, aren't they lovely, and settles down to work. She leafs through our information, maps, photos, and position papers, clearly wanting to understand the facts that we're asking her and the animal rights groups to carry around the Hill. Of course we realize the threat we've posed to the Endangered Species Act, I say, but we're doing all we can to make the darter a bulwark of the law rather than a fault line.

Stevens asks my thoughts on why a society should protect its endangered species—obviously a testing question like Martha Pope's, but different. In part it's for practical human reasons, I say, but also for much more—humans have a duty to steward vulnerable creatures with less capacity for conscious thought and action. I add that my father was born into a feudal setting in Europe and has raised his American family with a sense of legacy obligation to the land and wildlife, noblesse oblige, and an aversion to mindless and corrupt officialdom like TVA's. She smiles and nods vigorously.

I hope I'm not being hypocritical or prostituting myself in my alternating approaches to Pope and Stevens. Both demeanors feel true, and both end up in the same place. Within a day the materials I give to Stevens are being carried around the Hill by Defenders of Wildlife and other groups allied with her.

The National Audubon Society visit goes well, too. Audubon staffers Ann Graham and Steve Young take extra copies of our documents and borrow topographic maps to photocopy. Young pores through the cost-benefit ratio and pronounces it hooey, and shows emotion hearing stories about the displaced farm families. Graham worries that the snail darter decision might weaken Audubon's fight against the Dickey-Lincoln Dam—reporters might seize upon the Furbish's lousewort story and overlook that dam's shaky logic. But both see the linkage. If the darter shows the nation that environmental arguments bring common sense to boondoggles, that will help both cases and reinforce the Endangered Species Act.

The national office of Trout Unlimited signs on as a major ally. Saving the Little Tennessee is the number one priority for its southeast chapters, and Joe Congleton in Tennessee is one of the group's national directors. The World Wildlife Fund is generally uninterested. The Fund was at the center of the coalition that wrote the United Nations Convention on International Trade in Endangered Species, a hugely successful international environmental treaty, the direct catalyst for the Endangered Species Act in the United States. But at this point no one at the Fund's headquarters near Dupont Circle is ready to take on an endangered species crusade. The reception is warmer at the other groups on Anne and Brent's list, plus we make connections with the Native American Rights Fund and with Rural America, an advocacy group representing family farmers and noncorporate agriculture.

Is all of this schmoozing with citizen groups useful? "You bet," says Anne. "None of these groups was eager to welcome you into their circle. It's not just the darter. They were wondering who the hell you were—the farmers, you and your students, you're not part of any organization or network. You don't have any track record they can look at to see where you fit in. And you, Zyg, you're single-minded, pushy. They've wondered why you're doing this. Ego? Will you keep their confidences confidential? Thanks to Brent and me you've been hanging around for weeks, but you aren't being paid, so they don't know whether you'll follow through on what you promise. Will you be here if they get tough questions on Tellico, or if some committee announces an emergency oversight hearing? But it seems you're doing alright. Some of them probably wish you'd go away, but you've made it clear you won't. They may not be happy, but they'll fight on your side. You've put them in a pickle where they're going to get skewered along with you if you lose."

By my third week in Washington, all the environmental lobbyists I bump into on the Hill are carrying our message and information packages. Support starts appearing in their newsletters and, later, in their monthly magazines: "Don't let Baker pass a quick amendment cutting the snail darter out of the Endangered Species Act." We hear rumors that Baker is backing off his quick-strike threat. The word is, he wants to run for president and he knows the snail darter issue is being watched by the national environmental groups. Those groups helped get Carter elected, and their opposition would be trouble for his presidential campaign. Good.

## The White House, via the Old Girl Network

We've been bumping into the usual good old boy network on the Hill and in the agencies. But there's an "Old Girl" network developing too: intelligent women not yet in the top ranks but who, according to Anne, are all over Washington, know what's going on, stay in contact, and make things happen. Through her links to this network, we get to do intensive briefings in more than two dozen House and Senate offices and three federal agencies.

But Anne's most important Old Girl maneuver is to connect us to the White House. Joe Congleton in Knoxville tried fruitlessly to forge a connection with White House staff through a Georgian he knows, an old friend and confidant of Jimmy Carter's. On Monday of the second week, though, Anne announces that she's engineered an appointment for us with Kitty Schirmer and Kathy Fletcher, who work for Stu Eizenstat on the White House Domestic Council. Anne drives us over in her beat-up 1967 AMC Hornet, with its gearshift and right front door secured with duct tape. "No, not over there," she says as I get her wheelchair out of the backseat and start pushing it toward the West Wing. "The Domestic Council people are in the Old Executive Office Building," a five-story Victorian-Palladian monstrosity beside the White House. It's not wheelchair-accessible, so Anne has to leverage herself backward on her haunches up a long ramp of sandstone stairs to the first floor before she can climb back into the chair and wheel into a rickety elevator.

Anne introduces me to Kitty Schirmer, who in turn introduces me to Kathy Fletcher and then leaves for a meeting. Whether out of courtesy or interest, Fletcher is stuck with us for the next hour. She's a relatively young Old Girl but has a lot of campaigning experience. Before Eizenstat brought her into the President's Domestic Council she worked with a variety of citizen groups. She was clearly hired as a professional who could handle volumes of facts and policy analysis.

"You realize all of Washington thinks you're insane?" she immediately challenges us. "It's hard for this new administration to start a dialogue on the need for broad improvements in national environmental policy when everyone is laughing at your fish. Why shouldn't we just let this go away so we can get to work on the big things ahead of us like the Clean Air Act, and clean water, and toxics?"

"Yeah, we hear that a lot," we say. "It's a problem, but we can't go away. The case and the principle are too important. We're not going to let go of the injunction."

"You will if Interior delists your darter, or writes regs saying the Act only applies to future projects," Kathy interjects. She obviously knows the pressure points in our position, and knows Interior is leaning that way. Interior could officially acknowledge the transplants TVA has made to date, allow a couple more transplants, and then accept the TVA experts' testimony that the fish is no longer threatened with extinction and that the original river is no longer a viable habitat. We'd have to fight that in court, and we'd lose even if we filed the challenge outside Tennessee. What judge wouldn't defer to federal biological expertise in a convoluted case like this? Or if Interior issues authoritative regulations interpreting the law as *non*retroactive, that would immediately lead to a motion for rehearing in the court of appeals, which likewise would probably defer to Interior's specialized expertise in interpreting the law. Either way, we're toast.

"Now look, Kathy," Anne leans in. "Sure, it would be nice if this was a whooping crane case, or the issue didn't come up for a couple more years. But the environment doesn't line up its issues to suit the political calendar. This one's happening right now. It has to be confronted. If this case gets swept under the rug, everyone on the Hill will see the Endangered Species Act as just a paper tiger that dissolves under pressure. It'd be as good as repealed. This is the first national test of the law. If the Carter administration doesn't take it seriously now, it will never be taken seriously again. Besides, when you look into it, Tellico's a great case. Zyg, show Kathy the economics."

Out onto the table goes the map of the Tellico project area, showing the home shoals of the darter at Coytee Spring, the large swaths of farmland being taken by TVA for resale, the small, narrow reservoir, and the little dam down at the end of the river. Fletcher pulls her chair up to the map. This is a good sign. We've noticed that when people move to the map it means they're opening themselves to the analysis. We go through the project's cost-benefit ratios and alternative river-based development possibilities. "As you describe it, this dam doesn't make any sense," Fletcher muses. "But what would TVA tell me?"

"They'd say it was being built for shore land economic development, and wouldn't tell you the model city plan has been abandoned. Recreation is actually the major claimed benefit, but they don't talk about that now that the case is getting national publicity. The press wouldn't make much of this controversy if they knew it was a recreational dam. With the current energy crisis TVA will tell you about electric power from water going through the canal, but if you push them they'll admit the power part is trivial."

"So why, really, are they fighting for this dam and ignoring your alternatives—which, by the way, I'd never heard of?"

"Two reasons. Internally this is Red Wagner's swan song, an obsession he launched to rebuild the morale of a depressed agency. He and his senior staffers get apoplectic at the thought of local citizens talking back to them about how to run the valley." I tell Fletcher about the crack from a TVA insider who claimed that Tellico was suffering from "male menopause," with the old goats getting hot flashes when their potency is questioned. She nods a wry smile, understanding that phenomenon too well.

"But there's also the pork barrel. Tenn-Tom. The Corps and other construction agencies are building a lot of projects that couldn't survive public economic scrutiny. Federal pork water projects are a way of life for an entire political network, especially in regions linked to the Mississippi. Our Tellico case and the Endangered Species Act pose a direct threat to that way of life, and the coalitions here in Washington know it. Our case might bring the pork into the public eye. If America ever looked into the economics of Tenn-Tom or Tellico, many other projects—most of them—would be hooted out of the hall and the whole pork game would lose its meal ticket."

"So what do you want this administration to do?" Fletcher asks.

"Stop Interior from caving in. Secretary Andrus has been nothing but a disappointment on this. His proposed regulation gives a pass to all ongoing projects, and Interior itself drafted a Tellico exemption bill for Howard Baker."

Fletcher's eyes widen at this detail. "What? *Who* did that?"

"Keith Schreiner. Associate Director of Fish and Wildlife. He drafted a political exemption bill and gave it to Jim Range. . . . And you need to get the other agencies in line, and make sure whoever the president nominates for the TVA board vacancy knows what's at stake here. Help the environmental groups build the political case." Defending the snail darter and the Endangered Species Act serves Carter's own interests, we argue. Carter wants to make commonsense rationality a policy priority, with "zero-based budgeting" for wasteful and inefficient federal programs. In environmental policies he says he believes good ecology is good economics, and this is a perfect example. He can show a national audience that environmentalism isn't a fringe movement. It's good, sober national policy.

Throughout the hour Fletcher listens, taking no notes, interrupted occasionally by phone calls. Finally she stands up and says she must leave for a meeting in Eizenstat's office. "Before you go, however," she says, "I'll tell you something I think you'll like. When your injunction was first announced on the news, Frank Moore—he's the Georgia pol Carter hired as liaison to Congress—was in the Oval Office and said to the president, 'Can you believe they're stopping a big electric dam for a little endangered fish?' And Jimmy Carter said, 'I can't think of a better reason.' You should take heart from that. Jimmy was one of the only state governors ever to veto a dam. It's safe to say this president isn't dismissing you out of hand.

"But I'm not promising you anything on this," she continues. "Remember, you're one little issue in truckloads we have to deal with. But it's intriguing. Let's talk some more. Be sure to send me updates."

We wheel off to the elevator, down to the ignominious sandstone steps, and out to Anne's old Hornet. I wonder out loud what will come from the visit. Anne reminds me you never know who'll come through for you. You've just got to keep on pitching.

We hear nothing from the White House for the rest of the week, but the third week after the injunction I get a call to come visit Keith Schreiner at the Fish and Wildlife Service. This is the Schreiner whose name surfaces every time we encounter an obstruction in Interior.

According to Jim Williams, it's Schreiner who's been telling his staff we're "the enemy." I've never met him face to face until now, and it's immediately evident we'll never be buddies. He has a steady bureaucratic gaze with no twinkle in his eye, no laugh lines around his mouth. Stolid, heavy-set, and wearing a thin dark tie and an anonymous dark polyester suit, Schreiner may once have been a limber field biologist, but years in the little offices along Interior's stone corridors have reshaped him into a bureaucrat. His manner makes it clear he wields power within the agency and is involved at many different levels of institutional politics invisible to the citizen's eye. He does not have patience for nonsense, nor is he concerned with his own ego, having built his present position by commitment to the internal culture of the agency. He is suspicious of unpredictable players from outside the Establishment—like us.

"So you're from Tennessee," he greets me.

"Not exactly. I got fired. I'm in Michigan now." He already knew this, I think.

"You people have been causing us a lot of concern, you know."

"Yes." I almost say "Yes, sir." I consider this man an opponent, one of the obstacles that make citizen enforcement of environmental laws so difficult and so necessary. He is not a top official in the agency's leadership, but the fact that he can make things happen or not happen more effectively than political appointees gives him gravitas. I'm face to face with significant power.

"You know you could end up destroying the Endangered Species Act with this lawsuit of yours."

"Mr. Schreiner, you here in Interior could destroy the Act by undercutting our case. If you look into Tellico you'd see it makes really strong common sense, economic sense as well as biological sense."

Schreiner pauses. "Well, we in the Fish and Wildlife Service aren't interested in undercutting your case."

"No? What about the bill you drafted for Howard Baker?"

Schreiner looks poleaxed and angry. "Don't say that. Whoever told you that got it wrong. We merely responded to a request from a senatorial office for information on what kind of procedures the Service would have to go through to implement a delisting."

"A political delisting, you mean, that's what it proposes, not a biological delisting, and you didn't just give information, you drafted a statutory amendment that could make it happen."

"Look," says Schreiner. "Can we stop talking about that document? It was a mistake, but it's history. You should give us some credit. Watch what we do over the next weeks and you'll see the Department taking a strong position against any exemptions not based on science."

"Since when? What about your proposed regulation?" I may be impertinent, but we both know Interior has been hoping our case would go away.

"In the last several days we have had very serious discussions about that regulation. I'm authorized to tell you the final rules will be shaped to accord with your court of appeals decision."

Whoa—something is changing in the secretary's office! It could be that Secretary Andrus is finally listening to his scientists, but it's more likely that Kathy Fletcher and the Domestic Council wedged themselves into the middle of this. Perhaps by naming Schreiner to Fletcher as the guy who drafted that capitulation amendment, we triggered the gut fear of a civil servant—being singled out for doing something out of line.

"What about the delisting petitions for the darter and the river?" I ask.

"Those will be decided on the scientific evidence alone."

"But what does that mean? Are you going to let TVA take the juvenile fish stuck below the dam and dump them in other rivers? This fish has a two-year life cycle. The natural population will be extinct in two years, and set a terrible precedent for transplanting whenever there's a problem."

"No, Professor, I agree. Transplanting is not a fix. You can't know for at least five years whether a fish transplant is going to take." Good. Now Schreiner is talking like the savvy field biologist he once was.

"But doesn't it make sense," he asks, "to let TVA establish some transplant populations just in case you lose your case?"

"No. If we lose, it'll take TVA a year to finish the reservoir preparations, and that's enough time to do transplants—however successful they're likely to be. But the natural population in its natural habitat is scientifically the best place for the darter to survive. And reopening the river channel is the best way to save it there—the sooner the better. In the meantime the stress on the population from moving the down-drift juveniles back up over the dam to the Coytee shoals means you need to give the natural population every chance to survive there. Besides, do you know about where TVA wants to move those juveniles?"

"Yes. The application says Holston and Hiwassee Rivers."

"Do you know anything about those two rivers?"

"Not much."

"Do you know that the Hiwassee River drains the most chemically polluted area in Tennessee?" I ask. The Hiwassee is fed by flowage from Ducktown, Tennessee, a classic industrial sacrifice area. Law students read the classic cases where farmers near Ducktown complain about chemicals killing most of the vegetation there. The area is marked "Barren Lands" on the official state aerial survey. Railroad tank cars filled with acids and other chemicals still roll down tracks along the Hiwassee's riverbank to reach the main line, and if one ever spilled it would knock out the river. "Did you know the Holston has the wrong substrate," I continue, "big boulders rather than gravel shoals, and it's home to Eastman Kodak and other chemical plants?"

Schreiner had not known this, and he's listening. "We'll have to check on this," he says. "Are there other things you think we should know?" Now he's asking us, the erstwhile enemy, for suggestions. A good sign.

I point out that the record of Interior's implementation of the law over the past four years doesn't exist. If there are going to be hearings, what's Interior going to say about how it has successfully handled potential conflicts between agencies and endangered species? "Your lawyer Lambertson made it clear he wasn't interested in building that kind of record," I say, once again naming a name, wondering whether it will prompt the Interior Solicitor's office to get in line. "If your staff won't do it, you could let a couple of our law students into your offices to collect that data archive for you."

Schreiner flinches. He's not interested in having civilians come into his offices to tell him what needs doing. "Thank you for the offer. It won't be necessary. But I agree we should have that data collected." When I leave, we shake hands firmly, looking into each other's eyes, not with amity perhaps but, it seems, with a pragmatic understanding reached. "And," Schreiner says, "I don't want to hear anything more about that bill drafted for Baker, OK?"

"So be it," I promise. "OK."

I walk out of his office feeling sky-high. It's clear the secretary still doesn't want to talk with us, but so long as Schreiner has been deputized to negotiate a supportive new agency position with us, that's fine.

He has clearly listened to our arguments in detail, and now it looks as if he'll let science and the merits of the case determine the agency's stance. But if we hadn't found Kathy Fletcher, a fortuitous connection inside a White House open to environmental enforcement, would Interior have come around?

## Poison Dart Dodged?

It works. Within a week we hear Interior is going to change the proposed regulation to clarify that the Endangered Species Act applies to ongoing projects like Tellico. I am warmly invited to a discussion meeting with a group of attorneys in the Interior Solicitor's office. A young attorney, John Jacobson, pulls me aside beforehand.

"Good things are happening," he says. "We're going to deny those delisting petitions from TVA, and the regs will exactly track your court decision." He warns me, however, not to speak openly at the meeting about our strategy on defending the law. "The associate solicitor will be sitting in. She's big in Republican politics and there's a rumor she's one of [Nixon aide John] Ehrlichman's people." Many political appointees from the previous Nixon administration are now burrowed into civil service jobs, where they try to perpetuate old agendas within the agency, presumably with an antiregulatory and antienvironmental bias. In the meeting, however, she just listens.

Ron Lambertson, on the other hand, the head attorney who'd stonewalled us ten days ago, now is eager to talk. He wants me to know how very supportive of the Endangered Species Act he's always been. He'll help start collecting field data on how Interior has worked out negotiated resolutions for project conflicts under the law. The group goes through the economic arguments and maps, and I ask them to block any TVA transplants of darters outside the home shoals. It's not just a scientific issue. Tellico is an important precedent. All the lawyers agree.

"If you hear that Fish and Wildlife is planning to allow some transplantation into other rivers," Don Barry, one of the solicitors, tells me after the meeting, "please just threaten to sue us, so some of us here can make sure it doesn't happen. Or call whoever it is you're talking to in the Domestic Council." Hmm. Two very revealing comments.

How are we doing with Congress? From the Senate side we get a late-night call from Culver's aide Dick Oshlo. Oshlo has become a trusted and trusting ally. His girlfriend coincidentally is a friend of my research assistant back in Michigan, Les Iczkovitz; Hill politics is made of such accidental linkages. Oshlo has good news. "Sorry I couldn't call earlier. But you're going to get hearings, oversight hearings. Days and days of them. Culver has gotten mad at the pork-barrel guys pressuring him to roll over on this. He told me today it's a significant issue and it's not going to be railroaded past his committee as long as he has anything to say about it."

"Was he serious?"

"His face was bright red and it looked like steam was going to come out his ears, so I'd say yes, he was. He says he's forced Baker to promise he'll go along with hearings. I think you can bank on it. There'll be Senate hearings, and Tellico will be at the center of them." This is great news. We start brainstorming how to design oversight hearings to dig into the complicated realities of Tellico and significant issues of the Endangered Species Act's implementation.

The following morning, Spensley and Potter in Dingell's new Energy Committee offices nod with satisfaction. These two Hill veterans, central in building the Endangered Species Act and other conservation laws, have become gurus to us, though from here on they'll be less involved. "It looks good," says Spensley. "We think you've done it." With Baker retreating, no one else in the Senate will push it. And Dingell screamed so hard against the House exemption bill that Representative Beard had submitted on Baker's behalf that the Speaker won't even send it to committee. Apparently one of the secrets to success on the Hill is finding a champion or two, like Dingell in the House and Culver in the Senate, smart enough to handle anything thrown at them and known for towering rages. "The Department of Interior is definitely not going to delist. So you can start working on the longer term, building a critical mass here on the Hill. A lot of your focus should be on building your case's public image, because that makes a big difference politically. There's a lot of work to do now, not just preparing for hearings."

It looks like we've survived the short-term threat, and we've learned a lot, including a repeat of the lesson that nothing in Washington happens unless someone makes it happen. TVA and its pork-barrel allies, especially Howard Baker, began maneuvering to snuff out our court victory as soon as they heard about it. If we hadn't jumped into action with critical assistance from Anne Wickham and other friends, none of whom had time to do it themselves, the darter story would probably be over by now, ended by the iron-triangle insiders. But not this time. We've held off the quick strike and are going to get hearings.

Back in Leggett's office in early March, five short weeks after the appeals court gave us our injunction victory, Jenna Christy and I start planning for oversight hearings on the House side. Skip Spensley has moved on, but Christy can do a lot as we wait for the committee to appoint a new senior counsel. In formal terms she is just a grad student intern, but her science background, her grasp of the arcane systems of the Hill, and the fact that the committee members trust her will make her an important player in designing the House hearing sessions. And Leggett's receptionist-secretary, Marvadell Zeeb, will be here to help us, one of those deft congressional staff veterans who know everything that goes on and can be strategically helpful if they like you.

We notice a young kid—sandy haired, pink cheeked, fresh-faced, long, lean, and gawky—sitting hunched on a chair in the committee office waiting room. I wonder if he's here looking for a summer internship, or for someone to give him interview material for a term paper.

"Can we help you?" Christy asks.

"Uh, my name's Rob Thornton. I, uh, guess I'm going to be the new chief counsel."

"He just turned up today," Zeeb whispers to us out in the corridor, rolling her eyes. "We had no idea. They say he's Mr. Leggett's nephew. Mr. Leggett says the kid will be taking over Mr. Spensley's work for the subcommittee." Replacing Skip Spensley, the gifted legislative counsel with years of inside knowledge of the Hill? Skip Spensley, who was part of the group that shepherded the Endangered Species Act into existence? "The kid's apparently just graduated from law school, no experience with anything."

It looks as if nothing in these coming months is going to be easy.

# CHAPTER 7

# Endangered, on the Banks
# of the Potomac

In the early 1800s, on the farmlands and river-edge marshes that border the Potomac River, the revolutionaries who had fended off King George III went about consolidating a capital for their young republic. They built government offices, residences, shops, and taverns—the structures of civil society—and raised only one small city defense, Fort Washington, on the riverbank downstream. The British army, when it returned in 1814, did an end-around behind the fort, marched into the young city, and burned it to the ground. The lesson was hard but remains useful: consolidate, but prepare to defend.

The snail darter's defenders need to heed that lesson. The injunction is holding and the congressional quick-strike attempts are repelled. Our strategy now must be twofold: consolidate our successes as much as possible back home in Tennessee, on the federal government record, and in public opinion. In addition, we need to prepare solid defenses in anticipation of the attacks that predictably will be coming. Our opponents remain a potent threat. There's much work to be done, in several different realms of national governance—at least four of them.

In the executive branch we need to ensure that Interior's Fish and Wildlife Service holds the line in protecting the darter in the Little T, build an administrative record to show the Endangered Species Act is working, line up federal agencies to support the law, and ideally get the farmers back on their land and tourism encouraged in the valley to consolidate the idea of river-based development. As for the White House, the president's position on the darter and endangered species protection law looks wobbly. It needs to be informed and secured.

As to the courts, we're one hundred percent certain that TVA will ask the Supreme Court to take the case on appeal and repudiate our injunction. In anticipation, we need to deepen the arguments that won the injunction, bulking up the scant factual record Judge Taylor left us on the dam's bad economics and good alternatives. It's not clear we can do so ethically, because normally no new factual evidence can be added to a case during appeals, but we may be able to put data into hearings that can be cited to the court.

In Congress our strategic agenda is clear: *hearings,* the prospect of which helped hold off the first wave of attacks. Both the House and the Senate wildlife subcommittees have committed to holding hearings in the coming months. These will have to show the public and Congress the gravity of the mistakes behind the Tellico Dam project, and demonstrate how beneficially the darter serves public values and interests.

But the press may be the most decisive sector of modern governance for citizen campaigns like ours. The Fourth Estate is deeply linked to the political process, especially with regard to Congress. If we finally get thoughtful coverage of our story, including the condemnations of family farms and the Endangered Species Act's positive record, the public will understand the realities of an agency mandate gone awry. When the media brings embarrassing facts about an issue to the public's attention, the reverberations in Congress can be rapid and therapeutic.

## Within the Agencies and the Administration

The most immediate challenge is to prevent TVA from removing the darter's breeding stock from the Little Tennessee. Maturing juvenile darters trying to return to their home shoals now are milling around below the dam understructure that obstructs their return migration. TVA wants to net them all and transplant them elsewhere. Red Wagner insists he rightfully can make that decision, rejecting the Department of Interior's role as the lead agency in endangered species law. He refuses to "consult" with Interior, as required by the Endangered Species Act, unless he's permitted to transport the captured darters away from the Little T. His lawyers have even threatened to go to Judge Taylor to get an injunction declaring that TVA can transplant the fish wherever it wishes.

Working with Keith Schreiner in the Fish and Wildlife Service, we see positive signs. His superiors were irate when they learned that TVA was considering suing Interior to block its order to return captured darters to the Little T. They officially told TVA that any transplants away from the river are illegal. TVA filed a formal request that the designation of the Little T as the darter's "critical habitat" be reversed. After several months of discussions about the importance of original natural habitat, that too was denied by Interior.

Getting information from inside Interior has been immeasurably improved, moreover, by a confidential source I've cultivated within Fish and Wildlife's middle management. A year ago I was engaged by a private consulting firm to do environmental law workshops for the Fish and Wildlife Service's field staff and managers. After one session in the Midwest, which inevitably included discussion of the Endangered Species Act and the darter case, a quiet man with a Southern drawl stopped me in the corridor and confided that he was involved in many of the Department of Interior's internal discussions in Washington. Could we talk?

"What you-all are doing is what's right," he said. "I want to help, but if you and I work together on this it's got to be clear—no one can ever find out. You're too hot." Easy enough. It's like with Jim Williams—we soon decide that when I leave a phone message at this man's office, I'll be "Bill Evans," and when *he* calls *me* at an environmental group he'll also give his name as Bill Evans. Throughout the snail darter fight we talk regularly, both over the phone and in person. He is a bountiful information source, and has also discreetly added his voice to regulatory decisions that have gone our way within the agency.

I am accumulating other aliases with government informants—I am Chuck Cook with Jim Williams, Andy Graham when working with certain federal economists, Chris Peebles when talking with the federal historic preservation office, and Darral Stein (an anagram for snail darter) in several other places. The cooperating staffers understand that this isn't a joke, it's protective discretion on their behalf.

There are other executive branch issues. Though Wagner's final term as chair of TVA ended on May 18, with cheering crowds applauding him as he walked out of the agency's headquarters in Knoxville, Tennessee, he continues to exercise influence over his former staffers. The White House has appointed a sharp technocrat, David Freeman, to fill the vacant TVA board seat, and we want him briefed on the river alternatives and on Tennessee's treacherous political landscape. At Interior and in the Council on Environmental Quality—to which Marion Edey has just been appointed, departing her position as chair of the League of Conservation Voters—we had briefly pushed for formal reviews of Tellico's merits, but neither agency would agree to invade TVA's internal accounting.

More important, however, we need to push the White House to consolidate each federal agency's official position for upcoming congressional hearings. Numerous agencies clearly resent the Endangered Species Act's potential restrictions, so lining up supportive administrative testimony will be critical.

Edey passes on distressing news. President Carter knows virtually nothing about the Endangered Species Act and his policy people are advising him that the law is economically toxic, that he should focus on bigger and more defensible issues. If this is the White House attitude, the administration's testimony in the upcoming hearings could be a disaster. Kathy Fletcher echoes the warning. "We need information for the president showing the Act is working sensibly, that species are not blocking human progress all over the place."

Unfortunately the Department of Interior's records on how the law has been implemented over the past four years are a mess. Schreiner had promised to collect the data, but Jim Williams reports that the room where records from around the nation are supposedly being compiled is in total disarray. "My boss, John Spinks, told the clerk this data collection wasn't a priority," he said. "So there's just random piles of notes scattered everywhere, a lot of them with no indication even where they came from. No way is this mess going to produce credible hearings data."

We call Keith Schreiner and say it's time to go to Plan B on collecting the record of Endangered Species Act cases: call in our emergency volunteers. After a moment's hesitation, Schreiner picks up the phone and tells Spinks to clear an office and two phone lines for environmental law interns who will take on the records collecting project.

The next day my student Debbie Labelle, who had come to Washington as Anne Wickham's summer intern, moves into this office and begins setting up a national system to request and process records on Endangered Species Act conflicts from the department's twelve regional offices. In another two days she is joined by Mardi Hatcher, my trusted research assistant from Detroit. Mardi's husband, Winston, was reluctant to see her go but agreed when he heard the federal government couldn't prepare its defense of national wildlife policy without help from citizen volunteers. Over the next few weeks Debbie and Mardi compile official data on more than four thousand potential conflicts between endangered species and federal agency projects. Only three conflicts haven't been resolved by good faith negotiation—including, of course, Tellico Dam. The other two, both cases filed by the National Wildlife Federation, involve beautiful, endangered cranes. Everyone around us must be wishing it had been these iconic birds and the powerhouse Federation, not us and our ugly little fish, that were focusing the national endangered species debate. In the evenings Debbie and Mardi help prepare lobbying efforts on the Hill.

As the data comes together we send it to the Domestic Policy Council as well as the Interior secretary's office. Kathy Fletcher is somewhat reassured, saying that a successful record of species conflict resolutions helps the administration push federal agencies to testify positively in hearings. It would be more comforting, however, if the president's advisers didn't regard endangered species issues as a distraction.

## The Court

Our TVA insiders report in early May that an official request to the Supreme Court to throw out our injunction would be submitted within a week or two. It seems likely the Court will issue a notice of appeal, probably late in the year. Our legal arguments are already clearly formulated, so we decide to prepare more on the common sense of the case. Judge Taylor's trial record provided facts to prove a technical violation of the law, but he allowed nothing on the record to show the commonsense benefits available from a river valley project without Tellico Dam. The Supreme Court justices will probably be far more willing to uphold the snail darter injunction if they know there are beneficial alternatives to the reservoir. On appeal, however, courts aren't supposed to listen to any new evidence that isn't already on the record. In this case we need them to. Our strategy verges on the unethical: if we can prompt a House or Senate committee to authorize studies of the issue and place material on the public record, we can probably ask the justices "to take judicial notice" of the official congressional publications. So that's what we'll do.

Chuck Beddell, a Republican staffer on the Fish and Wildlife subcommittee and a friend of Anne's, has persuaded Rob Thornton, the new young committee counsel, to push the chair to officially request an "Alternatives for the Little Tennessee River" study from the University of Tennessee School of Architecture. Dean Donald Hanson has agreed to produce a rush-job alternatives analysis for the valley, but only if we can pay $15,000 in expenses for him and his students. Where will we find the money? The snail darter campaign is barely funded as it is by T-shirt sales and my maxed-out Visa card. Late in the afternoon after the conversation with Beddell, we land an appointment at the World Wildlife Fund office of Thomas Lovejoy, a preeminent expert on Amazonian biology who's fascinated by endangered species. Shortly after our defeat in Judge Taylor's court he'd offered to help transfer the fish to a zoo-based captive breeding survival program; we'd thanked him but told him we'd defend the fish right where it lives. The World Wildlife Fund is not only a deeply respected environmental organization, but also one of the wealthiest. Also, conveniently, Lovejoy is married to my wife's cousin.

After a long, careful discussion about the biology and economics of the valley, and common in-laws, Lovejoy agrees that the Fund will fund the alternatives analysis if the House committee officially requests it. Wonderful. A professionally prepared, officially authorized study will be compiled to show Congress and the Supreme Court that the darter case is not foolish obstructionism.

## Preparing for Congress: The Citizen Groups

Besides the World Wildlife Fund, more than a dozen environmental nongovernmental organizations work in the capital, and part of most days in Washington is spent massaging alliances with those groups we hope will stand with the darter in Capitol Hill battles. These organizations all theoretically support the same objective: protection of the environment and the Endangered Species Act. Their diversity prompts explosive tensions, however, and Baker's aide Jim Range has been working behind the scenes to drive further wedges between the groups, particularly between the more conservative rod-and-gun types and the humaniacs. At the National Audubon Society, for example, Range finds a willing listener in Mike Zagata, a duck and grouse hunter who's just been appointed head of Audubon's Washington office. "Dr. Zagata hates you, says you are extremists misusing the Act," Audubon staffer Ann Graham reports. Range has told Zagata the same thing he jeeringly told me: "Yeah, the public supports endangered species, but *it's a mile wide and an inch deep!* If we show them the law hurts human welfare, they'll turn right against it."

Mike Berger, a National Wildlife Federation Capitol Hill lobbyist, also begins backing away from the darter case. Oliver Houck, the Federation's General Counsel, at first had also tried to convince me to back off the case, but after seeing the facts and our determination he sighed and said, "OK, fight on, and we'll be with you." He and his senior counsel, Pat Parenteau, say they'll work to hold Berger and Zagata on board. "You're risking a lot," Houck says. "Some people here aren't happy about this. But we'll do our damnedest to back you up." The Federation and Audubon both have thousands of members and great press offices, as well as respected Hill lobbyists with more Washington clout than all the other organizations put together.

The Environmental Defense Fund's stance is dicier. That organization's attorneys find our presence and participation in the environmental groups' strategy sessions intrusive. We have been agreeing with a strategy of advancing endangered species cases circumspectly, not having dozens of new cases filed. "But you yourself just went right ahead on Tellico!" Bill Bishop of the Environmental Defense Fund screams at me. "How can you say we shouldn't be starting endangered species lawsuits around the country now, just because of a so-called backlash?" His organization may not stand with us in hearings.

For their part, the animal rights groups aren't happy about coordinating with the more middle-of-the-road groups. "I'm going to try to head off a split," Anne says. She persuades five groups, led by the Sierra Club, to call a gathering of all the citizen organizations to hammer out a group consensus for the House and Senate hearings on endangered species and Tellico Dam. Meeting at the offices of the National Parks and Conservation Association, the discussion starts with a hard line from Zagata and Berger, both fervent that the groups should back off to a more moderate position. "You can't go on thinking only of your snail darter," Berger snarls. "You're making the Act into an extremists' law. It's going to be a curse for us to carry around long after you've gone home." Unfortunately he's not clearly wrong on that.

As usual, Anne finds some glue. She reminds Berger of an article he'd written on the resolution of a conflict between endangered red-cockaded woodpeckers and commercial tree farmers in South Carolina. "With good faith on all sides, you said the Act works out reasonable solutions," she explains. "If we back off the Act now we'll send a signal that undercuts all the arguments you made there in your article. The darter case makes exactly the same arguments: good faith can resolve conflicts with a win-win for everyone."

Zagata tries another tack, raising the portent of future backlashes against the law based on its as-yet-unused Section Nine. We haven't been talking about Section Nine, but it's even stronger than Section Seven. It penalizes anyone who "takes" endangered species, including private citizens on their own property. "When that hits the fan," Zagata says, "the Act's doomed, unless we all start looking more moderate right now." But the group eventually forges a uniform position—we'll all stress that the endangered species law is working reasonably, using the facts of the snail darter case and Debbie and Mardi's Interior data, and we won't mention a word about Section Nine.

## The Media

As we prepare for the hearings, however, the "fourth branch" of government—the press—continues to be most difficult. In noble, challenging terms, James Madison and Thomas Jefferson framed the critical role that journalism must play in a democratic society—providing essential information to the American public so that citizens can hold their government to its high calling. As Madison said, "A popular government, without popular information or the means of acquiring it, is but a prologue to a farce or a tragedy, or perhaps both." Jefferson, deeming "the good sense of the people . . . the only safeguard of the public liberty," counseled that "if we think them not enlightened enough to exercise their control with a wholesome discretion, the remedy is not to take it from them, but to inform their discretion." And how was the public to be informed, in Jefferson's ideal? "Give them full information of their affairs thro' the channel of the public papers, and . . . contrive that those papers should penetrate the whole mass of the people. . . . Were it left to me to decide whether we should have a government without newspapers, or newspapers without a government, I should not hesitate a moment to prefer the latter."[1]

As in the nation's early years, the press continues to provide the daily flow of facts and opinion that reach the public's eyes and ears. When a situation is well covered by the media, Congress knows it's on the radar of public opinion and tends to address it on the merits. If it isn't, what governs is business-as-usual, tribal, off-the-radar insider Capitol politics.

Realistically, we always expected Tennessee's regional media to be passive. Some local newspapermen are true Tellico Dam believers, like the crusading editor of the *Tri-County Observer,* Dan Hicks, who gained national recognition for countering the Ku Klux Klan. His paper maintains loud support for TVA's promises of economic modernization, going so far as to call the Tellico Dam project "just a godsend [and] the greatest thing that ever happened to this area!" TVA's press office dominates local print and electronic media. In a few cases, when reporters have daringly written articles indicating doubts about Tellico Dam, TVA has stifled their inquiries by hiring them away to work for the agency. In other cases it directly intervenes; after his editors were pressured by TVA, Sam Venable, a senior Knoxville reporter confides, "I was told *I would not* column on Tellico!"[2]

We expected that the national media would be different, but the only national articles we see examining the dam's negative economics, land condemnations, and river-based development alternatives are in environmental magazines, never in major media establishments. Each day we make calls to reporters around the country trying to prompt stories that will reverse the conventional wisdom that asserts the snail darter case's irrationality. The darter continues to appear almost daily in newspapers and newscasts around the nation, but the coverage is shallow and dismissive, feeding a drumbeat of ridicule. The *New York Times,* for example, in a feature article two months after our appeals court victory, reported the darter-dam story in a manner that exemplifies most of the national coverage. Carrying the headline "Giant TVA Stalled by Controversy over 3-inch Fish," the March 22 story declared—

[It's] a classic struggle between ecology and economics, [between] the huge earth-and-concrete Tellico Dam [and environmentalists] who reject . . . arguments that the dam would be an economic boon to the area. They are not concerned that they halted the impoundment . . . after more than $100 million had been spent, . . . [quoting Dave Etnier] "the fish is more important than the dam." . . . Nellie McCall is adamantly against the project. . . . "The whole thing is just a land grab." [A local businessman, on the other hand, says] "It's a mess. . . . Things have gone too far to turn back for a little fish and we ought to finish it." . . . Now at stake is the Endangered Species Act itself: as interpreted by the courts, the Act does not permit [sensible balancing].[3]

The article parallels the media's typical framing of the story: We need to choose between ecology and economics—we implicitly can't have both; the snail darter story is nothing more than a little fish causing economic losses by blocking a huge (and implicitly hydroelectric) dam; the citizens resisting the "more than $100 million" dam are identified as "the environmentalists" who either care only about the fish, or care about the fish only to stop development; and if the press quotes landowners like Nell McCall, it's always implied that their lands are being taken for a power generation reservoir. Like most articles, the *Times* story also adds the knowing prophesy that our case now endangers the survival of the Endangered Species Act itself.

Even more distressing, the *Times* reporter who wrote the article, Drummond Ayres, had visited Tennessee. Members of our little group had spent time briefing him, taking him around the valley and into their homes. His *Times* article, however, didn't question TVA's "economic boon" claims, nor mention that the fish's survival might bring far more lucrative river-based economic development options, nor note that most of the "$100 million" expenditure was for beneficial infrastructure, not for the dam. The *Times* article cited Nell's pain at losing her farm but didn't note that most of her land, like most of the thirty-plus thousand acres of private land condemned by the government, is actually being taken for private corporate real-estate development.

This kind of news reporting has too easily made the snail darter the butt of antienvironmental jokes and outraged oratory around the country. Paul Harvey, the acerbic faux-populist radio commentator, regularly uses the darter as an example of environmentalism and regulatory government run amok. Ronald Reagan, who after leaving the governorship of California has resumed his syndicated media commentaries for the electric power industry, complains that the darter's blocking of a "dam [designed] to generate electric power" shows "the absurdity of the present endangered species law which gives priority to tiny fish, weeds, and spiders regardless of the merits of any proposed project."[4] Editorials around the country echo the same cant.

Our efforts to drum up informed coverage affirming the Endangered Species Act as well as the darter gain little traction. Every week we put together a new press briefing packet. Volunteers spend evenings collating stacks of photocopied pages on the floor of Friends of the Earth, and mornings dropping these packets into mailboxes at the National Press Building and other media offices around town. No discernible changes in coverage come from these efforts, however. The Associated Press wire service—with its constant electronic feed to more than six thousand American newspaper, radio, and television newsrooms—continues to carry the standard boilerplate darter-dam clichés around the country, not the essential facts.

Newspapers around the country failed to consider the project's foolhardy goals and economics, the extensive condemnation of hundreds of private farms for resale and real estate development, and the rich public values of the river's resources and ecology. The "extremism" narrative that prevailed in the media—greatly fueled by industry newsletters and public relations—consistently served to strengthen political attacks against the Endangered Species Act, environmental laws, and progressive regulation overall. Clockwise from top: *Knoxville News-Sentinel,* December 3, 1977; *Milwaukee Journal,* February 2, 1977; *News-Tribune* (Rome, New York), May 9, 1978; *Spokane Spokesman-Review,* June 17, 1977; *New York Times,* March 14, 1977; *Toledo Blade,* June 26, 1978.

"If a tree falls in the wilderness, and it isn't covered by the Associated Press newswire, did it really happen?" one volunteer muses bitterly.

Every month a few carloads of farmers or representatives of the Eastern Band of Cherokees come to Washington. They try to get their story through to the media and also walk the halls of Congress. We set up news interview opportunities so reporters can see the real people who have a personal stake in the snail darter's case. One day in May we send a press packet to four dozen journalists' offices in the National Press Building, and post a major interview notice in the Washington press's "Daybook," the listing sent to all media offices each morning:

> 10:30 a.m. TODAY, Cannon House Office Building, Front Entrance Portico, Independence Avenue—Press Availability: ENDANGERED SPECIES— THE TVA TELLICO DAM—Meet with Tennessee farmer dam opponents whose land is being condemned, and with a Cherokee representative about the ancient history at stake.

We gather the group by the Cannon portico at ten a.m., rehearsing the elements of the story that we want to impress upon the reporters. As displaced farmers, Nell McCall and Jean Ritchey sharpen some barbed lines about the communistic nature of TVA's land condemnations. Nell is visibly frail. Her husband, Asa, died in April, but Nell insists on soldiering on. She will move up here soon to live with her daughter and son-in-law, Margaret and Joe Sexton, who are there at the portico with us. Laura King is a quiet but regal presence for the Cherokees, ready to speak with forceful passion when the time comes. We wait. And wait. As a dispiriting hour passes, no reporters come. The little group squares its shoulders and marches off to the corridors of the Capitol, Jean leading the way, looking for politicians to lobby.

This is hard to take. Since Nixon and Watergate we've been hearing about the notorious liberal press. Shouldn't they take an interest in a story like this? Where are they?

Over these months we talk with more than a hundred individual reporters working for the big networks, National Public Radio, the newswires, and a host of newspapers and magazines—we speak with some of them more than a dozen times. Walter Cronkite, the dean of American journalism, directs two of his CBS researchers to talk with us. We spend an hour going through the data with them; they take copious notes. That evening we tune in to the six o'clock news hoping to hear

Cronkite at last tell the American public the awkward realities of the Tellico Dam. It doesn't happen. Cronkite begins the segment with, "We all have heard about the three-inch minnow that has stopped a $150-billion [*sic*] hydroelectric dam . . ." and the story goes downhill from there, quoting politicians who say that our injunction was a fluke and will soon be reversed in the political process, because our case makes no sense.

Through contacts with a woman at the Clean Air Coalition, we get a long interview with a reporter from the *Wall Street Journal*. He pays close attention to details of the project's shaky economics, with the Tennessee maps laid out on the table to show the broad extent of condemned private farmlands. He's impressed. "I'd never heard any of this," he says. "This dam looks like a classic pork project, completely irrational in economic terms."

Great, we say. When will he do the story?

"Oh, I can't write this," he replies. "It goes against our editorial policy."

"But," I say, "you're in the *news* department, not the editorial page."

"Doesn't matter," he says. "Our policy is not to publish articles like this." He doesn't clarify what "articles like this" means, and after two wasted hours he departs. The *Wall Street Journal* later publishes an editorial criticizing the Endangered Species Act, noting "all the dams and energy projects" that have been foolishly halted by the Act.

Oliver Houck at the National Wildlife Federation sends a note reminding us how the media coverage on our case is causing troubles far beyond Washington:

> I was with Johnny Jones and a crew of half-trackers [off-road outdoorsmen] in the palmetto breaks. He's the head of the Florida Wildlife Federation, and a more profane and dyed-in-the-wool conservationist you never saw. In his time, he was the only green in the state able to deal with the state legislators, which is like wrestling gators naked. We're fighting a highway across the Everglades. . . . We built a fire towards sundown, sat down on some pine stumps and broke out the beers. Johnny looked over at me in the firelight and asked if we can win this road fight, and I said yes, I thought we could. . . . He spat at the fire and said, "No way, if you bring another snail darter case. I mean that's *killing* us down here. I just walk in the room and they start making darter jokes. '*Darter! Darter!*' they say. I mean, it's *killing* us."[5]

There are a few somewhat brighter spots. We occasionally get a story by Ward Sinclair or Margot Hornblower in the *Washington Post.* The pieces are short—they're accurate about political events, noting pork-barrel pressures, but don't develop the farmland condemnation or economic information we've given them. "I know your story is important, but I just can't get the editors to see it," Sinclair apologizes. "The way I got that last story into the paper was a total fluke. I wrote that your case is starting a *pork panic.* When the headline writers saw that, they put it up at the top of the piece: 'Endangered Species Pork Panic Touched Off on Capitol Hill.' The editor didn't want to run the story, but with a headline like that, he had to."

Lucy Justus at the *Atlanta Journal Constitution* writes a good cover story for its Sunday magazine, with poignant photos of the scalped lands and diminutive dam, and descriptions of the land condemnations and questionable economics—although she doesn't mention the alternative river-based development options. We thank her profusely nevertheless, and I carry copies of the article all over Washington hoping national journalists will pick up the theme. Colman McCarthy does a nice op-ed in the *Times,* arguing "The Snail Darter: There's More to It Than a Little Fish." But neither of these stimulates national media reporters to move beyond the fish-dam cliché.

My neighbor back in Ann Arbor, Charles Eisendrath, who teaches environmental journalism, had at one time been a *Newsweek* reporter. "You've got to start *a news climate* rolling," he says, "and the articles you've gotten just aren't doing it. The story needs to have *legs,* you need to find *hooks* for a continuing series of articles digging into the case."

Hooks and legs, but how? Late one evening I call former *Washington Post* ombudsman Ben Bagdikian, who is now teaching at Berkeley. Bagdikian is revered as the conscience of the journalistic profession. "I'm sorry," he says wearily. "I can't tell you how to reverse the way your story is getting covered. This is an era of industrial arrogance. There's a strong tide running against environmentalism in the press and in politics." He adds, however, that "maybe you could persuade Ruder & Finn to take on your case."

"Who's Ruder & Finn?" I ask.

"They're a press relations firm. They're talking about doing 'public interest public relations' work. Try them."

We call Ruder & Finn, explain the essential facts of our case, and ask whether it's true they help public interest groups like ours, gratis. "We do," says the young guy on the line, "and this sounds like a good case for us to get involved with."

Great. When can they start?

"As soon as you can get us a check, just to cover our expenses. Around $20,000."

No one, including the World Wildlife Fund, is going to give us money for public relations. If that kind of funding is what we need to bring information into the media and political processes, our fling with democracy doesn't look promising.

We do encounter, however, several other hopeful media breaks. As the summer begins, we think we've hit the jackpot: Both CBS and ABC send film crews to the valley to do stories on the snail darter battles. The farmers and other volunteers in Tennessee spend hours with each of them. CBS's Al Wasserman and his crew make multiple trips, getting to know many of the farmers and the mordant details of TVA's land condemnations for resale. ABC's Roger Anderson of the TV news magazine *20/20* is interested in the David and Goliath angle of the battle between local citizens and mighty TVA, and he loves the quip about TVA's "male menopause." Harry Reasoner's take on the story for CBS's *60 Minutes* focuses on the farmers losing their land to TVA's real estate scheme, and he also probes the project's economics. The crews go back to New York and we wait for the stories to run.

After a few weeks I call Kathy Moore, a CBS producer for the story, and ask why it isn't being shown. She sighs and tells me, "It's a great story, it really is, but we just can't find a niche to put it in." ABC producer Aram Boyagian has the same answer. "I don't know if we'll run it," he says. "We've done a lot of environment stories lately." When I note there's a Cherokee angle, he retorts, "And we've done a lot of stories with Indians, too. I don't see this as having enough of a different personality." So what would they need as a "hook" to run the story they filmed? The answer I get from Boyagian: if we "find Senator Baker *shtupping* a milkmaid along the banks of the Little Tennessee River," that would probably be enough of a hook.

Why is the press that Jefferson and Madison lauded as democracy's critical public information system so passive, so avoidant of publicizing significant, newsworthy realities? Part of the answer seems to be the ever-increasing shift of journalism from a societal vocation to a market-driven business where newsrooms, like network entertainment divisions, are supposed to earn advertising revenue. "Infotainment" is the evolving mode in every sector of the press. News coverage is designed to be easily engaging, generally upbeat, diverting, not depressing, and not politically irritating to advertisers or increasingly conservative owners. "Getting the whole story" for the public audience is no longer the proud professional objective.

In part, some problems with media coverage are direct reflections of political pressure, and not just in Tennessee. When Justice William O. Douglas presented his article on Tellico Dam to the *National Geographic* magazine, Red Wagner and his TVA lobbyists intervened and persuaded the editor, and those of other magazines, that it was too radical. Douglas finally had to publish the piece, "This Valley Waits to Die," in *True, The Man's Magazine,* where it was promoted on the cover alongside a blond starlet wearing a skimpy swimsuit and carrying a snorkel, a forum hardly befitting the work of a Supreme Court justice.[6]

But there must be other reasons. "Your story may be too complex, with too many issues," guesses the Sierra Club's Brock Evans. "It's impossible to sum it up in ten words. Reporters know their editors want stories to be simplified, easy for readers to understand."

The national convention of the Outdoor Writers Association of America is being held in Athens, Georgia. We decide it's worth a plane ticket to present the Little Tennessee story to reporters who might convey the facts of the river's threatened fishing and recreation values to the American public. Knoxville reporter Sam Venable lets me sleep on a spare bed in his hotel room and sets up a session where we both describe the river's resources and explain why the dam makes no economic sense. A number of writers seem interested but tell us their editors, like Venable's, don't want controversial political issues in the outdoor and sports pages. The foray doesn't produce a single published story.

In Washington, we observe, journalists are exposed to a constant flood of opinion and insider gossip generated by the press offices of industry groups that now are targeting endangered species. Texts of industry "newsletters" and research foundation "white papers" are remarkably similar. We regularly see the same message, often in exactly the same wording: "extremists" have been listing "hundreds" of previously unheard-of species like the snail darter, using them to "block economic progress" in dozens of important projects around the nation like TVA's Tellico Dam; the Endangered Species Act itself is an example of "inflexible government regulations" that are far too broad, a threat to the economy; and a "reasonable balance" needs to be restored to environmental law. These slick publications reflect the lobbying positions of multibillion-dollar business coalitions. From the U.S. Chamber of Commerce on down, the Endangered Species Act is a target of opportunity. Widely distributed, these communications create a cloud of establishment political opinion that reporters as well as members of Congress accept as conventional wisdom.

A friendly Hill staffer shows us a copy of a mass-mailing letter that appears to have been generated by right-wing strategist and marketer Richard Viguerie, who builds mailing lists using techniques he pioneered in the 1964 Goldwater presidential campaign:

> As you know, the anti-development forces of *left-wing environmental extremists* have been using the *extreme inflexibility* of the *Federal Government's Endangered Species Act* to halt some of the most important public works projects in our nation in their tracks! . . . *Private property rights* that made our nation great are *under constant attack* by *government regulators*! please consider joining *thousands of angry citizens* in the *Citizens Coalition for Endangered Species Reform* to tell Congress that *enough is enough!*[7]

It doesn't matter that this "reform coalition" has just been invented in a lobbyist's office. A deluge of such well-packaged and well-financed advocacy—disguised as "grassroots" movements—shapes the political climate. Without a PR firm, our homemade press packets and factual briefing papers delivered to office staffers are droplets in the flood. The environmental organizations' press efforts are a good deal better than ours, but from what we see, reporters are basing their articles far more on the deft campaign being waged by the other side.

The media's avoidance of complex thinking may also reflect a low opinion, apparently shared by many within Washington, of the intellectual ability and interest of the American populace. "You've got to realize," the Associated Press's Dave Espo tells us. "I'm not supposed to write anything at a higher level than Fogg eighth grade." Huh? The Fogg Index, it turns out, analyzes words used in journalists' stories, scaled in terms of relative education levels. According to Espo and other reporters, most American media target their text at a Fogg reading level of eighth grade or lower. Only a few national newspapers—the *Times,* the *Post,* the *Wall Street Journal*—target their text at a Fogg level of high school graduate or higher. In societal terms, the Fogg Index raises a larger chicken-egg question: Is it a self-fulfilling prophecy? Does a citizenry that's fed a stream of dumbed-down sound bites and predigested summaries lose the ability and desire to think beyond sound bites? Or are the media merely adjusting to the preexisting reality of a low-functioning electorate, where science and learning are regarded with suspicion rather than respect, a public with its head in the sand and its butt twitching in the air?

For whatever reason, many of the people we're meeting in the capital—reporters, lobbyists, politicians—exhibit condescension toward the mass of Americans outside Washington. It may indeed reflect an assumption that the majority of voters think politically at Fogg-8 or less. More kindly it may be that so many intricate issues and decisions are batted around in the capital each day that it's virtually impossible to stay current unless you're wired into a Washington network and also read the *Post.* By the time most of the flood of daily decisions in this city—many of them narrow but significant—could be communicated and explained to a nationwide audience, they would already have been replaced by new fast-paced issues. Thus most of the avalanche of daily political information, horse-trading deals, and gossip that goes on within the insulated Washington bubble stays there, while the rest of the country sees only edited summaries of half a dozen selected items that emerge each day.

The media's treatment of the snail darter does not seem to be dictated by the personal politics of reporters and editors. Some certainly are conservative, but many conservatives are also in favor of the conservation of nature. Other journalists hold generally progressive inclinations, which should help us, but we don't see it in the newspapers and newscasts. Perhaps most people in the media, like most of America, have always heard about TVA as a heroic national success story, the New Deal's brightest rose. Perhaps they feel hesitant to tarnish that image.

There are two common journalistic *styles,* however, that are clearly having an effect on our case—the "two-hand-balance" approach, and the truncation instinct. The "two-hand-balance" approach was evident in that *New York Times* March 22 article that merely noted on one hand TVA's claim of "economic boon," and on the other hand Etnier's contrary statement that "the fish is more important than the dam." Journalists and their editors and producers too often merely present juxtaposed sound bites from opposing sides of an issue, and leave it at that. Yet such an approach to journalism is not at all a "balance," and leaves no place for statements and discussions of relevant and unarguable fact.

Ross Gelbspan, a *Boston Globe* reporter, notes with exasperation that this kind of reporting violates a professional duty. If a controversy concerns only arguments over pure *policy,* then of course a reporter should quote both sides to give the audience access to the debate. But in matters of fact, reporters have a further obligation to investigate and to inform their audiences what is factually accurate and what is not—in other words, it would be completely irresponsible for a reporter to say: "Senator A says the water bill passed, and Senator B says it did not; there you have it, today's news on the water bill." It's the stark facts of the darter versus dam case that are most ignored.

"Truncated expansion," the second problem that dogs us, is equally problematic. As a British reporter tells us, "There's a standard formula for selling papers: *Simplify, then exaggerate.* You see it all the time. It grabs an audience but doesn't require them to be perceptive."[8] This helps explain the sad reality that once our story had been framed in a simplistic way, with a focal image and a set story line, it's been extraordinarily hard to change it. Hundreds of journalists thus continue to report on our case in truncated terms: the litigation is simply a conflict between a Very, Very Tiny Fish and a Very, Very Big Hydroelectric Dam—a lawsuit that violates common sense and is putting the whole endangered species law at risk.

We hope the approaching hearings will do better than that with the facts of the darter versus dam story.

## Working on Congress: Hearings

Preparations for the congressional hearings continue apace, including even some enjoyable moments. When the Tennesseans went to the Capitol after their failed press event, they cornered Mississippi Senator John Stennis, wizened champion of dozens of Corps of Engineers dams. Backed into the wall by Nell McCall, Stennis had to listen to several minutes of a small, smart old lady's righteous indignation before extricating himself and shuffling away as fast as he could. Next they decided to confront Howard Baker. Alfred Davis tells the story:

> We were . . . trying hard to find Senator Baker, who was avoiding us, and somebody figured out he was going to a meeting upstairs in the Capitol building. There was this hallway lined up with some guards and lots of reporters, people . . . at least ten deep. I'm thinking, how are we going to get to Baker? We have on our best Sunday suits, mind you, but we probably still look a little bit like hillbillies. And Wendell Perry's son from Vonore was with us, he's about sixteen. When we got to the front, there was a big guard. He looked over at us and said, are you all reporters? And before I could say anything, the young Perry boy said, "No, we're just farmers." And I thought, "Well, we're going out the door now." But he turned around and said, "Son, don't ever let me hear you say that. Farmers feed the world. What are you all doing here?" And I said, "We're from Tennessee, and we're against Tellico Dam, and we've come to see Senator Baker, and he don't want to see us."
>
> The guard says, "Well, that little weasel is right over our heads; he's got an office right up there," pointing up above his head. And he said, "He'll be coming down here in just a few minutes, and if you want to see him, go back down that hallway there, and he'll come down that back elevator. Be standing in front of it. And when that door opens and when he starts to shut the door on you, you just step in the elevator with him."
>
> So we quickly got Miz McCall and a bunch of the others and just got together when the door opened—I really didn't realize 'til then that Baker was just about my chest tall—but he saw us, stepped out of the elevator, and guess what? He said he had heard we was in town, and was so glad to see us![9]

Baker listened to them with a warm smile on his face, then shook their hands and hurried away. Even though he surely wouldn't change his mind, it was a satisfying ambush.

It's clear to everyone, however, including the press, that there will soon be action in Congress on the Endangered Species Act and the snail darter, and most of the American public is hearing that the commonsense outcome will be reversal of the injunction and a weakening of the "extreme, inflexible" statute itself.

Looking to broaden political support, we engineer meetings with a series of nonenvironmental organizations that might lobby for us down the road if they knew the facts of the case. Tom Garrett, who himself had drafted part of Section Seven, now works on sustainable agriculture; he sets up meetings with the National Farmers Union. Laura King comes back to Washington for a meeting with representatives from numerous religious groups at the National Council of Churches' conference room; she talks movingly about the Cherokee cultural and religious sites facing destruction. At the National Congress of American Indians, Ella Mae Horse takes an immediate interest in the dam's threat to the Cherokees and will try to get information out onto the Native American networks. An executive at the Association of American Railroads, Richard Briggs, tells us that his rail company members will oppose any federal project or program that subsidizes barge traffic. He'll see if any southeastern railway lobbyists will actively take on our issue, but doubts it because no barges are likely ever to use the narrow, antiquated eastern Tennessee waterway to access a remote dead end on the Little T.

On the Hill we find interest from the congressional Environmental Study Conference study group, where the staffers provide a welcoming forum for our briefings on water projects, the Endangered Species Act, and our case. Though these study group people are already with us when it comes to prospective votes, it's useful for them to absorb the complexities of the Tellico project and the law. They'll pass on information to other representatives and senators whenever Endangered Species Act debates occur.

The congressional study group provides some satisfying moments. It invites TVA's Capitol lobbyist, Larry Calvert, to come to an afternoon workshop on Tellico Dam, and three of Red Wagner's staffers immediately fly up from Knoxville. Lawyer Charlie Wagner stands awkwardly in front of a roomful of sharp staffers and delivers the standard agency line: "Tellico is an important project, with industrial development, flood control, and barge navigation being blocked by extremist environmentalists." But here, with an intelligent audience that knows some of the right questions to ask, the TVA arguments accepted with blind credence in Tennessee and the pork committees fall flat.

The Hill staffers pepper them with questions: "Isn't the Timberlake industrial city a bust? Hasn't Boeing pulled out? Isn't flood control a negligible element? Is there any evidence that barge navigation will ever be practical in the foothills of the Smoky Mountains?" The TVA representatives stutter and stumble, and after a painful hour beat a re-treat to the friendlier confines of the appropriations committee offices.

Appropriations committees continue to welcome TVA warmly; the farmers and other citizen-opponents who come to testify at the annual money hearings continue to be rebuffed. As they have done every year, the appropriations committees continue giving the dam additional funding, and their committee reports echo the members' anger at the snail darter lawsuit: "The Committee does not view the Endangered Species Act as prohibiting the completion of the Tellico project at its advanced stage and directs that this project be completed as promptly as possible in the public interest."[10] According to House and Senate rules, however, appropriations committees do not have the power to make or amend substantive law on money bills, so, in terms of author-ity as well as meaning, their words in the reports don't undercut our legal position.

Anne Wickham tells us, however, that I need to register as a lobby-ist. Unregistered, I may be breaking the law: we're clearly making orga-nized efforts to influence legislators and legislation on the Hill. Anne is terminating her own lobbying registration. She's just been appointed to a position in the Carter administration's State Department, working in the office of Oceans and International Environmental Affairs—although, skeptical about an appointee who had been earning less than $10,000 a year, the General Services Administration has been holding up her personnel clearance. (Awaiting Senate confirmation, Anne must also discontinue her nocturnal guerrilla public-works project: driving her old Hornet through town looking for intersections with handicap-inaccessible sidewalk curbing; when she finds one, an accomplice jumps out and dumps clumps of wet Sakcrete to harden by morning into rough wheelchair ramps.) Anne continues to be a wise and vigilant adviser, and her introductions continue to open doors for us around the capital.

Within a week of our lobbying registration, the *Christian Science Monitor* runs a comical feature on the annual report of Washington lobbyists, noting a horde of newly registered lobbies ranging from the Bendix Corporation on a brakes issue, the Australian Wool Corpora-tion on a textile bill, down to "the Zygmunt Platter [*sic*] Lobby . . . interested in conservation and enforcement of environmental laws" (missing a chance to note the funding line on the form: "SOURCE OF FUNDS: sale of T-shirts"). Our entire annual budget probably totals less than any corporate lobbyist's golf budget for courting legislators.

In what by now has become our standard practice, every day includes visits to congressional offices in the House and Senate. Of the 535 offices, the 100 or so clearly on our side just get occasional updated information packets, regularly delivered by volunteers. We ignore the 200 or so irretrievably committed to the pork barrel. For the rest, we and our green group allies allocate assignments for visiting individual members. Getting access to members is not easy, however. Appointments are rarely available. You go to the office and try to catch the member coming in or going out, or between visitors. When ambushed in their offices, members will usually shake hands, listen for ten seconds, then say "Good, why don't you talk to my LA [legislative aide]." Often, it seems, the member looks over your shoulder and sees a well-dressed lobbyist who's followed you in, and with a quick wave of the hand he leads the potential source of campaign finance donations past you and into the inner sanctum. In our experience, a remarkable amount of members' schedules involves time spent talking with potential campaign donors.

After trudging the halls of Congress it's easy to become cynical about one's elected representatives. The particular merits of the issues on which they vote don't seem to matter very much. Most can speak straight to the cameras, often wittily, stating things they often know to be untrue. One motivation is the simple desire to be reelected, and with that in mind they make deals and vote based on regional loyalties, party lines, horse trades for votes on bills they care about, campaign contributions, and lobbying treats. "When you get right down to it," Anne says, "a lot of them are hacks." Time spent in Congress is a ticket to a good life, honored and feted, with power and perks. When they leave Congress, if they've taken the right positions, there will often be a lucrative niche waiting in an industry-funded lobbying firm.

"Mom and Dad figured out pretty quick when they came to see the politicians in their offices," Margaret Sexton says. "They were all trading. You scratch my back and I'll scratch yours. It didn't matter what the facts were, they were just in it for themselves. Very few're guided by the facts. It's all about dealing, dealing to get things for themselves, get power, get money for their friends, get reelected."

Even when we're able to talk with some of the most principled members of Congress—Leo Ryan, Dale Kildee, Bob Edgar, or John Moss in the House, or John Heinz or Mark Hatfield in the Senate—there is a hesitancy to get into the merits. They are apologetic: the issue is interesting, they'll vote for us, but they can't take the time to understand details because they have multiple duties on their appointed committee assignments, don't sit on environmental committees, and the Tellico Dam is not in their home state.

Our most hopeful congressional initiative is a bit unusual. We of course have always wanted some kind of probative economic study of the Tellico project and have never been able to persuade one into existence. A while ago, however, the American Rivers Conservation Council's David Conrad suggested that for congressional hearings, and perhaps for the Supreme Court as well, we needed a credible economic analysis of the dam and its alternatives, "and the GAO might be the way to do it."

"What's GAO?" I asked.

"General Accounting Office. It's Congress's own investigative bureau, run by the Comptroller-General." The GAO was originally a group of accountants reporting to Congress on bookkeeping tasks. In the past decade, however, Congress has asked it to do technical investigative work on controversial questions on which politicians handling a hot potato need straight information. A GAO report sounded just like what we'd been praying for. But GAO generally won't respond to just any congressman's request, Conrad says. It has to be pushed by an official request from at least one committee chair, more if possible. So Brent Blackwelder advises us to persuade some chairs to issue a request letter—probably Murphy and Leggett in the House committee.

In practical terms, we have no idea how a GAO request letter gets drafted. We do know, however, that if a document is going to be significant, you should always try to draft it first yourself. A draft in hand gets the momentum going, frames the discussion, and usually shapes the structure of the final product—and you know better than anyone else what's in it, and what isn't. We needed a good draft letter, economically sophisticated and specific enough that the GAO investigators could not avoid digging into the tough truths about Tellico Dam.

Brent had been working with Paul Roberts, an economist drawn to antidam efforts by an aversion to the fictionalized economics of public works pork-barrel projects. Roberts said he'd consult for free if we'd take him to a nice place for dinner. It sounded like an excessive but necessary expenditure from the T-shirt-funded darter budget. In the hushed power atmosphere of the Monocle restaurant, with swank lobbyists and Senator Patrick Moynihan and his entourage sitting at nearby tables, we sketched out four paragraphs for a GAO study request letter. The GAO should be asked—

1. to quantify the value of past expenditures that would be lost if a dam was not completed.
2. to quantify the future value of resources and project expenditures that could be developed for public benefit without a dam.
3. to determine the accuracy of TVA's cost-benefit claims for Tellico, analyzing the dam in the context of the four adjoining dams already in existence.
4. to analyze the extent to which TVA's projected benefits could be achieved by alternative development plans without a dam.

The dinner tab was worth it. Roberts's approval of the language gave us confidence that our charge to the GAO would contain no technical errors.

The next day we're happily surprised to hear Leggett and Murphy both say yes, they're inclined to sign onto the GAO request for us. Murphy, the bare-fisted politico from New York City, who'd been buttonholed in his office by Hank Hill, had apparently bonded with the tough kid from the base of Lookout Mountain.

Murphy's chief aide, Carl Perian, looked at me quizzically when I'd asked about signing onto a GAO request. "What's in it for Murphy?" he asked. "He typically gets something when he does people favors." Perian was teasing. Murphy was widely rumored to take bribes from a number of foreign lobbyists, but he couldn't expect citizen environmentalists to play in the same league as Arab oil companies or the Korean merchant marine fleet. Winking, Perian opened a locker and displayed some past gifts to the chair from cash-strapped citizen groups. Front and center was a reddish-orange snake, lying coiled in a large glass jar, pickled in formaldehyde. "See this? Poison sea snake. Murphy got it from environmentalists when he agreed to hold hearings on a proposal to cut a sea-level canal from the Pacific through Nicaragua to the Atlantic." So I pulled out the watercolor print lithograph of the snail darter done by Dolores Roberson, Exhibit 12 at the darter trial. Perian looked it over and said with a grin, "I guess that'll be enough," sliding the print alongside the snake into Murphy's office locker.

But Leggett and Murphy say they won't sign the GAO request letter unless we have at least some cover from a member of Congress from Tennessee. They don't demand we persuade a Tennessean to actually cosponsor the GAO request, but to avoid being accused of meddlesome carpetbagging they at least have to be able to say truthfully that a member from Tennessee told them off the record to go ahead with this.[11]

Where could we go to get a Tennessee politician to sign on, even just verbally? The most promising was Harold Ford from Memphis, whose legislative aide, Scott Morell, had been my student in Knoxville. As an African-American member, Ford was closer to the Black Caucus than to the rest of his state's delegation, and had been raised in a progressive political family. But Tellico was far from his district, and Ford ultimately said no.

That left Albert Gore, Jr., who had been styling himself an environmentalist. Hank and Sara Grigsby's husband, Chuck, went off hunting for Gore, who a week earlier had given Hank and Peter Alliman the runaround. On that visit to the capital, Hank and Peter had phoned Gore's office, said they wanted to talk about Tellico Dam, and were told Gore was out attending hearings. After several fruitless hours searching for him at his various committee assignments, they went back to the Longworth Building and climbed the rickety attic stairs to Gore's stifling little headquarters; Gore was just a first-term congressman and had one of the lowest-status offices.

"It was funny," says Peter. "The receptionist was on the phone so we stood there waiting. She was talking on and on with a friend about how Gore is hiding out because he wants to duck some people from Tennessee who're looking for him to talk about a dam. She finally hangs up the phone and we grin and say, 'Hello. We're those people from Tennessee and we'd like to talk to Mr. Gore about Tellico Dam.' The embarrassed secretary insisted Mr. Gore was not in, but she promised he'd get back to us soon."

A week later Hank is back in Washington with Chuck Cook, and Gore is there to greet them with a big smile on his face. He says he'll give them five minutes, and ultimately he gives them almost an hour. Hank gives Gore a full recitation of the economic and environmental case against Tellico. In addition to his enthusiasm, Hank is firecracker-articulate, able to lock onto a point and drive right through it with personal power that comes from a temper under control but visibly lurking below the surface.

"Gosh, from what I've been reading in the papers I didn't know any of this," Gore says. "But you probably are right on the merits, because otherwise you surely would have lost long ago."[12]

Would Mr. Gore give his oral approval—oral is all we need—to the request for a GAO study? "Yes," says Gore. "You can tell Chairman Murphy I am behind the request *one hundred percent.*"

The minute they leave the attic office Hank phones me in the Merchant Marine committee office, where I am standing by, and reports that "Gore has just given his oral agreement to support the GAO request." When he hears that, Leggett signs the letter and says, "Chairman Murphy's over in the main committee room in closed executive session. Get a staffer to take this letter in for his signature."

At this moment a call rings into the committee switchboard. Committee secretary Marvadell Zeeb, who likes us, takes the call: "No, Chairman Murphy's not here. He's in a committee meeting." She writes down a message on a yellow note card, thanks the caller, hangs up, then turns to us: "It's from Mr. Gore's office. It's urgent. Mr. Gore wants Chairman Murphy to know that he's just told some Tennesseans they can say he supports a GAO study of the Tellico Dam, but he doesn't really want that study. He asks Mr. Murphy please not to issue the request." Zeeb shows the note to Jenna Christy, then turns to us and says, "Alright, Mr. Murphy is down the hall there, in executive session and [pause; wink] I guess I'll have to deliver this to him in another five minutes or so." Grasping the request letter, Jenna and I race down the hall to the back door of the committee room. She shows the letter to Murphy's aide, carries it into the committee session, and comes back smiling a minute later with signatures of the chair and the senior Republican member splayed across the bottom of the page. Signed and sealed, it's immediately delivered by hand to the General Accounting Office. An hour or so later, when Murphy's meeting is over, he phones Gore and wryly tells him, "Your message got to me too late."

And no, Murphy would not call back the GAO request. "Look, Albert," he says, as Hank stands there, listening. "Those boys from Tennessee beat you fair and square." We wonder why Gore, a bright young legislator with an altruistic environmental stance, would double-cross home-state citizens trying to prove one of his central precepts— that good ecology and good economics go together—on Tennessee's biggest environmental issue of the decade. It doesn't matter. We're finally getting an official economic investigation of Tellico Dam, and it's coming from Congress's own sleuth, the comptroller-general of the United States.

The head of the GAO study team, Monte Canfield, calls the day after the request letter arrives on his doorstep. He's started pulling a team together for the study. "Jeez," Canfield cringes, "we didn't want to get into this mess. How did you ever get Jack Murphy to sign this letter?"

"Well," I say, "in part it's because we gave him a bribe."[13]

# CHAPTER 8

# The Snail Darter Gets Its Congressional Hearings

Back in March, oversight hearings on the Endangered Species Act as a whole and the snail darter in particular had been tentatively scheduled for June in the House subcommittee and July in the Senate subcommittee. Having seen eruptions of public attention created by other congressional oversight hearings, we're salivating at the prospect. Walking the corridors of Congress we often pass hearing rooms crowded with reporters, bundles of TV cables duct-taped to marble floors and snaking out and down corridors to mobile broadcasting vans for remote feeds to the evening news. Imagine how this kind of coverage carrying Tellico Dam facts to the public could unmask the pork barrel.

The scheduling of hearings has been an important deterrent to congressional sneak attacks on our case. With a month to go, preparing energetically for our Tellico Dam hearings, we're working equally hard with the citizen groups preparing for general assaults on the Endangered Species Act. The data collected by Debbie Labelle and Mardi Hatcher from internal records in the Department of Interior will be critically important for the sessions focused on the law as a whole. They show thousands of successfully negotiated resolutions of species conflicts. The Endangered Species Act works well, and reasonably. Our major worry is strident criticism of the law from several federal agencies likely to appear at the hearings. We've heard that a number of agencies that dislike the law are preparing to lambaste it, while the

Carter administration has been losing whatever ability it had to control the political agenda.

For the hearing sessions focused on the darter and Tellico Dam, we think we'll have two big weapons to validate our lawsuit and the law as a whole—the General Accounting Office Report commissioned by the House committee over Albert Gore's objections, and the alternatives study being prepared by a group at the University of Tennessee's School of Architecture under Dean Donald Hanson. When Monte Canfield, responsible for preparing the General Accounting Office report, meets with us the morning after receiving the letter requesting an analysis of Tellico Dam, Jenna Christy helps overcome his instinctive distrust of working with citizen activists. "The committee has strong confidence in the integrity of the citizens' information," she tells him, and over the next few weeks it becomes clear that Canfield and his staff do need our help. The Tellico story is complex, and at every turn TVA tries to blunt General Accounting Office staffers' inquiries.

"Did TVA give you a map showing the project area boundaries?" we ask. Well, no. "Okay, take this one." We give them our topographic map that clearly outlines the full area condemned by TVA for the now-abandoned model city development, with the neighboring Great Smoky Mountains National Park noted to emphasize alternative development potentials. Over the following two months we stay in constant contact with Canfield and his staff, discreetly channeling most communications through Christy, who has been designated by Chairman Leggett as his committee's liaison.

The General Accounting Office crew gives the project a deep probe. They collect data and interview dozens of people around the valley, request our help in finding strategic pieces of data, and circulate report drafts to us and to TVA for comment and further suggestions. For their visits to Tennessee, Peter Alliman spends days arranging interviews, pulling together economic assessments of the valley's soils and agricultural values, and doing a requiem analysis of TVA's grandiose, deceased Timberlake model city. Tennessee activist Jeff Mellor undercuts the agency's inflated calculations of flood control benefits. Another local activist with energy expertise, Bill Chandler, deconstructs the trivial claims for electric power attributable to Tellico's canal. Joe Carroll, a professor from Pennsylvania, shares data showing that TVA has previously taken more than a hundred thousand acres of condemned lands around existing reservoirs—including more than forty thousand acres as "prime industrial acreage"—but over the past dozen years has found tenants *for only sixteen acres.*

From TVA, the comptroller-general's investigators are getting obfuscations and evasions. Irritated, the General Accounting Office group is becoming convinced that Tellico Dam is an economic write-off, and, even better, it seems they'll be willing to say so publicly. But their timing is a problem. Canfield tells us the report won't be finalized until October. "We're only prepared to give the committees raw data in June hearings," he says, "not any conclusions. This stuff is politically supercharged. We want the analysis to be impregnable before we present it." A delay until October, however, will smother critically important evidence. By then the hearings will be over and the report will fall between the cracks. We tell Canfield that "Leggett and Culver will be furious if some form of analysis isn't presented at their hearings." He reluctantly yields. He will give an oral summary of the draft conclusions at the hearings. That will have to do.

Then another problem. A month before House hearings, young Rob Thornton at the Merchant Marine and Fisheries Committee sheepishly tells us our hearings have been postponed indefinitely. There won't be House hearings this year on any controversial issues like the darter and the Endangered Species Act. "You can have your hearings over in the Senate, but not here." Jenna opines that Thornton isn't yet confident enough to run a major hearing likely to attract heavy hitters and explosive fireworks. The House committee will instead schedule a series of innocuous endangered species hearings—on penguins, state revenue sharing, and imports and illegal sales of skins, feathers, and ivory.

Worse, Thornton tells us that Chairman Leggett, far from being "furious" about General Accounting Office delays, is no longer interested in getting the analysts' conclusions; the report can wait until next year. This is terrible. The Senate committee won't feel free to consider the report in its July hearings if the House committee that requested the analysis hasn't yet accepted it. "Look, Rob," I tell him, "it's not just the GAO study you asked for. Your committee also requested the University of Tennessee's alternatives study. You'll have egg all over your faces if you ditch two big studies that you yourself requested."

"Alright," Thornton concedes. "But not hearings. We'll schedule an informal staff presentation for the GAO report and the alternatives study a day or two before the Senate hearings. Mr. Leggett and some of our House staff will listen to them summarize the reports and then thank them for their work."

With the two studies' presentations shakily assured, we turn our full attention to the Senate preparations. There's nagging uncertainty about the White House, however. We've been hearing that the Bureau of Reclamation, the Forest Service, the Federal Highway Administration, and the Army Corps of Engineers plan to line up in fundamental opposition to Endangered Species Act enforcement and the public scrutiny it can bring. Having President Carter on our side doesn't mean the federal agencies will be on the same page. The president's political honeymoon is over, and his power over national agendas has eroded. In 1972 Reverend Jerry Falwell negotiated an alliance between the nation's evangelicals, the U.S. Chamber of Commerce, and the Republican Party. The GOP would adopt family values and the evangelicals would support initiatives against government regulation. In 1976 Carter, himself a genuine born-again evangelical, had hijacked the New Right strategy, temporarily pulling Falwell-recruited evangelicals into the Democratic column.

In office, however, Carter not only has coalesced GOP resistance by his willingness to tighten business regulations, but more significantly has offended evangelicals by his unwillingness, despite his personal religious convictions, to push mandatory federal restrictions on abortion. Evangelicals are deserting Carter for the newly Christianized business bloc on the Right. The GOP stokes the heat by escalating issues surrounding abortion, Carter's support for a Department of Education, and his decision to return the Panama Canal to Panamanian ownership under international law. Returning the canal, they say, will undercut America's global stature and undermine a quasi-biblical theory of American exceptionalism. A federal Department of Education will enforce secular humanism within the nation's schools and undercut homeschooling. These issues, endlessly hyped, are major obstacles to Carter's policy agendas.

Within the agencies, Carter's liberal appointees are having trouble changing the internal cultures of the departments they're trying to lead. In Agriculture, our friend Rupe Cutler, assistant secretary for the Forest Service, has been grinding against coordinated resistance from timber industry lobby pressures within and outside his agency. After a few months of fifteen-hour days, he's taken to a hospital on a stretcher late one evening, laid low by bleeding ulcers and exhaustion. As he explains to me later, "Try as I might, I can't budge my own bureaucracy. I've worked and worked at it, but they've just been treating me like a *mushroom,* you know what I mean? They keep me in the dark and feed me a lot of manure."

The Carter administration is having much the same experience in other agencies where good-government outsiders who don't understand Washington have been appointed as department heads. "There was bound to be trouble," says my colleague Bill Goldfarb, who teaches environmental law at Rutgers. "They should have known what happens when you put hens in charge of the fox house."

But perhaps most destructive of the president's political credibility is a "hit-list" mess. During the New Hampshire primary, candidate Carter said, "I personally believe we've built enough dams in this country and I will be extremely reluctant as president to build any more." Whether or not Kathy Fletcher and Kitty Schirmer at the Domestic Policy Council were encouraged to do so by our visit, they clearly had made critical analysis of pork-barrel water projects an active White House agenda item. They helped arrange a letter to Carter from seventy-four senators and representatives urging him to reject economically wasteful projects. Carter had his Office of Management and Budget do a quick study of water project economics, and the initial review showed seventy projects that were questionable, including Tellico Dam. To capitalize on the new president's election victory it was essential to make an early, successful show of power that would give him credibility with Congress. The hit list could do this. But someone in the Army Corps leaked the list, and congressional anger quickly started building. Carter's staff cautiously whittled the hit list down to sixty-one, then to forty-five, then to thirty-eight, then to thirty-five, then to eighteen. Disappointingly, Tellico Dam wasn't on the shortened list. "We needed to focus our political resources," Kathy reports. "Stu [Eizenstat, her boss] decided not to go after projects like Tellico where citizen lawsuits are already doing the job."

When the president finally made a formal announcement cutting funds for eighteen dams and canals, including the $4-billion Tennessee-Tombigbee Waterway, senators and representatives from the impacted states erupted, not only because their projects were being cut but also because the White House hadn't told any of them that the cuts were coming. (Carter's congressional go-between, Bert Lance, had tried to call all of them the previous Friday afternoon, but they all had already left town for the weekend.) Old Democrats that Carter needed on his side, including John Stennis of Mississippi, Lloyd Bentsen of Texas, and Robert Byrd of West Virginia, angrily drafted and attached an amendment to a Senate employment bill, declaring any funding cuts would be legislatively reversed. "Carter doesn't understand," a Hill aide says. "It took a lot of political effort to get those pork projects authorized. You can't just throw them away overnight. He could've won by just going after one or two projects at the beginning, but now he's united Congress against him." Carter seems not to have realized that on the Hill everyone knows most projects' economics are hoaxes, but they don't care so long as the public is unaware of it. Early in his presidency he's already cringing. Almost no one fears him.

On a flight to Atlanta Hank Hill again found himself sitting near Hamilton Jordan, Carter's chief of staff. Jordan apparently didn't recognize Hank, because he continued chatting with his companion about the president's changing fortunes. Hank overheard Jordan say, "We're really catching it from Congress. We didn't expect those dam project guys to have so much clout. Jimmy figured if these projects really sucked in economic terms he could just cut 'em. We didn't realize how much pull the appropriations guys have with the rest of them, and now this thing is blocking other stuff on our agenda. We're cutting a deal. We were down to eighteen of the seventy projects Jimmy originally wanted to kill. We'll give them half of those if they'll agree the remaining nine won't be funded this year."

"Is that as stupid as I think it is?" asks Hank on the phone from Tennessee the next day. "Doesn't it send a message of weakness? Won't Congress in the next session just re-fund the nine projects that're temporarily cut?" Hank's right. People in Washington are smirking about the naïve White House's retreat. The zero-budgeting, commonsense president from grassroots Georgia backs down as soon as he crosses the pork establishment. We warn Brent Blackwelder, Anne Wickham, and the National Wildlife Federation people. They groan, and agree that Carter's people don't understand how to play the game. If you have to compromise, make sure you're getting at least a solid half-loaf, and leave your opponents with some bruises they'll remember the next time they come against you.

This president, however, has brought his Christian tolerance to the capital's political battlefields, with disastrous results. He seems to assume that all congregants in his new political community are motivated by good faith and shared common goals, or at least are open to redemptive change. But a player who turns the other cheek, we've learned, doesn't build political strength. "This president is a lamb," says Anne. "He thinks he can convince politicians based on what's good for the public, but they couldn't care less. When they undercut him, he caves and thinks they'll owe him one, that they'll give him the next vote out of guilt or pity. He just doesn't get it. You need to be tough. Your enemies have to know you can hurt them." A belief in technical objectivity and good faith bipartisan negotiation may have worked for Carter when he won a navy commission to command a submarine, but in Washington it marks him as politically naïve, a target, a true believer who doesn't understand the full complexities of the governing process of which he's suddenly found himself the titular head.

"I know, I know," says Kathy Fletcher when we tell her. "But Jordan and Eizenstat say we can't win this one. The pork guys have agreed to let the president have a water resources council that will examine project economics in the future, and we'll settle for that."

Will the White House be able to control the agency officials who testify at the Senate oversight hearings? "I don't think you'll need to worry about the federal agency witnesses," Kathy Fletcher tells Anne after a meeting at the president's Domestic Policy Council. "TVA will be allowed to present its position, but it will stand alone. Everyone else will toe the line. What we need from you is Endangered Species Act data on each of the agencies that'll testify—the number of potential conflicts that got resolved in each one." Debbie and Mardi immediately start polishing separate agency reports from their research, identifying for each testifying agency what its experience with the law over the past three years has been. They've almost finalized their survey of federal agency case files and are ecstatic about what they've found. Almost 4,500 potential conflicts catalogued—low-level and high-level cases where agency projects or programs potentially could have hurt some endangered species or critical habitat. In virtually all of them either there wasn't a problem, or the agencies were able to negotiate reasonable adjustments to work them out—changes in design, location, timing. This record is going to be critical for the Carter administration's defense of the law. We also need to get the data out to all the environmental groups that will be testifying.

"What are the odds these hearings will be our knockout punch against TVA?" we ask Brent and Anne. We're wistfully hoping that stripping Tellico economics naked in front of a national audience will delegitimize the dam and reinforce the law's political stature to such an extent that TVA will be forced to give up and shift to river-based development options.

"That could be," says Anne. "It all depends on how strong the evidence in those hearing rooms is, and how the press covers it. But no matter what, you desperately need to have the hearings be as good as they can be. And it's you who have to make them that." Hearings don't just happen, she reminds us. They're carefully prepared demonstrative productions, arranging the right evidence and the right issues so the right messages will come through on the official record. "The people who stage these hearings," Anne says, "the chairs, senior members, committee staffers—they already know all the essential facts. What they want to do is build a record, showcase the facts and policy conclusions they want their colleagues and the public to see. And embarrass their opponents."

Opposing members and witnesses will surely try to derail our defense of the endangered species law. We're lucky that hearings in our case will be chaired by Senator Culver, who supports the Endangered Species Act and thinks our case is right on the merits. Culver not only seems to care about the issue, he's now riveted on making it the first major hearing of his chairmanship. "But you can't rely on committee staffers to do the job," Anne says. "They're overworked, and none of them knows the facts as well as you do." We'll need to coordinate closely with Kathi Korpon and Dick Oshlo on Culver's Senate committee. The way the hearings are prepared will make a huge difference in how effective they are. "When you go into hearings it isn't enough to be correct in every detail," Anne continues. "You have to be sure you have the right witnesses and evidence to get it across in public."

Any hesitations we have about inserting ourselves into the committee's planning for the hearings are dispelled with three weeks to go. "Can you guys be discreet?" Oshlo asks. "Culver has told us to set up four days of hearings beginning July 20, and Kathi and I need a lot of help. Too many people already want to testify," he says. "For most of them we'll just have them submit a statement for the record. We want you to help us figure out who gets real time in the hearings. On both sides."

"Is this unethical?" I ask Anne later that evening.

"No way," she says. "It's how things are done around here. The staffers know you've been sitting in the bulls-eye for four years, and they trust you. You know who'll make good witnesses and who won't. For the opposition, too. Hearings have to be balanced if they're going to be persuasive. The staff won't follow all your suggestions, but they'll use a lot of them."

The hearings will be scattered over a week and a half. In Tennessee on a weekend in late June we start arranging our witnesses for testimony at the hearings. A major concern has arisen, however. The School of Architecture has done virtually nothing on its alternatives analysis. Dean Hanson ruefully explains he's been in the hospital, bitten by a brown recluse spider. "But don't worry," he says. "I'm OK now, and it'll be fine. We've done this before." Unconvinced, we nevertheless proceed to outline for Hanson what his report needs to contain, using some of Peter Alliman's planning ideas, sketching out suggestions for charts and maps showing the agricultural lands, alternate industrial park sites, a tourism highway running from the interstate up through the valley to the Great Smoky Mountains National Park, and a number of other catchy images. With trepidation we hope the Hanson study will materialize in time.

There's a potluck supper at the home of Fran Scheidt, an energetic volunteer from the Knoxville flower club, to strategize roles for the hearings. Forty people are at the supper, at least half of whom want to drive up to Washington for the occasion. Not all will be able to testify. Six carpools will make the trek, arriving two days before hearings start. Some people will camp out on friends' couches. The Davises, Ritcheys, and a dozen others will find an inexpensive motel in the Virginia suburbs. Nell McCall will stay with her daughter Margaret in the Maryland suburbs. Before they make the trip we'll pin down what each speaker needs to cover and what statements will be put on the record. We'll choose witnesses likely to make strong impressions and sway members' opinions, making sure the testimony doesn't just voice anger or duplicate what others have said.

Over the next two weeks there's a constant flow of phone calls with committee staffers, contacts in the agencies, the tense jumble of environmental groups, and other assorted players. Countless practical details for the hearings need to be covered—some quite delicate—and include establishing a list of those who will receive official invitations, figuring out which hearing rooms to reserve, outlining the testimony that is being drafted in each agency, devising the order in which environmental groups will speak, and determining which reporters can be pulled in for the hearings.

Dick Oshlo pushes us for media publicity to attract other senators to attend the hearings. "Culver doesn't know how many senators are going to show up," he says. "He's just a junior senator and can't insist." We call reporters from national and small-town news bureaus to let them know of the upcoming battles over Tellico and the Endangered Species Act, emphasizing the first two days' lineups—the congressional attackers, economic revelations on Tellico and dam project alternatives, gut-wrenching testimony from salt-of-the-earth farmers being thrown off their lands for a federal real estate scheme, the Carter administration versus pork barrelers opposing endangered species protection, and environmental groups standing together, drawing a line in the sand against enemies of the law. Hearings notices are posted in the daily Daybook listing sent to every news agency covering Washington politics, and calls are placed to dozens of specific reporters, from the *New York Times* to a news service covering rural Alabama.

Frenetic preparations are plagued by the fact that I've been hit by a strange illness. I'm spending sixteen hours a day coordinating hearing preparations with witnesses all over the country, doing virtually all communication by phone as I lie curled in fetal position in the sweltering top-floor bedroom of David Conrad's commune. I am unable to stand, I have a constant excruciating headache, and the left half of my face is contorted into a twisted, distended gargoyle leer that slurs my speech as I talk into the phone. What's going on? I don't know, but I won't go to a doctor; too much work to do. When the hearings are five days away, however, late in a painful evening the medical intern girlfriend of one of the housemates insists that she drive me to her neurology unit at Veteran's Hospital. There a series of apprentice neurologists are stumped by my half-faced grimace, until one discovers a wen in my ear and asks, "Have you been exposed to chicken pox?" Yes, my neighbor's kids all had chicken pox when I spent a few days back in Ann Arbor.

"Aha! Ramsey-Hunt Syndrome! Bell's Palsy!" the bright young intern exclaims. "You have a pock there in your ear," she says, "and there'll be a lot more inside your head along the seventh and eighth nerve stems. That's what twists your face and hurts so much."

A parade of young neurologists comes by to observe the unusual diagnosis. My question: how long will it last? "The Manual says 'Indefinite duration; may be permanent,'" they say, "but it's related to shingles, triggered by chicken pox, and both of those usually go away in a few days. Wait and see." I drag myself back to David's place, crawl upstairs to bed, and at dawn get back on the phone, still in fetal position. With two days to go, thank God, I'm able to walk again, slowly, and my facial muscles are stiff but almost normal, except when I grin. Back at my desk at the foot of the stairs at Friends of the Earth, we count down the hours until the start of the hearings. When the Tennesseans arrive the evening before the sessions, Anne jabs and teases me in front of them, wanting them to see how my face still twists into a loony leer if I try to smile.

We're optimistic as we head over to the Hill on the morning of the first day of Senate hearings. Most of the pieces are in place. The General Accounting Office report and—despite our earlier concerns—Dean Hanson's alternatives study report both had come together very well at the House briefing on Tuesday. The General Accounting Office chief sternly declared that TVA's arguments for the dam were full of "questionable assumptions," and Hanson presented eighteen graphics illustrating how attractive and lucrative a river-based development project could be. Anne promises she won't do anything to make my face contort in front of the committee, though I'm not entirely sure she can be trusted.

There's an immediate dampener as we arrive at the Senate committee chamber: no bundled TV cables extend outside the room's heavy doors. Continually glancing about for arriving senators and reporters, we huddle with Dick Oshlo and Kathi Korpon and a couple of other committee staffers at the back of the dark-paneled hearing room and go over last-minute details. The session was supposed to start at ten o'clock. At 10:15, besides our Tennesseans there's just a scattering of people in the audience, no reporters, and only two senators on the dais, Chairman Culver and Jim McClure, the committee's junior Republican.[1] Several Tennessee representatives from the House make a last-minute entrance, but no one else. Howard Baker is nowhere to be seen. At 10:20 Culver gavels the session to order and tells those in attendance that "Senator Baker is unable to be here. He must prepare for the campaign finance debate. But he wants to express his deep concern over the implications of the Endangered Species Act for the Tellico Dam." A short statement from Baker is put on the record, suggesting that the law "needs to be tempered by reason and flexibility," and should be amended to protect only "widely-known" species that have "significance," a polite form of the diatribe he's been using in private conversation. As the darter's primary foe in the Senate, why isn't Baker here?

Two congressmen from Tennessee deliver short speeches: TVA's plans will bring great benefits. . . . Tennessee needs the jobs and economic growth. . . . The dam is almost complete, and in polls asking whether it should be finished most people now say yes. . . . It's crazy that a big project like this could be stopped by a little fish. . . . The outsiders who brought this lawsuit are extremists who don't care about the community. . . . There are lots more snail darters in rivers and creeks all over the state. . . . The Endangered Species Act should be changed so this kind of thing won't happen again . . .

They both repeat the theme that it's too late to turn back, citing the recurrent sunk cost argument appearing in TVA lobbying and media stories, including the *Times* article: TVA has poured so much money and concrete into the project (most of it since Wagner found out about the darter) that it's no longer possible to rethink the original plan, so let's finish the dam.

We've been trying to come up with a metaphor over the past two years to counter the sunk cost argument. One not especially catchy attempt was, If you've stacked a lot of old furniture for a bonfire but then find out everything is valuable antiques, do you say, "Too late, the bonfire's been prepared," and light it up? That attempted metaphor gets no traction.

After the pro-dam legislators leave, the session works out well enough. The Interior and Council on Environmental Quality representatives don't know much about Tellico but they say the right things about its poor economics, and emphasize that the Endangered Species Act has worked well in more than four thousand potential conflicts, with only three instances of a recalcitrant agency, including Tellico, failing to work out acceptable adjustments. Portions of the testimony are lifted straight from our position paper and fact sheets.

At the strong suggestion of our clandestine source in Interior we've urged the committee to issue a specific request for Keith Schreiner to attend, and he handles a few nasty questions from McClure. "If agencies try to comply in good faith," Schreiner says, "only the rarest cases will ever have to come here to Congress for resolution."

Tellico is mentioned several times in the general discussions about the Endangered Species Act. As the discussions continue, not a single reporter has yet shown up, and Culver and McClure remain the only senators present. Then the chamber door behind the dais opens and Senator Jennings Randolph lumbers in and takes a seat. Great! Having the full committee's chair here makes an immediately tangible difference in the tone of the proceeding. Randolph sits there with a blank look on his face, however, clearly exhibiting little idea of what's going on. He fidgets for a while, then scrawls a note and, handing it to an aide, points to me. The piece of paper is delivered and I read it: *"Where's the* Post*?!"*

I'd tried to pull a fast one. I'd called his staffer yesterday, urging Chairman Randolph himself to come to the hearings. "Why should he bother?" asked the aide.

"Because this is his committee's hottest issue this year, and a reporter from the *Washington Post* will be there."

"Oh, okay, I think he'll come, then." The mention of the *Post* clearly made an impression, but in truth, Margot Hornblower of the *Post* had said only that she *might* be there. So I'd called her at home before breakfast this morning to say she should attend the hearing, because the full committee chair would be there.

"Okay," she said. "If Randolph's coming I'll be there."

Now Randolph's here, but the reporter isn't. Randolph fidgets some more, glances at me irritably. I shrug helplessly. Ten minutes later, however, Hornblower swishes into the room and takes a seat. All three senators immediately take notice and shift forward in their chairs. Randolph furrows his brow, focuses his gaze on the witness who is speaking, and to all appearances begins listening intently. But the hearing's first-day lineup—even the short ichthyologists' tussle between TVA's expert Ed Raney, whom we'd seen back at the trial in Knoxville, and our ally from the Fish and Wildlife Service, Jim Williams—proves to be fairly boring. Margot squirms. There's very little confrontation going on here.

When we open the *Post* the next morning, Hornblower's article is on an inside page and headlined, "Wildlife Species Act Endangers Project; Change in Law Opposed." It almost totally misses the point, focusing on the old saw of the law's supposed potential for obstructing economic development. "The ESA may be endangering 52 projects ranging from the $4-billion Tennessee-Tombigbee Waterway to small stream-dredging operations in Virginia and Maryland," she writes. Where in the hearing session did Hornblower get that? She apparently pulled it from a memo that Baker's aide Jim Range has been peddling around. To reinforce it she adds some of McClure's statements at the hearing criticizing the law's inflexibility. She barely notes Interior's testimony of successful conflicts avoided, and mentions Tellico only briefly at the end, saying there may be an economic reassessment. But maybe she'll write a sharper story probing Tellico Dam after the second day of hearings.

The second day is about the darter and the dam, and we dominate because TVA has brought only two witnesses. We'd suggested the committee invite two TVA biologists and several front office officials, including Mike Foster, whose theories were central in justifying TVA's industrial development claims. But Wagner has sent only Mayor Charles Hall, the agency's favorite local dam booster, and General Manager Lynn Seeber. Only two senators are present, Culver and Wyoming Republican Malcolm Wallop, so we must take our comfort from the strength of the official record we're building. The General Accounting Office representatives and Hanson present their briefings. Both contain vivid statements and important conclusions that we can cite in a Supreme Court brief. The General Accounting Office's Canfield speaks diplomatically but sharply:

> We examined the assumptions and logic used by TVA. . . . Generally we conclude that TVA's projections are not representative of actual benefits. . . . For example, TVA's projection of recreation benefits, which account for about 38% of all benefits, had several questionable assumptions and did not adequately consider [significant] factors. . . . *We expect to recommend that no action be taken on legislation which would exempt the Tellico project from the Endangered Species Act,* at least until Congress has had time to receive and assess updated information.[2]

In the wake of his hospitalization, Hanson's presentation is far more impressive than we'd expected. He has large, arresting graphics and text showing multiple configurations of potential river-based economic development designs. As he presents the analysis it's clear each of the alternatives is feasible and far more beneficial than a reservoir. I follow up with a summary of the potential river-based developments, including industrial sites and the history-oriented tourism route, plus the project's twisting history and the unfounded rationales being pushed by its adamant leadership.

Then comes a parade of Tennesseans supporting the snail darter case. Ben Bridgers begins with testimony from the Cherokee. Alfred Davis is first to speak for the farmers. "You just heard a representative of the Cherokee," he says. "Two hundred years ago my ancestors were probably fighting his ancestors. But today we both of us agree this valley has got to be preserved." He notes how most farms are being condemned for resale, not for a reservoir, at $300 to $400 an acre, "but it's impossible to find land in our area for less than $1,000 an acre." Dave Etnier is next, and he tells of discovering the darter and of the special qualities of this last surviving stretch of river habitat. Hank delivers a powerful assault on the dam's logic and economics, archaeologist Jeff Chapman details the valley's extraordinary resources in this area, farmer Dan Burgner excoriates TVA's high-handed condemnation tactics, and Tennessee activist Bill Russell describes forty years of TVA's environmental deficits. Surprisingly, Superintendent Boyd Evison, the charismatic federal director of the Great Smoky Mountains National Park, has volunteered to testify against TVA, and he now speaks movingly about the park as a sanctuary that could be far better protected if it were partnered with river-based recreational management and the rich cultural resources of the Little T.

Jean Ritchey goes last. She draws up her small frame like a warrior, squints at the two senators on the dais, and shakes a finger at them as she speaks.

> MS. RITCHEY: I am Jean Ritchey, and I don't mean anything derogatory to you, but if you gentlemen had done your homework years ago we wouldn't be here today. . . .
>
> SENATOR CULVER: I wasn't involved with the Endangered Species Act, Ms. Ritchey, but anything else you want to blame

us for, just add it to the list because it's a popular national pastime.

MS. RITCHEY: This is the truth.

SENATOR CULVER: That it's a national pastime?

MS. RITCHEY: No, that you don't search out enough.

SENATOR CULVER: Well, let's just go ahead without finger pointing.

MS. RITCHEY: Our land is being taken under false pretenses. The condemnation papers said "for the building of Tellico Dam and reservoir." We live miles from the dam, and only about one or two acres of our land will be for the reservoir, three at most, . . . yet they are attempting to take all 119 acres of our farm. . . . It's morally and legally wrong to take all our land and sell it for a profit! The landowners are as endangered a species as the little fish in the river. They may not be extinct, but they can't continue to farm for a living. . . .

As Jean speaks, Senator Wallop listens intently and nods sympathetically.

After the darter defenders finish their presentations Mayor Hall gives a short statement about how the local area desperately needs the industry jobs that the project will bring, and how most of the local population now believes the darter shouldn't stop the dam. General Manager Seeber delivers TVA's retort to our citizens' testimony. In a somewhat irritated voice Seeber presents an extended history of TVA's efforts to build its dam. Tellico, he says, is a necessary project that already would have generated thousands of industrial jobs and prevented $15 million in flood damages in Chattanooga if environmentalists had not been blocking it.

In the audience Hank snorts, "That's a lie!"

We shush Hank, but he goes on in a stage whisper, "Those jobs disappeared when Boeing pulled out, and even the Corps says no way would Tellico Dam have prevented flooding in Chattanooga. I know. I live there."

Seeber ignores Hank and in a condescending tone continues his prepared statement. When he finishes, Wallop leans forward and delivers the question Jean Ritchey's testimony has planted in his mind.

SENATOR WALLOP: I have only one question: How do you respond to the charges of the people who came here who said
to get two acres of their land you are condemning 200?

MR. SEEBER: You have to understand: We are not trying to
build a dam and reservoir alone. What happens to the
shoreline is very important.

SENATOR WALLOP: What is the matter with industrial people
coming and buying that land from Ms. Ritchey? Why do
you have to condemn those farmers' land for two acres of
reservoir?

MR. SEEBER: We used the word "condemnation," but in over 90
percent of the cases it is voluntary—

At the word "voluntary," Jean, Alfred, and Hank hoot wildly, which
triggers many in the room to break out in laughter. Mike Perry, another
farmer, shouts out, "You threatened *ever' single one of them farms with
condemnation!*" From the witness table Seeber turns and looks over his
shoulder at the audience, then turns back to the senators:

MR. SEEBER: Uh . . . but maybe not willingly.

This explanation causes everyone in the gallery except Seeber and
Mayor Hall to roar with laughter. Seeber then digs himself in deeper:

MR. SEEBER: To get to your point, Senator, the reason we felt it
necessary to acquire that land as part of the project is that
we have experienced that if you go out and build a reservoir and leave it in private ownership, what happens is
your industrial sites get used up immediately by home
sites and cabins and the local communities don't have the
money necessary to buy the land. . . .

SENATOR WALLOP: Are you telling me that the Boeing Company
doesn't have the money? [He's scowling.]

Seeber tries to explain why it's necessary for TVA to take acreage
that won't be flooded under the reservoir, not quite admitting to Wallop that Boeing has abandoned the Tellico project as unworkable. But
after a minute Wallop cuts him off.

SENATOR WALLOP: I tell you, . . . I think you answered my question when you said it was entirely voluntary, *but not really!*

Whereupon, with the audience chortling and Seeber shifting uncomfortably in his chair and smiling stiffly, the session ends. As the room clears, the Tennesseans are gleeful. The studies and factual testimony laid out in this hearing have convincingly put the case we've been making into the public record, a vindication of years of effort. TVA looks foolish, and Wallop, who has never been a friend of environmentalism, has seen the truth of the Tellico reservoir project. It's a good foundation for tomorrow's defense of the Endangered Species Act. Unfortunately, however, Margot Hornblower of the *Post* hasn't seen this lively morning, because she did not come for the second day of hearings, nor did any other reporter. We console ourselves with the thought that the written record the Culver committee is building will be a valuable resource in the future.

The next two days of hearings promise suspense. Will some agencies tell the committee they think the Endangered Species Act is unreasonable? What kind of opposition will industry coalitions present? Will the environmental groups indeed stand together in confronting attacks on the law's "inflexibility"? The evening before the third day of hearings Kathy Fletcher tells us the official statements of all but two federal agencies have been given final approval by the White House. In original drafts some of the statements had argued the law was irrational and inflexible, but those texts have been changed.

A little after nine o'clock the next morning we're standing in the corridor outside the hearing room when three men come striding down the long hall, tossing arch looks at us as they pass. On the attaché cases each man is carrying is the stamp "United States Department of Transportation." The three are intercepted by two men in gray suits who suddenly materialize at the hearing room entrance. "Who are you?" the gray-suited interceptors ask the newcomers.

"Department of Transportation. I'm deputy general counsel of the Federal Highway Administration," says the leader.

"Would you step over here to the side of the corridor, please, and show us your prepared testimony?" one of the gray suits orders. The testimony statement is taken out of an attaché case and held up against the wall. One of the gray-suited guys takes a felt tip marker and starts crossing out lines and paragraphs of text as we watch, fascinated. The three Transportation men stand blinking, deflating with every stroke of the marker on their prepared text. The statement is returned to them with a caution: "Tell the senators you'll not be able to submit a copy of your formal testimony today. Use this marked-up edit as the basis for what you say today."

When they're called to testify, the Department of Transportation counsel apologizes to Wallop, saying that his written statement is "not yet in final form," and he delivers a brief bowdlerized bit of testimony, a bland opening saying that in general the department has no quarrel with the public purposes of the Endangered Species Act, and that it believes implementation can be worked out over time to satisfy different statutory mandates, but that the department's representatives will unfortunately have to provide a clean copy of their statement at a later date. A few minutes later John McGuire of the Forest Service is put through the same felt tip marker filleting of his statement in the corridor outside the hearing chamber, then balefully presents bland testimony when called to testify. All the other agencies that testify support the endangered species law strongly; most of them cite Debbie and Mardi's statistics, which are clearly making their rounds in government.[3]

Who were those guys in gray suits who censored the agencies that wanted to testify against the Endangered Species Act? "OMB," says Brent, meaning the Office of Management and Budget. "OMB oversees the budget, but it also coordinates administration policy within the agencies. When the president's Domestic Policy Council decides it's the administration's policy to view the Act as reasonable, OMB will enforce it with a heavy hand and scissors if necessary."

Not for TVA, though. Red Wagner announces at the beginning of his testimony that the White House has specifically allowed him to proceed with testimony in opposition to the Endangered Species Act, and he delivers a long statement focused on the inflexibility of the law as interpreted by the court of appeals in our case. The law lacks "balance," and "America's resources are too valuable and too scarce to allow the waste [of throwing] away more than $105 million invested at Tellico." At this point it becomes clear that Wallop has understood our argument that river development would save most of that money. He asks Wagner, "Weren't you inflexible with regard to the pursuit of other alternatives to resolve this? . . . Would you now be willing to pursue some of the alternatives that may be suggested?"

"We investigated other alternatives before we undertook the project," Wagner replies. "The Tellico project is entirely dependent on the creation of a reservoir. [River development] is contrary to our instructions from Congress [from the appropriations committee] . . . and in our opinion is unreasonable."

Wallop turns to Interior's Keith Schreiner. "Was Fish and Wildlife given any cooperation by TVA with regards to alternative means of developing the project?"

"We vigorously pursued an effort with TVA to consider alternatives," Schreiner says, "including not closing the dam, using the project area for other purposes. . . . I am of course reluctant to be critical of a fellow federal agency. . . . Most of their consultation with us was preceded with this thought: 'We will consult until you people are sick of it as long as we do not talk about not closing the dam, because the gates of that dam are going to close January 1.'"

Bless you, Keith Schreiner.

Wagner angrily retorts that his agency has spent so much money that considering anything besides the dam "would be pointless."

Only two senators are in attendance on this third day of hearings, Republicans Wallop and McClure, because Chairman Culver has been pulled away. The two senators and most of the audience, however, seem skeptical of Wagner's defense of TVA's drive to dam the Little T. As the room clears, I approach Wagner and suggest that this whole controversy can be resolved in the best interests of TVA's mission as well as of the people of eastern Tennessee if we work together on river-based economic development. Wagner stares at me hatefully, veins pulsing in his cheeks and forehead. "Get out of my way," he thunders, and pushes past me into the hallway.

But Kathy Fletcher and the Carter administration have come through for us with strong affirmations from all the other federal agencies, putting testimony on the record that the law works well if agencies consult with Fish and Wildlife in good faith.

The final day, a Thursday session labeled "citizen groups and interested parties," is a four-hour anticlimax. Wallop, the only senator attending, presides. All the environmental organizations ultimately step up to the witness table and stake out the uncompromised uniform position we've been urging—the law is working, the darter conflict is a

consequence of TVA intransigence and not statutory inflexibility, and
the law should not be changed. National Trout Unlimited, which has
collected more than six hundred donations from fishermen around
the country to support us, adds some history on how its chapters have
been fighting on behalf of the river and the farmers for more than ten
years.

Even Audubon's Mike Zagata, who'd aligned with Baker's staff to
split the environmental front by calling for "reasonable amendments"
to the law, comes across as adamant as the humaniacs. "The Act isn't
broken so it doesn't need fixing," Zagata says. "Tellico demonstrates
agency inflexibility, not statutory inflexibility. . . . In the very rare case
where administrative mechanisms don't resolve conflicts, Congress
can do the job, with hearings like today's." He even ends with the classic
quote from Aldo Leopold's *A Sand County Almanac:* "A thing is right
when it tends to preserve the integrity, stability, and beauty of the bi-
otic community. It's wrong when it tends otherwise." Whew. Zagata
has been pulled back into the fold, perhaps by the Audubon Society
elder statesmen whom I'd called and begged to rein him in. The National Wildlife Federation follows suit, with Mike Berger eloquently
emphasizing the human utility of endangered species as warning signals for human welfare, and defending the solid biology behind Interi-
or's listing of species and critical habitat.

What about the industry coalitions that have been attacking the snail
darter and the endangered species law so relentlessly? Only three witnesses speak on behalf of American industry. A spokesman for the National Forest Products Association argues that the law's "absolutism . . .
poses a very real and ominous threat to scientific forest management."
Chris Farrand of the U.S. Chamber of Commerce advocates amendments to allow federal agency officials to grant themselves exemptions
from the law in order to avoid "irrational" cases like Tellico. We'd
talked to Farrand before he testified, reminding him that a decade ago
the Chamber had characterized TVA's land condemnations as a federal
agency running wild. Farrand blew us off, saying, "I didn't remember
we'd supported you, but it doesn't matter. That was then, the issues are
bigger now. And my testimony's already written." Jerry Haggard of the
American Mining Congress submits a written statement decrying the
Act's hyperprotection and inflexibility as demonstrated by the snail
darter. He testified that the law should be enforced "only so long as it

doesn't conflict with other national policies" such as mining on public lands, and every species listing should be accompanied by extensive "economic impact statements."

Does the fact that the industry camp had only three witnesses testifying against us mean they're backing off? "No," Brent surmises. "Industry often doesn't come out in force for hearings if they think that making hearings a public spectacle might work against them. They do most of their political work in private conversations in members' offices—money talk, election contributions, and public relations campaigns. In Washington politics," Brent continues, "things happen on the Hill in critical moments when everything comes to a head. These hearings don't feel like that. People are waiting to see what happens in the Supreme Court."

Our Senate hearings have produced some sterling moments. Americans, however, heard none of it. There was no TV feed, and the hearings were barely mentioned in the papers, getting just a few brief paragraphs. Details about Tellico Dam economics from the General Accounting Office, the bountiful benefits of river development demonstrated by the alternatives study led by Department of Architecture Dean Donald Hanson of the University of Tennessee, the farmers' land losses, and the Endangered Species Act's affirmative track record—none of these are picked up by the national press.

"Last year it was anticipation of hearings that persuaded the politicians to pause in that frenzy when they were threatening an immediate override," we say to Brent, puzzled. "But now these hearings were paid so little attention!" Are hearings in reality not functional, not decisional—just procedural rituals—unless their press climate is active and hot? "That's too harsh," Brent says. "Some hearings do more than others. Some do it without press attention. You've built a pretty good paper record and that's something. You've convinced a few more people, including six or seven staffers. And Senator Wallop. He's important—a Republican from the West. He could be a big help for you down the road. For all his sympathy for mining and ranching, he was clearly touched by the farmers' stories, and he realizes the dam's an economic joke."

Oversight hearings in the House might make a bigger bang, but not until next year. We return to the daily routine that Anne Wickham has counseled from the start: pound the corridors, keep after the media, and educate, educate, educate. With an advance from her new boss at the State Department, Anne has been able to rent a small townhouse near the Friends office, simple but clean. This means I get to live in her apartment's second-floor bedroom, which she can't use because of the stairs. Every evening Anne reviews the day's efforts with me and helps target plans for the following day.

In the executive offices, our case has certainly been heard. Kathy Fletcher is a strong advocate for us within the administration; water projects and the snail darter occupy a lot of her time and interest. (She and her fiancé, Ken, go to a Halloween party costumed as our Tennessee case: he as the darter, she as the dam.)

In November the Supreme Court announces it's taking up our case, with oral arguments scheduled for next April. That should help hold off attacks on the Endangered Species Act and the darter. The inclination in Capitol Hill offices—among foes and friends alike—seems to be to wait and see: Maybe the Court will clarify this mess so Congress won't have to get into it. We begin preparing legal arguments that we hope will prevent the injunction from being overturned in the high court.

As it turns out, however, the Senate committee announces it is scheduling more hearings, to be held four days before our Supreme Court arguments are to occur, on a dramatic new legislative proposal that sets up a procedure allowing species to be exempted from the Endangered Species Act on a case-by-case basis.

Can we never have a clear, calm moment when politics don't churn ominously just below the surface?

# CHAPTER 9

# The Highest Court?

NOVEMBER 1977—JUNE 15, 1978

The evening news gave us the word on November 14: the Supreme Court wants to hear the snail darter case in April. Immediately we were thrown into the turmoil faced by every lawyer who gets that news—weeks of labor preparing a killer brief and oral argument to sway the highest, toughest court in the land. (In our case, moreover, a month into our preparations we're hit with an almost unprecedented twist that looks as if it will make our day in the Court even tougher.)

It was obvious from the moment we won our injunction from the court of appeals that TVA would appeal to the Supreme Court, but it wasn't obvious the Court would take the case. It takes the votes of four of nine justices for the Supreme Court to grant what the legal profession refers to as a writ of certiorari to hear a case on appeal. In any given year they often turn down 99 percent of these petitions. We'd tried, but not very hard, to persuade the Court to turn this one down too. TVA's original request to the Court had put us in a dilemma. Did we want the Court to take the case? Normally, if you've won in the lower appeals court, you just want to hold your legal ground. If the Supreme Court takes the appeal, as Ohio State football coach Woody Hayes used to say about throwing a pass, three things can happen, and two of them are bad. You can win—but you can also be reversed or remanded to a lower court, possibly facing a whole new trial. For us, however, there was reason to think the Supreme Court would be worth the risk. Our continuing efforts to educate Congress and the press are not going too well. At any moment TVA might get its pork-barrel friends to change the law and strike down the Endangered Species Act's protections.

"It's not the courts that'll give you a permanent victory," Anne told us from the start. "To be taken seriously you needed a court injunction, but ultimately it's politics that will decide what happens to your darter."

We sensed that Supreme Court scrutiny could actually help us, holding off potential political attackers and prodding the press to scrutinize the dam's true demerits, allowing the public at last to take our case seriously. Without the Supreme Court, congressional pork barrelers will have a much easier time overturning the injunction so widely viewed as an extremist mistake. We'd not only lose the river and the fish, but also forever be saddled with the guilt of having stained the endangered species law with a reputation for foolishness. A Supreme Court victory would offer the best opportunity to finally make public the facts of the fish and the dam, simultaneously resuscitating the public image of environmentalism. So we wrote a ten-page brief formally asking the Court to deny TVA's request, secretly hoping we'd lose the attempt and get to present our case to the world in the big Court—and win.

Once the Supreme Court agrees to review a case, a tight schedule of legal preparations is kicked into motion. As petitioner, TVA has sixty days to construct a brief and pull together a comprehensive selection of relevant testimony, exhibits, and prior proceedings to be bound into an official appendix record of the case. TVA designated five-hundred-plus pages of trial transcript, reports, and testimony from their trial witnesses to be printed, all paid for by taxpayers. Thank God we're not the ones filing the appeal; the printing alone would have bankrupted us. We put in only twenty pages: documents showing that since 1975 Interior had repeatedly and unsuccessfully asked TVA to protect the darter in its natural habitat and consider development alternatives without a dam.

The bombshell landed in our laps four weeks after the Court agreed to look at the case, and it wasn't a problem with the Appendix. It was an upheaval inside the White House. We had wondered who exactly would prepare TVA's brief and face us in court. Because TVA is a federal agency, the Department of Justice has the right to take over the case in whole or part, or leave it to TVA. We had a realistic hope that Justice wouldn't take over the case, because Wade McCree, one of the appeals

judges who'd voted for us, had since been named solicitor general of
the United States and now held the number two chair in Justice's leadership. Wouldn't he tell the White House and the attorney general's office to take a pass, letting TVA's general counsel Herb Sanger write the
brief and do the oral argument? We hoped so, thinking Sanger would
be hapless in an appellate-level legal argument. Or perhaps they'd assign some junior solicitor from Justice to handle the case?

Kathy Fletcher in the White House delivered the news: "Secretary
Andrus has been trying to push Justice to step away from TVA's case,"
she said. "He's been arguing that TVA's a scofflaw and should be forced
to go it alone. But McCree removed himself completely from the case,
and Attorney General Griffin Bell is making the decision himself. He's
furious about Andrus's 'interference' in a decision he thinks is his
alone to make. He's complaining to the White House that this is dirty
Watergate politics. Bell reads the newspapers and thinks your case is
silly. He's so angry about Andrus's arguments that Justice is for sure
going to represent TVA. But it's not just that. It's likely the attorney
general *himself* is going to argue against you in the Court!"

This isn't good. Even if Justice represents an agency, it's extremely
rare for the attorney general himself to argue a case. When he was
attorney general in his brother's administration, Bobby Kennedy did
so in one or two carefully selected pushover cases, but Bell never has.
Having him there would raise the profile of our case, but, as far back in
American history as anyone can discover, no attorney general—none,
ever—has argued a case and lost.

With an increasing sense that we were out of our league—we're
clearly rank amateurs—we started building a Supreme Court litigation
group. Don Cohen and I (two untenured academics no longer in Tennessee), along with a dozen student volunteers from the environmental
law societies of Wayne State University and University of Michigan law
schools, began research for a brief to the Supreme Court.

We'd been pleased with the brief we filed in the court of appeals. Its
forty-three pages had covered the entire case with sharp logic and good
precedent citations, setting out the facts very well. It may in fact have
been this brief, not the oral argument, that won us our unanimous injunction. But we threw it away. Why? Because as veteran Washington
lawyers told us, "The Supreme Court is different. A brief you think is
excellent anywhere else just won't do here. You've got to ratchet up

your expectations." We would have to rebuild our brief from scratch, with twice as many legal citations, argued twice as well, plus sharp maps and charts, and clear text, forcefully expressed, all befitting the highest tribunal. Our brief had to build a solid structure of arguments justifying an injunction, but also had to do much more. Arguments made to a court supposedly turn on legal doctrines alone, not on policy issues, but winning arguments must come across as solid common sense. You capture judges' gut feelings, using compelling facts and policy to convince them your position is the most reasonable. Then you provide them with enough legal doctrine to capture their pens so they can write their decisions your way. That's legal realism.

We expected the Justice brief to make the same four arguments we faced in the court of appeals from TVA. They'll say the Endangered Species Act doesn't apply to our case because the dam construction was under way when the law was passed; in other words, the dam is grandfathered because the law is "not retroactive." Second, they'll say the law doesn't apply because it's been "implicitly amended" by the subsequent pork appropriations bills authorizing continued funding for Tellico Dam. Third, even if the law applies it would be "absurd" to interpret it to stop important projects like this one. Fourth, there'd be the equity law argument—that because the trial judge made a full, careful "equitable balancing" of the merits (which of course he'd expressly refused to do), an injunction to stop the reservoir should be denied even if the law is violated, because the trial judge has determined that the public's interest in the dam is far greater than the importance of the fish.

The first two, the retroactivity and appropriations issues, are technical arguments saying the law didn't apply to the dam. The other two are deeper legal questions that could open the door to policy arguments about common sense. On all points we can expect the Justice Department lawyers to do a far better job than TVA. If our own brief is sharp enough, however, matching them point for point on the law, maybe the dramatic facts we pour into the latter two arguments could open the eyes of the Court and the public. Judge Taylor's trial record excluded most of the commonsense evidence showing our reasonableness, so we began combing through agency data and other official references that could be slipped into a brief to show the dramatic economic realities behind our legal arguments.

While we waited for the TVA brief, we also had to continue working the Washington corridors. On the legislative side we anticipated continuing pressures against the law. Our volunteers maintained a flow of fact sheet updates to offices on the Hill, using the data from Interior showing that the law was working well. Within the bureaucracy we worked to ensure that Interior would reject the latest petition from TVA. Red Wagner's lawyers were again arguing that the fish could no longer reach its spawning shoals on the Little T, so Interior should delist the river as the darter's critical habitat. That would at least partially undercut our legal case. Interior had been greatly irritated, however, by TVA's refusal to consult and by its transports of darters to other locations without permits. TVA would almost certainly be denied.

But another, happier surprise was coming from Foster Knight at the Council on Environmental Quality. He called and told us to "go over to Interior, quick. Talk with Bill Garner in their solicitor's office. My boss has been talking with Secretary Andrus. They're both so ticked off at TVA that they're asking the White House for permission to file a federal agency brief *on your side, against TVA!*" We ran over to Garner's office at Interior. It's confidential, he said, but we should know that Andrus and Charlie Warren at the Council on Environmental Quality had been comparing notes about TVA's stonewalling, its refusal to consult under the terms of the law on any project modifications that didn't include the dam. Now they wanted to argue on our side. What did we think of that? Great! No one we've talked to has ever seen a federal agency coming into the Supreme Court supporting citizens against another federal agency. Could the White House, we asked, also give permission for Leo Krulitz, Interior's solicitor, to make an oral argument along with us in the Court?

"Back off," Garner said. "Let us do the pushing. We're talking hard with the White House Domestic Council." In the following twenty days we worked with Knight and Garner on the shape and content of the brief that their agencies might file on our behalf, and held our breath.

The official federal brief packet was delivered to us by certified mail at the beginning of February, but there was only a single brief in the packet—TVA's. No brief supporting us? Then we saw it. Not a separate brief, no request for separate oral argument on our behalf, no Council on Environmental Quality. But there it was, bound into TVA's big brief as an "Appendix": a tight, punchy, thirteen-page brief from the Department of Interior, burning like a fuse at the back end of TVA's arguments.

The texts of both briefs were actually a bit perplexing but heartening all the same. The brief for TVA made only the first two arguments we'd expected—saying that there was no violation because the law didn't apply to ongoing projects, and that Tellico had been exempted from the law by continued appropriations. The Justice attorneys wrote articulately on the two technical points they were making and cited five dozen cases, but their brief seemed pretty dry. Reading it carefully, we couldn't find anything in its legal or policy terms that we couldn't handle. It just laid out their two defenses and the litigation history of the dam, with no practical political arguments against our position, no mocking references to little fish, and no "common sense" balance-of-equities arguments against our injunction. Where were those balance-of-equities arguments? Maybe Justice had decided to back off on them? Or maybe the Justice lawyers assumed from the press coverage, like their boss, Griffin Bell, that the irrationality of our lawsuit was so obvious it didn't require analysis?

And there, right after the pages of Justice's brief for TVA, was Interior's brief. Labeled "Views of the Secretary of Interior," it hammered each of TVA's arguments unmercifully. "Beyond taking a position that would result in the extirpation of an endangered species," Interior declared, TVA was asking the Court "to disregard the plain meaning of the Endangered Species Act" and to violate three basic rules prohibiting appropriations bills from changing existing laws. Case for case, the Interior brief refuted each of Justice's arguments for the dam, and then went a little bit further. It noted Debbie and Mardi's data showing 4,500 potential conflicts under the law, with TVA's stonewalling on Tellico as the only unresolved impasse, and it included quotes from the General Accounting Office study showing the errors in TVA's cost accounting and the existence of economic development alternatives to the dam. It didn't mention TVA's refusal to consult. Overall, however, it was an unexpected gift, a legal land mine planted right there within the covers of TVA's message to the Court.

Now it was our turn to prepare a brief in response. We started divvying up responsibilities. The Michigan students didn't know enough about Tennessee to work on the history and policy sections of the brief.

They all had access to the law library, however, and free use of the library's electronic search programs that were revolutionizing legal research and the practice of law. (We assumed, deciding not to raise the question openly, that students could ethically use those library services to help on our case because we weren't a profit-making venture.)

The Michigan students formed subgroups and started to collect relevant cases. For each section of the brief we decided to amass at least a dozen strong case precedents to shape the arguments. Law student Les Iczkovitz led the research focused on proving that pork-barrel appropriations for the dam didn't override Endangered Species Act protections, while fellow student John Dernbach's group focused on retroactivity. We decided to make balance-of-equities arguments, even though the Justice brief didn't raise them, because the Pacific Legal Foundation, one of many "public interest" legal groups funded by industry groups, had filed a friend-of-the-court (amicus) brief on equitable balancing. Receiving an informational query from a Pacific Legal Foundation attorney, I asked why his conservative group was supporting government condemnations of private farms for resale. From his evasive answer it appeared that his organization considered consistency on principle less important than the opportunity to strike down environmental regulation. The foundation's brief strenuously argued, inaccurately, that Judge Taylor had fully balanced the equities when he denied the injunction. So my research assistant, David Hiller, headed a group researching the balancing issue.

As the filing date drew near and the pressure mounted, our daily routine took shape. The little crew would meet late afternoons in the basement office of the University of Michigan Environmental Law Society, and assignments would be given out. Back home I would work up longhand first drafts of various subsections, and Dernbach, at the dining room table or in the Society office, checked citations, logic, and scansion, typing out new text and much smoother second drafts. Student workers would arrive at the door after the library closed, delivering copies of cases and legislative documents. We would analyze the new data and start working it into the drafts. I was the weak link, unable to work through the night. I'd sit drafting new subsections and polishing the final third or fourth draft of the text, but could never make it beyond three a.m. Dernbach, Hiller, and a couple of others sometimes worked until dawn. I'd get up at six and review what they'd done, and we'd set an agenda for the day's work. Then we'd all go off to classes, at the end of which our brief-writing labors would begin again.

The brief had to be postmarked by March 1. On February 24 we started ferrying sheaves of our final draft to a printer in Detroit, where it would be typeset in law-brief format. Our text had eight sections, each with passages of commonsense economics and policy woven into the legal arguments. The brief was coming together smoothly, but there was still too much to do. The tables of citations—more than a hundred cases and legislative documents—required nitpicky care. If only February had a couple more days.

At one point the head typesetter complained, "This is all too long. Our boss gave you a flat rate based on a regulation Supreme Court brief of fifty-five pages, but you're way over ninety pages if you count your footnotes. Nobody files court briefs with so many footnotes."

"Please," we said, "law professors need lots of footnotes." More to the point, the text was long because we'd larded it with chunks of facts, analysis, maps, and charts not in the trial record. We'd told ourselves it was ethical to slip these in because all our cited materials—mostly from the General Accounting Office report and committee hearings data— had been published by the U.S. Government Printing Office. Truthfully, however, we ourselves had submitted most of the official document materials we're citing. Yet how else can you show the facts if the trial court hasn't let you put them on the record?

"And ours is a public interest project with no money," we pleaded. "Please cut us some slack?" The compromise: the footnotes were printed in very small type, renumbered by section so the press's business manager and the Court won't realize there are ninety-five in all, and we cut out the section on balance of equities. The TVA brief was completely silent on the equity balance, but we nevertheless thought we ought to have enough of it in our brief to argue if necessary, so in went a single long footnote, footnote 40: if a full, accurate balancing had taken place in the trial court, we wrote, the darter would have won there. But equitable balancing is unnecessary: Congress itself should properly make the decision. Our argument uses the 1944 *Hecht* case that both we and TVA had used at trial, plus an article by my mentor Joe Sax on "remands to the legislature," holding that a court's job is to enforce tough laws so legislatures will do the job of rethinking them, and we added an old decision written by Chief Justice Warren Burger when he was a court of appeals judge, *Mosinee Paper*. With this footnote on injunction balancing, our work on the brief was complete.

With a day to spare, we went to press.

"What color cover?"

"Green!" we said.

"There's no green. How about French Blue?" Okay.

Late the next afternoon—March 1, the deadline for sending the brief—ninety copies had been printed and were ready. We packed up seventy-five to mail to the Supreme Court, keeping the rest for us and our allies. They were beautiful. We proofread the brief one last time and discovered three ugly typos—"assure" was printed "assuze," a paragraph began "En the facts here," and a law review citation was misprinted. They were all minor mistakes, but they imply incompetence. We quickly unpacked the seventy-five copies, laid them out on the living room floor, carefully masked each error in every one of the copies with correction fluid, being careful that the pages didn't touch and smear as they were drying, and carefully lettered in the corrections. Then we packed them up again and drove wildly for the airport, where the post office is open all night. But we arrived too late—it was past midnight, so the date was now March 2. But luckily we remembered that someone had told us a guy named Sidney at this post office will turn back the meter clock if you beg him. We did. He did. Our brief flew off dated yesterday, March 1.

With six weeks until our final day in Court and not much left to do in Washington, we assumed we could spend more time preparing for classes and a lot of time preparing for the Supreme Court oral argument. Not so. With two weeks to go, we heard that the Senate committee was going to hold its hearing on a new bill that included a species exemption procedure. Back to Washington for more battles on the Hill—we would be testifying in the Senate four days before the Court arguments—but we needed to spend time back in Michigan as well, mooting our legal arguments with an informal advisory brain trust in Ann Arbor.

The traditional preparation for a Supreme Court argument is to do a "moot court" simulation in front of a group of supportive but incisive critics. We pulled together a bench of colleagues from the Wayne State and Michigan law faculties—Beth Eisler, Bo Abrams, Don Cohen, Phil Soper, and Lee Bollinger, the latter two particularly important because both had clerked for Supreme Court justices and knew the battlefield from the inside. Meeting in a classroom in Ann Arbor one evening in March, we first held a scoping session analyzing each justice, one by one, and then did a moot session where I presented the best oral argument I could muster while being hit by their piercing questions. Our oral argument had to be much more than a mere recapitulation of the brief. We needed a vivid, ringing presentation, our finest opportunity yet to present the real case to the judicial system and the American public. If the oral argument flopped, on the other hand, it would have sad consequences in both legal and policy terms.

There are things you can do in an oral argument that you cannot do in a brief. We expected Bell to use the oral argument to undermine us by making fun of the silly fish that was stopping this dam, and emphasizing that it was he himself, the attorney general, who'd been forced to step up to argue against this irrationality. We had to counterbalance his eminence with the gravity of what was at stake, the words of Congress. If we were lucky, we could bring in a lot of dramatic off-record facts about TVA's bad faith, the solid economics of our snail darter injunction, maybe even take a whack at the pork-barrel realities of the appropriations committees.

TVA's short reply brief, submitted in response to ours, would give us one more piece of ammunition. It includes a very helpful letter from David Freeman, the progressive TVA board member recently appointed by Jimmy Carter, advocating river development to keep Tellico a "dry dam" without a reservoir. "The choice is not the snail darter or the dam," Freeman wrote. "The industrialization and other benefits to the economy can take place without another lake."

Our oral argument, done right, could pull together economic as well as ecological themes into a commanding case for the darter. But the moot court simulation was a disaster. In fifty-five minutes—twenty-five minutes longer than we'd actually be given in court—I expressed less than half of what had to be said. Stumbling and stuttering, wordy, pedantic, and vague, I had no conviction in my voice and no punch to my logic. My answers to probing questions were insubstantial and unconvincing. From the strained politeness in the faces of my colleagues, it was clear they thought that our darter case was a gone goose. It was difficult to make the case clearly—so many facts, arguments, and layers of legal and political strategy, not to mention judicial politics. So many complex questions of tone, pitch, and rhetoric. The evening's saving grace, however, was a further brainstorming session: How might each justice view our case, which would shape the questions we'd face in oral argument and the ultimate outcome? At least four justices must vote for the appeal to be granted, and conventional wisdom has it that they vote to take the case in order to reverse the lower court. Who were the four justices predictably against us? "You have no chance for Rehnquist," the ex-clerks told us. He'd be an implacable foe behind the scenes as well as in oral argument. A famous law review study of more than five hundred of Rehnquist's judicial votes demonstrated that the only consistent explanation for his positions had little to do with law or precedent but rather was the result of his personal politics: *who* was at bat in each case? He had *never* voted in favor of citizen environmentalists. To support the side he favored he'd misstate facts on the record, twist precedents out of context, and use his domineering facility with administrative law to slide shaky logic past his brethren. He'd never vote for environmentalists against TVA.

Worse, Rehnquist apparently carried more than one vote. By his ability variously to browbeat or charm his fellow justices, Rehnquist could often sway others, especially Chief Justice Burger. According to reports from Supreme Court clerks, Rehnquist often fed Burger the questions he wanted the chief justice to ask in oral argument. So Burger tended to follow Rehnquist's lead. However, Bollinger, who'd clerked for Burger, offered some sage advice on the best tactic for getting the chief justice's vote: "Sometimes if you cite Burger to Burger, you can get Burger." Unfortunately the only citation in our brief to a Burger opinion is buried in that footnote 40.

Lewis Powell was also likely to vote with Rehnquist. Shortly before he was nominated to the Court, he wrote a confidential memorandum to the U.S. Chamber of Commerce protesting "socialistic" causes like consumer protection and environmentalism. Powell was intelligent and cared deeply about private property rights, which might help us if he ever focused on the farmland condemnations, but he wasn't likely to see the merits of an environmental citizen suit against an agency that had become a solid part of the energy industry establishment.

So who else had voted for the appeals petition? Not Justice Brennan. We counted him firmly on our side. Nina Totenberg of National Public Radio informed us that Brennan had told a fishing companion he thought the snail darter injunction was exactly right. Brennan is getting old and speaks less often in oral arguments now, but he's a traditional progressive, hospitable to citizen enforcement initiatives—not to mention he's a fly fisherman and maybe even a member of Trout Unlimited. Our brain trust group also figured that Blackmun and Marshall would be with us. As a court of appeals judge in Minnesota, Blackmun had written notable decisions supporting environmental laws. Marshall, though mercurial, had written one of the Court's strongest environmental decisions in the *Overton Park* case, affirming the right of a small group of neighbors in Memphis using federal law to block a highway destroying a local park. He, the engineer and hero of a twenty-year civil rights litigation campaign, was the Court's strongest progressive and would surely be on our side.

That left Stewart, White, and Stevens. They're not predictable, although we suspected the person who told Totenberg about Brennan was Justice Stewart, talking off the record—implying that Stewart too might be with us. White was a liberal Kennedy appointee, but he seems to be growing irascible and impatient with the increasing flow of issues being brought to federal courts for resolution. Stevens is a cypher. Which of the justices is most likely to read the briefs before oral argument? Who would come to the case seeking its legal merits, instead of as a partisan? It's Stevens, the junior justice, we're told. He's the only one who regularly reads the briefs. And Stevens, our observers guessed, is most likely to vote on the facts and law as he sees them in each case, rather than on personal politics as Rehnquist does. This, we hope, means that Stevens's vote will tilt our way.

Thus our best guess, needing five, was three, three, and three. Rehnquist, Burger, and Powell against us. Brennan, Blackmun, and Marshall for us. Stewart, White, and Stevens in the middle, too close to call. That shows how much we knew.

## Into the Temple of Justice

It's four a.m. The officer on the night watch doubtfully scrutinizes the scruffy faces staring up from sleeping bags on the portico at the front doors of the United States Supreme Court.

"Please, officer, we've come all the way from Tennessee," Sara Grigsby begs the cop.

It's the misty-cool predawn hours of April 18. Sara, Peter Alliman, Les Iczkovitz, University of Tennessee student Pam Reeves, and a few others have climbed the marble stairs and are huddled between the columns to be sure to get seats to hear our oral argument in the morning. The Court chambers have limited space for visitors: if it's a big case and you aren't in line early, you're relegated to being cycled in to watch for a random five minutes or so. These students who are camping out have lived the case for four years and want to see the whole thing. The cop is stern at first but eventually says they can stay, so long as they behave.

Meanwhile, on a sofa bed at Friends of the Earth staffer Liz Raisbeck's house in the Adams-Morgan neighborhood of Washington, I'm staring at the ceiling, ruminating on the arguments that are going to be thrown at us in six, five, four short hours. It's going to be a rough day.

At dawn I get up and shave—twice, to be sure. For luck, I put on green boxer shorts from my Peace Corps years in Africa, and a white snail darter T-shirt, inside out so its vivid logo doesn't show through my new white dress shirt. I have a dark, striped three-piece suit bought for this occasion. I meet family at the Court's front steps, and give them audience passes. Hugs and exhortations. Kick butt, says brother Marek. David Hiller and Hank Hill (who'd just learned he'd passed the bar exam) hadn't slept out on the Court's marble porch because they'd gotten two of our allotted six passes. The ones who did sleep out there are waving now from the head of the line as we walk past them and into the building. I find a bathroom—it has lots of marble—to make sure that my bladder is profoundly empty. Then, at 9:30, the sergeant at arms says we can go up to the front well of the courtroom, a classically proportioned, high-ceilinged amphitheater lined with pale Romanesque bas-reliefs, draped in rich maroon velvet, already crowded with observers.

We're motioned to the table at the left of the well—the north side, to the justices' right. We turn and look back at the crowd. In the first public row, a dozen feet away, are Hank, Les Iczkovitz, Sara, Hiller, and four other supporters, grinning and waving. Camping out has rewarded those of our group lacking passes with the best public seats in the house. Don Cohen and Boone Dougherty settle in at the counsel table, and I walk over to the middle of the well and try out the feel of the lectern. It stands just below and in front of the seat of the chief justice.

Behind the wings of the curving bench are eight more chairs, four on each side of the chief justice's domain. When you stand at the podium you have to look upward to see the justices. On top of the podium are two small, bright lights: a white one that winks when you have five minutes left to finish your argument, and a red one that means "Sit down *now!*"

The table is set with a pitcher of water (don't drink from it . . . I have to remain undistracted for two hours) and two white goose feather quill pens traditionally provided for each side arguing before the Court. We give the feathers to Boone for his daughters. Don pulls out his legal pad. He's going to take running notes to identify which justice asks which questions through the morning, because the Court's official transcript doesn't. We lay out a small three-ring binder containing ten different briefs filed in the case by us, by TVA, and by outside friends of the court; the trial record appendix; a thick binder carefully tabbed for quick reference to a couple dozen cases and statutes (is it realistic to think it can be perused under fire?—not likely); and an open folder sheet covered with squiggles, balloons, and buzzwords, spread out like a road map, tracing paths through all the arguments we anticipate.

We walk over to the south side of the well, where the attorney general is laying out his own materials. Bell is stately and tall, wearing a sleek long-tailed morning coat. We introduce ourselves to Bell and Dan Friedman, the intense acting solicitor displaced by Bell's decision to argue this himself, who sits hunched and with a worried look on his face. Good.

"We're glad you're going first," we say to Bell. "This is an intimidating courtroom!" This is intended to be just gentlemanly banter.

"Professor?" He holds up a little bottle of formaldehyde. "I was planning to show the Court this snail darter. It's an exhibit from the trial. Do you have any objection?" Dammit. We know he's not going to use this exhibit for any scientific point. That little bottle is going to be used to trivialize our case.

"No. Fine with us." We could quibble, but who wants to look like a low-class brawler in the well of the Supreme Court? We shake hands with Bell and Friedman. We also nod our heads toward TVA's lead attorney, Herb Sanger, a man for whom we have no respect, hoping that he's been Bell's dominant source of preparatory information, because he's not legally sharp and is viscerally incapable of acknowledging the weaknesses in the dam's factual merits.

We hasten back to our table as the justices are announced: "Oyez, oyez, oyez . . ." At precisely 10:12 a.m. we stand as the justices enter and settle into their seats. They are all smaller than expected, except Chief Justice Burger, who leans forward, the floodlight lavishing his proud face and cloud of silver-white hair. He looks like Zeus. He clears his throat, a basso profundo rumble. (In summing up Burger's merits when he was nominated by President Nixon, a White House staffer noted: "He looks like a chief justice, he sounds like a chief justice.")

> CHIEF JUSTICE BURGER: "We'll hear arguments first this morning in *Tennessee Valley Authority against Hiram G. Hill.* . . . Mr. Attorney General?"[1]

Griffin Bell walks to the lectern. He carefully lays out his papers and the glass vial with its unfortunate little passenger. He gathers himself, and begins:

> The ATTORNEY GENERAL: "Mr. Chief Justice, and may it please the Court. I appear on behalf of the government in this case. My colleague, Mr. Daniel Friedman, appears with me, as does Mr. Herbert S. Sanger, Jr., who is the general counsel of the TVA. In this unusual case, as attorney general I agreed that the secretary of interior could take a position opposite our position in this Court. And I've included—I've stated his position in writing as an Appendix

A Supreme Court "rogue's gallery" of characters involved in the battle over the snail darter, April 18, 1979: (from left), David Etnier, the author, TVA Chairman Aubrey "Red" Wagner, U.S. Attorney General Griffin Bell, Chief Justice Warren Burger, and TVA board member David Freeman. (Courtesy of *Knoxville News Sentinel*)

to our brief. I will, of course, not argue the secretary of interior's position, but it is well stated and I know the Court
will take note of it . . ."

Oh, how Bell must hate having to start this way! But he was overruled
by the White House and had to accept this embarrassing split in the
federal position, so he'd best get it out of the way.

The ATTORNEY-GENERAL: "This case presents a conflict between the snail darter, an endangered species under the
Endangered Species Act, and the Tellico Dam project . . .
a multipurpose project, designed to free a navigable body
of water, electric power, industrial development, flood
control, and recreation on the Little Tennessee River . . ."

Bell begins reciting the geography of the project, but is visibly unsure of
himself. "*Free* a navigable body?" He stumbles too on the dam's location and history, and Burger and Rehnquist (no surprise) jump in to ask
him some easy questions to help settle him down.

JUSTICE REHNQUIST: "General Bell, am I right in thinking that
the Tellico Dam itself is on the Little Tennessee prior to its
confluence with the Tennessee?"
The ATTORNEY GENERAL: "Right, just before the confluence.
[Pause] Now I think it will help if I give a brief chronology
of the project. . . . Construction began in 1967 . . . In 1972
there was a lawsuit . . . Finally TVA prevailed [and] commenced working—"
JUSTICE BURGER: "That was before the discovery of the existence of the snail darter, was it?"
The ATTORNEY-GENERAL: "Yes, sir. In '72 that began. In August '73, the snail darter was discovered. The snail darter
is of the darter—of the perch family. There are 130 known
varieties of darters. There are 85 to 90 in Tennessee alone.
There are 11 in the Little Tennessee River. There have
been 8 to 10 darters discovered these past five years. I have
in my hand a darter . . ."

Here it comes. He wants to underscore the image of an inconsequential
fish, just one of hundreds more just like it. Bell grasps his little bottle,

waves it in the air, and immediately the argument becomes perceptibly more engaging to everyone in the room. Justices and audience alike shift forward in their seats, focusing on the little bottle.

> The ATTORNEY-GENERAL: ". . . a snail darter, Exhibit No. 7 in the case when it was filed. And we brought that with us so you could see it. It's three inches. It is supposed to be a full grown snail darter, about three inches in length."
>
> JUSTICE BRENNAN: "Is it alive?" [Laughter]
>
> The ATTORNEY GENERAL: "I've been wondering what it's in, if it is. It seems to move around. I've been puzzled over that." [More laughter]

Dammit. It's a stupid joke, but already you can feel the start of the comic tone that will kill us if it takes over. Why is Justice Brennan, who is supposed to be on our side, being so flippant?

> JUSTICE STEVENS: "Mr. Attorney General, your exhibit makes me wonder. Does the government take the position that some endangered species are entitled to more protection than others?"

Ah, a chastened quiet immediately returns to the courtroom. Thank you, Justice Stevens! His is a tough, serious question, carrying a not-so-veiled point: *all* endangered species are protected by the law, whether Bell finds them laughably small or not. Stevens's question nips the comedy act in the bud. So Stevens is on our side?

> The ATTORNEY GENERAL: "Well, I don't take it this morning, because I don't have to reach that point—"
>
> JUSTICE STEVENS: "The statute, the Endangered Species Act, doesn't distinguish as among various priorities in the different species, does it?"
>
> The ATTORNEY GENERAL: "It does not. Once it gets on the list, it is an endangered species—"
>
> JUSTICE STEVENS: "And the snail darter is on the list. There's no question about it."
>
> The ATTORNEY GENERAL: "It's on the list, and this particular area has been designated as a—"
>
> JUSTICE STEVENS: "Critical habitat."

The ATTORNEY GENERAL: "—critical habit."

JUSTICE STEVENS: "Right."

Thank you again, Justice Stevens. He's not messing around with the comic stuff. He has clearly read the briefs and is trying to pin down the elements of the statutory violation in order to see Bell's argument. If Stevens is indeed on our side, that probably gives us at least four votes.

> JUSTICE BLACKMUN: "Attorney General Bell, there is something in the briefs about efforts at transplantation, and, I wondered, can you bring us up to date on that? Have they been successful? And secondly, I would like to know whether the construction already done to the dam has so endangered the species that it is not going to survive anyway."

Ouch. Here is Blackmun, whom we figured would be with us and whose first question pulls the discussion away from the violation facts proved at trial and echoes TVA's "common sense" transplantation argument. His second question echoes an amicus brief, filed by the Southeast Legal Foundation, that supports TVA's argument that the darter's natural population is already doomed in the river because of the way the dam's footings block the juvenile fishes' return to their spawning shoals. Are we back down to three justices?

Bell grabs Blackmun's first question and runs with it. Yes, he says, TVA has successfully transplanted two thousand darters to another river, the Hiwassee. He implies that the darter isn't really endangered any longer because of TVA's good-faith efforts to move it to new homes, so an injunction against the dam is unnecessary. But then Justices White and Marshall both ask why, if the fish isn't endangered, it hasn't been taken off the list.

> JUSTICE WHITE: "You say this . . . it's not in the record in this case?"
>
> The ATTORNEY GENERAL: "Not the success story. It's in public documents that were filed with the secretary when TVA tried, to take the . . . there's a petition filed to take the snails—"
>
> JUSTICE WHITE: "Of course, everything in those documents may not be true . . ."
>
> JUSTICE MARSHALL: "But TVA did ask for it to be taken off?"

The ATTORNEY GENERAL: "They did, and after a year the secretary denied it, just in the last two or three months."

Bell is forced to say that Interior, the expert agency, has rejected the transplantation success story. White and Marshall seem to be interested in the details, which is good.

The ATTORNEY GENERAL: "The issue presented is over the construction of the Endangered Species Act, Section 7 of the Act . . ."

Finally he's getting to his legal argument.

The ATTORNEY GENERAL: "The district court went about it on a balancing of equities. . . . Now, we—our argument is that, by the way, the language of the statute itself can be construed to support the district court and allow this dam to be completed and operated, and then there are certain other things that I'll argue that support that. . . . So that's the issue that is presented, the issue that must be resolved: Can there be a balancing of the equitable factors in deciding whether this action taken in the meaning of the statute can be taken."

This is confused. Is he arguing that the Endangered Species Act doesn't apply in the first place and thus is not violated, or that it applies but because of a balancing of equities the violation doesn't deserve an injunction remedy? The second argument, balancing, seems to be a major part of it, which is ironic given that the trial judge *didn't* balance, and Bell's brief for TVA completely avoided that theory. Or is he making both arguments, with the no-injunction argument as his fallback? It certainly isn't easy to think and speak precisely in this tense setting, but at this point Bell isn't making clear what his argument is.

JUSTICE REHNQUIST: "General, when you say 'balancing the equitable factors,' is one of the ways that that would be done the decision of the district court or the court of appeals whether an equitable injunction would issue?

The ATTORNEY GENERAL: "That's it. Yes, sir . . . I think, in essence, that's what the district court judge here did, he took all the factors. He said this dam is finished for all intents and purposes. They have moved these darters, snail darters, over to another place. We do not think that the statute was intended to be applied retroactively. . . . Taking all those things into consideration, I hold that the dam can be used, and the project go forward. In other words, he applied the Endangered Species Act."

Still confusing. Bell picks up on Rehnquist's attempt to help him by saying that, yes, there's a balancing of equitable factors on whether you get an injunction, but he's also arguing both that the statute didn't apply, and that it did.

> JUSTICE BURGER: "What you're saying, I take it, is that the Endangered Species Act is not to be applied, was not intended by Congress to be applied, to projects that were already under way."
> The ATTORNEY GENERAL: "Well, I think it does apply—No, I'm not saying it doesn't apply. It does apply, but then you consider what stage of development the project is in. What are the reasonable alternatives? Could you change it? Could you change the design?"

So now it's back again to balancing? There's no way Bell is going to say there are alternatives available. That would crack TVA's case wide open. Hope we can get to that . . .

> JUSTICE BURGER: "Is one of the factors to be weighed the fact that $120 million has been spent?"
> The ATTORNEY GENERAL: "Exactly. The next argument . . . is the secretary's own regulation at that time . . . which was in effect when the district court decided this case, . . . a tentative regulation, not a final regulation, . . . it said: 'the Department of Interior [doesn't intend] that Section 7 bring about the waste that can occur if an advanced project is halted.' . . . The regulation has since been changed to cite the Sixth Circuit ruling. . . . Now, that's one argument."

Bell's citation to this draft definitional rule seems to be arguing "no violation," but he's showing his integrity: He could have cited the proposed regulation as if it was law, leaving it up to us to take the time and effort to correct it or let it slide. Instead he's honest, saying it was only a proposed rule, and tells the Court that Interior's final rule agreed with us, not with TVA. And how nice it is that ship came in. Had we not won in the court of appeals, the agency's official definitional rule would have interpreted all ongoing projects right out of the law's protections.

> The ATTORNEY GENERAL: "The third is that Congress three
> times—'73, '76, and '77—said 'Go forward with this project.
> We know about the snail darter'—this was in committee
> reports, granted, not on the face of this statute, but—'Go
> forward. We intend for you to complete this project. . . .'"

Bell is implying that in the mind of the congressional appropriations committees there was no violation. This actually should help us, because it would mean *they didn't think they were changing the law* when they passed the money bills. Again Bell is showing integrity here. He clarifies to the Court that the committees did not purport to change the statute, but only inserted a statement in their reports. Bell seems to want to say that technically the law is violated but on balance an injunction remedy should not be ordered. His brief took exactly the opposite tack, however, arguing that there was no violation, and saying not a word on the injunction balance.

> JUSTICE WHITE: "So on any of those grounds that you are
> suggesting, you're suggesting that the statute itself be con-
> strued so that there's no violation here if these gates are
> closed?"
> The ATTORNEY GENERAL: "That's it."
> JUSTICE WHITE: "There's no violation of the statute at all?"
> The ATTORNEY GENERAL: "Right."

Now his argument is clear. The law doesn't apply to a project that's so far under way, or because it was amended by the money bills.

> JUSTICE WHITE: "Your argument *isn't* that it's a violation of the
> statute, but an injunction isn't authorized?"
> The ATTORNEY GENERAL: "That's it."
> JUSTICE WHITE: "That isn't your argument, is it?"
> The ATTORNEY GENERAL: "That is my argument."

Whoops. Now it's back the other way—that there is a violation, but it doesn't deserve an injunction.

> JUSTICE WHITE: "You don't concede there's a violation of the statute, though. You construe the statute so that closing the gates wouldn't violate the statute?"
>
> The ATTORNEY GENERAL: "No, not unless . . . the factors, the facts, taken as a whole, would prevent there being a violation of the statute. I don't concede—I concede the statute applies, though. I think it does apply. I—excuse me."

Ouch. Poor Mr. Bell. He seems to be squirming, unable to argue straightforwardly that the statute does not apply. Why? Could it be that the White House has told him that administration policy—contrary to what he said in his brief—is that the law applies to *all* projects, even those that were under way, and that appropriations don't amend the law? So is Bell now only supposed to argue about injunction balancing, even though his brief said nothing about that, and he's not allowed to make the arguments that his brief makes?

> JUSTICE BLACKMUN: "Mr. Attorney General Bell, I understood your principal argument to be that the statute could not fairly be construed to apply to a project that was either completed or substantially completed."

Blackmun is trying to bring Bell back to make the retroactivity argument, but his question isn't clear. Is Blackmun suggesting the law didn't apply in 1975 when the darter was listed, which would be a statutory construction question, or doesn't apply now, three years later, which would shift it to a commonsense balancing argument? Either way, ouch. We'd counted on Blackmun, but here he is clearly trying to advance TVA's arguments.

> The ATTORNEY GENERAL: "Well, but that would be like . . . you'd have to have a hearing to see if the statute could be read as applying to those particular facts."
>
> JUSTICE BLACKMUN: "I understand you'd have to have a hearing. But . . ."

For the next several minutes, despite Blackmun's earnest attempts, Bell refuses to say simply that the law doesn't apply retroactively. And when

Blackmun shifts to the other tack, inviting Bell to say that the law was amended by appropriations to TVA for the dam and transplanting the darter, Bell again refuses to argue that the funding bills exempted Tellico from the law, even though that was the central argument of his brief. It's becoming clear to us that Blackmun is not with us, and that Bell, for some reason, will not or cannot make the argument that his brief does—that the law doesn't apply. The attorney general seems to be saying that the retroactivity issue, the appropriations bills, and the congressional intent arguments are relevant only to the balancing question.

And he isn't digging deeply into that balancing argument either. Why? Maybe because as a man of integrity he knows he cannot truthfully say the trial judge carefully balanced the comparative merits. Maybe he doesn't know the facts, or suspects the dam isn't so great. Maybe it's just because it's not in his brief because the White House told him not to put it in there. Poor Griffin Bell. He either doesn't know what he wants to argue, or has been told by the Oval Office that he cannot argue what he wants to.

> JUSTICE STEVENS: "Did Congress ever grant an exemption from the Endangered Species Act for the snail darter?"
> The ATTORNEY GENERAL: "They have not."
> JUSTICE STEVENS: "Might it have been the most unambiguous way to resolve the whole thing? . . . Much better than just hiding it in a committee report in an appropriations bill?"
> JUSTICE MARSHALL: "Generally, it is easier to dump it on us, and we've never even seen the snail darter."
> [UNKNOWN SPEAKER] (aloud but not into microphone): "Yes, we have!" [Laughter.]

It looks as if Justice Stevens understands the pork committees, and he buys our argument that implying statutory changes from money bills isn't the way law is supposed to be made. He's telling Bell it's up to the full Congress, not the Court and not the pork-barrel committee report, to rewrite the law.

> JUSTICE STEWART: "Well, the statute requires more than just consultation in good faith. It . . . requires, in rather clear and unambiguous words, the agency to take such action

234 THE HIGHEST COURT?

'*necessary to ensure* that actions authorized, funded, or carried out by it do not jeopardize the continued existence of the endangered species, or the destruction or modification of its critical habitat.' And as I understand it, it's conceded that the completion of this dam will jeopardize the continued existence of this endangered species . . . or the modification of its critical habitat."

Stewart is laying out the violation. He's with us?

The ATTORNEY GENERAL: "Well, unless this moving over to the Hiwassee River makes that into a noncritical habitat."

JUSTICE STEWART: "But the secretary has determined *this* to be the critical habitat, has he not?"

The ATTORNEY GENERAL: "At the time, yes."

JUSTICE STEWART: "And has determined this little fish to be an endangered species."

The ATTORNEY GENERAL: "Right."

JUSTICE STEWART: "It seems—the language of the statute that I just read aloud for my own information and to refresh your memory—seems to me to be an unambiguous requirement."

Yes, Stewart is definitely with us!

JUSTICE MARSHALL: "Mr. Attorney General, what would happen if they found snail darters in the basement of this building? Would they tear the building down, this building?"

Ohmigod. What? Another joke, interrupting Stewart and making fun of the Endangered Species Act. Or worse, is Marshall buying TVA's argument that our reading of the law is too extreme?

The ATTORNEY GENERAL: "You'd have to ask the Sixth Circuit that. I think they'd enjoin you from functioning if they found it to be a critical habitat."

No laughter this time, a good sign. Maybe the audience can sense here that a serious point is getting interrupted by Justice Marshall's comments.

JUSTICE STEWART: "Has there been any proposal in Congress to amend Section 7 of the Endangered Species Act? . . . Not to generally amend the language, but a specific exemption?"

Thank God. Stewart pulls it back to sanity, the question of *who* should have the job of amending statutes, the Court or Congress?

The ATTORNEY GENERAL: "Yes there has, to exclude this snail darter."

JUSTICE STEWART: "And what's the status of that bill?"

The ATTORNEY GENERAL: "It's pending in the committee, and has not come out of the committee, as I understand it."

JUSTICE STEVENS: "Of course. . . . Mr. Attorney General, if we were to sustain the injunction, Congress could always exclude the snail darter later. But if we let the snail darter be extinguished, I guess the choice is irrevocable. . . . I mean, what assumption do we make for the purposes of deciding? Is the snail darter going to be extinguished or not?"

The ATTORNEY GENERAL: "Only the secretary under the law can find that."

JUSTICE STEVENS: "And he has found it will be, hasn't he?"

The ATTORNEY GENERAL: "That's what he found at one time . . ."

Justice Stevens is really nailing it down. Whose job is it to make the law? Congress. And whose job is it to determine biology, whether the fish is really endangered? The secretary of interior. And Justice Stevens has the political realities right too: if the citizens lose in court they have no prayer of getting Congress to revise the law in their favor. If TVA loses, they surely will have the political pull to get a congressional rehearing.

But where is Rehnquist? Burger? And Blackmun has also gone silent now as Bell is pulled into the question of who should properly determine the facts. Having helped Bell at the start with friendly questions, are they now saving their hot fire for us environmentalists? Powell doesn't like judicial activism. Maybe he's leaning our way. Marshall is unpredictable. And what about White?

> JUSTICE WHITE: "Well, Mr. Attorney General, why shouldn't there—why shouldn't the Court remand this case to have the record brought up to date? A lot of things have happened since the court of appeals decided it."
>
> The ATTORNEY GENERAL: "Well, I—that's exactly right. You might well want to do that. I'm not objecting to it . . ."

Uh-oh. What's this? "Remand" means send it back to ol' Judge Taylor in Tennessee, for what? More facts? But nothing has changed. The secretary just decided two months ago that the fish was still endangered despite TVA's efforts to transplant it. What will we say if White asks us about a remand? He seems to want to get the decision out of this court. But if it stays here, is he leaning our way or TVA's? If we go back to Tennessee, we're in a hostile court, with no money to litigate. Time will drag on, and time is our enemy: so long as the river channel remains blocked by the dam's base plates, each seasonal cycle is going to kill off further chunks of the Little T's darter population.

For several more minutes White and Stewart muse back and forth with Bell about the proper way to figure out whether the fish is still endangered. Their discussion peters out with the recognition that if TVA believes the fish isn't endangered, the agency should be arguing with Interior in a separate district court case, not with us in this enforcement action.

> JUSTICE POWELL: "Mr. Attorney General, may I ask you a friendly question? Let's assume that in order to resolve this issue, somebody introduced a bill in Congress saying explicitly that Section 7 shall apply to every completed federal project in the United States. Do you think many congressmen who voted for that clarification of this statute would be reelected? . . . And doesn't that suggest that nobody, really no one rationally, could apply this to a completed project?"
>
> The ATTORNEY GENERAL: "It does to me. . . ."

OK. Now we hear from Powell, and it's not good. He clearly thinks our view of the law is nuts.

> JUSTICE POWELL: "May I ask you one other, maybe less-friendly, question? You commenced your argument—and I felt for

you—by saying that it was not without precedent for two
departments of the government to come to our Court in
an antagonistic position. It's not easy for us to resolve—I
speak for myself—it's not easy for us to resolve issues of
vast importance to our country when two Cabinet-level
departments are at sword's point. I wonder why these
things aren't determined at the Cabinet level rather than
submitting them to us?'"

The ATTORNEY GENERAL: "You say that's not so friendly. It's
a very friendly question. It gives me an opportunity to say
that I do not favor this system. We have one attorney general and one solicitor general, and I think that ought to be
it. But as long as you can do it, people will ask you to do
it. . . . It's the only time we've done it since I've been attorney general. I don't favor it. But I'm glad I had a chance
to say so."

Interesting. The Rehnquist conservatives are still remaining silent,
and Powell, who sounds like a certain reversal vote against us, is shifting the argument away from Bell's argument for TVA onto an irrelevant
procedural issue—whether the U.S. government should speak with
one voice. Nevertheless, this question of dueling agencies seems to interest some justices, and Bell's response reveals an unspoken riddle.
What exactly is the role of the attorney general when he decides to
represent TVA against another federal agency's position? Is he taking
that position as attorney for TVA, or as attorney for the entire federal
government? Bell seems to think that, short of the president, he as
attorney general should be allowed to decide what the position of the
entire administration on the Endangered Species Act is to be. No
wonder Secretary Andrus reacted violently and submitted a counter-
brief.

JUSTICE STEVENS: "But Mr. Attorney General, are you suggesting that if the secretary of the interior has placed a species
on the endangered species list, that the attorney general
should have the power to take it off the list?"

The ATTORNEY GENERAL: "No, no, I'm not suggesting that."

JUSTICE STEVENS: "No matter what we do, that part of the
record is before us. The secretary of the interior has

238 THE HIGHEST COURT?

> determined that this is an endangered species. . . . We
> can't second-guess him on that, can we?"
>
> The ATTORNEY GENERAL: "No, that's his prerogative. I'm not
> denying that."

Justice Stevens is so sharp. He is reminding Bell and the Court about separation of powers. The secretary of interior is the statutory agent who has determined the fish is endangered by the dam, and any talk of transplants and nonendangerment is beside the point. Whatever Bell's arguments are, he should be focusing on legal points, not biological arguments.

No one seems to have any more questions for Bell about TVA's case. Justice White makes a comment, thinking out loud about other occasions when the Court has seen federal agencies opposing each other, and then the chief justice signals Bell to sit down: "Thank you, Mr. Attorney General." Unhappily, Bell sits down. He's never made clear exactly what his legal argument is. Is he regretting now that he demanded the right to represent TVA himself? Dare we be a little bit optimistic?

> CHIEF JUSTICE BURGER: "Mr. Plater?"

Okay . . . I walk up to the podium, lay out the argument chart alongside the three-ring binder and the briefs. I adjust the glass of water that will not be touched. Attorney General Bell hasn't seemed to set any difficult traps for us, and now we know which judges are going to throw some tough questions at us, so best get right to it. Just try to lay out the darter's case as clearly as possible. Grasping the sides of the podium, clenching my bowels, I look up at the leonine head of the chief justice. He nods.

> COUNSEL: "Thank you, Mr. Chief Justice, and may it please the
> Court. I am Zygmunt Plater for respondents. In this case
> the respondents quite simply support the unanimous deci-
> sion of the Court of Appeals for the Sixth Circuit that the
> TVA must obey the law. Although the case arises from a
> conservation issue, it essentially turns on traditional ques-
> tions of separation of powers and administrative law—"
>
> JUSTICE BLACKMUN: "Mr. Plater, Judge McCree did write sepa-
> rately below, didn't he? Did you feel that he was, however,
> joining the majority opinion?"

Ouch. Only twenty seconds into the argument, and Justice Blackmun nails me. It's not a friendly question. He means I'm exaggerating the facts: It was *not* unanimous. Judge McCree wrote a short separate opinion, and he didn't fully agree with the reasoning of the other two judges.

> COUNSEL: "Yes, Your Honor. Judge McCree below said that he concurred with the result of the court's opinion. The fact, also, that, indeed, the TVA project must be enjoined, because it would eliminate the species from the face of the earth."

I'm flailing already.

> JUSTICE BLACKMUN: "Well many times, when we appear particularly to concur in the result, it means we think the majority opinion was rather poor, and we have reasons of our own."
>
> COUNSEL: "Your Honor, I don't want to second-guess Judge McCree, but it might be noted—"
>
> JUSTICE BLACKMUN: "Well, you said it was a unanimous opinion. It may be a unanimous judgment, but I wanted to—"

—to nitpick? And to do it in a way that undermines the fact that Judge McCree, now Bell's second-in-command as solicitor general, voted for the darter when he was our judge in the court of appeals?

> COUNSEL: "Unanimous *position* taken by the Sixth Circuit that this project should be enjoined. Thank you, Your Honor."

With this and the leading questions you gave Bell, we kiss your vote goodbye. I press on.

> COUNSEL: "The unanimous position, then, taken by the Sixth Circuit, and the position taken by the Department of the Interior and by the respondent, comes down essentially to two basic points: The first point is that Congress, in 1973, when this species was discovered, wrote a mandatory statute to the agencies, . . . prohibiting those agencies from taking actions which would jeopardize or destroy endangered species. . . . That section is clearly violated by this dam portion of the Tellico project. And secondly, Congress has not changed the law. Although Congress is reviewing

public interest resolutions for the conflict, Congress hasn't changed the law, and the *Court* should not amend the law. And yet that is precisely what TVA's position is asking the Court to do, to construct some form of implied, informal, grandfather clause exemption for this project. . . . And to construct some sort of informal statutory amendment, overriding the Endangered Species Act, based on appropriations funding."

That's it. They let me lay out the entire basic argument. Make it clear: the Court should just enforce the law. It should reject TVA's jumbled request that the Court in some way should rewrite Congress's law.

> JUSTICE MARSHALL: "Suppose you found snake darters [*sic*] around Chickamauga Dam on the TVA? What would you do?"

Ah. This is a real question. Thank God he's not asking about snail darters in the Supreme Court basement. Marshall is asking whether the law's prohibition is so extreme that it would mean tearing down a finished, operating dam. It's like Powell's question to Bell that showed Powell thinks our interpretation is irrational and extreme. But now the head count shows you desperately need Marshall's vote.

> COUNSEL: "Your Honor, that is a question also like the question asked by Mr. Justice Powell. And the point is, biologists tell us that if you would find a species in a completed project, that would be a biological indication that that population was not endangered by the dam, because indeed it was living there, established there and breeding. And of course, no completed dam would have to be taken down."
>
> JUSTICE MARSHALL: "Well suppose the Department of the Interior said it was?"
>
> COUNSEL: "Your Honor, the Department of the Interior—"
>
> JUSTICE MARSHALL: "You'd have to tear Chickamauga Dam down."
>
> COUNSEL: "No, your Honor, all they have is biological authority to assert that the endangered species is there, and is threatened by the present circumstances."

What should I be arguing here to get around Marshall's fear of interpreting the statutory language too extremely? I'm not speaking smoothly.

> JUSTICE MARSHALL: "Well, suppose, they say that?"
> COUNSEL: "Well, Your Honor, the Department of the Interior—"
> JUSTICE MARSHALL: "—and they're wrong?"
> COUNSEL: "If they're wrong, then—this answers a question posed also by Mr. Justice White—there are proceedings currently under way in district court in Tennessee challenging another listing of an endangered species, arguing that the Department of the Interior is wrong. That is the way to do it. The biological opinion of the secretary, once established, is established, and is not to be overturned by lawyers trying to debate biology."

That's a good response. But, uh, on second thought it's self-contradictory. I deride the idea of lawyers debating biology, but agree that the secretary's biological decision *can* be reviewed in a court, which would require lawyers to debate biology, wouldn't it? Wasn't there a better answer we wanted to make?

> JUSTICE STEWART: "You concede there is judicial review of the secretary of the interior's action? Whether in putting a species on the endangered list, or in saying that a certain area is its critical habitat? Is there judicial review of either finding?"

Stewart to the rescue! He pins down for himself and for the Court that we are not making the extreme argument that the secretary's findings are absolute. They are reviewable in a proper action, and we can now make that clearer.

> COUNSEL: "Yes, Your Honor. There appears to be. The current pending action seeks a delisting of the species. . . ."
> JUSTICE BURGER: "Let me pursue a question that Mr. Justice Marshall put to you. Suppose that you have a $300- or $400-million dam—I don't know the . . . cost of the one he mentioned—and you are confronted with a showing that originally there were 300,000 of a particular species, and

now by the operation of the dam over a period of years, it's
down to 10,000 and it's about to become extinct. Are you
suggesting that Congress intended that that dam should
be torn down?"

Burger, as expected, wants to make us look fanatical. It's a touchy
question.

> COUNSEL: "Your Honor, that of course is not this case."
> JUSTICE BURGER: "Well, I know. I'm asking you hypothetical
> questions to test your argument. As we did with the attor-
> ney general."

Yes, and we'd be happy to get the kind of cream puff questions you
gave Bell to help his case. Burger is posing this hypothetical question
to make us look like extremists. What was it I was supposed to pull into
the argument here?

> COUNSEL: "Your Honor, that is certainly a question that would
> have to be raised. We do not take a position on that argu-
> ment. But the point is, Congress appears to have cared very
> clearly about the prevention of the extinction of species.
> There were two prior statutes, in 1966 and 1969, which gave
> agencies discretion, and the courts reviewing them to bal-
> ance the question, and those statutes did not work, so that
> Section 7 was written in 1973 as mandatory . . ."

Flailing again. They already know it's mandatory. That's why the drastic language scares them.

> COUNSEL: "Your Honor's question is one that is certainly diffi-
> cult to handle . . ."

Right. It makes us look apocalyptic. What do I need to say here?—the
killer argument that it's *Congress* that should make those hard choices.
I should have jumped into the Congress argument as soon as Burger
popped his question: "If the language of the Act is too drastic, it's up to
Congress, not the Court, to fix it, so send extreme cases back to Congress by enforcing the law with an injunction."

Is it too late? Maybe I can slide Burger's question over into the Congress point . . .

COUNSEL: "I think that the easiest way to handle that is perhaps to take the hypothetical that General Bell ably brought out, and that is this: There may be cases where the public interest is so intimately involved with a case, and a species would be jeopardized, that indeed there must be a hard decision taken, and the species rendered extinct. Now, that's never had to occur. There's never in human history been a conscious extinction of a species. But we say that indeed that may be the case. The point is, however—"

JUSTICE MARSHALL: "—Do we know the facts right now? Do we know how many snail darters are there?"

Argh. I was just about to say, "The point is, it's *Congress* that should do this," but Marshall is cutting me off and going off again on whether the darter is really endangered.

COUNSEL: "We know approximately, Your honor. And this is—"

Here I am again about to say, "And this is what *Congress* properly should review," getting it back to separation of powers, but I'm cut off again.

JUSTICE MARSHALL: "Well, how many have been removed?"

Dammit, I don't know. But who cares so long as the secretary says it's still endangered?

COUNSEL: "In the present case, Your Honor, we do not have a full record on the transplantation. But—"

JUSTICE MARSHALL: "—Don't we need that? Suppose where they're now living, they are six and eight inches long, and just having a ball? [Laughter] Would your argument be the same?"

COUNSEL: "Your Honor—"

JUSTICE MARSHALL: "—Would your argument be the same?"

COUNSEL: "No, Your Honor, it would not be, if the secretary of the interior—"

JUSTICE MARSHALL: "—You wouldn't have any argument, would you?"

COUNSEL: "Your Honor—"

JUSTICE MARSHALL: "—Shouldn't we find that out?"

This hurts. Marshall is a vote we need, and he's hammering me to say either that I don't care about whether the darter is really endangered—which would make me look like a devious cynic—or that this case needs to go back to Tennessee to see what the darter's numbers are today. If he understood the law he'd realize what White, Stevens, and Stewart already concluded: given the secretary's official findings, the question about darter numbers should be irrelevant to this court. Even the trial court said the secretary was accurate. If TVA wants to sue the secretary, fine, but not here in our case.

> COUNSEL: "Your Honor, if the secretary of the interior changes the listing of the species and the critical habitat, then clearly this case is no longer—"
> JUSTICE MARSHALL: "—That was not my question."
> COUNSEL: "Excuse me. I misunderstood."

I understood perfectly well but thought the question was a red herring.

> JUSTICE MARSHALL: "My question was: Should we know what the transplanted snail darters . . . how they are faring? Shouldn't we know that before we decide this case? . . . I'm not talking about the secretary of the interior. I'm talking about us."
> COUNSEL: "All right. Your Honor, the factual situation presented in our brief is up to date as well as is known by anyone. And that is this situation: TVA claims that approximately two thousand fish now exist in the Hiwassee. But as they revealed in Senate hearings, and noted at footnote 26 in our brief—"
> JUSTICE MARSHALL: "—Well, then, how can we—you're now getting ready to say that what they say is not true."
> COUNSEL: "Your Honor, that is based—"
> JUSTICE MARSHALL: "—How can we know what's true?"
> COUNSEL: "Because—"

Please God, get us out of this cul-de-sac. Rehnquist is sitting there grinning, probably because he knows Marshall is wasting large amounts of our time on a side issue, and he senses from Marshall's tone that maybe Marshall doesn't like this case and is going to vote with him.

JUSTICE MARSHALL: "—We're not a fact-finding body."

OK. Give him some data and maybe he'll let go.

> COUNSEL: "Your Honor, that's correct. The TVA's biological data perhaps is determinative here. In December of last year, they did transects in the Hiwassee River, and they revealed, out of 710 fish that were put in, 5 fish left in the transects on the original shoals, and I believe it was 9 juveniles near the flowage of the Ocoee River. That is the latest scientific evidence on how many fish are in the Hiwassee."
>
> JUSTICE MARSHALL: "If I may correct you, that's the latest scientific evidence that you know about."
>
> COUNSEL: "Your Honor, I've checked the records of the secretary of interior."
>
> JUSTICE MARSHALL: "Well, I mean, suppose there are some other records available. Do you seriously object to this going back?"

Yes, we do! How to explain Judge Taylor to him, or that this little group of citizens cannot endlessly carry on the burden of doing the government's work enforcing the laws, building more and more evidence of violation, trying to get a decisive order out of the Court while every week TVA pours more and more tax dollars into its reservoir development construction, and smugly watches the darter's natural population dwindling toward oblivion.

> COUNSEL: "Your Honor, there may be reasons for this case to be remanded. However, transplantation is not a fulfillment of the Act, and therefore that would be an incidental inquiry. We believe—"

I'm about to say, "We believe the Court should enforce the law, then let *Congress* resolve this case on the merits," but again Burger cuts me off.

> JUSTICE BURGER: "—Do you mean that even if a successful transplant took place, you'd still be opposing the functioning of this dam?"
>
> COUNSEL: "Not at all, Your Honor."

Yes, of course we'd still oppose it. One transplant doesn't guarantee survival, and that last large natural population at Coytee Spring is trying to tell America something about this river. But Burger is clearly insinuating that environmentalists don't care about the darter. We are, just as Paul Harvey says on the radio, a bunch of eco-communists trying to stop progress.

> COUNSEL: "We would request that legal procedures be followed. If the transplantation were a success so that the species were no longer endangered, the secretary of interior, petitioned by TVA, would review the biology data for this Court and for Congress, would certify that it is no longer endangered, take it off the list, and that would be the end of the case."
>
> JUSTICE STEWART: "If the fish thrive in the Hiwassee River?"
>
> COUNSEL: "Your Honor, if the fish thrive in the Hiwassee River, then indeed, as Mr. Chief Justice Burger suggested . . ."

Sucking up to Burger . . .

> COUNSEL: ". . . as Mr. Chief Justice Burger suggested, through this procedure this case would come to an end. But that does not appear to be the biological evidence. As a matter of fact, it appears that the best place for a species to live is in its only known natural habitat—"
>
> JUSTICE BURGER: "—Well, that's not historically true for every species. There have been all sorts of species transplanted into new areas where they did much better then they ever did in their original homes. Isn't that the history of evolution?"

Hmmm. Burger has jumped back in at the sound of his own name, and seems as if he wants to talk science. But what he's saying implies that because biodiversity is dynamic, you may not need protections for natural populations. After all, extinction too is natural. Better give him some science that favors keeping the fish in its natural home.

> COUNSEL: "Your Honor . . . the Hiwassee River is connected geographically to the Little Tennessee. Biologists tell us that if the Hiwassee were a good habitat for the species, it would be there already by the process of evolution, but

that, rather, this species turns out to be a highly sensitive indicator of precisely the qualities of the habitat that the citizens were fighting about in this case for years before the snail darters were known to exist."

Sloppy, but I'm trying to turn the argument toward the canary-in-a-coal-mine point, that endangered species protections provide rational corollary benefits for humans.

JUSTICE POWELL: "Mr. Plater?"
COUNSEL: "Yes?"

Powell is smiling graciously. Maybe he's not trying to nail me, after all.

JUSTICE POWELL: "May I interrupt you right here? Apart from the biological interest—which I say we do not challenge—what purpose is served, if any, by these little darters? Are they used for food?"

Wrong—he's indeed trying to nail me. But his question is helpful. This is the classic "common sense" utility question: "Isn't this little fish worthless to humans? Why should we care about protecting it?" These are policy questions, not legal, but it's good. Powell's giving me an opportunity to tell how saving this fish makes human common sense:

COUNSEL: "No, Your Honor. When Congress passed the law, it made it clear that the purpose of the Act was to prohibit the extinction of species for a variety of reasons. One of them was where there was a food value or a direct economic value; others—for scientific study; the philosophical question—that, indeed, a species should not be eliminated; and biological diversity. But ultimately there's a utilitarian purpose that is served precisely by the snail darter. That is to say, even though it doesn't have food value . . . it is highly sensitive to clean, clear, cool flowing river water. And after sixty-eight dams through the TVA river system—sixty-eight of them, one after the other—the range of the snail darter has apparently been destroyed, one by one, until this last thirty-three river miles is the last place on earth where the species, and human beings as well, have the quality of that habitat."

That was pretty good. I've been able to present the darter as canary, my major rational policy argument for saving the darter, bolstering the legal argument. I still haven't gotten to the send-it-back-to-Congress argument, though.

> JUSTICE POWELL: "So that's the last place it's been discovered, I take it?"
> COUNSEL: "Your Honor, TVA has looked *everywhere* for snail darters." [Laughter]

Hallelujah. We've transferred the laughter and mockery onto TVA. The courtroom audience is laughing with us, not at us, and that makes a significant tonal difference.

> JUSTICE MARSHALL: "They haven't searched the basement of our building yet. That's what I'm worried about."

This crack gets no laughter. Another good sign.

> COUNSEL: "Your Honor, if snail darters were in the basement of this building then I suspect they would not be in danger."

Lame, but keep it going.

> JUSTICE POWELL: "Mr. Plater? Are they suitable for bait? I'm a bass fisherman."

He's a fisherman. Be nice. This line of talk may be way off the point, but if the dynamics appeal to Powell, maybe he'll come back to our side.

> COUNSEL: "Your Honor, the Little Tennessee River has a fine bass population in its lower stretches, both smallmouth and largemouth, but they don't appear to be interested in the snail darter, which perhaps is why the snail darter has survived."
> JUSTICE MARSHALL: "They're indigestible."
> COUNSEL: "Pardon me? . . ."

What the heck, Justice Marshall? Just keep going . . . bring this back to something logical.

> COUNSEL: ". . . The snail darter holds over very shallow shoals. It's a highly specialized fish, as I was indicating, an indica-

tor of water quality. Instead of a dead one, I've left with the clerk several prints, which were Exhibit No. 12 at trial, which show the species in its natural habitat along the bottom of the river; and this would be eliminated. There are now 2,500 miles of dammed-up river in the Tennessee area, more than twice the coastline of all the Great Lakes combined. And this is the last such stretch of river which is left."

Hot damn! As I'm talking here, the Clerk of the Supreme Court stands up and edges along behind the bench, handing each justice a copy of the Exhibit 12 lithograph that I'd left with him. It's a lovely print, showing the crystal clear beauty of the river shoals. Perhaps the justices will look into the beautiful brown eyes of the two little darters in the picture and feel some empathy. Far more meaningful than a dead fish in a vial!

> JUSTICE REHNQUIST: "Mr. Plater, isn't it at least an arguable part of the intent of Congress that the government simply leaves certain areas of nature alone, without necessarily having a reason for leaving them alone, but just that they didn't want any more elimination of species, and so forth."

What's this? Rehnquist has come in, and he's mentioning Congress, but what in God's name do congressional nature reserves have to do with it? Maybe he's suggesting that protecting species doesn't make sense except inside parks? That's pure policy, not law. . . . Can I pull this toward the separation of powers issue? And where is Justice Brennan, whom we've been told is on our side, but who has said only one thing, his joke with Bell about whether the fish in the bottle is alive?

> COUNSEL: "The Devil's Hole pupfish case, which this Court decided, was such a case, where there was one small area that was made into a reserve. This Court unanimously upheld that reservation."

And Rehnquist himself wrote that decision.

> JUSTICE BURGER: "We weren't faced with the conflict between the pupfish and a $120-million dam, though."

Excellent—Burger thinks he's taking a swipe, but he's giving us a great chance to overthrow the pernicious cliché that is cursing us every day in the media. It's *not* a big dam!

COUNSEL: "Your Honor, that isn't the conflict in this case either. The $120 million which Your Honor refers to is the total project cost. But the project is not primarily the dam. As a matter of fact, the dam structure cost $5 million, a large part of which was labor, . . . plus earthworks. It is talked about as a dam, because that was certainly the focus for TVA's planning. The $120 million, Your Honor, is for the purchase of thirty-eight thousand acres of land, less than half of which was to be flooded, that was condemned for resale at a profit to pay off the cost of the project. Twenty-five thousand acres of those are prime agricultural land. And to say that that would be lost by destroying this darter—not to consider the fact that the project includes land purchases, roads, and bridges which are immensely beneficial to the people, and to focus on the dam itself, which Congress itself is now reassessing completely—is to lose sight of the realities of the situation . . ."

Yes, Burger has given me a chance to lay out the startling truth: The dam is small, only a lousy $5 million, most of TVA's project involves condemning family farms for resale, and most past project expenditures are beneficial to the public even without a dam. Will this make some of the conservative justices—and reporters—prick up their ears?

COUNSEL: ". . . The conflict in this case is between an agency which has, since 1973—when there was only a little bit of that concrete there, out of $120 million to be spent—in 1973 they took the position that they would not comply with the Endangered Species Act, and, as we noted on page 13 of our brief . . . doubled the amount of money spent. . . . The conflict in this case is between an agency that did not want to consider anything but the original dam as proposed."

It's a new story we're giving them: The media cliché is wrong, private property rights are at stake too, and TVA is full of bad faith.

JUSTICE BRENNAN: "I take it—what did you mean when you said Congress is now reconsidering what?"

Ah, here's Brennan finally, and he hits right on our argument on the role of Congress.

> COUNSEL: "Yes, Your Honor. Once the injunction came down, the Sixth Circuit said the law will be enforced—that is the role of the courts—and there were immediately a series of actions taken in the proper committees with jurisdiction over the Act, that is to say the House Merchant Marine and Fisheries Committee, and the Senate Public Works and Environment Committee. They requested a GAO study to review the cost evaluation of the dam project— and they found it was highly unreliable—and secondly, to look at what alternatives there were, even today, for resolving this issue.
>
> Mr. Justice Powell talked about it as a dam which is fully completed, no other alternatives. That is the way petitioner would characterize it. But Congress is not doing so. The GAO study indicates there are a series of project modifications which were suggested to TVA as early as 1974, which they have rejected again and again, which still today appear to be even more profitable than the dam. Farming, for instance, is the first industry of Tennessee, and it would be destroyed in the valley area. Tourism is the second, and, I note in Appendix B, this dam project is up against the Smoky Mountains."

Boy, they're letting me roll along on this now, and I'm killing two birds with one stone: this is all relevant to the "Let-Congress-do-it" argument, but it is also giving the Court and the media reporters some of the dramatic commonsense policy facts on why the darter should win on the economic merits. If they're listening.

> JUSTICE MARSHALL: "You couldn't call roads endangered species, could you?"
> COUNSEL: "No, not at all, Your Honor."

Oh shoot, not this again.

> JUSTICE MARSHALL: "Well, that's what we're talking about. We're not talking about closing down roads."

COUNSEL: "Your Honor, the Congress is weighing, on one hand, the original dam project, which includes valuable investment in roads, bridges in the valley, and—"

JUSTICE MARSHALL: "—Well, I thought the question was, Is Congress considering what was going to be done about this particular matter, including snail darters—"

COUNSEL: "Precisely."

JUSTICE MARSHALL: "—like this one here. Not roads."

COUNSEL: "That's exactly right."

Marshall doesn't get it. No one thinks this case can be decided by focusing only on the darter. Congress could find that we can protect the darter in its river habitat, abandon the dam, and the new roads and bridges will be valuable without the dam.

JUSTICE BRENNAN: "Are you suggesting, Mr. Plater, that Congress may finally decide we better abandon this whole dam? At least the dam?"

God love you, Your Honor.

COUNSEL: "Yes, Your Honor. The dam has always been only a small portion of the project. The project wasn't passed— not for hydropower purposes—electrical power—barge— those were all minor. It was passed to create industrial subsidized lots, and more recreation in an area where you've already got twenty-two recreational lakes within sixty miles. Congress, indeed, is saying that although we've lost . . . not $120 million but something far less than half of that, the value of the remainder may be several times greater than the purported claims for the dam. That is to say, Congress is reviewing it. And I'm pleased to announce— . . ."

Ouch. Why did I say "announce," which sounds inappropriate and grandiose?

COUNSEL: ". . . that the agencies are reviewing it as well. In the reply brief of TVA, it is noted that the new director of TVA has agreed that the dam is not integral to this project. The project has benefits which can be achieved as well or better

without destruction of the valley by a reservoir. And sec-
ondly, I was informed just today, Your Honors, that the
secretary of the interior has requested—"

JUSTICE MARSHALL: "—Well, just speaking for myself, I'm not
interested in what you discovered today. I've got a record
here."

Marshall didn't seem to care about the record in front of him on the
transplant issue. But now he can make me sound grandiosely off the
record because of my "announcing" and my news flash tone about
the secretary.

COUNSEL: "Your Honor, our case is fully sufficient on the record. It shows that there is a violation, it shows that Congress, in the law-making committee, is considering exactly
the question that Your Honor—"

JUSTICE MARSHALL: "—But doesn't the record also show that
this dam was not for hydraulic purposes?"

What's going on here? Is Marshall just being nasty for the heck of it?

COUNSEL: "That's exactly right, Your Honor."

JUSTICE MARSHALL: "Why don't you say that instead of what
you were told today? Because that's in the record."

COUNSEL: "Your Honor, it's clear in the record that this project
was being made for general regional economic development. It's the last dam in Tennessee Valley Authority's history. It's the most marginal. It's the last one on the list of 1933
dams to be built."

Help. Would somebody please jump in and help get this back on track?
And now the goddam white light is on, saying I'm going to have to sit
down in five minutes, and I haven't yet gotten to the argument that I
absolutely have to make about Congress.

JUSTICE STEVENS: "Mr. Plater, let me interrupt you with just
one question. Because there's been an awful lot of discussion about things that have happened since the district
court tried this case. Is any of that relevant to our decision?
Anything the attorney general said, or anything you've
been telling us in response to all these questions? We have

a finding of fact that this closing the dam would result in total destruction of the snail darter's habitat. Do we have to know anything else?"

Thank you, God and Justice Stevens.

COUNSEL: "No, Your Honor. I agree completely with Your Honor's question."

Oops, a little too obsequiously, gushingly grateful here. But Stevens has put us right into the "Let-Congress-do-it" argument.

JUSTICE BURGER: "Well, let me put another question to you that I think is in addition to that. You haven't discussed it yet, and you don't have much time left. Do you suggest that any of the legislation passed here has abrogated the normal equity function of a United States district judge in granting an injunction, the very extraordinary relief that is sought here—that—are you suggesting that he should not function as he does with any other application for an injunction?"

—Argh. Burger's pulling us away from the Congress argument and tossing this judicial turf question at us like a grenade. He's saying we're trying to strip judges of their traditional powers. Out of the corner of my eye I see Rehnquist rocking forward in his seat, nodding his head and mouthing the words "abrogate the equity functions of a judge." Has Rehnquist set up Burger to ask this question, needling the chief justice that we upstarts are challenging the sacred turf of the federal courts? Burger finishes the question and leans back away from the microphone, muttering something sotto voce, something about how, darn right, judges still have those powers!

But bless you, Justice Burger. Though he doesn't realize it, he's helped us by raising the balancing-of-equities issue that's critical, even though the only mention of it in the parties' briefs was in our footnote 40.

COUNSEL: "Not at all, Your Honor. That question is an important one. We do not advocate the stripping of this Court, or any court, of their equitable powers. And indeed, Your Honor, we rely on Your Honor's decision in *Rondeau v.*

*Mosinee Paper Corporation*—that is to say, the equity courts 'have the full panoply of powers required *to enforce the laws of Congress.*'"

Hah. Footnote 40! Burger looks up quickly when he hears me cite his own opinion, just as Lee Bollinger predicted. Rehnquist suddenly looks frantic and pitches forward.

> JUSTICE REHNQUIST: "But *Hecht against Bowles* says you *don't* get an injunction automatically for a statutory violation!"
>
> COUNSEL: "That's correct, Your Honor. And we do not insist on an injunction. If petitioner agreed to obey the law voluntarily, as the Hecht Corporation did in that case, or as the Mosinee Paper Corporation agreed in Your Honor's case [nodding again toward Burger]—"
>
> JUSTICE BURGER: "—Then you don't need an injunction."

Yahoo! Burger's got it!—our argument relies on *his* prior decision.

> COUNSEL: "That's precisely right."
>
> JUSTICE BURGER: "It's academic."
>
> COUNSEL: "And the law would be complied with."

He's following our logic now. But he still worries that we're making a very extreme argument.

> JUSTICE BURGER: "But the question that I'm putting to you is, should not the district court, confronted with an application to enjoin the operation of a dam in which $122 million worth of money, one way or the other . . . has been invested, exercise the ordinary functions of an equity judge weighing and balancing the equities?"
>
> COUNSEL: "Yes, Your Honor, it seems to me that the Court does have equitable discretion. Let me describe, however—"
>
> JUSTICE BURGER: "—And that includes the equitable discretion *not* to enforce the statute?"

Okay: here is where I must make my stand.

> COUNSEL: "No, your Honor, it does not."
>
> JUSTICE BURGER: "You think it does not."

JUSTICE REHNQUIST [not into microphone]: "It sure as hell
   does!"

For the next minute or so, as I make a long response, Rehnquist is
engaged in muttered conversations to his left and right, clearly trying
to stoke irritation with our impertinent argument that the courts are
bound by the statute.

   COUNSEL: "Let me take the far-out hypothetical, taking the
      Tellico Dam today, and advancing it to the point of
      completion—that is to say, they would still have to cut
      down trees, bulldoze, scrape, and strip the valley, they
      would have to construct the canal, they would have to get
      the gates ready for closing. At that point, if, for instance,
      Your Honor, it were discovered that the whooping crane
      required that valley to breed . . . the district court could
      not, it seems to us in that case, Your Honor, take on the
      question, which is essentially a very legislative question, of
      what should be done with the Tellico Dam. For instance,
      the Court would then have to go into the full cost account-
      ing. Your Honor, it would have to consider, now, what is
      the true value of this dam . . ."

All right. I'm sounding wordy but reasonable on the facts—the dam is
far from complete, and I've brought in everyone's favorite species, the
whooping crane, to show how inappropriately *legislative* the courts
would be in trying to resolve this. This throws the accusation of "activist judging" right back in the face of the so-called conservatives who
want to quash environmental citizen suits. Wonder how Rehnquist is
taking this?

   JUSTICE REHNQUIST: "I don't agree with you, Mr. Plater. Be-
      cause you have a long history of equitable adjudication
      where, for instance, a building is built over a lot line, and
      there has been a contest throughout, but the chancellor . . .
      may say, applying the common law, which has the same
      sanction to him as the legislative laws passed by Congress,
      'I will give you damages, I will not give you an injunction.'
      Now why isn't this an appropriate case for that sort of an
      adjudication?"

Who's flailing now, me or Rehnquist?

> COUNSEL: "Several reasons. Number one is, as Your Honor
> [nodding toward Justice Stevens] noted, damages of
> course is not a remedy. Once a species is rendered extinct,
> as Congress said, it's extinct forever. Secondly, of course,
> that would be involving private parties under the common
> law. This Court has repeatedly said that in cases which
> involve a *congressional statute* . . . the principle which
> guides the Court in the exercise of its discretion is *enforc-
> ing the law,* which has not been set up by common law but
> by statute."
>
> JUSTICE REHNQUIST: "It's completely opposite in *Hecht against
> Bowles.*"
>
> COUNSEL: "No, no, Your Honor, we are not arguing that an
> injunction must be issued. Under the *Hecht* case—"
>
> JUSTICE REHNQUIST: "—That is, if there were voluntary com-
> pliance, and an injunction wouldn't be necessary. And
> that was *Hecht v. Bowles.*"

He's flailing, looking over at Burger now, trying to retrieve him, giving
him the big case law citation to show that we are wrong, that courts can
indeed adjust the law if they want to. But he's had to admit that in *Hecht*
there was voluntary compliance, as in Burger's own case.

> COUNSEL: "Yes, Your Honor. The *Hecht* case said if compli-
> ance with congressional statute *would otherwise be achieved,*
> the Court of course need not issue an injunction. We
> would be pleased if an injunction would not have been
> necessary in this case. Because in 1973, when all options
> were fully open—although Congress appears to indicate,
> and the GAO study indicates, that options are still open,
> today—we would be in a much better position to review
> the question."

Rehnquist leans back, shaking his head, but if anyone looks at the
*Hecht* case they will see we're correct and Rehnquist is wrong. And
now Powell is leaning forward to jump in again.

> COUNSEL: "Yes, Your Honor?"

JUSTICE POWELL: "May I come back to an argument you were
making a few minutes ago that this dam, after all, is not important to what Congress intended. I read a few words from
the Senate Appropriations Committee report last year:
'The project will provide needed flood control, water supply, recreational opportunities, improved navigation. . . .'
Now, without the dam and the water in it would any of those
objectives of Congress be attainable?"

COUNSEL: "Your Honor, it should be noted that the Appropriations Committee at no time has ever reviewed the GAO
study, the reviews taking place in the other committees,
and so on. It turns out—"

JUSTICE POWELL: "—That wasn't my question."

COUNSEL: "Your Honor, it is true that there would be no flood
control, there would be no electric power in the project—"

JUSTICE POWELL: "—No recreation?"

COUNSEL: "No, that is not so, Your Honor. The river is the last
place left in the river system that has high-quality water
conditions. It's the finest trout stream in the southeast of
the United States. People come from Alabama, Georgia,
and all over to fish—"

JUSTICE POWELL: "—You've got Mr. Stewart's vote already."
[Laughter]

I hope he's right.

COUNSEL: "Your Honor, it is the last place for flowing water
recreation. And as the GAO noted, because there have
been so many impoundments—"

JUSTICE POWELL: "—Do you think the Senate of the United
States, or the Senate Appropriations Committee, was thinking about maintaining this stream when it was appropriat-
ing money to close the dam?"

COUNSEL: "Your Honor, I believe that the relevant discussion is
in the committee that has lawmaking jurisdiction over the
Act . . . and they clearly are concerned about recreation
on the House side as well."

Damn. I'm not emphasizing that the primary justification was recreation, not electric power, and moreover, according to the GAO, river

recreation is worth more than dam recreation. But I've lost that chance, and now Powell is grilling me on Congress's intent.

> JUSTICE POWELL: "Is there any record that the members of that committee voted against this appropriation?"

Now Powell may be getting a little far out. Although I can't say it, everyone knows that most members of Congress don't read what they're voting on, and everyone votes for the final appropriations bills.

> COUNSEL: "Your Honor, the appropriation bill, on its face, does not purport to treat Tellico. It says nothing about Tellico."
>
> JUSTICE POWELL: "I understand the bill on its face doesn't. But do you think any rational person could read the reports of the committee for the last four or five years and conclude that there was any intention on the part of the Congress other than to complete this project?"

Les Iczkovitz's section of our brief nails the law on this.

> COUNSEL: "Your Honor, I believe that one reading those reports would find clearly and specifically that, indeed, Congress had no intent to amend the Act. . . . As a matter of fact, in 1977 Senator Stennis specifically said, 'If we put such an amendment in here, it would be subject to a point of order.' I think Your Honor's question, however, reflects the fact that, certainly, the Appropriations Committee, or certain members of it, probably didn't agree with the Endangered Species Act, or wished that it didn't apply in this case."
>
> JUSTICE POWELL: "Do you think that reflects any indication on the part of the Congress not to construe Section 7 as applying to completed projects?"
>
> COUNSEL: "I believe, Your Honor, that the appropriations bill—as every appropriations bill . . . presumes that the agency will comply with all applicable relevant laws. Because the agencies are creatures of Congress."
>
> JUSTICE POWELL: "You apparently didn't hear my question, so I'll put another one to you . . ."

He's being really snide. Powell keeps insisting that Tellico is completed, and was asking about congressional intent on retroactivity. I've replied that presumptively all federal agencies are supposed to comply with federal laws, and that was a totally appropriate response.

> JUSTICE POWELL: ". . . Do you think—it is still your position, as I understand it—that this Act, Section 7, applies to completed projects? I know you don't think it occurs very often that there'll be a need to apply it. But does it apply if the need exists?"

At this point the little red light telling me to sit down comes on. What do I do now? Will Burger stop Powell? Am I allowed to continue answering this question?

> COUNSEL: "To the continuation . . . ?"
> JUSTICE POWELL: "To completed projects. Take the Grand Coulee Dam . . ."

Powell launches into a barrage of questions trying to pin down how extreme our argument must be. He says we are saying the Endangered Species Act requires completed dams to be torn down. The duel drags back and forth about the Grand Coulee Dam. (Shouldn't this oral argument be over by now?) And then Burger jumps in too, saying our argument is too extreme because it applies to any agency action at any time.

> JUSTICE BURGER: "The actions might be the continued operation of the Grand Coulee Dam."

Burger either doesn't see the red light or doesn't care. Either way, I'm going to keep on answering as long as they keep interrogating. But how can I get away from this stuff about environmental extremism?

> JUSTICE STEVENS: "There's nothing that would require you to tear a dam down."

That's a start. Thanks again, Justice Stevens.

> COUNSEL: "If that situation would arise, Your Honor, it would probably be a biological rarity. . . . In the Culver hearings in the Senate last summer, it was again and again noted

that the biological expertise of the Department of the Interior is capable of handling many sophisticated such questions. And there has never been a case that could not be resolved through good faith and administrative consultation. There have been 4,500 potential conflicts. There have been hundreds of actual conflicts. But only TVA testified that the Act was unworkable. Every other administrative agency said that, although the Act was sometimes a bother, they could resolve these conflicts."

This is good. I get to paint TVA as a power-crazed maverick. And those numbers are nice, especially considering that the federal government wouldn't even have them had Mardi and Debbie not camped out in Interior last summer and done all that work themselves.

I'm a long way over the permitted time now—but they're still grilling me.

> JUSTICE MARSHALL: "Getting back to—why don't you rely on the fact that even though a facility is all built, if you know about it when you started building—isn't that what you say?"
> COUNSEL: "That was the situation in this case, Your Honor."
> JUSTICE MARSHALL: "That's what I mean. You're not leaving that, are you?"
> COUNSEL: "No, of course not, Your Honor. Thank you for reminding me."

Great! Marshall is onto the argument about TVA's bad faith, rushing ahead with the dam when it found out about the darter. He's not solely interested in torturing me with weird questions.

> JUSTICE BURGER: "Well, when this litigation—when this litigation first began to block the development of the project, there was no snail darter problem involved, was there?"

Burger again. Which means, first, that I can keep on talking, but second, he wants to say TVA wasn't in bad faith because it didn't know. It sounds pretty clear that we won't get Burger's vote. He wants to cast us as crazy environmentalists.

> COUNSEL: "The NEPA suit, Your Honor, which was filed in 1971, noted that there possibly were endangered species in

the river. TVA had notice. But at that time, of course, Your
Honor, it was the old Act, which allowed the TVA to have
the discretionary flexibility—that they're now trying to
read into this Act—applied."

JUSTICE BURGER: "When the snail darter was discovered, and
became a handy handle to hold onto."

Handy handle! Now it's out in the open. He wants to paint us as hypocrites who're just using the fish for our own goals of blocking progress.

COUNSEL: "Your Honor, the question of the snail darter clearly
went specifically to the qualities of this habitat, that as you
suggest, the citizens have been concerned about for years,
that is to say, the last free-flowing, clear, . . . big river left
in the region."

JUSTICE BURGER: "I'm sure that they just don't want this
project!"

Again he's making a patently personal crack. We obviously can kiss
Burger's vote goodbye. And with that little red light burning I should
be ending this now anyway. Say something that shows our good faith,
and then it's high time I sat down.

COUNSEL: "Your Honor, there are a combination of plaintiffs in
this case, many with different points of view. . . . One of
our plaintiffs, for instance, the Association of Southeastern Biologists, has no interest in the valley for conservation purposes, but for biological purposes is taking what I
believe is its first public stand to show that a biological
statute of Congress is important to be enforced. That agencies should not violate the law with impunity.

As a matter of fact, Your Honor, that's where we would
leave this case. The Act is working on the record, except in
this case. This is the only agency that has persistently declined to comply with the law. And of course, in 1973, there
were all options open. That is the relevant time to question
when, indeed, TVA should have looked at this Act and decided if they, like every other federal agency, would abide
by the law."

OK. Not great, but it feels like a good-enough exit line. Burger is leaning forward to tell me I may sit down. But, no, I get hit with one final
salvo:

> JUSTICE WHITE: "Nevertheless, your statement is absolutely
> incorrect unless the Act is construed the way you say it
> should be construed."
>
> COUNSEL: "Yes, your Honor, if this Act is discretionary the way
> the old law was written, if this Act doesn't mean what it
> says, then, indeed, this—"
>
> JUSTICE WHITE: "—But one of the issues in the case is, what
> does the Act mean. You're arguing that it should be con-
> strued in a certain way. But some other people disagree
> with you."
>
> COUNSEL: "They do. Thank you, Your Honors."

I back away from the podium and make a run for the defense table.

> CHIEF JUSTICE BURGER: "Thank you, gentlemen. The case is
> submitted."

"Whereupon," as the Clerk of Court records it, "at 11:22 a.m. o'clock,
the case in the above-entitled matter was submitted." Everybody rises
to their feet. The justices file out for lunch. They'll take our arguments
back to their chambers, where they'll mull them over for a couple of
months before announcing who wins.

## Coming Down from the Mountain

Back down in the well a mob is surging around us. Sara is jumping up
and down. "We beat 'em up! We totally beat 'em up!" Our group is convinced that, if oral arguments mean anything, we've vanquished TVA
again. If the justices were listening, didn't we have a winning answer
for absolutely everything they asked? And Bell? Didn't he seem hapless? He's standing over there, shaking his head. The suits around him
are trying to be reassuring, nodding their heads sagely. But no one is
smiling.

Bell's arguments were confused and unsure. The strength of our
case on the facts and the law seemed to come through in the oral argument, even if there was far more we could have said if we'd had a

chance. For the students, too, it's been intoxicating to hear the very arguments they'd researched late into the night poured out in the Supreme Court debate. Every part of our brief seems as solid to us now as it did before the argument.

"If you want to take home some leftover copies of your brief," says the Clerk of Court, who'd so energetically passed out the snail darter lithograph in mid-argument, "you'd better pick them up now, because this brief is a hot item."

There are a few words of worry. "You were wonderful, dear," my mother says. "But why did you have to use such showy words, *panoply* of powers?" Because, Mum, it was in the quote from Burger's own opinion. Margaret and Joe Sexton are worried, too. They'd been allowed to sit in the audience for only five minutes, despite their protests that this case was about *their farm*. They're eager to know if the farmers were mentioned and are sad to hear, "not much." The Council on Environmental Quality's Foster Knight grumbles, "Why the hell didn't you grab the remand idea when they suggested it?" From his read of the Court he obviously thinks a remand is the only compromise that will save us from getting overturned by Rehnquist and Burger. I tell Foster we're convinced we can and must win on the record today.

There's one more, quite trivial, item left. Not even an afterthought, because none of us thinks of it. It's the sergeant at arms who comes over and says, "You should leave the courtroom now and go out on the steps. They usually want to get a quote."

Who are *they?* I go out to the marble steps and see Griffin Bell standing in the sunlight halfway down the stairs, surrounded by Dan Rather and at least thirty reporters with camera crews, sound booms, and video hookups. Bell looks as if he's pulled himself back together. He poses in his black morning coat, waving his little bottle with the pickled darter. "This is what it's all about. A silly little fish. It just doesn't make sense to me."

A press gofer holds us back until they've finished with Bell. Still photographs have to be taken to be sure they all get a good shot of Bell's upraised arm and the bottle. Then Bell scurries off with his coterie. We move down into the circle. Reporters are waving microphones, shouldering themselves nearer, scribbling on pads. "How do you feel about today's arguments?" Jeez. I haven't thought for one second about what to say at this moment. Do I answer the question they asked, or offer a zinger of our own choosing? If I answered their question, I'd say, "We think Griffin Bell was a wretched mess, like TVA's case, and we really did well compared to him." But that would never do. Graceless, nasty, and just begging to be brought down a peg by any justice watching the news tonight.

With fifteen seconds of national, maybe even international, coverage, what are we going to do with it? Say something that will reinforce our case. Pity I don't have a visual to hold out for the cameras like Bell. For one crazy second I think of ripping open my shirt and showing the snail darter T-shirt underneath. But that would make us look completely flaky—and anyway it's inside out. So I pick up on the theme from the end of the oral argument: "What we're doing here today is trying to teach a federal agency to obey federal law." There. That's a good line. I repeat it a couple more times in different ways to stay on message and hammer the point home.

We leave. There's a picnic celebration on the Capitol lawn. Slowly, the hammering in my ears dies down and slips away. We'll take a break for a day or two. But it starts to sink in later that night. I've blown it. Really blown it. I may think I smashed Bell inside the Supreme Court, but as I watch the national evening news and monitor print coverage over the next few days, it's clear Bell has scored his own rebound victory right there in those moments on the Supreme Court steps. What does America see? Just one more confirmatory scene in the continuing ridiculous story of the little fish versus the power dam. Griffin Bell waves the fish. Then I come on and imply that we enviros are catching an agency on a mere legal technicality. Which side sounds like common sense?

Like Walter Mitty, I should have thought to say something defter: "Mr. Bell wants you to focus on the little fish, not on the facts of the case. Because if you did, you'd see this fish is protecting a valuable river and three hundred family farms being condemned for resale, not for a reservoir! It's a small fish, but it's fighting a hugely wasteful boondoggle, a federal land grab! TVA and Mr. Bell don't want you to look beyond their fish-in-a-bottle, but if you reporters investigated the case you'd find this little fish is proving that good ecology makes good human economic sense!"—something like that.

Too late. But there on the Supreme Court steps, did I learn a lesson?

We wait for the Court to announce its decision. We figure the vote will be close, probably 5-4. But which way? Voting against us will be Rehnquist, of course, and, thinking back over the oral arguments, we've come to accept that TVA will also get Burger, Powell, and Blackmun. For us will be Stewart, Stevens, and Brennan. (Justice Brennan for sure. We've heard surreptitiously from a Court clerk that during the oral argument Brennan and I were brothers under wraps: one of Brennan's clerks had gotten him one of our snail darter T-shirts, and during the oral argument he too had been wearing—under his robes—a snail darter!) That leaves Marshall and White. We need both, but the Rehnquist faction needs to gain only one. The more we ponder it, the more it just comes down to wishful thinking.

Meanwhile, there's still work to be done on the Hill and in the agencies. Another Senate hearing is to be held two weeks after the arguments, then four days of House hearings on the Endangered Species Act and Tellico, spread over the last two weeks of May and into June. While awaiting the Court decision the committees are not going to do much on any of this, but we must stay in contact with staff. We also need to step up the pressure on Interior to start making contingency plans for what to do if and when the Court upholds the Tellico injunction. It's amazing what an appearance in the Supreme Court does for your case. At last, people who always should have been active allies are listening to us seriously. We're talking regularly with our old Interior nemesis Keith Schreiner now, openly working with his biology staffers, whom we used to visit surreptitiously late at night.

Wednesday evening, June 14, the standard routine. Home in Michigan, finish grading and turning in exams, start preparing notes for the continuing Senate hearings and a discussion with Assistant Secretary Rupe Cutler at the Agriculture Department in Washington in the morning. Get up at 5:30, catch the jitney to Detroit airport, have a defrosted bagel and instant coffee for breakfast on the plane, land at National Airport at 9:50, take the Metro to Capitol Hill, and walk east down Pennsylvania Avenue toward the low rent area, to the Friends of the Earth office, our base. Push through the door, and . . . *bedlam!* "You won! You won!" the volunteers are yelling. The Clean Air guys are clapping. Liz Raisbeck is grinning. "You guys did it!" she says. "The snail darter won in the Supreme Court this morning! It was announced just twenty minutes ago."

"Holy cow! Hallelujah! OK. What was the count? Who did we get? We lost Rehnquist and Burger, right? Who wrote the majority opinion?"

"Wrong!" Liz Raisbeck says. "Burger wrote the opinion! It was 6-3!" That means we'd also gotten White and Marshall! "Burger announced the decision right at the beginning of the Court session. He sounded really sarcastic about it, though. The people there said it sounded as if he was inviting Congress to come in immediately and clear up this stupid case. And Powell said exactly that." Ann Graham calls a few minutes later and tells us she's heard from a clerk that, after the oral argument, Burger realized he was losing, so he'd switched to the majority so he could assign himself the opinion and water it down.

We quickly get a preliminary copy of the opinions. The majority opinion—Burger, Brennan, Marshall, Stevens, Stewart, and White—doesn't look watered down. It's quite wonderful, not only for us but for the Endangered Species Act as well, even though it does ignore every single scrap of commonsense fact and policy material on the darter case we'd put into the brief and oral argument.

Why protect endangered species, the majority judges asked themselves? Because the Endangered Species Act is "the most comprehensive legislation for the preservation of endangered species ever enacted by any nation. . . . Congress has spoken in the plainest of words [!?!], making it abundantly clear that the balance has been struck in favor of affording endangered species the highest of priorities, thereby adopting a policy which it described as *institutionalized caution*." Why should the Court enforce the law if it seems silly to some judges? The decision answered that question with a final, ringing quote from Robert Bolt's *A Man for All Seasons*, the story of Saint Thomas More, who was executed by King Henry VIII for insisting that judges must base their decisions on legal principle rather than personal opinions about what was right:

> "The law, Roper, the law. I know what's legal, not what's right. And I'll stick to what's legal. . . . I'm not God. The currents and eddies of right and wrong, which you find such plain-sailing, I can't navigate. I'm no voyager. But in the thickets of the law, oh there I'm a forester. . . . What would you do? Cut a great road through the law to get after the

Devil?. . . . And when the last law was down, and the Devil turned round on you, where would you hide, Roper, the laws all being flat?. . . . This country's planted thick with laws from coast to coast—Man's laws, not God's—and if you cut them down . . . d'you really think you could stand upright in the winds that would blow then? Yes, I'd give the Devil benefit of law, for my own safety's sake." [R. Bolt, *A Man for All Seasons,* Act I, 147 (Heinemann ed., 1967)]

So we devils celebrate for a few minutes, then call the Capitol media's Daybook scheduling office to tell them we're having a press conference outside the Friends of the Earth office at three o'clock, in time for evening news deadlines. The decision's going to get national publicity, and we better grab the spotlight while we can. At our sidewalk victory press conference, thirty members of our coalition stand in front of the office. Only four or five reporters show up, but they include CBS News's star reporter, Fred Graham, who's brought along his little boy to see the festivities.

We tell ourselves to remember the lesson learned on the Supreme Court's marble steps. We need to get the dramatic facts of Tellico through to the press. The Court's decision doesn't include the common sense of our case, but the victory gives us this opportunity to speak to the world. I speak for the darter. Anne Wickham for Friends of the Earth. Pat Parenteau and Ed Osann for the National Wildlife Federation. Jim Elder for the Sierra Club. Others, to whom we owe a lot for helping so much, also speak. Each of us delivers a brief talk about how this case shows how the Endangered Species Act makes sense in economic, ecological, and ethical moral terms.

But we're blowing it, again. "You're losing them," whispers Rafe Pomerance, leaning his Ichabod Crane frame out through the doorway and hissing into my ear. "This is too polite. These are *reporters!* You have to *grab 'em by the balls.* Give them some really good quotes, in ten seconds! 'This dam is *full of crap!* a *turkey!* This fish is *saving America a billion dollars!* The *Tellico Dam is just a bureaucratic land grab!* '" Ah, but no, I think we cannot do that. Too coarse and flaky. We have to show the world that we environmentalists are sober rationalists making a sensible case for the public good based on economic facts and data. So we talk on and on, about the farmers, about the collapsed land development plans, about the fish as an indicator of human as well as ecological welfare, about valuable economic alternatives. That evening, the next day, we watch. Nothing we say makes it into national news coverage. Rafe was right. Our press conference, which could have captured a national moment, didn't, because it was boring. There's another media lesson here. Why aren't we learning?

Imagine our horror later to learn that, six weeks before the Court agreed to review the case and scheduled the oral argument, Justice Rehnquist had successfully signed up a 5-4 majority for an order denying us oral argument and summarily reversing and dismissing our case without even allowing briefing![2] Only some mysterious infighting had prevented Rehnquist's sleight of hand from working. To get his five votes Rehnquist had urged the balance-of-equities argument—telling his brethren, untruthfully, that Judge Taylor had considered all the project options at trial before denying the injunction, and echoing TVA's arguments that the law didn't apply. White and Burger had initially gone along with Rehnquist. Throughout October Brennan had tried to block the maneuver. Along with Marshall, Stewart, and Stevens, he had threatened to write a long dissent opposing the summary reversal. It was finally Blackmun who'd turned the tide, even though he was against us, saying the diversity of internal debate meant it was improper for Rehnquist to reverse our injunction without briefs or oral argument.

We'd come that close to summary reversal! Without the voice of a Minnesotan of strong character—who from the start thought we were dead wrong, who attacked us bitterly in the oral argument, and who never changed his mind about the case—the snail darter would never even have had its day in Court. We'd mistakenly thought we had Blackmun's vote, and never won him over, but thanks to his integrity we'd had the chance to flip White and Burger, and that, it turns out, was enough.

# CHAPTER 10

## Another Trial and Vindication, in the God Tribunal

### APRIL 13, 1978–JANUARY 23, 1979

Here's a scene I wish I could have avoided: It's midafternoon and I was moving fast down a marble corridor in the Russell Senate Office Building when, rounding a corner, I almost plowed into a senator, Iowa's John Culver. As I backed away, I saw that he'd recognized me, and as soon as he did he exploded: "Goddammit, what is this crap you're putting out?" He cornered me up against the wall. I weigh about 149 pounds. According to the Harvard varsity football archives, John Culver weighed more than 215 pounds back in the 1950s when he played fullback on the Crimson gridiron team with Ted Kennedy, and it's safe to say that in the intervening twenty-plus years the bull-like body straining angrily toward me has gained a few more pounds as well as political weight.

"I'm trying to save your goddamn act, and you are going around saying I'm undermining it!? You know that's total bullshit!" His face was flaming red, and his booming voice was trembling. He was waving a copy of a position paper that I'd typed out two nights ago. It had been carried to offices all over the Hill by volunteers from Friends of the Earth and the American Rivers Conservation Council. It said that Culver was engineering "a dangerous answer to a problem that does not exist," and went on from there.

"But, but, but," I gurgle, "we're actually trying to help you," or something like that, to which Culver spits out "ungrateful idiots," and then, thank God, turns on his heel and, shaking his head, strides off down the hall, with his aide Dick Oshlo in his wake. Oshlo looks back over his shoulder with a pained expression on his face that says, "Now you've done it."

This scene occurs five days before our oral argument in the Supreme Court. The senator—who fortuitously decided last year to make the Endangered Species Act and the snail darter a major focus of his subcommittee agenda, despite the fact that his farm-country constituents probably don't have much interest in endangered species—has decided he must negotiate a compromise with Howard Baker of Tennessee. Baker is the Senate's most powerful Republican, TVA's most powerful representative in Congress, and the darter's archenemy. Culver has been our most fervent congressional convert and our champion in the Senate hearings. We deeply respect his intellect and his passion.

His aides tell us Culver has soberly concluded that unless something is done we and the Endangered Species Act can't survive the political firestorm that's been building since our court of appeals injunction. The Fish and Wildlife Service fears a backlash from the public reaction to a supposed avalanche of threats that species protections allegedly pose to human welfare. Given the insider politics, there really is a danger of losing the entire law to a fit of unreasoning congressional violence. Culver calculates that the existence of a legal exemption review process might build a barrier against assaults on the allegedly inflexible endangered species law.

As it turns out, Culver's thinking is about to bring the snail darter into an unprecedented godlike decision-making mechanism. Culver has persuaded Baker to cosponsor a compromise bill to create a tribunal with the power of life and death (extinction) over endangered species. If it works, Culver thinks it will take pressure off the darter and the Endangered Species Act.

Baker had again loosed upon us his chief legislative hatchet, Jim Range. Range is a powerful agent provocateur, and in offices all over the Hill and in the Department of Interior we've found his footprints. Educated at the University of Tennessee's law school, he is smooth and handsome, delivers rifle shot arguments with a subtle mountain twang, knows how to cozy up equally well to good ol' boys and female staffers, is very good at both reading and playing political cards, and is clearly riding Baker's train to a capital future.

As Baker's agent, Range is applying pressure to get Tellico exempted from the law in every place he can. He pushes the Fish and Wildlife Service to support major transplantations of the darter away from the Little T. He urges the House and Senate appropriations committees to twist arms for a Tellico override. In office after office in both House and Senate we're told Range was there before us. He demeans our "amateur" fact sheets with arch condescension, telling members of Congress and staffers that "TVA knows economic development in the Valley a lot better than those environmentalist amateurs," or that "the majority of people in Tennessee want that dam; would you like members from other states telling you what to do in yours?" Range lobbies hard, urging Republicans to follow his boss on Tellico and urging moderate Democrats to let this one small issue go, in order to assure bipartisan cooperation from Minority Leader Baker on other issues. He sets up duck hunting jaunts with important congressional figures and powerful lobbyists, laying *Sports Afield* buddy talk on them about how Tellico should be left to Tennessee's senior senator. He jabs away at the confidence of Environment and Public Works Committee staffers who had been convinced by our river defenders' case, and makes the same arguments face to face with us: "People in Tennessee want the dam. You're just a little group of college tree huggers. . . . Your environmental arguments are just wishful thinking. . . . I know a lot about ecology and Tellico Dam, and I can tell you that little snail darter doesn't amount to much biologically. Hey, if you just look at the importance of species in ecosystems, you'll see that *mosquitoes* are more valuable than those darters!" Range is effective wherever he goes, and, though he twists the facts, the subtlety of his battle plan reflects that he actually does know a lot of details about Tellico.

How does Jim Range know so much, we wonder? He's certainly in close contact with TVA lawyers, but he's making their arguments far better than they do. "Guess what I discovered!" Hank Hill shouts, calling in from Tennessee. "I was talking to Price Wilkins [veteran wildlife biologist who has long opposed the dam]. He tells me that *Range started out on our side,* back when he was a law student and the farmers first tried to stop the dam! He worked with Wilkins for the University of Tennessee chapter of the Association for the Preservation of the Little T. He was one of its most active student members fighting to stop the dam!" Now we know why Range knows how to present TVA's case so well. He knows how to speak with apparent authority about details, knows what *not* to say when talking to informed people, and knows what facts can undercut our arguments—like the fact that even though Tellico Dam indeed has no generators, the canal would carry some electric power potential to the nearby Loudoun dam, or that the transplants of darters indeed are showing indications of interim success.

Ever since that potluck dinner in old Fort Loudoun it's been clear to us that a political victory will be necessary; a Supreme Court verdict won't deter TVA. Even though Red Wagner is finally gone and David Freeman, Carter's technocratic appointee, is now chair, Wagner's people within TVA and the agency's internal instincts continue to resist all efforts to expose the demerits of the dam and acknowledge the river's beneficial alternatives. The Tennessee political establishments— local politicians, the governor, and the entire Tennessee delegation in Congress—are tied into TVA's traditional stance on this dam. They miss no chance to undercut Freeman, who simply doesn't fit the TVA ethos. Freeman is a cool, cosmopolitan technocrat, a policy wonk foisted upon them by Carter who is skeptical about TVA's beloved nuclear power and make-work projects.

For his part Freeman has let the Domestic Policy Council's Kathy Fletcher and other close friends in Washington know he thinks we're correct on the Tellico project's demerits. That's why, soon after becoming the junior member of the TVA board, he'd stuck out his neck to attach a contrarian statement to the agency's Supreme Court reply brief, declaring that the dam was unnecessary and river alternatives were attractive. To the Tennessee political establishment this marked Freeman as an irredeemable outsider, a heretic, a New Age environmentalist. Within TVA, a core of lawyers in Freeman's own law department has continued a clandestine war against their new boss's reformist inclinations. We repeatedly try to communicate with the new chair. If we had a linkage with him we could pass on pieces of critical data he doesn't know about, identify useful local pressure points, and help him identify his antagonists within TVA. Freeman avoids us, however, apparently hoping to keep his public stance of neutrality uncontaminated by contact with the maverick citizens opposing Tellico Dam.

By now, moreover, our political opponents in Washington extend far beyond TVA, which is only a small regional player on the national chessboard. Our Tennessee case has galvanized a horde of national heavies against us. The big antiregulatory political blocs in the capital and around the country are calling for the snail darter's blood and the Endangered Species Act's decapitation. The Army Corps of Engineers realizes its $4-billion Tennessee-Tombigbee Waterway could be stopped in its tracks if an endangered species there triggers serious public scrutiny of its skewed economics. Beyond the water projects agencies the anti-Endangered Species Act lobbying we encounter is coming primarily from the Edison Electric Institute, the U.S. Chamber of Commerce, the National Forest Products Association, and the National Association of Manufacturers, joined recently by the Heritage Foundation and the Pacific Legal Foundation, all hoping our case will be dismissively ridiculed as quixotic, discrediting the species law and government regulation in general along with it.

The battlefield for fighting against these political forces now shifts to Congress. We can't complain about that because we'd argued in favor of it in court, hoping the Court injunction would prompt Congress to address the real facts of the case. If the public finally sees the facts in a congressionally mandated review process, we win. If the old insider game rolls on out of public view, we lose. Congress could address the case in either of two ways. It could undertake the job of deciding each specific case itself, in a new set of hearings and floor debates on some sort of explicit exemption bill, or it could pass off the hot potato into some kind of specially delegated administrative process.

There are strong arguments for Option One, making the people's elected representatives in Congress do the portentous work of deciding whether one branch of God's creation lives or dies. We even draft a model bill for discussion, setting out standards that would be appropriate for a rational decision in favor of the dam, standards we know no hearing record could satisfy in favor of Tellico Dam. Our experience with congressional hearings, however, doesn't make this a compelling proposition, and for their part, moreover, Baker and TVA show no interest in anything that involves more congressional investigation of Tellico. Legislators of every stripe tell us they don't relish the idea of having every species standoff come to them for embarrassing and burdensome votes. The House, the home base of pork, has two bills before it from local Tennessee representatives seeking peremptory overrides of the darter injunction, but for some reason—perhaps the case's newfound prominence and the fear of being seen as high-handed?—even the House is shying away from passing a surgical midnight bill exempting the dam.

Alternatively Congress can toss the hot potato to the executive branch. A compromise bill could set up some separate administrative decision process to review and exempt species from protection. This is what Senator Culver chooses to do. Culver has persuaded Baker that the darter case and all such species conflicts should be sent to a special high-profile, interagency Endangered Species Committee with the power to issue extinction verdicts. Amending the Endangered Species Act to create that apparatus will get these cases out of Congress's hair and satisfy any clamor from animal lovers around the country, who probably would be equally infuriated by a congressional extinction vote as by wholesale repeal of the law.

On April 12, just six days before we argue in the Supreme Court, Baker and Culver, with several tag-along cosponsors, submit their bill creating the process for an extinction exemption committee, almost instantly christened and referred to as the God Committee and later, less reverently, as the God Squad. A hearing is held two days later. In the politically charged atmosphere in which we find ourselves—with the darter being portrayed in editorial cartoons, media opinion pieces, water-cooler conversations, and even Sunday sermons around the nation as a symbol of irrational extremism—the God Committee bill is actually a fabulous stroke of good fortune for us and for the Endangered Species Act. It could have been designed as some lowly bureaucratic device hidden away in the bowels of Interior—or even delegated to agency officials themselves to decide whether their pet projects should proceed or cease. Instead the God Committee decision process proposed by the Culver-Baker bill is tough! It's an unprecedentedly high-level panel, at the presidential Cabinet level or equivalent. Its members are to include the secretary of the interior as chair, the secretaries of agriculture, transportation, and army, and the administrators of the Environmental Protection Agency and the National Oceanic and Atmospheric Administration, plus the chair of the president's Council of Economic Advisers—all of whom must sit together and deliberate in person, no delegates, plus a representative of an affected state. This eminent proposed tribunal would be allowed to exempt a species from the Act's protections only if it commands a special majority vote of "not less than five of . . . seven members voting in person."

The decisional standards, moreover, are strict and specific. When an agency asks for an exemption from the law, the Endangered Species Committee is ordered to give the project an intensive review on all its merits—the kind of review we and most project challengers have found difficult or impossible to generate. A decision for extinction would require a special majority to vote that

- the action is of regional or national significance (we'd have no quarrel with that), and
- *there are no reasonable and prudent alternatives* to the agency action, (precisely the realistic official commonsense investigation into alternatives we have so fruitlessly been seeking for years), and
- *the benefits of such action clearly outweigh the benefits of alternative courses of action* consistent with conserving the species or its critical habitat. . . . (The committee must explore alternatives! And it can't vote to exempt the species unless it finds a strong imbalance in favor of the project, a burden few pork-barrel projects will be able to survive.)[1]

Within ninety days of passage, the snail darter injunction would have to survive or fail in an immediate God Committee process, along with another case, an injunction that the National Wildlife Federation's Pat Parenteau had won against the Greyrocks Dam in Wyoming. The Greyrocks case has gotten far less play than the snail darter in the media, probably because it protects the whooping crane, a species far less subject to ridicule than our small fish.

The God Committee bill's proposed tests require exactly what we have so long wanted. By remarkable coincidence, moreover, we find that they were initially drafted by a Senate aide who, during her junior year at the University of Michigan, had been a student in the environmental law course a colleague and I had organized. As part of the course the aide, Patty McDonald, learned about the classic *Overton Park* case, which involved a balance between a Memphis, Tennessee, park and a section of interstate highway, a case illustrating the necessity of looking at projects' rational alternatives as well as at alleged benefits and costs. Going to Washington straight out of college, McDonald now happens to be working in the office of Wyoming Senator Malcolm Wallop, who is interested in the Endangered Species Act, perhaps in part because of Jean Ritchey's Senate hearing testimony about land condemnations. Baker happily accepted fellow Republican Wallop as cosponsor on the bill and used Wallop's staff in the drafting process. McDonald was asked to shape the God Committee standards.

This bit of serendipity aside, however, we do have some concerns about the committee. Look at the appointments beyond the obvious choices of the heads of Interior and the Environmental Protection Agency: the secretary of the army represents the Army Corps of Engineers, the worst federal agency in terms of physical destruction of wetlands and waterways—not to mention that it is also wedded to Tenn-Tom. The secretary of agriculture represents agrichemical interests, and its Forest Service fears that Endangered Species Act scrutiny will threaten net-loss timber clear-cutting sales around the nation. The secretary of transportation runs afoul of species conflicts in interstate highway planning. The head of the National Oceanic and Atmospheric Administration, based in the Department of Commerce and historically inclined toward business interests, has authority over fisheries, where protections for endangered turtles conflict with the fish-netting and shrimp industries. The chair of the president's Council of Economic Advisers? Senator Culver's initial draft had specified "Chairman of the President's Council of *Environmental Quality*." Baker said no, insisting "this is fundamentally an economic decision, not an environmental decision." He forced out the environmental appointee and penciled in the fiscal official, assuming that hard economics would favor the dam's steel and concrete.

Overall, however, the God Committee bill could be a boon for our case. We're excited. If it stays strong in the legislative process, it can provide the potential walk-off economic verdict the farmers and their allies have been denied for more than a dozen years. I ask Anne Wickham what we should do about this bill that does so much for us. "That's easy," she says. "You oppose it!" After she explains why, I draft a strong position paper—the one that enrages Culver—and it's distributed on the Hill and to reporters by the environmental organizations and our volunteers. Our position paper argues that the God Committee should never be allowed to see the light of day:

PROBLEMS with S. 2899:
The Baker-Culver amendment is a dangerous answer to a problem that does not exist! . . .

> Opponents of the Act are rushing the amendment through on rhetoric and wolf-crying. . . .
> This loophole procedure would undermine enforcement of the Act. . . .
> It will create yet another wasteful and unnecessary executive agency. . . .

Why, if we really like the bill, are we opposing it? Last summer's Endangered Species Act hearings had deeply eroded our respect for politicians as fact finders, at least when the press and John Culver weren't riding herd on them.[2] If extinction decisions are to be made, we think the expert administrative committee tied to clear statutory standards, whose actions can be directly challenged by citizens in court, would be far better than a review process in Congress. "That's the point," Anne says. "The boys in the pork barrel will never accept Culver's bill if they think our citizen groups support it. That'd identify the bill as liberal, and they'd instinctively attack it."

If, on the other hand, we attack the bill from the liberal Left, the legislation will be perceived as a centering compromise. Our public opposition to the bill will strengthen Culver's position, helping him sell the compromise and hold Baker as a partner in the deal. The Sierra Club's David Brower and I had once joked about this positioning tactic: going into a negotiating session with opponents, you decide which one will be the "junkyard dog," and which will play the sensible voice of reason who'll pin down a good compromise deal. Our position of protest against the bill is like Br'er Rabbit's plea when he was cornered by ol' Br'er Fox: "You can kill me, Br'er Fox, eat me up, but please, whatever you do, don't throw me into that sharp and spiny briar patch." When Br'er Fox, smirking evilly, is induced to do just that, Br'er Rabbit happily frolics off through the thorns singing, "Hah. It's jes' what I wanted, Br'er Fox! I was born and raised in a briar patch!" We don't want the law to be eaten up, and will be quite happy if Br'er Baker is encouraged to throw us into John Culver's tough briar patch. We can hardly believe that Baker is going along with the compromise.

Adopting this tactic, our environmental position paper, nominally backed by a rough coalition of environmental groups, denounces "the Baker-Culver compromise" bill (notice whose name we always put first) as "unnecessary" and "unwise." We cite the Endangered Species

Act's successful history, compiled from Fish and Wildlife's files by students Debbie Labelle and Mardi Hatcher, showing the resolution of those 4,500 potential conflicts. Meanwhile the environmental groups' lobbyists surreptitiously signal our disingenuous stance to friends on the Hill. Publicly, however, our criticism needs to be maintained until the compromise passes.

I'd explained this positioning strategy to Culver's aides, cautioning them not to let the Baker deal slip away. It appears, however, that the tactical message didn't get through to Culver. Culver's rage in the corridor is repeated the next day when I testify in his hearing on the God Committee bill. Culver's home state newspaper, the *Des Moines Register,* has printed a nasty editorial against him using arguments from a copy of my position paper relayed by some overeager volunteer. Ouch. We need to have some of our farmers write rebuttal letters praising Culver to the editor in Iowa, but in the meantime the senator, shaking his finger at me, roars his anger. Elizabeth Drew, a reporter who is following Culver around for her forthcoming book *Senator,* acidly notes that "some of the environmental groups assured him and his staff that they recognized the political realities the Act had encountered, and that the compromise was a 'constructive' approach. 'The problem is,' Culver says, 'those assurances didn't stay stuck, and the newsletters and press releases went out saying this was a know-nothing attack on the ecosystem!'"[3]

Neither Culver, a freshman senator, nor reporter Drew seems to realize how our tactical opposition strengthens Culver's political position. Culver is just flat-out infuriated at us for, as he sees it, trying to make him look bad in the court of public opinion. Culver's anger at the April 14 markup hearing is one more unwelcome tremor in my gut as we prepare for the Supreme Court argument four days hence, but it does make us hopeful that a tough God Committee bill can hang together.

The God Committee bill comes to a final vote on the Senate floor a week after the Court's decision. John Stennis of Mississippi, the thirty-year veteran Senate godfather of countless Army Corps of Engineers water projects, offers a right-wing amendment to the Baker-Culver bill: the Endangered Species Act, he says, should apply only where it is "practicable" and "consistent with [agencies'] primary responsibilities." This would implode the law, returning it to its weak pre-1973 form. Agency heads, like Red Wagner, could themselves decide whether a species' welfare outweighed their prize projects. The Stennis amendment excludes the God Committee provision, and says the Endangered Species Act would not apply to any project where 50 percent of the estimated budget had been spent, consecrating the sunk cost strategy. Loyal to his compromise with Culver, however, Baker successfully holds most of the Republican bloc to defeat the Stennis amendment, which loses 76 to 22. Watching from the gallery, we grin.

An amendment to protect only "substantial" species, offered by Senator William Scott of Virginia (who, when the Washington press corps had voted him our least intelligent federal legislator, called a press conference to deny it), goes down to defeat, 87 to 2.

Then comes an impossibly excellent environmental amendment to further strengthen the law, offered by our strong ally Senator Gaylord Nelson. Nelson was an original sponsor of the Wilderness Act, Earth Day, and of a host of environmental statutes. But we know his amendment doesn't have a prayer of actually blocking the God Committee compromise. Nelson speaks eloquently about the Endangered Species Act's success, citing the familiar statistics from Debbie and Mardi, and argues they show that the God Committee mechanism is unnecessary. Culver forcefully defends the need for a compromise, and Nelson's amendment loses 70 to 25. We're not distressed because the Baker-Culver compromise then passes on a final vote of 94 to 3. Riding a mood of inevitability, sixty days later the Senate bill overrides a weak House version and emerges almost unscathed from the conference committee. President Jimmy Carter signs the Baker-Culver compromise into law on November 10.[4]

What now? There's never before been a God Committee, with life-and-death powers over endangered species. No one's quite sure what to make of this new creature. What kind of process will it have? How deep will its scrutiny be, how public its investigations and deliberations? How neutral, or politically biased, will its votes be? As secretary of interior, Cecil Andrus takes charge within the agencies. Interior Department economists will be the dominant committee task force staff. They will arrange for public hearings to be held in Tennessee to receive testimony and evidence from any interested parties. The main analytical process will be firmly based in Washington. The actual work will be done by a small team led by senior economist Robert K. Davis, based in his sequestered office on the fifth floor of the agency's marble mausoleum off C Street.

Interior staffers already know many basic physical facts about the darter-dam conflict. The day after the Supreme Court verdict, TVA's new boss, David Freeman, had asked Andrus to assign Department of Interior analysts in Washington to a joint effort developing "Alternatives for Completing the Tellico Project." During the following weeks Freeman tried to force his TVA staff to cooperate with Interior. The joint TVA-Interior alternatives study could make a dramatic difference, openly acknowledging the weakness of the dam's economics and the project's attractive alternatives.

Some very savvy Interior staffers were selected for the joint task force. "Guess who just got appointed to travel down to Knoxville to straighten out TVA?" our source "Bill Evans" within Interior chuckled on the phone one evening. Secretary Andrus had chosen him to lead a major sector of the joint agency reanalysis. Soon we started getting clandestine reports from within the task force down in Knoxville. The team discussions didn't go well, however. Many TVA staffers bitterly resisted the suggestion that Red Wagner had been wrong over all those years. TVA members of the task force continually circulated memos spinning data in favor of the dam and denigrating the feasibility of river-based development. Because our source often worked alone in the TVA executive offices late into the night, we regularly received information about TVA memos he saw on Freeman's desk.

Soon enough the TVA staffers' cant and foot-dragging persuaded Andrus to abort the attempt to draft a consensus report with TVA, and the two staffs went their separate ways. "Bill Evans" returned to Washington. Interior's God Committee staff will prepare the official analysis of the dam and its alternatives. TVA's staff will prepare its own report.

The intensive fact-gathering, number-crunching mission of the God Committee staff working in Washington raises practical problems. The committee has to reach a final verdict in less than ninety days. There are only four full-time employees on the staff, and their analysis presented to the committee will have to be solidly based on explicit empirical evidence. A public hearing held in Knoxville contributes very little. It has a very strange format: just a tape recorder sitting on a desk against a wall, with a podium for people who want to speak to the recorder and the wall. A secretary positioned in the corner to change tapes as needed is the only "official" present. When thirty people, pro and con, have had their say, the clerk collects the tapes and sends them to Washington. It's not clear that anyone will ever listen to them.

Returning to Washington, we wonder if we can push our way into the internal committee process within Interior to channel key information and suggestions to the staff. We fear the Interior staff will be at the mercy of TVA expertise unless we can help orient their research with some practical local insights. We face two main obstacles in our desire to insert ourselves into the God Committee staff's internal administrative process. One is ethical, which gives us pause. The official channel for presenting information to the committee was the public hearing in Knoxville. The interior secretary's office has made clear that the committee staff in this controversial, first-ever administrative process is supposed to work in secret, isolated in Davis's office at Interior. A lawyer from the solicitor's office has lectured the staff on external contacts: "You must be very careful who you talk to." When contacts approach them off the record, they must avoid "even the appearance" of impropriety. Our overt attempts to set up appointments with the staff are rebuffed. This is Washington, however. There are always ways to contact sympathetic staffers informally. Can we do that, ethically, passing material in to the staff? And could friendly staffers keep us informed about details of their investigation and of what TVA is offering them? Can they ask us for clarifications and our reactions to issues as they arise?

If the God Committee process had been held to trial-type procedures, it would clearly be unethical for us and the staff to speak to each other ex parte—without notice to opposing counsel. But because Baker had slightly watered it down to a less formal standard, I decide we can ethically do at least as much as TVA is doing, which is almost boundless contact with the staff. TVA is just as much an interested party to litigation as we are, isn't it?[5]

Still, we need to be very discreet. That's because the second obstacle we face is the skittishness that Interior's leadership still exhibits toward us. "You're loose cannons," our source in Interior tells us. "They know you're not part of any established organization. They see you have this obsessive drive to save your darter and the river. No other issues, no political balancings, no trade-offs. Even people who care about the law worry because they think you might torpedo the whole Act trying to save your fish. With the facts on your side, the Carter people can't dump you. But the public's perception is all the other way. The lobbyists and the press are making you and anyone who works with you look unreasonable, crazy, radical. Interior's leadership sees you as trouble no matter how good your case is. They don't want to be seen working with you, because then they'll be seen as radicals like you." It's true. The broad populist momentum of late-'60s Earth Day environmentalism by now has largely been marginalized. The industry-oriented public relations efforts have tarred environmentalism with the image of a narrow quixotic cult of love-beaded hippies, and political condescension, scorn, and reprisals are heaped on those who are too closely identified with it.

What this means is that our involvement in the God Committee preparation can be intensive, but will have to be surreptitious. Through an intermediary, with luck we're able to open a link to the chief of the committee task force himself, Davis. He is very professional, realizes we can provide some useful help, but is cautious. "I'll talk with you in this process. But you know you're considered controversial." We agree on camouflage: starting in November, and for the next two months, Davis's secretary's log of incoming messages records a series of calls back and forth with "Andy Graham." In this clandestine flow of communications we feel a pleasant, unfamiliar sense of being heard and valued as solid, rational public critics of a fundamentally unsound project. As the "Day of The God Committee" approaches in January, however, apprehensions increase. Davis will not slip us any drafts of the staff report being prepared for the committee, and none of the basic number calculations. Moreover, he reveals some fundamental decisions that could be bad news. Most devastating, Davis says that, under current national accounting principles, he will weigh in the balance only the *remaining* project costs against *total* project benefits. "Past expenditures are irrelevant," he tells me. "We'll analyze the full actual benefits predictable for the dam against just the 5 percent of remaining costs that TVA needs to complete it."

"But that rewards bad faith!" I argue. "It rewards TVA for trying to moot the whole case with sunk costs—bullying ahead with all that construction and spending in defiance of the Act."

"Good faith, bad faith—not in our jurisdiction," says Davis. "That stuff is politically relevant, maybe, but to an economist it makes no difference. We're going to analyze and report the development benefits and costs of the reservoir and the river as they stand today in the national interest."

"But," I groan, "that means you won't make this dumb project take account of 95 percent of its actual costs—TVA gets to weigh any project benefits as if they were almost costless, against our river development alternatives, which are going to need funding."

"Yes, that's the way it is in economics, if done properly. *Prospective* accounting, not retrospective. You'll just have to live with it and take your chances." Davis does, however, pick up on our leads about the economics of the valley's prime agricultural soils, flood control economics, barge lock inadequacies, and dam safety requirements.

But there's more bad news on the river benefits side: *tourism development benefits*—the biggest pot of gold the river can deliver—are going to be totally ignored. We're confident we can win on national economics or local economics, but only if *all* the valley's true resources are counted, especially the tourism potential. "You have two problems with tourism," Davis tells me. "Tourist gains at one place tend to be pulled away from other existing destinations, so on a national economic balance they don't count as a positive benefit. It's the same way you argue Tellico reservoir recreation should be ignored if it's drawn from existing reservoirs."

"Our tourism benefit plans are different," I plead. "It's not just shuffling existing tourism. The proposed Cherokee Trail will create an entirely new destination opportunity. We can pull travelers from the two interstate highways, from the millions of people driving back and forth who'd otherwise just keep on driving. We'll give them a great new attraction, a beautiful loop off the interstate up through the valley, visiting Native American sites and archaeological digs, touring the fort, float-fishing for the day, spending the night in a tourist lodge or camping, then continuing on their way around or through the Smokies Park and back onto their interstate highway. It's an add-on, not a redistribution."

"You may be right, but that raises another problem: You have no numbers, no professional design for the tourism plan. You just have a route map you drew yourselves, a catalog of potential tourist and recreation sites along the river, and a conceptual description of what tourism and recreation developers could do."

Shoot. With five or six weeks to go we don't have enough time or expertise to create new baseline data. TVA, of course, hasn't done any such calculations, so without numbers from us the committee won't be able to take account of tourism benefits. Unable to communicate with Freeman via back channels, we're stuck. The history-tourism "Cherokee Trail" plan, paired with three-hundred-plus family farms, constitutes the biggest, most compelling economic argument for the river in terms of local Tennessee politics. But TVA Chairman Freeman doesn't know about the river alternatives study headed by Department of Architecture Dean Donald Hanson of the University of Tennessee. If we could prompt him to order some of his TVA employees to design and publicize the proposed tourism economy option for the river, it would have an immediate visceral effect on the local political climate. But Freeman remains withdrawn. TVA's dam boosters have sarcastically tagged him "Dry Dam Freeman" because of his tentative suggestion that development might be accomplished without a reservoir. He's staggering under withering pro-dam politicking and public relations pressure orchestrated by antagonists within his own agency and their local allies. But if the Tennessee public started to hear from TVA about possibilities for better economic benefits without a dam, and if they heard official acknowledgment that the dam is a dud, the political picture could quickly turn around. "If you can change the local party line that the dam's the only way money is going to come into the local economy, then you'll win this thing," says Mary Hendershot, a daughter of the Monroe County judge and an acute observer of Tennessee politics. But Freeman doesn't get the message. It doesn't happen.

Cash-register economics are going to be the heart of the committee's decision process, and that may mean trouble for us. No one besides TVA has ever had the time, money, agenda, or staff to collect data on Tellico economics, and since 1966 TVA's data has been fundamentally skewed to justify the dam. Two highly respected economics institutes— Resources for the Future and the Conservation Foundation—volunteer expert critiques that tear apart TVA's draft report submitted to the God Committee. The trouble with these reviews, however, is that they can analyze defects only in what they're given; they cannot generate new affirmative data. The General Accounting Office study we got last year was likewise limited to undercutting TVA's data, not producing forward-looking economic data. Our Little Tennessee River Alliance, led by

286 VINDICATION IN THE GOD TRIBUNAL

Peter Alliman, has put together its own "Plan for River-based Development," emphasizing agriculture, tourism, and industrial parks. Like our
prior analyses of the project and alternatives, it's done as best we can. It's
largely conceptual, however, lacks comprehensive economics, and isn't
professionally slick. The Hanson-led river alternatives study is a purely
conceptual compilation of "might-be's," likewise with no fiscal data.

Comes the day of the God Committee, January 23, and we anxiously
cross our fingers. A couple hundred people file into the auditorium off
the C Street entrance of the sprawling 1930s Interior building. Andrus
is walking around giving impromptu directions. Folding chairs have
been set up in rows facing folding tables set end-to-end with name
cards for the Cabinet officers and state reps, who amble in awkwardly
shortly after nine a.m. They've never been in a situation like this before, pulled out of their cloistered offices to sit with Cabinet colleagues
reviewing reams of technical data for half a day, then casting votes
as superjudges. Will their newly created God Committee be a wise
tribunal—dealing rationally, even soulfully, with clashing streams of
evolution? Or will it be a sordid distillation of human politics?

Pat Parenteau's injunction against the Greyrocks Dam in Wyoming
comes first. A complex settlement has been reached between the parties:
if the power authorities reduce plant size and accept federal regulation
over river flows to protect the whooping cranes' migratory resting places,
buy irrigation water rights to supplement flows, and set up a $7.5-million
river fund, that dam can be completed. The committee takes Greyrocks
first and gives it a quick disposition, accepting the settlement. Parenteau,
sitting beside us, leans over and whispers stoically, "I think I've just
bought you your river." But volatile politics and uncertain economic
algorithms mean we can't be sure what will follow for the darter.

"We will now move to the Tellico project," says Andrus. "The staff
will give us a brief background, and then we will move into disposition
of that question."

Davis begins the staff presentation. He moves methodically through
a summary of his staff's fifty-three-page report, supplied to committee
members three days earlier. He notes serious problems with TVA's accounting of benefits in flood control, recreation, barge navigation, and
in industrial development where "equivalent . . . development opportunities exist in this area whether there's a reservoir or not." Good. "Agriculture and forestry, which would be limited with the reservoir, present

opportunities for intensive development under the river alternatives." He doesn't say, however, how substantial those farmland values are. Then he repeats TVA's claim of two hundred million kilowatt hours in electric generation through the diversion canal without explaining its relative expense and insignificance in the TVA system. And, agonizingly, the staff report completely ignores all the tourism alternatives we consider to be the project's most lucrative and realistic economic resource.

Worse, Davis then presents his overall conclusions on net economic benefits for the reservoir and for the river. "This brings us back to the total annual benefits: $6.5 million for the reservoir development, and $5.1 million for the river." Ouch. Their analysis has accepted a lot of TVA's facts and, by completely ignoring the river's developable recreation and tourism values, has severely diminished our river alternatives. If past expenditures are set aside, Davis concludes, "net measured annual benefits for the reservoir are about one-half million dollars larger than for the river alternative." He does mention that the river has "certain unmeasured benefits which must also be weighed, . . . cultural, history, archaeological values, . . . trout fishing," but he doesn't mention tourism, and none of these resources has numbers attached to them. Everyone in the room knows that in modern governmental processes most things without price tags are treated as things without value.

Davis finishes presenting his extensive economic analysis. No one else seems to have anything to say. Decision time? Andrus peers up and down the table. "What is your pleasure, gentlemen?" No one moves.

Finally Charles Schultze, chair of the Council on Economic Policy, clears his throat and leans forward. Uh-oh. He was put on the committee at Howard Baker's insistence, displacing the president's environmental adviser in order to bring hard-nosed economics to the table.

"Mr. Schultze?"

"Well, somebody has to start," says Schultze. "I can't see how it could be done, to say there are no reasonable and prudent alternatives to the project. The interesting phenomenon is that here is a project that is 95 percent complete, and if one takes *just the cost of finishing it,* against the benefits, and does it properly, it doesn't pay! Which says something about the original design." His comment is greeted with laughter and applause.

William Willis from Nashville raises his hand. This could be a problem. Willis was appointed by Tennessee's Governor Ray Blanton to represent the state's position on Tellico shortly before the governor left office under a cloud of criminal charges. Blanton had been a TVA fan, and we expected his appointee to be equally bad news for us.

"Dr. Davis," Willis asks, "could one not infer from the TVA report submitted to you in December that TVA itself feels that river development is a viable alternative?"

Whoa! Blanton's appointee is making a decisive point *for us!* The way he poses it, under the God Committee test the precise comparative economics may actually be irrelevant! The question instead is whether there is a reasonable alternative to the dam which is "not clearly outweigh[ed]" by TVA's project design.

"I'd have to leave the inferences to the committee," Davis replies cautiously.

A member of the committee then asks Willis what the state of Tennessee's official position is.

"Well, I really can't state that," Willis says. "There are some for and some against." More laughter. Willis continues: "It might be helpful for the committee to know as a matter of history that the Tennessee Wildlife Resources Agency has consistently deplored the completion of Tellico Dam. . . . Governor Winfield Dunn in 1971 began voicing opposition to the project. . . . I am not aware of the position of our new governor who took office on Saturday."

Not only is Willis *not* being antagonistic, he proceeds to validate our case: "Please don't hold me to this math, but if you take the TVA figures on benefits, . . . they give quite a spread, like on navigation from zero to 620, . . . and take the average of the figures, according to my math you come out with a benefit for reservoir development of 2.2, and a benefit for river development of 2.3!'"

There's a shocked silence. Clearly everyone expected Willis to be the voice of the TVA pork barrel. Instead he's laid out a nonexemption case for the river.

It's Schultze, the economist, who ends the suspense. "I move that we deny an exemption."

"All those in favor of the motion, say aye," Andrus intones. There's a chorus of ayes. "Opposed?" No one. Andrus continues: "If I might be given the right of editorial comment, . . . I think I would be remiss if I did not point out to the American people that in more than 5,000 instances [here's Mardi and Debbie's data again] we have had consultation under the Endangered Species Act, and they have all been resolved, with the exception of the one we have handled today. . . . I hate to see the snail darter get the credit for stopping a project that was so ill-conceived and uneconomic in the first place."

Jubilation and knowing chuckles are the prevailing reactions as the crowd breaks up and heads for the door. Schultze tells a reporter, "It'd cost $7.22 million a year to operate the dam, but the total benefits would only be $6.5 million." We, the motley citizen critics of the water project establishment, have been vindicated. The environmentalists clustering outside the hall are beaming. Against all odds, finally, we've gotten a high-level verdict from a congressionally designed review publicly affirming our oft-repeated snail darter mantra that "good ecology makes good economics." The darter and its river have prevailed.

And the knowing chuckles? Most Washington insiders always understood that this dam project, like so many others, was a crock of spin. But this is a first. Never before has the nation's political system allowed a project from within the steamy world of public works appropriations to be held up openly to the light of economic and logical scrutiny as this one has been. And now, with the raw truth laid out in the open on the public table, even many of the crowd of attendant insiders probably are wryly experiencing schadenfreude, witnessing their country-cousin TVA's pork-barrel tricks publicly revealed. The long-standing collusive veils have been parted, the light has been turned on, and poor old TVA has been caught standing there with its hand in the pork pie.

Outside the C Street doors I squeeze forward through the departing crowd toward David Freeman, who is looking for a cab. He does not look at all unhappy until he hears who I am. "Mr. Freeman," I say, "we need to talk now about getting the farmers back on the land and—"

"Some other time," he barks, clearly not meaning it. Seizing the elbow of his companion, Bobbi Hornig, a reporter from the *Washington Star*, Freeman bundles her into a cab and they zip away. This is the only conversation I will ever manage with Chairman Freeman. But as we meander along in the noonday glare, enjoying a pleasant cathartic glow, it seems possible that the God Committee's unanimous decision will finally grant the snail darter its long-awaited national "aha" moment. The American public can now see the sharp reality: this was never anything but a crooked dam project that didn't make sense in the first place.

# CHAPTER 11

# 140 Days of a Slow-Ticking Clock, Ending in 42 Seconds

JANUARY 24–SEPTEMBER 10, 1979

Will the God Committee's dramatic verdict create a breakthrough for the little fish and the Endangered Species Act? On its face the clear economic victory for the darter and the river is legally the final chapter; no more procedures remain to be satisfied. It's time to consolidate the lessons so painfully learned about the dam project into positive and enlightening action. Get farmers back on their farms, start a tourist flow up through the valley's historic sites to the national park, and make sure the darter is securely back on its Coytee shoals.

The committee's high-level vindication of our years of opposition is a glowing opportunity to change perceptions. The public can now see and appreciate a remarkable reversal of conventional wisdom about the darter and "environmental extremism," proving that good ecology and good economics indeed go together. We of course don't expect anything like a thoughtful reaction from pork-barrel insiders, so while we try to consolidate our victory we must continue to defend it. As predicted, Howard Baker and other public works politicos had immediately reacted with anger. An immediate statement issued from the senator's office: "If that's all the good the Committee process can do, . . . put us right back where we started from, we might as well have saved the time and expense. I will introduce legislation to abolish the Committee and exempt the Tellico Dam from the provisions of the [Act]."

"That committee was not supposed to make its decisions on economics," Baker tells a reporter, though he himself had insisted that the chair of the Council of Economic Advisers be on the committee instead of an environmental official. Baker must be wondering how he let our champion, Senator John Culver, sucker him into the committee review process. Perhaps Baker, enraptured by the pundits' notion that he had a shot at the presidency, figured the Baker-Culver bill would make him look like a national statesman, rather than a regional politician, on this hot issue. He apparently presumed that the internal dynamic of the committee would be to grant exemptions, not deny them, and he hadn't even bothered to lobby the issue.

"No one came to me," William Willis tells a friend in the Tennessee wildlife agency. "As the state of Tennessee's representative on the committee I didn't get pressure from anyone saying I should vote for the dam. So I just approached the thing on its merits."

The political alliances supporting water projects will support Baker. Their fears are justified. As soon as the God Committee verdict was announced, an Alabama environmental group announced it was filing an endangered species complaint against the Tenn-Tom Waterway. This news scares us. The law's not politically secure yet. A parade of endangered species attacks on big public works projects could bring the roof down. We dearly wish our green friends in Alabama would hold off a bit for the sake of the Endangered Species Act's political health. But it's disingenuous for us who leapt into court with the darter case against the wishes of most environmental groups now to urge restraint upon those who want to use our precedent as a magic bullet against their own boondoggle foes.

Because of the darter, other Iron Triangles are agitating against the God Committee. Endangered species exist in all fifty states, especially in the vast public lands of the West. That could trigger critical reviews of a host of pork projects and programs—timber sales and ranching operations cosseted by the Forest Service and Bureau of Land Management (BLM); mining projects under Interior's Minerals and Mining Service and BLM; irrigation syndicates allied with the Bureau of Reclamation; the National Association of Home Builders with the Commerce Department and Housing and Urban Development; and oil and gas with the Mineral Management Service. Meanwhile the U.S. Chamber of Commerce, representing industries that resent federal controls of any sort, continues using the species law as a prime argument for rolling back government regulation in general.

But what about the effect of the God Committee decision beyond the special interests? Won't the economic revelations about Tellico make people rethink the clichés attached to the snail darter? In Tennessee, people who'd been mourning the Little T's impending death are surfacing joyfully. Hearing the committee's decision, fishermen have flocked back to the Little T. The river's in good shape. "There were fifty-seven cars parked at Hoss Holt's dock on the river on Saturday," Joe Congleton, our Knoxville attorney friend, happily reports. The water is running clear again, and fertile soils in the bulldozed areas are coming back to life. Where TVA had wiped out shoreline willows and cottonwoods, the hundreds of young willow trees planted by David Scates are swaying upward in the breeze, some now more than eight feet tall. A few large, old trees stand uncut in the ribbon of land straddling the river on both sides. A dozen or more farmhouses and farm buildings are still occupied, a testimony to the landowners who have fought on against TVA. Natural spawning of trout in the tributaries is continuing uninterrupted. The Little T darter population is holding strong. Currents have cleaned the shoal at Coytee of its mud and silt, and at least ten thousand darters are swimming around the gravel bars where they were born. The breeding population is sustained by continuing transport of juveniles up and around the dam structure's obstructions, monitored by Dave Etnier and by Jim Williams in Interior's Office of Endangered Species.

Alfred Davis reports the area's farmers have been reenergized by the God Committee verdict. "We got more than a hundred people to come to a meeting this week at the fort. We formed a Tellico Landowners Association to get us all back on our land." Alfred was elected president. That's what we need—a tangible presence of farmer families back on their fertile bottomlands, making it clear that the river valley, as it exists today, is still the heart of a vibrant community with a solid economic future. We need to get that through to TVA Chairman David Freeman, too. Personally, Freeman clearly wants to support the committee decision and river-based development, but he needs political arguments to back him up, and nothing would be more likely to anchor the river the way it is than getting the farmers back on their land.

A disturbing problem continues to haunt us, however. As so often before, there's virtually no acknowledgement of the God Committee's damning economic verdict reflected in local or national papers, on news shows and local talk radio, or in letters to the editor. Three weeks after the committee's verdict, Tennessee Congressman John Duncan called for a protest meeting in Madisonville near the river, and hundreds of local citizens came to jeer the little fish. Local schools canceled classes so students could attend. Not a single comment or news story mentioned the God Committee's findings on the dam's economic failings, nor the tourism and alternative development designs that could revitalize the area far more than just one last murky reservoir. To cheers, Duncan promised the crowd he'd author a bill to exempt the darter from the law. The continuing local support for the reservoir is frustrating. When we ask people what they make of the economic verdict on Tellico Dam, most say that from what they hear TVA's plan probably is the best option. The committee's review is perceived uncertainly if at all, or is explained as "just Washington politics." It's difficult for many to acknowledge that the little fish that so many Tennesseans have mocked for so long could make more sense than TVA's dam.

Why doesn't the Tennessee media report the details of the God Committee's economic analysis? As with the General Accounting Office report two years earlier, Tellico's embarrassing economics are

Left: 4-H Club members from Madisonville, Tennessee, demonstrate in favor of Tellico Dam in 1978 (one demonstrator holds a sign saying "Finish the Dam or *We* will be the Endangered Species"). Right: Protesting the dam as an act of patriotism. As a result of TVA public relations and shoddy media coverage, most eastern Tennesseans probably opposed the Supreme Court decision, considered the river defenders extremists, and knew nothing of the God Committee's economic verdict against the dam. (Courtesy of *KnoxNews* and *Knoxville News Sentinel*)

apparently not a subject that the local media will acknowledge. In part it may reflect the history of this region: the local press knows that when major initiatives have been accomplished, it's TVA that has done them. There is an understandable sense of inevitability: TVA, which has dominated the region for forty years, in the end will get its dam. Freeman is the chair of the three-person TVA board now, but Wagner's retirement left one slot empty and Bill Jenkins, the other board member, has resigned, so Freeman doesn't have a quorum to take any substantive actions—having vacated his member position on the board to assume the chairmanship position, he is now the only one on the board. Freeman, the newcomer from Washington, won't—can't—change anything.

Perhaps there's another, more human, reality behind the media's failures. For reporters and their editors in Tennessee and around the nation (as well as for most eastern Tennesseans), there may be a visceral resistance to changing their previous convictions about the Tellico project and the snail darter. Once the story was framed by TVA's impressive publicity machine—as a trivial fish versus a valuable dam, with extremist outsiders whining about the region's most eminent governmental agency—it's understandably difficult to reverse perceptions. Over the past five years, in probably thousands of daily conversations and talk radio phone-in shows, people have expressed their belittling dismissal of the silly minnow and the environmentalists using it to oppose progress. Maybe it's as hard for reporters as it is for private citizens to change their minds on something they've accepted as truth, and even harder if it means not only that they were wrong but that, further, they've been gulled, played for fools. In this context it's unsurprising that public opinion doesn't easily swing toward the farmers and the fish, and that reporters and their editors, beyond their tendencies to parrot TVA, are hesitating to acknowledge that they'd been patsies, failing to explore the most basic facts of a major controversy in their backyard.

The national coverage of the God Committee verdict is as disappointing as Tennessee's. Where previously the darter's quixotic legal victories had regularly been featured, with ironic photos, on the front pages of the nation's newspapers, or as a lead story or final story on the nightly news, this latest and most upbeat chapter of the darter story is downplayed. The *New York Times* ran the darter's Supreme Court victory on page one, but the God Committee verdict has been covered only briefly and buried on page twenty-two. The revelations of shifty economics are hardly mentioned. Charles Mohr of the *Times,* recently assigned to the Washington environmental beat after superb war reporting from Saigon, listened to us, examined the maps showing vast acreages taken for resale, and was clearly interested, but ultimately told us, "I don't see a workable hook for the *Times.* These new facts completely change the story that people have been hearing, but it's too difficult, saying to our readers that now they've got to understand a whole new version." The *Washington Post* put the God Committee's economic verdict on page twelve. The *Wall Street Journal,* which had angrily called for sober economic analyses to resolve species controversies, put it on page eighteen. The God Committee story did not make most radio and TV news shows. It went out on the Associated Press wire service, which failed to mention any of the economics, but many newspapers didn't run it anyway.

The dramatically revised darter-dam story is brimming with legal, political, economic, even philosophical import. It could shape a long-running news cycle with successive stories on all the intriguing features of the saga—farmers, Native Americans, agency pork, corrupt officials, junk science, fraudulent economics, David and Goliath. There are implications for other federally subsidized boondoggles, and an affirmation of American pluralist democracy in having local citizens with no political power carrying an issue to the highest levels in the land and winning. . . . As far as the American public is concerned, however, the silly little fish story remains completely unchanged.

We increasingly sense we're in an uneasy calm before a predictable storm rumbling ominously in the distance. There will surely be a counterattack, and we need to secure the darter's position in national power politics, or the fish, the river, the farmers, and our citizen coalition can lose it all. We need to drive a stake through the heart of Tellico Dam. Otherwise it will rise again from the dead and destroy everything we've been fighting to preserve. As it turns out, we have 140 days.

For a brief time after the God Committee decision the opposition forces seem to hesitate. After Baker's press release threatening to "abolish the Committee and exempt the Tellico Dam," we don't hear much from the antiregulatory lobbies. Perhaps they're holding their breath, waiting to see what Baker will do, or gauging public reaction to the pork chicanery revealed by the God Committee verdict. In practical terms we continue broad defensive preparations in Washington. At any moment we may need to fight off a quick amendment bill in Congress. We also try a flurry of further potential initiatives within the federal government, more nails to hammer into the Tellico Dam's coffin.

Dave Conrad of the American Rivers Conservation Council advises Interior Secretary Andrus's staff to designate the Little T as a National Wild and Scenic River, which would preserve the valley, turning it into an economically attractive tourist destination. The secretary doesn't show much interest. Bennie Keel, who works in Interior's National Historic Preservation program, proposes that the National Park Service designate the Little T valley as a National Native American Historical Park. It richly merits that designation, and Interior has been under pressure to protect more Native American cultural sites. Keel's novel proposal goes nowhere. We learn from archaeologist Jeff Chapman that TVA's work in the valley technically violates the National Historic Preservation Act. The historic preservation statute, however, doesn't have enforceable provisions except in a Nixon executive order that probably exceeds statutory authority. Interior isn't in a mood to push it.

A call comes from our Interior informant, who shocks us with the news that he is now working for TVA in Knoxville. TVA officials were so impressed by his expertise during the joint planning group that they hired him to work for them. In his new position he has more information on Tellico Dam's engineering safety violations, confirming what we had previously argued: in the event of a 150-year storm centered on the western Smokies, the spillways of the dam would likely fail, undermining the dam structure and sending a wall of water into a residential neighborhood four thousand feet downstream.

This dam safety issue could be big. But a staffer at the Army Corps of Engineers, responsible for dam safety regulation, tells me the Corps is not interested in enforcing it. "If anyone is going to address that violation, it'll have to be you." After some research Peter Alliman and I conclude that, yes, a Tellico lawsuit based on dam safety is possible. Even if it isn't likely to win at trial, the dramatic risk of drowning families downstream might trigger greater media scrutiny of the project.

But another citizen lawsuit, launched just for media impact, would require another huge investment of time and effort from all of us. "Don't do it," advises Joe Congleton. "It'd be too much for us all to take on, and isn't necessary. We've got an injunction that stops the dam. What more do we need?" Congleton is right, legally. There's no legal reason to pile another injunction on top of the one we already have. And it would be exhausting for our tired river defenders to take on an unnecessary second lawsuit, even if it might improve our political position. We back off the idea of proving the dam violates more than endangered species law.

Working with Culver's resource protection subcommittee staff and our environmental group allies, we send out information packets to offices on the Hill and prepare defensive strategies for an anticipated Senate fight. But we also heed advice from many quarters that we need to focus proactive strategies back in Tennessee. "A lot of people on the Hill ask whether your position has support in Tennessee," Anne Wickham says. "They don't like to push a national agenda where it isn't wanted. You need to get traction with the general public in Tennessee."

We launch a series of local initiatives, with me flying down regularly to help the local crew. The university group continues to sell T-shirts and agitate for protection of the farms and river. Peter Alliman and Hank Hill continue to attend TVA's monthly public meetings, where they remind Freeman and public attendees about Tellico Dam's deficiencies, and the ample benefits of river-based development without a dam. Starting in late February, Sara Grigsby, as a leader of the Tennessee Endangered Species Committee, our university group, coordinates an effort to get the state government back on our side. The new governor is moderate Republican Lamar Alexander, who knows the Little T, and Sara arranges meetings for us in Nashville with Ann Tuck, Alexander's conservation commissioner who, it turns out, had been Sara's Sunday school teacher and a family friend. Tuck will support proposals for coordinated planning efforts for river-based development of the valley. Veteran Nashville pol Walter Criley, an old friend of the new governor, tells him that our river alternatives can make the Little T "a phoenix rising from the ashes." He tells us the governor is interested.

Tony Campbell, the head of the state's conservative rod-and-gun-club group, the Tennessee Wildlife Federation, works on business lobbyists in Nashville. In a meeting with the Tennessee Manufacturers Association, the head industry lobbyist complains to him that our lawsuit is a prime example of antibusiness environmentalism, "and that law professor is the Obstructionist of the Year." He expresses surprise when Campbell tells him there's an industrial park larger than TVA's at the heart of our river-based development plans, and our potential designs are economically far more lucrative and realistic than TVA's.

In March Peter and I go to the McMinn County Rotary Club in Athens, Tennessee, the Loudon County Chamber of Commerce, the Tri-County Committee of 100, and a number of other gatherings of local business interests skeptical about the darter. We show them the tourist development potential of a Cherokee Trail into the national park, the agricultural economy that can rebound, the industrial park sites, and the dam-break threat from the dam safety violation we have discovered. We even show a map depicting how the flood surge from a breach in the dam would cover portions of Lenoir City.

None of the groups, however, reacts with much more than skepticism. We're peppered with variations on the question "Are you sure? How come we've never heard about any of this from TVA?" They know nothing of the God Committee's economic analysis. I'm a Yankee and Peter is just a University of Tennessee student. The local instinct is to believe the agency, not citizen critics, and TVA hasn't publicly admitted the dam's economic problems. A young reporter from the Lenoir City paper comes up to us after the Rotary meeting. "I know you're right about the dam," he says, "but my publisher won't let me write a story that raises any doubts about it." Local newspaper editors and TV and radio producers, according to reporters we talk to, won't authorize investigative reporting on this, the region's biggest environmental controversy.

Perhaps a scandal will trigger press attention? Hank has discovered deeds showing that TVA General Manager Lynn Seeber and his wife bought more than a dozen land parcels around the project area during the time that Seeber was making decisions whether to halt the project in compliance with federal law, a clear conflict of interest. The TVA official responsible for policing ethics and conflicts of interest is Seeber himself! This is juicy stuff, but no Tennessee media will run it. "It implies Seeber's bad faith," says Ernie Beazley, a sympathetic *Knoxville Journal* reporter. "My editors would say it's slander. We won't touch it."

Attempts to get the Seeber deeds story into the national press fare no better. Charles Mohr at the *Times* explains to me that the connection to the dam controversy is too indirect. Another reporter is very excited at first. "This can be a scoop!" he says eagerly, but then he starts to worry that maybe he would be *too far* out in front. "Have there been any prior stories about personal corruption in TVA?" he asks. No. He never writes the story. Turning to Jack Anderson, the national gadfly muckraker, we get some interest, but after reviewing our photocopies of the deeds he tells me it's a local matter, with too many complicated details for a national audience to understand.

We keep trying with the Tennessee press. Letters to editors. A satirical op-ed, "Where Is the Monster Dam?," tries to make the point that the huge hydroelectric dam that TVA depicts as an economic dynamo is nowhere to be found, its fictional ghost haunting the bars and newsrooms of eastern Tennessee. Nothing gets traction.

Some local offers of help we reject: Alfred Davis calls from his farm, where he and Virginia are still holding out. A number of condemned landowners had received an offer "from a fella with experience in South America who said he could blow up the dam for us real quick." We'd received the same sort of offer in Knoxville from a self-described Vietnam vet with explosives expertise. Stupid attempts to entrap us, aligning us with radicals? Both were ignored.

More meetings with local gatherings. We attempt to arrange a conciliatory low-profile conversation with ex-Chairman Wagner at his church, the Tennessee Valley Unitarian Universalist Church, to which many of our activists also belong. Wagner says no. We invite Chip Carter, the president's son, to come float the Little Tennessee. We contact Dolly Parton's agent, hoping the country music star might help resolve a hometown tragedy. A letter to Robert Redford asks: would he help show America what's at stake in the snail darter's river valley? Nothing transpires.

Freeman remains skittish, refusing to talk with us. Isolated from his natural Washington habitat, he realizes that the old TVA culture is woven into the region and the depths of the agency of which he is the titular head. Much of the opposition and sniping which Freeman has endured over the past year is still being aided and even directed from within his own organization. He's been burned by an atmosphere of ridicule his law department and its local allies have orchestrated against "Dry Dam Freeman." The local newspapers don't mention the development alternatives but are happy to report on Freeman's local political travails. President Carter has not backed up his TVA chair, either. Instead of providing a supportive colleague, the president is in the process of filling the recent vacancy on the board with Bob Clement, an old-style

Tennessee politician whose father served as governor of that state for many years, and who has publicly declared the river should be impounded as soon as possible.

Freeman's only substantive communication with us was relayed through the Tennessee Wildlife Federation's Campbell: "The citizen group should hire a public relations firm to turn local public opinion toward river development," the chair advised, plus he said we should organize demonstrations of thousands of people backing the darter case. Thanks, Mr. Freeman. How does he think we'd find the money to hire a PR firm? And how are we to organize big demonstrations when his agency's press juggernaut has so thoroughly marginalized our river defense group's local efforts?

We have a number of practical tactics ideas Freeman could implement to undercut the dam project, based on strategic information he doesn't know: the dam safety violations; how his attorneys, who helped marshal ridicule against his river-based alternatives, are manufacturing a specious legal argument that river-based development is illegal because appropriations forbid it; how the National Park Service can coordinate with him in designing and funding a "national resource development commission" for the Little T valley. We have discreet linkages—Freeman doesn't—with the national park leadership, which is eager for such a joint initiative.

And if TVA cleared the way for farmers to get back on their lands, that alone would anchor the case for the river. Once farmers are again planting crops in the valley's soils, the human reality of the story and its history would make evicting them a second time politically impossible. Contrary to what Freeman's attorneys are telling him, TVA has statutory authority to return possession to the farmers immediately. And most publicly persuasive, we'd push Freeman to describe the extraordinary tourism development actions that could almost instantly provide an economic jolt to the counties traversed by the river.

But though Freeman knows the dam is a loser, he's not willing to work with natural allies. He won't meet with Peter, Hank, and me, nor with Alfred Davis and the farmers' group. He won't let Campbell or Joe Congleton, with whom he has had several conversations, bring us together clandestinely, or channel our information to him. Pushing in frustration for contact, we've only scared him. (At one point we thought we were actually being given a back-channel opening, but it turned out to be something else entirely. Sara got a call from Freeman's secretary, who said that the TVA chair would like to arrange a meeting. Wow, was this the linkage we had been waiting for? Not exactly; Freeman had seen Sara at a swimming club and wanted his secretary to arrange a date with her.) Our best tactic for changing the public debate in Tennessee—TVA simply acknowledging the facts already on the record—thus went nowhere.

In early April Ollie Houck and Pat Parenteau at the National Wildlife Federation tip us off that Senator Howard Baker is about to bring an override amendment to the Senate Committee on Environment and Public Works. This is it—the Donnybrook moment where the dam proponents open a frontal attack on the Endangered Species Act, overriding the verdicts of the God Committee and Supreme Court. We spend the next month back in Washington in battles over Baker's override bill.

Our political efforts finally start paying off. Baker brings his bill to the committee, where we've had long conversations and have organized grassroots efforts with Republican senators as well as Democrats. By the day of the committee vote on Baker's override bill we get the strange sense we're winning. Baker opens the committee hearing on a wry note: "This snail darter is becoming the bane of my existence, the nemesis of my golden years!" He expresses dismay that the God Committee did not override the fish, which "is what Congress intended." He declares that the darter is "not really endangered," because many people in the papers and talk radio have said they've seen snail darters in creeks and puddles across the land. But he doesn't press hard against the committee members, Republican or Democrat. Is he pulling his punches because he worries about his potential run for the presidency? As the vote approaches after an hour of discussion, Baker makes a short summary statement and excuses himself from the room saying, "I have to meet with the president." Chairman Jennings Randolph of West Virginia calls the vote. We win, 10-6, with Malcolm Wallop and three other Republicans voting with us.[1]

There's one more congressional round to be fought. In mid-June Baker announces he'll try to do on the Senate floor what he was unable to do in committee. With our citizen group allies and Culver's subcommittee staff we've been running an anticipatory lobbying effort with a base of operations in the Friends of the Earth office. Student volunteers make briefing packets in the evening for Hill offices and press corps in-boxes, and then deliver them the next morning. Margaret and Joe Sexton continue to volunteer their efforts in walking congressional halls to lobby legislators, often accompanied by Margaret's mother, Nell McCall. In her eighties, Nell is fading. She no longer has the strength to back Senators James Sasser and John Stennis into a corner, but the trio's Tennessee accents get them sympathetic listeners in many offices.

As we make our way back and forth through the Capitol halls between office lobbying visits, we frequently see—and are awed by—Brent Blackwelder of the Environmental Policy Center and American Rivers and other high-ranking citizen group leaders stationed at the doorways to the House or Senate chamber. There they stand, armed with a handful of our briefing packets along with an armful of their own, waiting to pounce when key members come into either chamber on roll-call votes. Brent knows almost all 535 members of Congress by sight, and he waits in ambush in the milling crowd, stepping into the flow to intercept members he knows may be leaning toward green votes like ours and need a push. You cannot buy this kind of expertise and effort, at least not if you work in the public interest community. Tom Kimball, the president of National Wildlife Federation, targets a number of old-boy senators, telling them that their rod-and-gun-club constituents care that a prime trout-fishing river is at risk. Marion Edey again gets the League of Conservation Voters to announce that our issue will be counted for the annual Dirty Dozen ranking.

We're not so lucky with the media. Dave Espo of the Associated Press is lured out for a picnic with us on the Capitol lawn by one of our female ecolobbyists, but he isn't fooled. "You'd like me to do a story, right?" he laughs. "You think it's important to get information out now *before* the vote. Forget it. We won't do it. We aren't supposed to *make* news, we just report it after it happens." So much for Thomas Jefferson's solemn mandate that the press must inform the public of the ongoing affairs of state.

After a week of collective effort by our volunteers and allies on the Hill, the day arrives for the Baker amendment's Senate floor fight. The bill has been put on the calendar for two hours of debate before a vote. Accompanied by a dozen student volunteers and a couple of environmental group staffers, we go up to the Senate gallery to watch the showdown. Culver—our hero—begins a powerful soliloquy about the law: "The Endangered Species Act is a profound law. . . . The chilling tragedy of the massive losses of species will never be fully understood because among the species irreversibly lost are some whose existence we never realized, and whose contributions to science and mankind will never be known." He recounts the successful history of endangered species protections, including the snail darter's God Committee scrutiny. Good stuff, written by his aide Dick Oshlo.

"But look, there's almost no one here!" I whisper to Anne Wickham, "and the ones who are here aren't listening." Only a few senators can be seen in the chamber. They are walking around, talking to each other, or sitting quietly reading, and only a few seem to be paying occasional attention to Culver.

"What did you expect," she asks, "the Lincoln-Douglas debates?"

John Chafee of Rhode Island rises as senior Republican on the committee and continues the positive theme. Chafee is a Teddy Roosevelt conservationist, resolutely out of step with, and only begrudgingly tolerated by, the modern GOP. "This Act is important not just to us but to future generations. . . . A strong Act is absolutely necessary, whether we are talking about spindly-legged spiders or the majestic bald eagle." Ten more minutes of prepared speeches, then Culver and Chafee give the floor to Howard Baker.[2]

Baker, standing at his desk with Republican Jesse Helms of North Carolina, introduces his amendment exempting Tellico Dam and the darter from the Endangered Species Act. There still aren't many senators in the chamber. Baker delivers his prepared speech, which doesn't mention the God Committee's economic analysis. Instead he implies dirty dealings by us, the environmentalists: "Oddly enough, nobody ever heard of this darter at the time this dam was started. When the darter was discovered, somebody—I rather suspect intentionally—set out to find a species to stop this dam using this Act. . . . What I am doing today is what that review committee should have done . . . a consideration of practicality and common sense." Baker speaks scornfully, wielding facts about the dam's economics he knows are untrue. He implicitly admits he'd intended the committee process just to overturn the Court, not to examine the merits seriously. He builds upon the standard refrain—silly fish, silly lawsuit.

More senators have been arriving on the floor as the time for a vote nears, maybe sixty by the time Baker finishes. Helms stands and adds his views. "Completion of the Tellico Dam is absolutely essential. . . . It would add 7,900 jobs to an area in desperate need for employment. . . . The Endangered Species Committee . . . was not established to rule on economic benefits of public works [again forgetting it was Baker who'd insisted on the economics expert]. We cannot allow [the Act] to expand to the point that it can be used to challenge all federal projects."

Culver and Chafee stand and say how much they respect Baker, the senior senator from Tennessee, and his long-standing environmental record, then call the vote against him. Because the upcoming vote has been signaled to every senator's office, the chamber now is almost full, the last few dozen rushing in from the underground tramways in the past five minutes. It's clear that most of them don't know much about what's going on. Will their vote be determined by some last-minute encounter with a friend or lobbyist, or by the memo from their legislative assistants that some are clutching in their hands? For most, their votes certainly won't be shaped by any of the past hour's unheard speeches.

Sitting on clenched hands in the gallery as the roll is called, we start to see a pattern. Most Republicans and all the pork Democrats are going with Baker, but a critical number of Republicans are shifting our way, and not just the relic liberal Republicans. Most of the subcommittee Republicans who shifted to us earlier stay with us. All the Democrats except eight Southern pork barrelers vote with us. Baker loses, 52-43.

Right after the vote we talk with Baker's staffers. Do we need to prepare for further battles with the senator? No, comes the direct answer. "Off the record, Senator Baker made his override try today, but he's decided that after this he doesn't want to force the issue further." Before the vote this morning, his aide Jim Range had told the senator, "Twist five arms and you can get it," but Baker had backed off. His staff begs us to be discreet about this news, however. If we appreciate the senator's decision not to go further against the darter, could we please be politically sensitive enough not to speak publicly of it, to protect Baker from the old-boy TVA crowd back home? Okay, we say, it's a deal.

Baker is in an ambiguous position. Houck and Parenteau remind us that on one hand he's deeply tied to the TVA cohort in Tennessee and the public works political machine in Washington. On the other hand he wants to be president and wants to nurture a reputation as "the Great Conciliator," brokering wise national compromises. For Baker, co-father of the God Committee, to overturn his own committee's verdict to save a pork-barrel project—which might, if the press ever looked into it, become a symbol of corrupt politics—would make him look like a tawdry politico in the eyes of the public rather than a national statesman. A quiet peace? That's fine with us. And now perhaps we can rest a bit.

Holding off two major assaults from the Senate's top Republican is a major accomplishment. Time to take a breather. I do some housekeeping in the cubbyhole command center at the Friends of the Earth office, make some phone calls trying to push Washington reporters to get the straight story out to America, and then fly back to Ann Arbor, planning to return the following Wednesday.

Three nights later, on June 18, however, the phone is ringing as I return home after a Monday night class. It's Ernie Beazley, the *Knoxville Journal* reporter who has long sympathized with our case though never been allowed by his editors to tell the story. He does not have good news: Tennessee Congressman John Duncan just attached an amendment to an energy and water appropriations bill that exempts Tellico from the Endangered Species Act. On the House floor late today, when virtually nobody else was in the chamber, he and committee members attached the amendment—which, in these situations, is referred to as a rider—to the money bill. Waiving the rules, they put it in by voice vote without reading it out loud. "Duncan's office just called me to brag about it," Beazley says. "They say the money bill has so many goodies in it that it can't be stopped."

Dammit. We'll fight this, I say, but if the bill passes, we'll file suit on the dam's other legal violations. "No you won't," Beazley says. "The amendment doesn't just override the Act. It says finish the dam, and it overrides any other law that might prevent that."

I book a flight back to Washington for the next morning.

From the airport I go straight to the House clerk's office and try to get more details about what happened. How did the appropriations committee and Duncan slip a stealth rider into a multibillion-dollar spending bill? The clerk in charge of the House videotaping says I can buy a copy of yesterday's official podium videotape, but it costs $1,000. Then, against the rules, he lets me skim the full day's tape master, so my check pays for just the fifteen minutes we need, $184.

I run the tape. In a hurry to get home, most members are noisily streaming out of the House chamber after the last record vote of the day, with the exception of a small, tight group that has moved down the aisles to sit together conspiratorially in front of the lectern in the well of the House chamber: the House Appropriations Subcommittee on Water Projects, all ten members, both parties. In this day's session the annual appropriations bill funding energy and water programs around the nation has been moved along under the gavel of a freshman representative from Indiana exercising the Speaker's role. Hour by hour, the provisions previously negotiated in the appropriations process receive pro forma affirmation by voice votes. As the subcommittee members gather in the well, Representative Ted Weiss of New York steps to the podium to express dismay that a prior vote failed to require tougher nuclear evacuation plans. As Weiss finishes his statement for the record, Duncan steps to up the House clerk, gives him a piece of paper, and asks to speak. Weiss yields the lectern to him.

Like most of his peers we always had taken Duncan lightly—a legislator who rarely spoke and had no clout on the Hill, but whose steady services to constituents back home got him voted back to Congress every two years. Duncan's voice is somewhat indistinct on the tape, though the chair apparently could hear him well enough.

"Mr. Chairman, I offer an amendment . . ."

The clerk begins to read from the sheet of paper: "Amendment offered by Mr. Duncan of Tennessee. On page 28, line 18, strike the period and insert: '*Provided* that notwithstanding the provisions of 16 USC chapter 35 or any other law, the Corporation is authorized—'"

"Mr. Chairman, Mr. Chairman!" Duncan breaks into the reading of his amendment. "I ask unanimous consent that the amendment be, uh, read, and, uh, in the *Record*."

The clerk stops reading the amendment.

The chair looks over toward the seated appropriations subcommittee. "Is there an objection? . . . The gentleman is recognized for five minutes," but Duncan says nothing more.

John Myers, the senior Republican subcommittee member, jumps to his feet and says, "The minority has reviewed the amendment and accepts it."

Tom Bevill of Alabama stands up for the subcommittee Democrats: "We have no objection to this amendment."

"The question is on the amendment of the gentleman from Tennessee," says the chair. "All those in favor?" One cannot hear the little group's voices but they all apparently call out "Aye."

"All those opposed?" No one. "The amendment is agreed to." And placidly the bill moves on.

The span of this entire episode, from beginning to end: forty-two seconds.

What happened in that brief moment? Checking the text of the *Congressional Record,* page 15301, we find that the tape doesn't agree with the official text. On the tape Duncan says only "Mr. Chairman, Mr. Chairman!" and stops the reading of the amendment after "authorized." In the *Record,* however, there follow more than two hundred words of amendment text and a short speech by Duncan describing the amendment.

The unread rider amendment's key phrases: "[N]otwithstanding the provisions of [the Endangered Species Act] or any other law, the TVA is authorized and directed to complete construction, operate and maintain the Tellico Dam . . . including maintenance of a normal summer reservoir pool of 813 feet above sea level."[3]

And there, maybe, goes five years of all our volunteers' labors on the darter litigation, and the farmers' twenty years of painful, persistent, sacrificial effort to get the American legal system to reverse an ongoing mistake. We see the hand of TVA's attorneys in this, drafting the amendment for Duncan behind Chairman Freeman's back. On their own, Duncan and the appropriations committee would never have known to say "normal . . . pool of 813 feet above sea level," which negates Freeman's suggestion about retaining a drawn-down dam. Nor would they have known to exempt the dam from "any other law." Only we and the TVA attorneys know the full range of the dam's other legal violations—dam safety, diking permits, historic preservation, cemetery protection laws, and more. The stealth rider is a very well-designed missile.

Congressman Jim Weaver, a progressive green legislator from Oregon, was furious. He happened to still be in the chamber and was standing near the podium but had no idea that something dramatic was happening. If the clerk had read just nine more words before Duncan

308 140 DAYS, ENDING IN 42 SECONDS

stopped him, Weaver would have heard "Tellico Dam" and he would immediately have made a point of order. The parliamentarian clearly would have rejected the amendment. House Rule 21 forbids "any provision in any [appropriation] bill . . . changing existing law," and this amendment clearly does exactly that. A violation of the rule is moot, however, if no member makes an immediate point of order. It can't be made later. Nor can the violation be taken to court. The rules are enforceable only by Congress itself, not by judges.

"Dammit," George Mannino, a friendly staffer for the Senate subcommittee, says to us later that week. "On Tuesday I was griping at dinner about this lousy trick, and my wife told me she was the one who'd typed it up for the appropriations committee! She's a secretary there; she thought we knew all about it." And what about the House parliamentarian, who sits beside the podium and is supposed to tell the chair when a proposed amendment violates House rules? He can't do anything if he never sees or hears the text. Stealth ambushes are far easier than open combat.

"This isn't the first time this trick has been pulled," *Washington Post* reporter Ward Sinclair tells us. "The old boys have done it a bunch of times. It's how tobacco price supports were added last year. Teddy Kennedy's done it, too, sneaking liberal items onto money bills in the Senate. Usually each party has somebody stationed in the chamber to look out for sneak riders so they can block them with a point of order." On Monday afternoon, however, the subcommittee's Democrats were colluding with the Republicans, and Representative John Brademas, who was supposed to be the Democrats' general lookout, had gone home for the day.

And what about the two-hundred-plus words added to the *Congressional Record* that never were spoken? "The *Record* isn't really a record of what's said in Congress," Sinclair tells us. Members often insert material into sessions they didn't even attend. These insertions are typically tagged to denote this distinction, but if the members actually speak at least three words on the floor, they're then allowed to "amend and extend" their remarks for the *Record* without specifying that they never actually spoke the added text in the session.

"Sometimes they cut out parts of what they said, too," says Hank. "Last year Representative Marilyn Lloyd from Chattanooga stood up and told the House that the dam was needed because her house had been destroyed by a flood two years ago. It was a damn lie; the water never reached her house, and Tellico Dam wouldn't have made any difference. She pretty quick decided the lie might get her in trouble, so she had it removed from the *Record*."

Most judges don't realize, as we hadn't, that the *Congressional Record* doesn't necessarily reflect what's actually said in Congress. In courtrooms all over the nation judges decide cases about the meaning of statutes by referencing the words of legislators printed in the *Record*. They say that such-and-such a statement was made on the floor of the House or Senate before a law passed, so the members assembled must have agreed with that interpretation. In reality no members may have been present in the chamber at all, except for the chair and the speaker, who may have uttered but three words. A law professor at the University of Chicago Law School, Antonin Scalia, has been criticizing judges and lawyers who foolishly rely on a law's printed congressional history. They "assume conclusively that statements recorded in the *Congressional Record* were in fact made. That assumption of course does not accord with reality. . . . There is no basis either in law or in reality for this naïve belief."[4]

Scalia is right about the vagaries of legislative history. On one occasion we ourselves helped Senate staffers write a conference report *after* the full Senate had already voted to approve it. And what does this say about cherished theories of democratic governance? If, as is practically inevitable, most members of Congress vote most of the time on bills they've never read and on issues they've never studied, then don't many of their votes come down to pure insider politics? If the press isn't looking over their shoulders, members' votes can be cast based upon the influence of campaign donors, party whips, or gym buddies' opinions. If the public interest is to intrude upon legislators' usual motivations, it depends a lot upon (God help us) the press, or upon the energies, brains, and integrity of individual members' staffers, too often likewise a crapshoot.

But here we are. The rider is attached to the money bill, a Christmas tree statute loaded up with so many earmarked goodies that it will indeed be very hard to stop. And by hitching it to a pork appropriations bill, the matter has been transferred away from the subject-matter committees where we have friends and supporters—Culver's Senate resource protection subcommittee and the House fisheries and wildlife subcommittee—and shifted over to the House and Senate pork committees that are the bonded friends of TVA. The override amendment will now go from the House to the Senate and we'll fight it there, and if the Senate stays with us, it will go to an appropriations conference committee of the two chambers to iron out the differences, and we'll fight it there too. If we lose that battle and the money bill passes with the rider still on it, the American legislative system gives us one more place to fight it—1600 Pennsylvania Avenue.

Our source in Interior relays some good news. He's overheard discussions within the Carter White House—"They're planning to veto the entire bill." The White House staff is in shock at the appropriations committee's maneuver, and not just because they care about our case. When they looked at the *Congressional Record* the morning after the rider was slipped into the money bill, they discovered that the subcommittee had pulled yet another fast one, double-crossing Carter by torpedoing the economic reviews that were part of their hit-list deal on water projects. Sixty seconds after the snail darter rider had been stuck on the money bill the appropriations team had added another stealth rider: "None of the funds appropriated for the Water Resources Council may be expended by the Council for the review of any . . . proposal or any preconstruction plan for a federal . . . water resources or related land resources project *unless funds for such review are authorized to be appropriated by Congress*" (italics mine).

"You know what that means," American Rivers's David Conrad says wryly. "They'll fund reviews of water projects when Hell freezes." The White House is aghast. Secretary Andrus immediately issues a statement saying he has spoken with the president, and if the bill passes a veto is probable.

The Carter administration, however, is in political disarray. Most of Carter's legislative initiatives have stalled, and many liberals have been encouraging Teddy Kennedy in his widely whispered threat to run against the president in the primaries. On the Right, Jerry Falwell's evangelicals are irate over Carter's reluctance to impose antiabortion laws. Antiregulatory interests are mobilizing around ex-California governor Ronald Reagan and persuade him to be the rallying figure that will pull the evangelicals back into the Republican alliance. Reagan has changed his positions on astrology and abortion, now declaring that he is a born-again Christian and will support abortion bans.

Through all of this the press has not been kind to Carter. During a fishing excursion last spring in a muddy pond back home in Georgia, a bewildered swamp rabbit swam up to the president's johnboat and tried to climb aboard. He pushed it away with his paddle. The *Washington Post* screamed, "President Attacked by Rabbit!" and the mocking "killer rabbit" story made all three network newscasts and reverberated for a week.

If political scientists were worried that Lyndon Johnson and Richard Nixon had ushered in an era of imperial presidencies, Jimmy Carter had now singlehandedly cured that fear. Congress stands dominant, a fulcrum of peremptory power. Not a good situation for us. We've seen too much of Capitol Hill and how it works to sleep well at night knowing how congressional politics run rampant.

The Senate appropriations committee will bring the bill to the Senate floor. We're optimistic, because our long-standing champion, Senator Culver—as pugnacious as he is bright—knows our case and says he'll fight the amendment despite the fact that he's deeply involved in strategic arms limitation treaty negotiations and a farm bill. "He'll stand tall for you," promises Martha Pope, who has left the National Wildlife Federation to work for Culver's committee. "But he says you damn well better be behind him one hundred percent. It's now or never, Katie bar the door."

The appropriations pressure Culver will face in the Senate is not as powerful and adamant as that on the House side. Because all money bills start in the House, the Senate hasn't traditionally been the center ring for money bill politics. Several leading appropriations senators, moreover, are far more progressive than their House counterparts. Warren Magnuson of Washington and Mark Hatfield of Oregon are usually supportive of environmental protections unless the northwest timber industry is directly concerned. Dennis DeConcini of Arizona and two other fiscal conservatives have regularly voted with us. Moreover, Howard Baker's staff signals that the senator, having made his symbolic attempt in June, won't go full force against us on the rider deletion vote. James Sasser, Tennessee's much less potent junior senator, is on the appropriations committee; he'll speak for TVA.

Six farmers come up from Tennessee to work the Senate. They visit several Midwest senators. Once again we try to get the press involved. The *Post*'s Ward Sinclair agrees to do an interview with the farmers and persuades Sasser to be part of the interview, holding it in the senator's office. Sinclair brings along a buddy, John Chambers, who writes for a Kansas newspaper. "Well, now, I'm a Chambers myself!" declares Nell Chambers McCall when the reporters are introduced. "So you'd better write some good things about this here case we've got!" The farmers lay out their story, and Nell again makes Sasser squirm. When Chambers is astonished by her account that most of the condemned farmland is being taken for resale, Sasser is forced to say he knows about that and agrees that the project should never have included excess condemnation beyond the reservoir.

Later, in the corridor, Sasser's aide Martha Ketelle gives a stunning explanation of why the senator still supports the dam. "The senator can't count on enough support from liberal voters," she says. "Liberals vote with their brains, on facts. He needs to depend on the majority of voters who just stay on blindly even when he's voting against their interest." Neither Sinclair nor Chambers is able to get his respective editor to run the story. A national story does appear, written by conservative commentator James Buckley, mocking "The Snail Darter Syndrome."

But we get increasing feedback from Senate offices expressing anger about the House's trickery. Don Cohen, who has moved from Michigan to Tacoma, Washington, reports that the northwest delegations say they'll go with us on the motion to strike. Jim Elder, an energetic friend who lobbies for the Sierra Club, reports that South Carolina's Senator Ernest Hollings, a member of the appropriations committee, is with us. "Hollings checked with David Freeman at TVA about where we'd gotten our data, and Freeman said, 'You can trust the data; they got it from us.' Hollings says don't worry, the Senate is going to hold for you." And the *New York Times* publishes a short editorial: "This Kind of Trick Endangers More Than Fish."

Even more heartening, we hear from our Interior source that "Secretary Andrus is really p.o.'ed. He can't believe what the House is doing, that all his work on the God Committee is like it never happened." The White House has told Andrus to fight on for the little fish. He's written a powerful letter and delivered it to every member of Congress:

> Congress created a special seven-member Committee which I chaired.
> After full consideration we found that completion of the project is *not*

*justified.* . . . The . . . Committee unanimously concluded after an intensive three-month economic analysis, that the value of the project did
not outweigh the value of the River alternatives which were available
if the dam were not closed . . . In the event of a large flood, the dam
would be *overtopped and breached,* resulting in *more significant destruction* than if it had not been built . . . The darter transplants are *not
yet successful* if they will ever be. . . . I urge you to review those conclusions when you vote on this legislation to override not only the decision
of the Supreme Court, but also the unanimous verdict of the Committee you created to resolve the difficult questions presented in these
cases.[5]

Exactly one month after the override amendment is stuck on the
appropriations bill, Culver brings his motion to strike the rider to the
Senate floor. His angry speech has more listeners this time and goes far
beyond the economic merits:

To exempt the dam now would subvert [the God Committee]
mechanism . . . and put each and every conflict back in the hands of
Congress. Before you vote to exempt the Tellico Dam . . . you should
ask yourself if you are enjoying this debate. Because I can assure you this
is just the beginning, just the first of many if we ignore the decision of
last year. . . . What happened over there in the House? . . . This amendment on an appropriations bill, if it were offered in the daylight would be
ruled out of order. . . . Only 15 Members present. . . . 42 seconds. The
skids were greased shamefully, shamefully!

Baker says very little. His junior colleague, Sasser, forgetting what
he'd said last week to Nell McCall and the reporters, carries the load
and launches into a rambling commentary alleging the project's benefits, saying we opponents had sought out "a back door mechanism to
thwart the will of Congress," that the dam itself cost $111 million, which
would all be lost if the Court decision stands, and he's heard from
friends in Tennessee that snail darters live in many other parts of the
region but TVA hasn't looked hard enough for them.

After Massachusetts Senator Ted Kennedy, well briefed as usual by
his staff, delivers a few remarks—about the dam's waste of money, loss
of farmlands, and destruction of Cherokee sacred sites including Sequoyah's birthplace—Culver's amendment goes to a vote. It's fast and
sweet. We win, 53-45, carrying most of the Republicans on the environment committee with us.[6]

A week later, July 25, the Senate conference committee members—all of them appropriations legislators—refuse to accept the override amendment, agreeing with our argument that the Senate has twice voted against it and that the full House has never even debated it, let alone voted on it. So the battle shifts back again to the House, where an explicit debate on the override amendment is scheduled for the week before the summer recess. "You're becoming a political ping-pong ball," Pat Parenteau laments. "House to Senate, then back to the House, then it'll probably be back to the Senate, and yet another House-Senate conference committee session. This is brutal." Ouch. Yes, we do have another chance to convince the House, but it will be tough. All the members will be antsy and distracted, eager to clear their desks and get away from steamy Washington.

The Friends of the Earth office has no air conditioning, and we're exhausted. Unhappy calls start coming from volunteers: "Most of the offices on the Hill don't care about the darter. Staffers are being told that the God Committee economics were biased. What should we say?" Jeez, all the staffers have to do is read Andrus's letter, which was sent to every member. Or look at the God Committee report. If they can't find it we'll bring them a copy. "Tell them that Carter is threatening a veto. . . . Tell them that the Tennessee delegation is split." If the Tennessee delegation cracks open we'll automatically get another fifty-plus votes from representatives otherwise loath to vote against a solid block of colleagues from a project's home state. But if they ask *who,* we can't tell them. Two Tennessee representatives—Harold Ford and William Boner—say they'll vote against the dam, but they won't allow us to give out their names before the vote.

"Tell them the Tellico Dam has serious safety defects," says University of Tennessee engineering professor Bruce Tschantz. He's been bravely publicizing an analysis of the dam's capacity to fail. On Tellico and other reservoirs with earthen berms, a freeboard (the space above any projected flood's high-water mark) of at least three feet is necessary. Tellico Dam would have zero freeboard, and the spillway capacity is insufficient. "You can *assume* it will fail in the maximum flood," he says. So-called maximum floods happen all the time, with two in nearby river systems in the past year alone.

Is this too much for student volunteers to get across? We have a two-track problem. To be considered credible in this complex case we have to be comprehensive and detailed on the facts, but to get through to congressional members, harried staffers, and reporters we need simple sound bites. It's hard for anyone, let alone our casual volunteers and interns, to pull that off.

On the Hill I try our arguments on some middle-of-the-pack votes. The staff of Representative Dick Cheney from Wyoming thinks he may go with us. He's an avid fly fisherman and has repeatedly posed with Trout Unlimited leaders in outdoor magazine photos. "Cheney will be interested," they say. "He likes to go along with Trout Unlimited on these issues."

Southern California archconservative Bob Dornan has sponsored several animal welfare bills in the House, Brent Blackwelder tells us. Sitting in his inner office—which features a one-way mirror mounted on a wall to enable him to survey his staff—surrounded by miniature fighter planes and models of bombs, Dornan says he believes that TVA has indeed cooked up corrupt economics for the dam. He's somewhat interested in the farmers, and he chuckles at the dam's lousy engineering. He takes an information packet. Will he go with us? "I'll think about it," he says. "By the way, what's your position on abortion?" Uh, abortion's bad, I say, but government probably shouldn't be making decisions about a woman's body. Dornan's face clouds. I should have demurred. "I'll think about your darter," he says.

In the halls of Congress we constantly bump into fervent, clean-cut, antiabortion evangelical lobbyists carrying anti-Carter, antiregulation political tracts along with antiabortion messages. The antiabortion activists and the proenvironment groups have very different political stances and influence; the prolife lobbies are considered political heavyweights, the long-haired environmentalists not so much. And for legislators like Dornan, if you're for one, you tend to be against the other.

Caucusing back at Friends of the Earth each evening, we can see that the fight ahead will be rough, as volunteers report that nobody on the Hill worries about Carter's veto threat. The situation looks bleak elsewhere as well. Jim Williams phones from Interior. "Bad news," he reports. "The darter population in the river is way down, terrible. We can't find any young-of-the-year back on the breeding shoals at Coytee. If we can't remove the channel blockage by spring, you can forget the darter in the Little T." Martha Pope calls next. She sounds dispirited too, and tired. She's been talking again to Baker's aide Jim Range, who tells her the House is going to kill us, and that Baker has an economic study showing the dam breaking even. "We have lots of other things to fight, that we're losing," she says. "Your Tellico Dam is like flypaper. It sticks to us more every time we touch it, and doesn't ever let go." I also get a call from Alfred Davis back in Tennessee. Nell McCall "is feeling sicklity," he says, and other farmers have cropping to do. They'll write letters to farm-state newspapers and thank-yous to legislators who voted with us, but no farmers can make it to Washington this time.

But one gloomy morning several days before the vote, the door at the Friends office flies open and a burst of light and noise floods in. Eight people pile through the entranceway, whooping and hollering. "Let us at 'em! We're from TU Georgia, and we're going to set 'em straight!" I don't recognize most of them, but these are down-home Trout Unlimited members, and they know and love the Little T. When they'd heard about the approaching House battle they decided, unasked, to fly up to Washington and help us out. This feels so good on a day that was feeling so bad. Itching to lobby, the visitors are immediately given a printout of Southern legislators who just might respond to their regional voices and their shit-kicking anger over "that dumb dam."

They look over the list. "Hey, you don't have Newt Gingrich on here." We explain to them that Gingrich is tied to the New Hard Right corporate crowd and is a lost cause. "Hold on!" they say. "We're going to go in to see Newt, and we're going to open his eyes. Just wait. You'll see!" Sure they will. They don't understand the intimate networks that tie these new Hard Right Republicans together. But these lovable grassroots visitors will be here for two full days, and they'll hit at least thirty offices that would never have welcomed our pony-tailed student volunteers. Heartened, I turn back to my work. I call reporters, making sure they have Andrus's letter, and call a Corps engineer to discuss, off the record, the dam's violation of design safety and other regulations. I'll spend the weekend in Washington writing a clutch of speeches for friendly members of Congress to deliver on the floor whenever a vote is scheduled.

Joe Congleton calls from Knoxville: William Willis, the Tennessee representative on the God Committee who, surprisingly, had spoken and voted for us, is so disturbed by the way things are going that he's pushing hard on his Tennessee House colleagues Albert Gore and Bill Boner. Maybe we *can* crack open the Tennessee delegation.

Monday morning the circus recommences. A call from the *Post:* they've been thinking about doing an editorial for us and want to know when the vote will be. Then, Representative John Dingell, sponsor of the original law, sends a message: he'll speak for us, he says, but "can't stand out there for us" because he'll need a lot of conservative votes to defeat an upcoming auto safety airbag bill opposed by his hometown Detroit carmakers.

Through Monday and Tuesday the feedback from visits to House offices continues to be troubling. Albert Gore's staff passes word that he understands the details and merits of the God Committee's judgment in our case, but he can't publicly support us and feels obliged to vote against us to maintain solidarity with the others in the Tennessee delegation. Duncan has sent around a "Dear Colleague" letter, his first ever, telling all members of the House that the Tennessee delegation, including Gore, supports the dam against the fish. I call Congressman Harold Ford's office, which reports that, no, Ford's still with us. He'll do a letter saying he doesn't agree with Duncan, but it'll take a few hours, and please don't release it publicly; we can make only fifty copies, which have to be handed out discreetly. Ford won't give a floor speech unless TVA Chairman David Freeman asks him to. Boner's office tells us that the congressman is willing to give a pro-darter speech if the president himself calls him. Who do they think we are? Carolyn Isber at the White House says she'll try but it's hard to get the president's staff focused until it's too late, and "we may be on slippery ground here," meaning that his close advisers may be hesitant. Late in the day she succeeds in getting Andrus to call Boner, and it sounds as if we'll get Boner's vote. Another White House staffer says he'll try to get TVA Chairman Freeman to call Gore and Ford, but when Freeman is asked he demurs, explaining that he feels lost down in Tennessee and that his old Washington friends don't understand how embattled he is. We write a new fact sheet refuting Duncan's letter; in the evening, volunteers and interns stuff it into all 435 House mailboxes.

The House, trying to finish everything and leave town, will stay in session until at least 9:30 p.m. That's bad. When issues in Congress run late in the day they usually get railroaded in a hysteric rush to make quick decisions and go home. Martha Pope and National Audubon Society's Ann Graham intercept members at the door and report dismally that of the two or three dozen they've spoken to, at least twenty have no idea of the facts on the upcoming vote.

With Margaret Sexton and her husband, Joe, we go around to several more offices, all seemingly in bedlam. There are dozens of votes today and no one seems to be able to focus on our darter for more than a few moments. At seven o'clock that night we go up to the Visitors' Gallery above the House chamber and hunch over the railing. We can see that on each representative's chair has been placed a photo of the Tellico Dam structure with a crude photocopied handwritten caption attached: "This is an actual photo of Tellico Dam—99% complete at a cost of $111 million—vote for completion!" Duncan has figured out that photos are the way to send a message. "If they paid $111 million for that little thing, someone got took!" we overhear one old boy say, but he doesn't look bothered by it. Tom Bevill, the appropriations subcommittee chair, rises and makes the motion that the House insist on keeping the rider on the energy funding bill.

John Breaux, the new wildlife subcommittee chair, is a traditional pork politician from Louisiana, but, backed by young Rob Thornton, the new committee counsel, he stands and defends the law, the darter, and his committee's turf: "I do not think anyone . . . who knows the record . . . can in any way, shape, or form classify me as being a crazy environmentalist. . . . I . . . have myself voted to support this project in the past. But I do not do so today. If you look at it from an economic standpoint, it is a turkey!"

A series of our allies rise to speak in support of Breaux in the mostly empty chamber. Dingell notes how the darter has revealed the dam project's lousy economics. Silvio Conte, a liberal Republican from western Massachusetts and a member of the appropriations committee, puts Andrus's full letter into the *Record,* reading salient lines. Representative Bob Edgar, a Methodist minister from Pennsylvania who is widely disdained for his idealism, speaks firmly for us, echoing Dingell's economic arguments for the darter, reminding the House of Andrus's warning about a presidential veto, then adding solemnly, "While you may not like the looks, the shape, or the size of the snail darter, it has a right to exist."

The appropriations chair introduces a parade of statements from politicians and public works spokesmen from around the country decrying the darter injunction, and calls for a vote. It takes ten minutes

THIS IS AN ACTUAL PHOTO OF TELLICO
DAM — 99% COMPLETE AT A COST
OF $111 MILLION — VOTE FOR COMPLETION

Tellico Dam photograph that TVA lobbyists placed on the
desks of all House members, urging them to override the Supreme Court verdict and the God Committee decision. (Photo
of dam by Tennessee Valley Authority, 1978)

for representatives to start arriving in answer to the intercom voting
call, and, one by one as they hit buttons on their desk to record their
votes, little colored lights flick on beside the 435 names on the huge
electronic board hanging on the eastern wall—green for *yes* on Breaux's
motion to strike the rider, red for *no*. Harold Ford, who has promised
he'll support us, sits at his desk and hasn't spoken. On his knee is his
nine-year-old son Harold Jr., brought along to see Dad vote. His father
lets little Harold push the button to cast his vote. A green dot for us
appears on the board beside "Ford, Tenn."

More representatives pour in to vote. There are jams at the entrances
to the chamber. Standing at one door is appropriations subcommittee
Chairman Tom Bevill and at the other House Majority Leader Jim
Wright of Texas. As the representatives break through the scrum into
the room in singles and pairs, blinking at the board, they ask, "What
vote is this?" Signaling with their thumbs down, Wright and Bevill

shout out to each representative entering: "It's *yes* if you want min-nows, *no* if you want electricity."

"Anyone who thinks Congress is a deliberative body should come watch them vote," says Dave Conrad.

The red dots pretty quickly start outnumbering the greens. As the red count climbs and the number of uncast blanks diminish, Harold Ford gets up and leads his son out of the chamber. The little light left glowing beside his name has been changed from green to red. We are losing, badly. Margaret Sexton is crying softly. Joe looks stricken. Jan Schoonmaker, an aide for Louisiana Democratic Representative Lindy Boggs, leans toward me in the gallery and says, "Lindy had to vote against you, but she knows you're right. You remember what Bismarck said: 'Anyone who cares about laws and sausages shouldn't watch them being made!'"

We lose, 258-156 on the last day before the congressional vacation, August 1.[7] Most of the people we had hopes for go against us. Ford. Gore. Boner. Kemp. Leach. Murphy. Cheney. Bennett. Panetta. Stock-man. Aspin. Gephardt. Glickman. Daschle. Dornan. But guess who voted *for* the snail darter? Newt Gingrich! The Trout Unlimited guys from Georgia did it. They understood some of "the intimate complexi-ties" of Washington far better than I.

We cannot rest during the month that Congress is in recess, because we know the House-Senate appropriations conference committee will meet a second time to consider the override in early September. "And don't expect any rational decisions in the second conference," Anne Wickham warns. "The porkers are all working together this time." Unfortunately Anne is right, as usual. The conference committee votes overwhelmingly for the override amendment.

So back again to the full Senate we must go to see if the conference committee's override vote will be accepted by a Senate majority. The little fish has become a shuttlecock in a congressional game of badmin-ton, and our allies are wearing down. If you're working for the public interest, not for the insider players in the political marketplace, you have to keep on defeating their attacks, time after time. As my mentor Joe Sax tells us, you can never expect once-and-for-all victories: "Money can always wait."

Although the Senate has voted twice against the dam, things now happen in a rush. Howard Baker returns to the attack. What happened to the deal we'd made? Perhaps now that TVA's attorneys and Duncan have thrown the Supreme Court's Endangered Species Act decision back onto the front burner, Baker figures he needs to join his traditional allies in incinerating the precedent. Also, we grimly realize, Baker has seen over the past six months how little the press has been telling the American public about the merits of the darter's case in the God Committee's economic verdict. If the public never hears the story, Baker must reasonably conclude, his presidential fortunes are not likely to be dimmed by his support for this regressive pork override.

As the final Senate vote approaches, we still hear enthusiasm from the darter crew in Tennessee. They're writing letters to editors and to the senators, and they're once again ready to make the long drive to the nation's capital. "Let us know when we should come up to help you fight." In Washington, however, our allies are more somber. Only the animal welfare Monitor group, combining several of Christine Stevens's organizations, is gearing up its full lobbying staff. In the other groups it's mostly our closest stalwarts who rally round. Martha Pope on the subcommittee staff sounds petulant. "Don't push me. I'll take your ideas and follow through if I think they're worthwhile. Culver will stay with you, and if you win it'll bounce back to the House and you can fight there again. But we're worried about the whole Act now."

In some offices, our work over the past two years has had an effect. "Wallop will be with you," his staffer tells us. Wallop remembers Jean Ritchey's testimony about the Tellico project's farmland condemnation. Her family's farm should not be confiscated just to be resold to a corporate developer. In many Senate offices, however, we hear a sense of grim inevitability. "The story has taken on a life of its own," says one empathic congressional staffer glumly, meaning the trivial fish-dam caricature, "and the facts don't matter." At the White House, Kathy Fletcher isn't enthusiastic about our chances in the Senate. Will Carter veto? "Most of the advice he's getting is for the veto. But when he does, you'd better be ready to work hard for us."

On September 10, the day of the Senate vote, the speeches sound familiar. Culver again lays out the facts of the God Committee verdict and adds an extended economic analysis from Carter's Office of Management and Budget ripping apart the TVA's economics. John Chafee speaks about the importance of the Endangered Species Act and the advantages of developing the valley without a dam.[8] Sasser retorts at length about the importance of the dam and says that talk-radio callers throughout the southeast have been reporting snail darter sightings all over the place. Howard Baker presents his position more jovially, repeating the jokes he'd made in committee: "The awful beast is back! The Tennessee snail darter, the bane of my existence . . ." Appropriations committee Chairman Bennett Johnston, a Louisiana Democrat, adds sardonic comments about the fish, and passes on a threat from the House—if no dam, no money bill.

Looking down from the gallery as the Senate record vote is called, however, we note with surprise that the atmosphere seems very different from the flippancy in the House. The Senate chamber is nearly full throughout the floor speeches. Senators are listening to the arguments, and seem to be picking up on Culver's scorn for the corruption of pork politics, and his hope that senators hearing the facts will vote for what's right.

We listen as the clerk calls the roll, senator by senator, and votes are shouted out. Keeping score, a miracle is occurring. The vote is very close, and with most senators now counted we realize we have forty-nine votes against the override amendment. Because three senators are out of town, that means that, against all odds, we've won again!

But Howard Baker leaps to his feet. He and his aide Jim Range, who has been sitting beside him, clearly have also been keeping score, and they know that the senator must do something fast. "I ask that the [vote] clock be stopped for three minutes!" Baker calls out. His request is granted, and Baker moves quickly around the room. We watch as he approaches Wallop. Baker is intent. Wallop shakes his head no. Baker then puts his hand on Wallop's shoulder and whispers fervently. Wallop, who, remembering Jean Ritchey and the farmers' property rights, has always voted for us, steps back, slowly turns and walks down to the clerk to change his vote. Four others get Baker's pitch and change their votes too. The clock is restarted. We lose, 48-44.

It's done. Congress has now passed the bill overruling the Endangered Species Act and all other laws protecting the darter and its river. We sit stunned, our wistful hope that the American legal system was going to decide this long battle on the merits now dashed.

The majorities who voted against the darter in both chambers did so knowing the sordid facts about the dam: Andrus's dramatic letter had been sent to every single one of them and repeated in the floor debates. Over many months every member had received heavy doses of the core facts behind the decisions of the General Accounting Office, Supreme Court, and God Committee. But they also knew that the American public *didn't* know the facts. As with so many other politically driven projects and programs, so long as the public doesn't know, Congress's insiders are free to play power games, stoop to tribal alliances, and defer to campaign contributors. Science and objective data are ignored or, worse, disrespected.

"It's one of the sad little secrets of government," Sierra Club's Jim Elder says. "Most of the votes cast by most members of Congress are based on short-term pressures, nothing to do with the real public interest merits."

Over in the House, Albert Gore releases a statement: "It was unfortunate that the controversy over the snail darter was used to delay completion of the dam after it was virtually finished. I am glad the Congress has now ended this controversy once and for all."[9]

What shall we do now? It's obvious—presidential veto. Carter knows the facts and has threatened to veto the bill. We need to stiffen his resolve. It takes a vote of two-thirds in both chambers to override a veto. We'll need to line up votes from at least one-third of the members in the House or Senate to guarantee that the president's veto is sustained.

We're not worried. Given the tally of past votes we've won in both chambers, we know we can do that.

# CHAPTER 12

# A Phone Call from Air Force One

SEPTEMBER 10—NOVEMBER 29, 1979

A little after nine on a Tuesday night two weeks after Congress passed the override bill, the phone bank rings in the cramped upstairs office of the Sierra Club. Drew Diehl, a Sierra Club staffer who was working late, answers the blinking line, then turns to me and says, "It's for you."

"Professor Plater? We have a call for you coming in from Air Force One, the president of the United States. Will you take it?"

Is the White House communications guy kidding? For the past two weeks we've been waiting for this call.

Shortly after the Senate accepted the House's exemption of Tellico Dam from all the laws of the United States, President Jimmy Carter's Domestic Council contacted our coalition of environmental groups. The White House staffers told us to start working Capitol Hill to guarantee enough votes in at least one chamber, Senate or House, to block congressional override of an impending presidential veto on the bill. We know Carter wants to veto, because his instincts are green and, beyond overturning our Supreme Court injunction and the God Committee's economic verdict, the appropriations bill rider also terminates his water project pork reform process. It seems clear the president's credibility will suffer yet another emasculating loss if the old-boy network can successfully strike down these symbols of the president's merit-based reforms.

In the subsequent two frenzied weeks we've worked the Hill and the press to sustain the presidential veto. With the press, we continue to be unlucky. Reporters and their editors seem content just to say there's a potential veto on the horizon. CBS and ABC continue to decline to run the video exposés they've filmed. They'll wait and see, opting to cover the matter when and if Carter acts. In a context where national decisions are shaped by polls, the president wants to be confident that the public knows the facts behind a potential veto decision. Concerning the darter, they don't.

On the Hill, however, we've been extraordinarily successful. Focusing on members who supported us in the House and Senate battles, congressional staffers tell our volunteers in office after office that the appropriations rider process offended their bosses. The crude maneuvers and shallow arguments on the Tellico override have tainted the legislative process even in the eyes of some cynics.

To our surprise and delight we've been able to line up solid blocks of votes to protect Carter's imminent veto in *both* chambers. On the Senate side you need 34 of 100 senators to block the two-thirds majority that can override a veto. Forty-one senators of the 44 who supported us in the last Senate vote have firmly committed to us, and some who voted against us will vote with us now, like South Dakota's Tom Daschle, whose aide said he hadn't realized what his prior vote had meant. In the House, which has been generally unfriendly, you need 146 out of 435—but we've got strong commitments from almost 170. That means appreciably more House members have decided not to override the president on the veto than the 156 who voted with us in the prior House vote.

Brent Blackwelder comes back from a meeting at the White House and is as happy as we've ever seen him. "Kathy Fletcher says it's time to stop lobbying the White House," he tells us. "Just keep working on Congress. There's an overwhelming likelihood you're getting your veto. Jim Free [a White House staffer on resource policy] says it's a sure thing." Democratic Representatives Mo Udall of Arizona and Richard Ottinger of New York talked with the president and got a good reaction when they pushed Carter for the veto. Brent has gotten a national railroad union to announce its support. The Cherokee got a resolution from the National Congress of American Indians at their annual convention in Sarasota. Retired Justice William O. Douglas is too infirm to issue a blistering statement on our behalf, but Cathy, his young wife, contacted Stu Eizenstat in the Domestic Council to tell him the old man cares deeply and expects Carter to do the right thing. Gus Speth at the Council on Environmental Quality has sent three memos to the White House, along with clippings of an editorial he wrote for us. Sue Irving, an aide to Council on Economic Policy Chairman Charles Schultze whom we'd met at the God Committee, said not to worry about White House staffers, like Frank Moore, who clearly would prefer to trade away the darter for congressional votes. "Tough shit," she said. "Almost all the advice Carter's getting is for your veto." Interior Secretary Cecil Andrus has been telling Carter that this is also a prime opportunity to stick it to Howard Baker, who may be his opponent in the 1980 election. "You don't help yourself by ducking this one."

Andrus has also been working to get our message into the press. To grab reporters' attention he's inserting juicy sound bites into his public appearances. "Yes, it's a little fish, but that Tellico Dam is clearly a turkey!" "You know, this is the only fish story I've ever heard where the fish keeps getting *smaller!*"

There are some worrisome notes, however. Senator John Culver's wildlife subcommittee staffer Martha Pope is peeved at how much attention our issue is getting. "This is politics, not a religious issue," she gripes to me. She and Ann Graham at Audubon are wringing their hands at the amount of political capital invested in our case. Brent goes over and firms them up. The Tellico case will be a pillar of environmental credibility for the future, he says, if we do this right.

Other rumors swirl about the tight squeezes Congress is putting on Carter's legislative agenda. The president desperately wants Congress to ratify the treaty giving Panama legal title to the Panama Canal, and the GOP is rounding up evangelicals to oppose him (Jesus, it seems, wants the United States of America to maintain ownership of the canal). Carter also wants a Department of Education, which the Right considers a first step toward socialistic school policies. On top of these issues, a major nuclear reactor needs its appropriation renewed; as a former nuclear submarine officer Carter likes nuclear power, and the threatened halt of nuclear funding concerns him. And the Endangered Species Act itself needs to be reauthorized. The public works lobby will try to block that too.

But heck, our friends in the White House say, there's nothing unusually threatening here. Votes for the canal treaty and education department look strong. As for the nuclear plant renewal, the pork barrel loves nuclear power even more than Carter does, so a nuclear cutoff threat isn't credible. And even if the Endangered Species Act and nuclear funding reauthorizations were not to go through, Congress would give them continuing resolutions to carry on, as it always does.

Our confidence grows with every passing day. Picking up on a suggestion from Margaret Sexton, Asa and Nell McCall's daughter, in mid-September we draft a paragraph for Carter's veto message, urging that the Endangered Species Act reauthorization bill contain a provision that "confiscated lands shall be returned to their former owners."

"The public doesn't know about farmers being condemned for private corporate development," Margaret says. "Carter can really grab public opinion and turn it around by making that part of his veto." We pass the draft to the White House and use the idea of private property repatriation as a persuasion point in lobbying congressional offices.

At noon on the twenty-fifth we hear the veto decision is imminent. Carter is flying to New York City to speak to a national public transit meeting and shore up support from Mayor Ed Koch to help stave off the escalating likelihood that Ted Kennedy will challenge the president in the primaries. We're told the president has drafted a veto message. Here we go!

As the afternoon hours tick by there's no news. Carter makes several speeches around New York City, holds a series of conversations with local politicians, then heads for Kennedy Airport. I've been told to wait for a call to kick off the veto defense campaign, and I have given the Domestic Council staffers the phone number at the Sierra Club office, where I'm still waiting at 9:15 p.m. Five minutes later the phone rings. It's Hank in Tennessee. He sounds staggered. "Dick Lodge, [Tennessee Senator] Sasser's guy, just called me. He says the president called Sasser a few minutes ago and said he'd signed the bill."

"Oh, God, no. Was he sure?"

"Maybe not. Have you heard anything?" And then the other line rang . . .

"Deacon is coming on the line now, Professor."

"Huh? Excuse me?"

"Oh, sorry," the White House operator says. "*Deacon*'s the code name we use for the president. Hold, please. Hold for Deacon . . ."

"Professor Plater? . . ." The voice with the Georgia accent is there just as it sounds on the evening news clips.

"Mr. President? . . ."

There's a short time delay between each spoken clump of words.

"Professor Plater, I wanted you to know that after careful analysis and soul-searching I have determined to sign the bill. I think it's the best decision."[1]

He's not vetoing. Then why is he calling? There's no point. He's overturning years of work by us and his own administration, not to mention his own declared merit-based governing principles.

And why's he calling *me*? He must know I have no political power. Is he just being polite? I don't think so. His voice is shaky, not a confident voice graciously addressing a loser. My immediate sense of it is that Jimmy Carter is calling to ask for understanding, for Christian forgiveness. I have two immediate reactions—one, that maybe I can convince him to change his mind before the plane lands back in Washington (can a bill be legally unsigned?); and two, I'm going to hold his face in this, not letting him get off the phone without suffering.

"Mr. President, you are making the wrong decision. Hundreds of Tennessee farmers, and sportsmen, and conservationists have worked hard on this, for more than ten years, building a record to support your veto. And the citizen groups have gone out and lined up a minimum of 170 House votes to sustain it."

"Well, I think it was in the country's best interests and the best interests of conservation."

"Mr. President, I don't know of a single conservationist who thinks so."

"Well, I am a conservationist. And it's a close question."

"Not on this record, it isn't. You have the votes [to back up the veto]. You don't build leadership strength on a record like this by taking a position of weakness."

"I don't think it was weakness. This vote [meaning his non-veto] will help protect other environmental laws from congressional attack."

What is he thinking—that by his turning the other cheek, the porkers and other antienvironmentalists will owe him one, and protect other environmental laws?

"Mr. President, you don't help the Endangered Species Act by overturning its major symbolic case! Like you wouldn't strengthen environmental law by overturning the Storm King case. [*Storm King* on the Hudson River was environmental law's first big court victory.] Remember in 1977, when you were persuaded not to veto the public works bill? You subsequently said that was a big mistake. This is, too."

"We won't know that for some years, Professor."

"But you clearly had the votes [to uphold a veto]. More than forty-five in the Senate!"

"Yes, but subcommittee Chairman Bevill's already put it [another override] onto another bill."

"We could circumvent that by legal means . . ." [Not sure what I mean by that. Maybe that a further episode of violating the House rules would be rejected.]

"But Professor, the subcommittee chairman is insisting on this—"

What does this say about Carter? He's the president of the United States, but he can't stand up to a subcommittee chair? He could stand up strong, telling the public what they have so long never heard. Imagine what he could say to the press and the American people.

Instead he says, "I think I've made the right decision."

"I don't know any conservationists who think so." I'm repeating myself, but I want to hold him in this painful position. "You don't build strength by not exercising leadership when you're in a position of strength."

What else should I be saying? I notice I've stopped calling him "Mr. President." My tone borders on condescending. I'm feeling a flood of sadness and exasperation. Is this the end of our story?

"Well, Professor, I just wanted to call to make the gesture, because I know how much you cared about this."

What is one supposed to say at a moment like this, "I understand"?

"It's not the gesture I was waiting for," I say.

Silence. Then, "Well, I have to go now, Professor," he says.

Click.

I'd held him twisting for almost five minutes of pain. I start kicking myself for not being more articulate, not pulling out some big moral gun. If only I'd said, "Mr. President, do you realize that if you don't deliver a veto when you get off that plane, you'll be the first person in human history to hold a species created by God in his hand and consciously condemn it to extinction?" That would've gotten under his theological skin, tilting a veto our way, wouldn't it? Why hadn't I said it?

I sit in the darkened office, choked up, empty. Drew offers some consoling words. I ask him to write down everything he'd heard in the conversation so I can record it accurately. I too scribble the whole thing into my notebook.

What now? We've lost. Every statute that could give us legal leverage against this misbegotten project has now been removed from the Tellico Dam. Our government and a self-described conservationist president have failed us, and themselves. There's nothing left but to go home, lick our wounds, and try to get back to our lives—isn't that so?

Hell, no! Maybe it's blind stubbornness, or a mean-spirited desire to lash back at one's conqueror, but knowing that the Tellico project is a stupid and destructive mistake, and that the decision to override the laws so tawdry, how can we stop now?

Fight on.

Back to the phone. Call Peter, Hank, Sara, and Alfred in Tennessee and tell them what's happened. Talk with the North Carolina Cherokee, several of whom are up here in Washington. Let's get the word out to all the faithful about Carter's failure. This isn't over yet. We plan a press conference for tomorrow to launch the next battle. The Cherokee will be there with us, angry. Our most constant Washington allies, too, Dave Conrad from American Rivers Conservation Council and Liz Raisbeck from Friends of the Earth, along with Ed Osann from the National Wildlife Federation and Jim Elder and Brock Evans from the Sierra Club. "There's still hope, if we are all willing to keep going." Into the night, every single phone call says it: "Fight on."

Three hours later, after midnight, I stumble down the narrow Sierra Club office stairs, totally spent, once again with the acrid taste of defeat in my mouth, steadying myself with a hand on the stairwell's ancient brick wall. The calls have been made, a notice of tomorrow's press conference is posted on the reporters' Daybook, and in the morning we'll pull plans together early for what we'll do there. But late this night it's hard to avoid the feeling that this is the endgame. Four years ago our odds had started at nil, but they'd improved more and more each year. Now it feels they're back close to nothing. My hand brushes across a paragraph from a speech by the ecoactivist writer Edward Abbey; someone had typed it out and taped it to the bricks on the stairway wall. I stop to read it—

One final paragraph of advice: do not burn yourselves out. Be as I am—a reluctant enthusiast, a part-time crusader, a half-hearted fanatic. Save the other half of yourselves and your lives for pleasure and adventure. It is not enough to fight for the land; it is even more important to enjoy it. While you can. While it's still here. So get out there and hunt and fish and mess around with your friends, ramble out yonder and explore the forests, climb the mountains, bag the peaks, run the rivers, breathe deep of that yet sweet and lucid air, sit quietly for a while and contemplate the precious stillness, the lovely, mysterious, and awesome space. Enjoy yourselves, keep your brain in your head and your head firmly attached to the body, the body active and alive, and I promise you this much; I promise you this one sweet victory over our enemies, over those desk-bound men with their hearts in a safe deposit box, and their eyes hypnotized by desk calculators. I promise you this: you will outlive the bastards.

Next morning, more phone calls from all over. Our friend and supporter Ginna Mathews in Tennessee is grim: this government doesn't care about facts, just images. Sara is crying—long, wracking sobs. TVA has announced they can start flooding the reservoir over the farmland and Cherokee sites within thirty days. What do we do now? Alfred calls. He and other farmers had planned a tractor motorcade demonstration to support Carter's veto. Useless now? Yeah. Scrap the plan . . . No, wait. Roll 'em! Get angry! Later today a bunch of tractors—and maybe they'll pull "honey-wagon" manure spreaders behind them—will roll through the streets around TVA's Knoxville offices. "It'll take more than one punch to get us down," one of our Chattanooga activists, Randy Brown, says. "They're going to have to beat us to death."

From different corners of Washington comes more news. In exchange for the non-veto, Marion Edey of the Council on Environmental Quality, past president of the League of Conservation Voters, thinks that the president got probably twelve Panama Canal votes, plus a hollow oral promise from the appropriations subcommittee chair that he'll not defund Carter's Water Resources Council. The president had called Edey shortly after he talked to me (his call hadn't reached Tom Kimball at the National Wildlife Federation), and then Russ Peterson at Audubon; clearly Carter was hoping that environmentalists wouldn't turn against him over this. Hank reports that Sasser threatened to support Ted Kennedy in the Tennessee primary if Carter vetoed the dam—a ludicrous proposition to anyone who knows Kennedy's image in Tennessee. Andrus thinks Carter also got a promise of congressional

One of the Little T valley farmers who drove tractors to TVA headquarters in Knoxville in protest of Tellico Dam. (Courtesy of *Knoxville News Sentinel*)

passage of the bill to create a Department of Education. Does this mean the White House set us up, asking us to build credibility for a threatened veto so they could cut some deals?

"I don't think so," Edey says. "I talked to the Domestic Council. Eizenstat wanted to make deals. He thinks the environmental groups will have to stay with Carter. But the president was really torn on this one. Before he left to get on the plane he'd prepared two messages, one for the veto and one for signing the bill. And get this: they told me Carter had decided to veto, go our way, until Frank Moore got to him just before noon as he was leaving for New York."

Frank Moore is the president's longtime Georgia buddy and his stumblebum congressional liaison man. Apparently Moore had said, "Mr. President, I understand you're going to veto that bill," and Carter had replied, "Yes, I've decided it's the right thing."

"Mr. President," Moore reportedly said. "If you veto that bill, tomorrow morning every editorial cartoonist in the nation will have a drawing of you holding a snail darter in one hand and a killer rabbit in the other. You just can't stand that kind of ridicule in the press." And that, perhaps, was what finally pushed Carter to sign. What a demoralizing and sad story, especially because it could be true. At the end of such a long, hard road doing all the right things, did we lose in the legal system to a media caricature and an unfunny joke? A president who knows what's right—backed by law, facts, economics, common sense, and more than enough votes to support his veto—can't do it because of his own shaky media stature and because public opinion has been skewed by years of lazy press?

Brock Evans from the Sierra Club stops by our Friends of the Earth office and hugs me. "Remember," Brock says, "You're down, but you're not out. What you've got to do at times like this is to figure out a path to victory. Find one, and then do it."

So here is our best remaining strategy: The bill overrides only *statutes*. Congress and Jimmy Carter cannot override the United States Constitution. Let's try the *constitutional* argument: that the Tellico project violates clearly recognized First Amendment religious freedom rights of the Cherokee.

From the beginning we've talked about the Little T valley as the center of the Cherokee religion, and the site of Chota as the holiest Cherokee place, its Jerusalem. The Sequoyah brothers, Ammoneta and Lloyd Sequoyah, great-great-great-grandsons of the great Cherokee leader—both of them "traditionals" who don't fully assimilate into contemporary culture, and both medicine men—still get their herbal medicine from the Little T valley near Chota.

Over the past six years Bob Blankenship, one of our Cherokee friends from North Carolina, had been suggesting we add the First Amendment count to our lawsuit, buttressed by the Native American Religious Freedom Act, which specifically recognizes those rights. We'd always demurred. "Let's stay with the statutory case we have, and hold back the religious case in reserve." That's not bad faith. That's strategy. Now, though, it's time. If the Cherokee tribal council agrees later this week, we'll get a constitutional lawsuit rolling.

Through the morning we put our heads together with Blankenship, Dean Suagee at the Bureau of Indian Affairs, Dan McCoy (the current chief of the Eastern Band), and our citizen group buddies. Because of Carter's non-veto we hope to get a roomful at the press conference. We'll tell them the whole tawdry story of Tellico Dam, and then we'll tell them how the dam is unconstitutional.

This time our hopes for a press conference are fulfilled. The room is jammed with reporters. Why now, finally? According to my notes, over the past three years I have been in contact with more than 120 reporters, some more than a dozen times, and have never been able to entice a journalist to do a national press story on the Tellico project's critical details. Maybe they're all here today because they sense the final day of a long-running story. Maybe they think we'll declare a rejection of Jimmy Carter, stoking Kennedy's presidential hopes. Or maybe it's just that when they checked the Daybook there wasn't much else scheduled. Anyway, they're here, more reporters than we've ever seen in all these years, even after the Supreme Court verdict.

And they listen! They scribble notes as the Cherokee representatives describe the valley and its place in their history and culture. We show the old map of Cherokee towns and forts. They take notes and ask questions as we roll out our talking points about how this isn't a hydro dam, it's a recreation project and a land grab. Proven diseconomies, we say. Condemnation of farmland to give to private developers. The farmers: "They've broken their backs carrying the case all the way to this point, and now Washington has broken their hearts." Pennsylvania Representative Bob Edgar speaks eloquently about how this is "government by a runaway appropriations committee," a sad threat to democracy. Brent lays out a few pithy statements on national water policy cursed by insider pork politics. The National Wildlife Federation's Ed Osann quietly tells how environmentalists everywhere are disappointed by this president, who knows the importance of these issues but has apparently been sucked into "a cynical bargain, and such a weak bargain." Brock Evans echoes Osann: Carter is selling out his original supporters to try to mollify his enemies.

Doesn't this seem like a huge mistake, we ask? How could Carter, how could Congress, how could the agencies, how could *the press* have let this happen? A reporter in the front row reacts with a yelp. It's Phil Shabecoff of the *New York Times,* a pioneer in covering environmental stories.

"How can you say that?" he challenges. "How come it's only *now* we hear all of this? About the farmers' land being taken for real estate development, about benefits getting so inflated, about Cherokees? Why didn't you tell us this long ago? This is a story that the American people needed to hear!"

I lose it. Poor Shabecoff, who seems like a nice guy, gets hit by the blast of years of our media frustration. "Goddamn it," I fume, "are you out of your mind? We *have* been trying to get you reporters to cover this story *for almost three years!* We've distributed more than a dozen information packets at your press buildings. I've personally put several of them in *your* in-box—with photos, maps, explanations of how this dam is an economic disaster. We handed you quotes and information from the God Committee decision. We set up press conferences with farmers and Cherokee tribal members here in Washington, put them right there in your Daybook, and *none* of you came. No one. And you blame *us* for not getting the story across?" I am shaking with the anger of futility. Our environmentalist allies look over at me with some embarrassment, it seems, but they understand.

Phil Shabecoff looks chastened. What can he say? There's an awkward pause. Another reporter asks, "Well, what will you do now?"

I look over at Blankenship and McCoy. "How about explaining the religious freedom law to them, and American Indian religious rights?"

The Cherokee representatives launch into an explanation of how constitutional law protects Native American religious sites and practices. They say that Cherokee sites on the river aren't just historical, they're tied to deep religious beliefs and practices. They repeat the Sequoyah brothers' words. The valley lands, and especially the site of old Chota town, are the heart of the Cherokee religion. In the Cherokee language, a dammed river is "dead water." If the river at Chota stops flowing, the Cherokee religion will die, and the brothers as medicine men will die with it. We say the First Amendment legal argument builds on good precedents. It's been explicitly reinforced by terms in the recent Native America Religious Freedom Act, which, we argue, isn't reversed by the statutory rider because it's an express congressional recognition of long-standing constitutional religious rights. It's our judgment that federal courts reviewing cases like these will have to issue injunctions against any government action that destroys those rights.

"So you'll bring another lawsuit against TVA?"

I look over at McCoy. It's the Cherokee who must carry the ball now. McCoy smiles at the reporter and says calmly, "Just you wait."

Back on the North Carolina side of the Smokies, the Cherokee Eastern Band tribal council quickly authorizes a lawsuit. An activist Cherokee group from Oklahoma, the United Ketooah Band, joins in as well. Under the leadership of the Carolina tribe's local attorney, Ben Bridgers, we design a complaint and enlist Bunky Echohawk and Curt Bluedog from the Native American Rights Fund in Colorado to argue the case in an accelerated trial for preliminary injunction. The complaint is accompanied by the religious practices affidavits from the Sequoyah brothers, written in Cherokee. It'll be Judge Taylor again.

Is this Cherokee lawsuit proof that we never really cared about the little snail darter—that it was only about the river and the valley farmlands, and that we just used anything to save them? It doesn't feel that way. The darter and the river and the farmers and the Cherokees and the trout and the family float trips are all inextricably connected. The

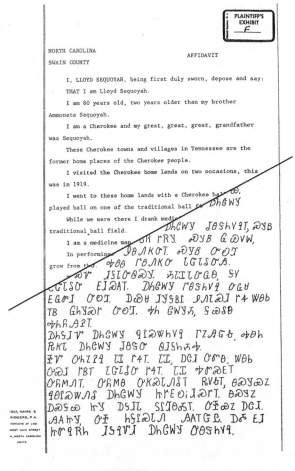

Affidavit filed in the lawsuit *Sequoyah, et al. v. TVA,* based on the Constitution's religious free-exercise clause; medicine men Ammoneta and Lloyd Sequoyah affirmed the Little T and its valley as their necessary source of traditional religious spirit medicine. (From court files, U.S. District Court, Eastern District of Tennessee, Civ. No. 3-79-418)

fish was our best chance to protect everything linked to its river. As Jimmie Durham, a northern Cherokee with the International Indian Treaty Council, says, "That little fish is my brother."[2]

On October 20, a week after the Cherokee file the lawsuit, four or five hundred people rally for River Day at Chota meadow on the Little T. Taciturn Cherokee and farm families with kids running around mix with raucous college activists, scientists from Oak Ridge National Laboratory, plus a contingent of student volunteers from Michigan who carpooled down to meet the river and the people they'd been fighting for.

Before dawn some local thugs scattered thousands of roofing nails over the dirt road approaches to the river, clearly with the goal of disrupting the mass gathering. Hank's car and a half-dozen others are disabled before warnings can be posted. Why would these vandals disrupt our David versus Goliath rally? Probably because Red Wagner's team has successfully painted the darter, the river defenders, and even the holdout farmers as interlopers. We're regularly depicted in the local press as extremists opposing the local community's best interests. One local paper's op-ed page runs a picture of a human hand cleverly photographed emerging upward from a puddle of mud and is captioned, "This is the hand of a *real* endangered species!" TVA's refrain that its model city will provide thousands of jobs is still repeated and believed, years after the plan imploded. Despite our best efforts the array of attractive non-dam alternatives for the river valley is completely unknown, and the sorry details of the dam project's economics unacknowledged. An atmosphere of knee-jerk antagonism has reached the point where the local community's remaining river defenders scarcely talk publicly against the dam.

TVA Chairman David Freeman shows some class, sending a TVA magnet sweeper to remove the nails: "We want to ensure our protesters stay safe." As the River Day gathering swells into the hundreds, there are Cherokee dances and storytelling; home-style potluck dishes; bluegrass bands singing "Dam the TVA and Save the Little T!"; and fiery speeches ("God bless the snail darter, God bless the Cherokees, and God bless the Little T"). The day also happens to be my birthday; a couple hundred people sign the back of a darter print for me, a copy of that Exhibit 12 from the trial. The odds are now formidably against us, but the opposition to this destructive mistake hasn't been eradicated.

Midway through the rally, agents from the Bureau of Alcohol, Tobacco, and Firearms rush up to the flatbed truck we're using as a stage and tell us to evacuate the area immediately: an anonymous caller has reported that sticks of dynamite have been planted in the field where we are rallying. We announce the threat over the loudspeaker and say those who want to should leave. Only one person does, Charles Easterbrook, a reporter from the *Atlanta Constitution* who'd hastened up to see the river, telling us excitedly that the darter's untold story "is Pulitzer material." But now he is clearly terrified. Soon the agents find twelve sticks of dynamite tucked within a bush near the flatbed, but there are no detonators. The feds take the dynamite away and we party on. Hours later darkness enfolds the valley and dozens of young people spread out their sleeping bags around the meadow and along the riverbank, nighthawks screeling above unseen and the river's cool currents whispering through the night.

Ten days later the Cherokee case brings the Tellico Dam to Judge Taylor's court for the last time. Bunky Echohawk and Curt Bluedog, clad in three-piece suits and with their jet-black hair in long ponytails, explain the offense a reservoir would do to more than a dozen Cherokee religious sites. A large blowup I've made in Ann Arbor of the old 1782 Cherokee map is entered into evidence; it shows the sacred sites,

River Day demonstration, October 20, 1979, in Chota meadow beside the Little Tennessee River. Several hundred farmers, Cherokee tribal members, fishermen, students, and local environmental clubs participated. (Courtesy of David Scates)

all of which will be destroyed. The trial hearing seems to go well. The continuing Cherokee religious practices in the valley are clearly shown.

As soon as the oral presentation is finished, however, Taylor reaches into his drawer and pulls out his written opinion dismissing the case:

> The question [is] whether the denial of access to government-owned land considered sacred and necessary to plaintiffs' religious beliefs infringes the free exercise clause. . . . The free exercise clause is not a license in itself to enter property, government-owned or otherwise, to which religious practitioners have no other legal right of access. Since plaintiffs claim no other legal property interest in the land in question . . . a free exercise claim is not stated here.[3]

This theory—that one must have ownership rights or explicit access rights in order to claim protection of religious values on a particular piece of land—is strained and hitherto unknown. It would surprise the Native American Religious Freedom Act's congressional sponsors and their Native American supporters, who designed the law to protect sacred sites throughout the West, most of which are on federal land. But Taylor isn't concerned by lack of logic or precedent. He's clearly irritated that his earlier ruling was reversed. Here's a final chance to quash the opposition to TVA and Tellico Dam. No balancing of competing rights, normally the rule in religious cases. Case dismissed.

The U.S. Court of Appeals for the Sixth Circuit in Cincinnati again hears the appeal from a Taylor dismissal decision. We try to tell ourselves there's still a glimmer of hope, still a path to victory. The appeals court could recognize the desecration of Cherokee sacred sites and enjoin the dam once more. As the appeal approaches, we're buoyed by a searing article that finally reaches a national audience: Peter Matthiessen, renowned for his prize-winning essays and books on nature and indigenous cultures, persuaded the *New York Review of Books* to publish his exposé "How to Kill a River" revealing the Tellico Dam's impact on the Cherokee. It's too late.

In the court of appeals, the vote goes against the river, 2-1. The judges all reject Taylor's reasoning that the Cherokee need to own the land or legal access in order to claim religious rights in the valley. But two of the three substitute a new theory, saying our case fails nevertheless because we needed to prove "centrality"—in other words, get a trial court ruling that the river sites around Chota are central to the

Cherokee religion. We had in fact presented evidence of Chota's centrality on the trial record, and could easily have presented much more
if we'd known of this newly invented judicial test that didn't exist when
we were litigating the case. The lone dissenting judge recognizes the
irony: "The District Court . . . did not explore, develop or find any

**The Smile of Satisfaction**

Former TVA Board Chairman Aubrey J. Wagner, wavered in his support for the project. The Nov.
wearing a hardhat signifying his role in the fight to 12, 1973, date on his hat represents the date TVA
finish the Tellico Dam, smiles with approval as TVA crews resumed construction after the first injunction,
crews lower the gates on the dam. Wagner, a which halted the project between January 1972
retired 44-year veteran of TVA, was chairman of and November, 1973, was dissolved in Federal
the TVA board that authorized the project in 1966. Court. (Staff photo by J. Miles Cary.)
Throughout the fight that ensued, Wagner has not

Retired TVA Chairman Red Wagner enjoying the final closure of Tellico Dam, November 29, 1979. "I'm glad to see it finally filled. It's potentially *the best hydro project* TVA has ever
built!" he said. (His claim was ironic, to say the least; from the
start the Tellico project was designed and promoted for recreation and real estate development, not hydroelectric power
[emphasis added].) (Courtesy of *Knoxville News Sentinel*)

facts concerning the role that this particular location plays in the Cherokee religion. . . . I believe the case should be remanded to the District Court to permit the Cherokees to offer proof concerning the significance and centrality of their ancestral burial grounds [and Chota] to their religion." But the two-judge majority seems to be saying this controversy has dragged on long enough. A morbid air of inevitability has settled upon the case.

We desperately file an emergency petition to the Supreme Court, asking the Justices to hear our appeal—another writ of certiorari—still pretending it's possible to prevent the filling of the reservoir. Very quickly the United States Supreme Court issues its order of decision: "Certiorari denied."[4]

On November 29, 1979, Red Wagner witnesses the completion of his dam, surrounded by a cluster of long-time acolytes. A photo in the evening paper shows him grinning—"Smile of Satisfaction," reads the caption—as the final act proceeds.[5] Acetylene torches cut through steel cables holding up six heavy gates; one by one they drop into place in the dam. Immediately the waters of the Little T begin to rise. A flattened slick with a roiling edge of flotsam creeps steadily upstream, marking the line where a flowing river dies.

# A Few Years Later, on the
## *CBS Evening News*

**SEPTEMBER 1, 1981**

"The final story on *CBS Evening News* tonight comes to us from Tennessee. . . ."

"For four years," anchorman Dan Rather reminds his national audience, "the snail darter, a finger-sized endangered fish, blocked completion of the Tennessee Valley Authority's $150-million Tellico Dam project on the Little Tennessee River. . . ." (The camera shifts away from Rather to an aerial view of a low dam in Tennessee farm country. Backed up behind it, a serpentine reservoir twists thirty-three miles up the middle of the valley into the misty distance, where the Smoky Mountains rise up from the plain.)

The TVA, Rather says as the camera returns to him in the studio, had to fight more than twenty years to complete its Tellico Dam project because of the dogged opposition of local farmers and trout fishermen who fought to save the last undammed stretch of the cool, clear, historic river and the valley farmlands lying along it. Toward the end the citizens used the Endangered Species Act, defending the valley by protecting the last natural population of the previously unknown darter that lived in the river. (The television screen switches to film of several darters swimming at the bottom of a white plastic bucket.) Rather notes that, after twenty years of court cases, five years of fish-versus-dam confrontation, a Supreme Court verdict, and an economic thumbs-down on the dam from a special review council, TVA bureaucrats—with the aid of a climate of public ridicule—finally won the fight by getting Congress to pass a loophole bill overriding all the laws that stood in their way.

Dan Rather now cues a report in Tennessee from correspondent Bernard Goldberg, who is standing in the middle of the Tellico project lands along the river, interviewing Nellie McCall, now a scrappy eighty-year-old widow. Of the ninety-plus acres she and her late husband, Asa, farmed, only three have been covered by the narrow, muddy reservoir that wiped out the snail darter's natural habitat. It turns out, Goldberg says, that virtually none of the development benefits TVA had claimed in order to justify its sixty-ninth dam were realistic. (The camera displays views of the project area today, with lonely silos of drowned farms sticking up forlornly here and there in the shallow reservoir, surrounded by vacant project lands.) The agency, which received $150 million in taxpayer dollars for the project, is now starting to auction off the condemned farms to land speculators and a Walmart-affiliated developer that will build vacation home subdivisions.

Squinting at the CBS camera, Nellie curses the federal agency. "What would be any diffr'nce 'tween what Russia does, and what *they* do?" she asks. "Not *any* diffr'nce at all . . ." On the television screen, a bulldozer is shown crushing the McCalls's home.

The reporter then turns to Beryl Moser, who also lost his home and farm to condemnation. Now the local mail carrier, Beryl shakes his head; he doesn't want to do an interview. "It's a hell of a country, ain't it," he says quietly, turning and quickly walking away.

"Jean Ritchey and her family had a 119-acre farm," continues the reporter. "Only three of those acres were flooded for the lake. The rest of the land was to be part of the model city that doesn't exist." The camera shows Jean pointing across a field toward the bulldozed remnants of her family's home, now overgrown. "We still go back there. It's just like we went home—"

"But there's no house there anymore," interrupts Goldberg.

"That's true," says Jean. "But we go there and stand. Where it was. We were ever so into that land. Children were born, grew up there. We could be living right there now, just like we always were, farming. . . . They'll sell it for a lot more than they gave us for it." Jean is right. The

In a smoldering hole into which TVA bulldozed her house and left-behind furnishings, Nell McCall finds burnt and crushed parts of a table that had been made for her by her late husband, Asa. (Courtesy of Margaret McCall Sexton)

farm families, some of whom had lived here for eight generations, can't afford to buy their lands back at the auction.

The screen shifts to TVA headquarters in Knoxville, Tennessee. Spokesman Richard Morgan is clearly nervous. The Tellico project, he says, was designed to revitalize the region. It hasn't exactly worked out the way TVA had hoped, but his agency figures that maybe in a few more years the project will begin to produce some economic gains, if not the scuttled model city that TVA had repeatedly used to justify its claims for the dam. And the darter has indeed survived in some transplant areas.

So this is what the battle between the TVA dam and the little fish had really been about? Not a hydroelectric project, but farmers trying to avoid being thrown off their lands by a federal agency land development scheme that seems to have been ill-considered from the start?

Although the farmhouses and barns were bulldozed, TVA left barn silos standing in the waters of the shallow reservoir; some swimmers use them as diving platforms (they call this "silo-ing"). These three silos, just beyond the golf course and marina that were built after the valley was flooded, were part of the farm owned by Jim and Yvonne Graham. TVA paid them $500 an acre for their 425-acre farm, of which 150 acres were flooded. When Jim Graham confronted Senator Howard Baker, Baker replied, "That's politics, Jim. It's just politics." (Photograph by Marika Plater)

Nell McCall is fighting back tears. "I don't believe nothing they tell," she says. "The biggest bunch of liars I ever heard talk . . ." She won't get her land back. It sells today for more than ten times what the agency paid her for it just two years ago. "I'm going to be hurt and angry about this as long as I live," Nell sighs.

Back in the studio in New York, Dan Rather has a catch in his voice as he signs off for the night. He continues to sit grimly at the news desk as the closing credits roll. When the "Live-On-Air" light finally winks off, he jerks around in his chair and barks at Kathy Moore, the producer who had prepared the segment. "Goddammit!" Rather yells. "*We missed the fucking story! How in hell, over all those years, did we miss the whole fucking story?!*"

"Dan Rather had tears in his eyes," Moore recounts later. "He was choked up and angry. I didn't have the heart to tell him that we *had* filmed the story. Harry Reasoner had done the reporting. We had it ready in the can for *60 Minutes.* I don't know why CBS didn't run the story; somehow they could never find the time."

Indeed, in no other country in the world could a small group of people so lacking in power and influence have challenged a politically powerful mistake so long and so far through the highest levels and through so many branches of national government—and we came so close to winning. With just one or two additional happenstances, the river could still be flowing today, the farmers still farming, the valley's economy prospering with tourism and agriculture far better than at present, and the darter still darting among the cobblestones beneath the riffles of the Little Tennessee.

The multiple plots of the story continue to play out. For those interested in further information about the complex history of the battles to save the Little Tennessee River, extensive materials are available on an archival website—www.bc.edu/snaildarter—including updates on the snail darter, the Tellico project, and people mentioned in the narrative who played a significant role during the years defending the darter and its river—plus oral history video interviews, photographs, maps, a glossary of useful legal terms, court decisions, bumper stickers, excluded draft text, and more, including an MP3 clip of the protest song "Dam the TVA and Save the Little T."

Here's what has happened in the years since the gates on Tellico Dam closed and the Little Tennessee River was impounded—

- The snail darter: When its role as canary in a coal mine was ended, the darter became extinct in its natural habitat in the Little Tennessee River when the river became a reservoir. All the individual darters that could be netted (primarily juveniles blocked below the dam structure in their life-cycle migration) were transplanted under Department of Interior supervision, most to the Hiwassee and Holston Rivers, where they appear to have prospered, although both rivers are somewhat at risk because of upstream chemical manufacturing activity. A small remnant population was discovered in Chickamauga Creek near Chattanooga. In 1984 the Fish and Wildlife Service changed the darter's legal status to "threatened" from "endangered" (49 FR 27501), but it still lives under the protections of the Endangered Species Act.

- The holdout farmers: Asa McCall died while still occupying his condemned home in April 1977. Nell McCall was moved out by marshals on November 13, 1979. Boone Dougherty comforted Nell as she stepped off her porch, and they stood by and watched as her house was burned and bulldozed into a pit. Nell died at the Florida retirement home of her daughter, Margaret Sexton, in 1994. Margaret and her husband, Joe, moved back to Tennessee; Margaret died in 2011. Jean Ritchey's family was able to buy another farm—"but the soil is nothing like our old place." She spoke in 2008 at the 30-Year Symposium on *TVA v. Hill.* Jean died in 2009. Alfred and Virginia Davis shifted their livelihood to running an equipment supply business. Alfred also addressed the 30-Year Symposium (footage can be viewed on the website).
- The Cherokee: The two medicine men who were plaintiffs in the eleventh-hour Cherokee lawsuit against the dam, Ammoneta and Lloyd Sequoyah, descendants of the great Cherokee leader, both prophesied that they'd die within a year if the river and its sacred places died. The reservoir filled in spring of 1980. Lloyd Sequoyah passed away January 25, 1981, and his brother, Ammoneta, on August 22, 1981. Bob Blankenship became tribal chair and has authored five "roll books" on Cherokee genealogy (see www.cherokeeroots .com).
- The Tellico project: TVA completely scrapped the Timberlake model city idea and transferred major sectors of project land to a "development agency" allied with local politicians. After two embarrassing years without any development interest—the Boeing Corporation, TVA's major partner, having pulled out back in 1975 and no further development interest appearing—in 1982 TVA proposed to use large portions of the valley for regional toxic waste disposal. This plan was abandoned less than a day later, however, when the author passed leaked information about it to the local United Press newswire. Eventually major portions of the project area were transferred to real estate developers, including Cooper Communities, Inc., a second-home development

Some of the dam-resisting citizens and farmers and their Tennessee allies as they appeared at the time: (top row, left–right) Mary Ann Ritchey, Sally Ritchey, Carolyn Ritchey, Ben and Jean Ritchey, Ginna Mathews; *(second row)* Beryl Moser, David Scates, Price Wilkins, Peter Alliman, Hank Hill; (third row) Doris Gove and Jeff Mellor (from a later year), Nell and Asa McCall, Sara Grigsby, Alfred and Virginia Davis; (fourth row) Larry Crisp, Fran Scheidt, Bob Blankenship (from a later year), Randy Brown (from a later year), Wayne Starnes; (bottom row) Kirk Johnson, Joe Congleton, Margaret and Joe Sexton, Boone Dougherty, David Etnier. (Montage by Nathan Bress; photographs courtesy of the subjects, plus: *Knoxville News Sentinel* [Beryl Moser]; © Roger Simpson [Nell and Asa McCall, David Etnier]; David Scates [Larry Crisp]; the author [Bob Blankenship]; Chattanooga Arboretum and Nature Center [Randy Brown]; *Knoxville News Sentinel* [Boone Dougherty])

Some of the active Washington, DC, allies of the Little Tennessee River campaign as they appeared at the time: (top row, left–right) Jim Williams, David Conrad, Marion Edey, Pat Parenteau; (second row) Brent Blackwelder, Anne Wickham, Oliver Houck, Liz Raisbeck; (third row) Jenna Christy, James "Skip" Spensley, Kathy Fletcher, Brock Evans; (bottom row) Keith Schreiner, the anonymous source at Interior, Senator John Culver, Christine Stevens. (Montage by Nathan Bress; photographs courtesy of the subjects, plus: courtesy of Wickham family [Anne Wickham]; U.S. government photos [Keith Schreiner and John Culver]; Animal Welfare Institute [Christine Stevens])

firm with ties to Walmart. Much of the shore land around
the reservoir is now lined with expensive vacation and retirement homes. A dozen businesses have located in the industrial park, in the same industrial site area proposed in the
citizens' alternative plans. Three boat enterprises use reservoir access, having chosen to locate at Tellico rather than
at adjoining reservoirs. Warmed by impoundment, the waters of Tellico Reservoir have been vexed by widespread algae growth and invasive Eurasian water milfoil and hydrilla.
Slowed by impoundment, the reservoir's bottom sediments
have cumulated toxic pollutants from upstream hydro generators. No barge freight traffic has occurred. Flood control
benefits and electric power generation via the canal to the
adjoining reservoir have been relatively minimal. Belatedly
acknowledging that Tellico Dam could not survive a maximum probable flood, as the citizens had argued back in 1979,
in 2011 TVA installed extensive sand works to protect the

Three of the dozens of ostentatious properties that various real estate development companies built around Tellico reservoir on condemned farmland. (Photograph © Roger
Simpson)

rim of the insufficiently designed dam and levees from failing under the strain of high water.

- Back to Judge Taylor: After resignation settled in, the plaintiffs returned to Taylor's court one last time to try and recoup some of the expenses of their attempts to enforce the Endangered Species Act. Under the law the court "may award costs of litigation (including reasonable attorney and expert witness fees) to any party, whenever the court determines such award is appropriate."[1] (The majority of our citizen enforcement expenses—the agency and congressional work—were not subject to reimbursement.) Taylor refused to grant compensation for our enforcement effort, but before an appeal to the court of appeals in Cincinnati could be decided, TVA asked to settle out of court. Boone received $25/ hour for his work. The author received $14,000, which he donated to National Trout Unlimited for river protection work in recognition of the organization's commitment to flowing water and of the many Trout Unlimited volunteers who had fought so hard for the river over the years. Taylor died in 1987, to the end expressing his belief that the snail darter litigation was "foolish."

- The Endangered Species Act: Despite fears during the snail darter battles that the law would suffer from a political backlash, the Endangered Species Act doesn't appear to have been weakened by the case. Paradoxically the law may have been made more credible by the purported extremism of the snail darter case and the injunction's enforcement by the Supreme Court. The terms of the God Committee exemption amendment are so strict that only one subsequent attempt has been made to use it to undercut Endangered Species Act protections. Section Nine of the law has been given a somewhat similar flexibility mechanism. Despite continued targeting by business lobbies, the law and its stringent requirements continue to be taken very seriously by developers.

- TVA: Completion of the Tellico Dam project, wrote Tennessee historians Bruce Wheeler and Michael MacDonald in their 1986 book on the Tellico project, "marked the death of the agency as it had been known. . . . [TVA's] victory . . .

Silo marking the dairy operation that belonged to Ben Clark and his family, midway on Tellico reservoir near the Tennessee State Highway 411 bridge. (Photograph by Marika Plater)

constituted a fitting, if limited, end to the American obsession with technocratic power. . . . In its uncertain future, whichever of many roads the TVA chooses to travel, the ghosts of Tellico will always go with it."[2] The agency was shaken in 2008 when a huge coal-ash waste lagoon it maintained at Kingston, Tennessee, ruptured and sent a billion gallons of slurry downstream through homes and fields. TVA has since worked hard to restore its image; one such attempt was to fund a lavish course package with DVD and glossy text for distribution in high schools around the nation. The materials laud TVA's historic accomplishments and minimize the negatives of the Tellico Dam case.[3]

Today, silos still jut up here and there from the impounded waters of the shallow Tellico reservoir, marking—for those who remember—the resources, farms, human lives, and very special fish that once were here when the waters of the Little Tennessee River still flowed free.

# Notes

The URL referenced for the book's website is www.bc.edu/snaildarter.

## Preface

1. See James Salzman and J. B. Ruhl, "What Are the Greatest Hits in Environmental Jurisprudence?," *Environmental Forum* 26, no. 6 (November/December 2009): 36, 39. In an online poll of environmental law professors in 2001 on the most important Supreme Court case, *TVA v. Hill* received the highest number of votes, twice as many as the runners-up; in 2009 the same poll had *TVA v. Hill* as one of the national law professors' top two (the other was *Massachusetts v. EPA*, in which the Supreme Court ordered the Bush administration to address climate-changing greenhouse gases).

## Introduction

1. Staff Report and Transcript of Proceedings, U.S. Department of Interior, Endangered Species Committee, January 19, 1979 (staff report), and January 23, 1979 (proceedings) (both unpublished, accessible on book's website).

2. Tennessee Valley Authority, *Tellico Project Environmental Impact Statement*, I-i, 1972, available on the book's website.

3. Transcript of Proceedings, U.S. Department of Interior, Endangered Species Committee, Washington, DC, January 23, 1979, 24–29.

## 1. Of Time, a River, and the Tennessee Valley Authority

1. William Bartram, *Travels Through North & South Carolina, Georgia, East & West Florida & the Cherokee Country* (New Haven: Yale University Press, 1958), 347–48.

2. D. E. Lilienthal, *TVA: Democracy on the March* (Harmondsworth, UK, and New York: Penguin, 1944).

3. William U. Chandler, *The Myth of TVA: Conservation and Development in the Tennessee Valley, 1933–1983* (Cambridge, MA: Ballinger, 1984).

4. William B. Wheeler and Michael J. McDonald, *TVA and the Tellico Dam, 1936–1979: A Bureaucratic Crisis in Post-Industrial America* (Knoxville, TN: University of Tennessee Press, 1986), 3–4.

5. Wagner admits that hydropower benefits from Tellico Dam would be "relatively insignificant" (*Knoxville Journal*, September 23, 1964, 1, col. 2). See also Darren A. Shuler, "On Our Land: Progress, Destruction, and the TVA's Tellico Dam Project" (master's thesis, University of Georgia, 2000), 97.

6. Kenneth M. Murchison, *The Snail Darter Case: TVA Versus the Endangered Species Act* (Lawrence, KS: University Press of Kansas, 2007), 16.

7. Ibid., 21.

8. Wheeler and McDonald, *TVA and the Tellico Dam*, 92–93.

9. Under the terms of Senate Document 97 issued by the Kennedy administration— "Policies, Standards, and Procedures in the Formulation, Evaluation, and Review of Plans for Use and Development of Water and Related Land Resource Projects," May, 15, 1962— all federal water projects had to have documentation supporting an affirmative economic benefit when compared with federal monetary investment. The agencies' cost-benefit claims have been widely criticized as enthusiastic fictions, but no branch of government has proved interested in reviewing them. A project's claimed ratios often varied from year to year. TVA's official cost-benefit ratio for the Tellico project in 1973, for instance, was:

| Direct Annual Benefits Claimed | |
|---|---|
| Flood control | $505,000 |
| Navigation | 400,000 |
| Power | 400,000 |
| Recreation | 1,440,000 |
| Fish and wildlife | 220,000 |
| Water supply | 70,000 |
| Shore land development | 714,000 |
| *Redevelopment* | *15,000* |
| Total direct annual benefits: | $3,760,000 |
| | |
| Annual Costs: | |
| Interest and amortization | $2,045,000 |
| *Operation and maintenance* | *205,000* |
| Total annual costs: | $2,250,000 |

Cost-benefit ratio: 1.7:1.0

*Source:* Tennessee Valley Authority, Tellico Project Environmental Impact Statement, vol. I, 1972, 1–49 (available on book's website). (Both the General Accounting Office review [1977] and the God Committee review [1979] concluded that all figures in this ratio were inaccurate.)

10. Shuler, "On Our Land," 73–75.

11. Frances Brown Dorward, *Dam Greed* (Philadelphia: Xlibris, 2009); Kirk Johnson, "A History of Opposition to the TVA Tellico Dam" (unpublished; available on the book's website). At the Greenback public meeting, Wagner had assured the obviously hostile crowd that Tellico was intended to help them, and "that the project would be dropped if local sentiment were against it," but when Judge Sue Hicks proposed a local referendum on the dam, Wagner backtracked. No local referendum, he said, because the dam's benefits would reach far beyond the local community (*Maryville-Alcoa Daily Times*, September 24, 1964).

12. William O. Douglas, "This Valley Waits to Die," *True, The Man's Magazine,* June 1969, 40–43, 91–98.

13. Johnson, "A History of Opposition."

14. Tennessee Valley Authority, *Tellico Project Environmental Impact Statement,* vol. I, 1972, available on the book's website; Murchison, *The Snail Darter Case,* 55, 62–63, 178.

15. Gov. Winfield Dunn, 1971 letter to Chairman Red Wagner, and Wagner quotes in response, Tennessee Valley Authority, *Tellico Project Environmental Impact Statement,* I:3–42 to I:3–51.

16. Tennessee Valley Authority, *Tellico Project Environmental Impact Statement,* I:1–46.

## 2. At the Old Fort

1. As with most of the reconstructed conversations in this narrative, thirty-plus years after the fact, the comments attributed to Etnier were read and confirmed by the speaker while the book was in manuscript.

2. "Congressional Comment on ESA Enforceability," 119 *Cong. Rec.* 42913 (1973) (testimony of Representative John Dingell [D-MI]); "Hearings Before Subcommittee on Environment," 93d Cong., 1st sess., 7, 68 (1973).

3. 16 U.S.C. § 1536 (1974).

4. Thomas Beryl Moser (in some settings spelled "Burel") quotations are in Darren A. Shuler, "On Our Land: Progress, Destruction, and the TVA's Tellico Dam Project" (master's thesis, University of Georgia, 2000), 53.

5. Jefferson Chapman, *Tellico Archaeology: 12,000 Years of Native American History* (Norris, TN: Tennessee Valley Authority, 1994).

6. William Wheeler and Michael McDonald confirm the Worth Greene–Corydon Bell informant linkage in William B. Wheeler and Michael J. McDonald, *TVA and the Tellico Dam, 1936–1979: A Bureaucratic Crisis in Post-Industrial America* (Knoxville, TN: University of Tennessee Press, 1986), 150.

## 3. Pushing the Snail Darter onto the Endangered Species List

1. Administrative Procedure Act, 5 U.S.C. § 553(3) (1946).

2. Ray Blanton, after serving as governor of Tennessee from 1975 to 1979, was convicted on corruption charges and served several years in prison. He died in 1996.

3. Richard Nixon, "Statement About the National Environmental Policy Act of 1969," January 1, 1970, American Presidency Project, Signing Statements, http://www.presidency.ucsb.edu/ws/?pid=2557 (accessed July 13, 2012).

4. Powell Memorandum, "Attack on American Free Enterprise System," http://www.webcitation.org/64jAmJkKB (accessed July 13, 2012); also on the book's website.

5. Richard J. Lazarus, *The Making of Environmental Law* (Chicago: University of Chicago Press, 2004), 75–78; J. Brooks Flippen, *Nixon and the Environment* (Albuquerque: University of New Mexico Press, 2000).

6. Congressional Budget and Impoundment Control Act of 1974, 2 U.S.C. §§ 601–88.

7. Fred Powledge, *Water: The Nature, Uses, and Future of Our Most Precious and Abused Resource* (New York: Farrar, Straus Giroux, 1982), 286–87.

## 4. Trial and Tribulation in TVA's Home Court

1. A partial transcript of the trial is kept in the Boston College Little Tennessee River archives (accessible from the book's website).

2. Hecht Co. v. Bowles, 321 U.S. 321 (1944).

3. Hill, et al. v. Tennessee Valley Authority, 419 F. Supp. 753 (E.D. Tenn. 1976). For clarity the text combines text from Taylor's preliminary and permanent injunction

decisions and court sessions. The trial court decision dismissing the permanent injunction lawsuit is at 419 F. Supp. 753 (E.D. Tenn., May 25, 1976); the "$15 million" finding, incorporated from a shout in the courtroom, appears in the earlier decision denying the preliminary injunction, CIV. No. 3-76-48, U.S. District Court for the Eastern District of Tennessee, Northern Division, February 26, 1976 (available on the book's website).

4. Hill, et al. v. Tennessee Valley Authority, 419 F. Supp. 753 (E.D. Tenn. 1976).

## 5. An Appeal for Justice as Bulldozers Roll

1. Transcripts of U.S. Court of Appeals for the Sixth Circuit arguments are destroyed after its judges have taken final action; the colloquy reported here is reconstructed from notes and memory.

2. The expletive in Judge McCree's limerick wasn't revealed to me.

## 6. The Snail Darter Goes to Washington

1. Muskie, one of the preeminent environmental pioneers in the Senate, was in a quandary as he attempted to reconcile his past support for the Endangered Species Act and his current backing of the U.S. Army Corps of Engineers' plan to create a large dam with publicly owned power generators on Maine's St. John River. The National Audubon Society was fighting the dam but was focusing its arguments on the project's basic economic and ecological demerits—not on the endangered species issue concerning the oddly named Furbish's lousewort plant, discovered by amateur botanist Kate Furbish in 1880. It was Army Corps officials, not environmentalists, who publicized the issue of Furbish's lousewort, presumably to encourage public mockery that would undercut the Endangered Species Act in general and strengthen the agency's political case for the Dickey-Lincoln Dam.

## 7. Endangered, on the Banks of the Potomac

1. James Madison to W. T. Barry, 1822, in Ralph Louis Ketcham, ed., *Selected Writings of James Madison* (Indianapolis: Hackett, 2006), 308; Thomas Jefferson to William C. Jarvis, 1820, quoted in Roger Osborne, *Civilization: A New History of the Western World* (New York: Pegasus, 2006), 324; Thomas Jefferson to Edward Carrington, 1787, quoted in John Nichols and Robert McChesney, *The Death and Life of American Journalism: The Media Revolution That Will Begin the World Again* (New York: Nation, 2011), 119.

2. Quote from Sam Venable, silenced by *Knoxville News-Sentinel,* confirmed to author by Venable, July 4, 2012, and noted in Darren A. Shuler, "On Our Land: Progress, Destruction, and the TVA's Tellico Dam Project" (master's thesis, University of Georgia, 2000), 45; Carson Brewer, a respected veteran eastern Tennessee journalist, ceased writing skeptical articles about Tellico when TVA hired him to write its official history, as did freelancer Jim Dykes, regretfully, when he likewise joined TVA's payroll; William B. Wheeler and Michael J. McDonald, *TVA and the Tellico Dam, 1936–1979: A Bureaucratic Crisis in Post-Industrial America* (Knoxville, TN: University of Tennessee Press, 1986), 141–42.

3. R. Drummond Ayres, "Giant TVA Stalled by Controversy Over 3-Inch Fish." *New York Times,* March 11, 1977.

4. Ronald Reagan, radio broadcasts, October 18 and 29, 1977, quoted in Kiron K. Skinner, Annelise Anderson, and Martin Anderson, *Reagan's Path to Victory: The Shaping of Ronald Reagan's Vision: Selected Writings* (New York: Free Press, 2004), 214, 231, 367.

5. Houck provided his recollection of this conversation in a message to the author, March 17, 2011.

6. Wheeler and McDonald, *TVA and the Tellico Dam, 1936–1979,* 84–85; William O. Douglas, "This Valley Waits to Die," *True, The Man's Magazine,* June 1969, 40–43, 91–98.

7. The solicitation letter was shown to the author by the legislative assistant for Rep. Floyd Fithian (D-IN).

8. "Simplify, then exaggerate" had apparently been the classic advice of an editor at the *Economist* to his reporters in the 1950s. It is repeated in the *Irish Daily Mail,* March 31, 2012, 25.

9. An audio file of Alfred Davis telling the Howard Baker ambush story is available on the book's website.

10. S. Rep. No. 94–960 at 96 (1976); H. Rep. No. 94–1223 at 83 (1976).

11. At the time the snail darter team did not know that the local congressman, John Duncan, had sent a request letter to the General Accounting Office several weeks earlier, confident that it would not be granted because of his lack of stature in the congressional hierarchy. Had we known it existed, the situation would have been eased for us, for Murphy, and for Albert Gore.

12. The odd behavior of Representative Albert Gore (he referred to himself as "Albert" until he shifted his sights to a national stage) as a first-term member of the House trying to launch a political career in his father's footsteps—giving his express approval for, and then surreptitiously attempting to block, the committee's request for a GAO economic report on Tellico Dam—occurred on or about the afternoon of March 2, 1977. The facts are reflected in the author's notes as confirmed by Peter Alliman and by Hank Hill, who conversed directly with Gore and then made the phone call relaying Gore's approval, and by Jenna Christy, who was present in the House committee office when the call came from Gore's office attempting to reverse the approval Gore had just given. The resulting GAO report, *The Tennessee Valley Authority's Tellico Dam Project—Costs, Alternatives, and Benefits,* EMD-77-58, October 14, 1977, is available on the book's website, and contains a facsimile of the official request letter in its appendix.

13. "It's a shame the FBI caught Murphy in the ABSCAM sting," Hank says a few months after the GAO letter. The FBI had caught Murphy in an undercover operation taking bribes for legislative favors from an agent disguised as an oil sheik. "Sure, Murphy was a crook," Hank said, "but he was our crook. He helped us when we needed it."

## 8. The Snail Darter Gets Its Congressional Hearings

1. *Endangered Species Act Oversight Hearings,* Senate Committee on Environment and Public Works, 95th Cong., 1st sess., S. Rep. 95-H33 at 17–178 (1977).

2. Ibid., at 179–331 (Monte Canfield testimony, 178–89; Jean Ritchey testimony, 224–28; Lynn Seeber testimony and questions, 263–67).

3. Ibid., at 332–1025.

## 9. The Highest Court?

1. The official transcript of *TVA v. Hill* oral arguments is available at the book's website; for audio and rough transcript see "*TVA v. Hill,*" http://www.oyez.org/cases/1970 -1979/1977/1977_76_1701; and D. Cohen, Oral Argument in *TVA v. Hill, Puget Sound Law Rev.* (1978), 89–136.

2. The fact that Rehnquist had almost engineered a reversal without oral argument was revealed in Marshall's papers after his death; Blackmun's and Brennan's papers also

have fascinating details to reveal about the internal court maneuvering prior to and after the briefing and oral argument.

## 10. Another Trial and Vindication, in the God Tribunal

1. The drafted God Committee standards passed into law as an amendment to Section 7, now located at 16 U.S.C. § 1536(e) (1974).

2. We'd come to view Congress as erratic and unpredictable, carried along by its own internal momentum, ignoring rational processes whenever insider deals or short-term whimsies arose. In her new job in the State Department's environmental office, Anne Wickham was forced to spend three months lobbying to turn around a House vote slashing State's environmental funding in half. A minor Arkansas congressman, annoyed when State declined to hire his buddy's girlfriend, got the whole House to slice the agency's appropriations.

3. Elizabeth Drew, *Senator* (New York: Simon and Schuster, 1979), 33.

4. The only significant slippage in the compromise was a technicality: God Committee decisions are not prescribed to get full formal judicial scrutiny as Baker promised, but only the quite deferential "arbitrary and capricious" review.

5. One case, Home Box Office v. F.C.C., 567 F.2d 9 (United States Court of Appeals, District of Columbia Circuit, March 25, 1977), concluded that contacting staff ex parte is unethical even in informal circumstances, but most jurists consider it an outlier.

## 11. 140 Days of a Slow-Ticking Clock, Ending in 42 Seconds

1. The Senate hearing on the Baker amendment was held May 9, 1979. An extended description of the citizens' lobbying in the committee is available on the book's website.

2. The Senate floor debate: "Energy and Water Development Appropriations, 1980," 125 *Cong. Rec.* 14572–73 (June 13, 1979). For a time line of congressional actions, see also the book's Little Tennessee River Chronology.

3. The rider: "Energy and Water Development Appropriations, 1980," 125 *Cong. Rec.* 15301 (June 18, 1979).

4. For later published representations of Professor Antonin Scalia's views on legislative history see: Conroy v. Aniskoff, 507 U.S. 511 (March 31, 1993); and Zedner v. U.S., 547 U.S. 489 (June 5, 2006), 510–11.

5. Cecil Andrus, "Letter to Members of Congress: Re: Tellico Dam Decision of the Endangered Species Committee," July 16, 1979, available on the book's website.

6. The Senate floor debate and vote: "Energy and Water Development Appropriations, 1980," 125 *Cong. Rec.* 18934-18939 (July 17, 1979).

7. The House floor debate and vote: "Conference Report on H.R. 4388, Energy and Water Development Appropriations, 1980," 125 *Cong. Rec.* 21987-22002 (August 1, 1979).

8. Final Senate debate and vote: "Energy and Water Development Appropriations, 1980," 125 *Cong. Rec.* 23866–72 (September 10, 1979).

9. Albert Gore's statement on the Tellico Dam override was quoted in Jeffrey St. Clair, "Al Gore, the Origins of a Hypocrite," *Counterpunch,* March 3, 2007, 3-5, http://www.counterpunch.org/2007/03/03/al-gore-the-origins-of-a-hypocrite, accessed October 27, 2012.

## 12. A Phone Call from Air Force One

1. "The Daily Diary of President Jimmy Carter," September 25, 1979, 9:20–9:24 p.m., Carter Presidential Library, http://www.jimmycarterlibrary.gov/documents/diary/1979

/d092579t.pdf. The substance of the phone call—not noted in the Daily Diary—as quoted here is based on notes taken by Drew Diehl while listening to the conversation, and on the author's notes taken immediately afterward, available on the book's website.

2. *Endangered Species Act Reauthorization, Hearings on HR 10883, Before the Fish and Wildlife Subcommittee of the House Merchant Marine and Fisheries Committee,* 95th Cong., 2d sess., (February 15, 1978), 648, statement of Jimmie Durham, president of International Indian Treaty Council.

3. Taylor's dismissal of Cherokee lawsuit: Sequoyah et al. v. TVA, 480 F. Supp. 608 (November 2, 1979).

4. The text's timing is condensed; the final appeals court and Supreme Court decisions were issued after the dam was closed in November 1979: Sequoyah et al. v. TVA, 620 F. 2d 1159 (Sixth Circuit, April 15, 1980); Sequoyah et al. v. TVA, 449 U.S. 953 (November 30, 1980).

5. Aubrey Wagner quotation: *Knoxville News-Sentinel,* November 29, 1979.

## Epilogue

1. Endangered Species Act, Section 7(g)(4).

2. William B. Wheeler and Michael J. McDonald, *TVA and the Tellico Dam, 1936–1979: A Bureaucratic Crisis in Post-Industrial America* (Knoxville, TN: University of Tennessee Press, 1986), x, 220.

3. "Protecting Our Ecosystem: It's the Astonishing Story of the Tennessee Valley," Currents of Change, http://www.currentsofchange.net/lessons/.

# Index

Helms, Jesse, 303–4
Heritage Foundation, 65, 274
Hicks, Dan, 168
Hicks, Sue, 20, 354
Hill, Hank: at the old fort, 31–55; suggests darter as term paper topic, 34; petitioning for listing, 60; trial preparation, 90, 93–94, 106; defending the injunction, 130–31, 142; GAO request, 184–87, 193; Senate hearings, 202–04; at Court argument, 223; lobbying, 272, 297–98, 308; night of non-veto, 327, 330–31; River Day protest, 337, 348, 357
Hiller, David, 217, 223
Historic Preservation Council (in DoI), 296
historic values, sites, preservation efforts, 6–11, 31–32, 37–38, 46–47, 93, 202, 296
Hit list, water projects, 192–93, 310
Hornblower, Margot, 173, 200–201, 205
Houck, Oliver, xv, 145, 166, 172, 301, 304, 349, 357
House Rule 21, 308
Humane Society of the U.S., 148

Iczkovitz, Les, 158, 217, 223, 259
informant (DoI/TVA), 162, 200, 281–82, 296, 310, 312, 349
injunctions: NEPA injunction, 27–30, 33, 89; planning for ESA darter injunction, 39, 52–53, 90; trial, no injunction, 92–96, 106–10; appeal stay, and successful injunction, 116, 119–21, 137; TVA defies, 137; defending injunction in Washington, 123, 134–37, 159–62, 216–19; in Supreme Court, 228–32, 235, 242, 251, 254–57, 269; overridden, 324; seeking Cherokee injunction, 335–36
Internal Revenue audits, 26
International Indian Treaty Council, 337
iron triangle, 78–79, 159, 291

Jefferson, Thomas, 167, 302, 356
Johnson, Kirk, 348, 354
Jordan, Hamilton, 142, 193–94

Keel, Bennie, 296
Kefauver, Estes, 37

Kennedy, Ted, 270, 308, 310, 313, 327, 331, 334
Kildee, Dale, 183
killifish, 74
Kimball, Tom, 144, 302, 331
King, Laura, 171, 180
Knight, Foster, 215, 264
Korpon, Kathi, 123, 139, 141, 195, 198

Labelle, Debbie, 163–64, 167, 188, 194, 206, 216, 261, 279–80, 288
Lambertson, Ron, 85, 142, 156–57
land condemnation. See condemnation
larval drift. See snail darter, life cycle
Leggett, Robert, 83–85, 127–28, 130, 138–40, 159, 183–91
Leopold, Aldo, Sand County Almanac 208
life-cycle of darter. See snail darter, life-cycle
Limbaugh, Rush, xi
limerick of darter, Judge McCree's, 119
listing darter on federal endangered list, 57–63, 67–69, 84–87
Little Tennessee River: history, 6–12; contrary development plans, 15–21, 24–25, 28, and See alternatives; descriptions, 9–11, 31–32; trout and fishing, See fishing; darter habitat, See snail darter; at trial, 99; partial impoundment, 118; in Supreme Court, 249; dies, 341; retrospective, 352
lobbying against darter and ESA, 170, 175–76, 209, 285, 293; and See Range, Jim
lobbying for darter and ESA, 123, 126–41, 158–59, 171, 178–83, 301–02, 311–17
lobbying registration, 182–83
Lovejoy, Thomas, 165

Madison, James, xiii, 167, 174, 356
male menopause, TVA, 29, 152, 174
Marlin, John, 81–82
Mathews, Ginna, xv, 331, 348
Matthiessen, Peter, 339
McCall, Asa, 2–3; at old fort, 39–40, 53–54; passes his hat to start the battle, 53–54; deceased, 171, 348